no in rock /

WHO'S WHO IN ROCK

WHO'S WHO IN ROCK

BY MICHAEL BANE

Researcher: Kenny Kertok

Facts On File, Inc.
460 Park Avenue South
New York, New York 10016

Who's Who in Rock

Library of Congress Cataloging in Publication Data

Bane, Michael.
  Who's who in Rock

  Bibliography: p.
  1. Rock music—Bio-bibliography.   I. Title.
ML102.R6B36   784.5'4'00922 [B]   80-20304
ISBN 0-87196-465-1

Printed in the United States of America

10   9   8   7   6   5   4   3   2

To Cory Medlin for his friendship

CONTENTS

INTRODUCTION

We all float in a self-created ocean of popular culture. Perhaps more than we would like to admit, we take our cues on the way we act, the way we dress, maybe even the way we think from what we hear on the radio or what we see on television or what we read in the press. For those of us born in the 1950s and raised in the turbulent years of the 1960s, rock and roll looms as one of the most momentous influences in our lives. From its very beginnings, rock set out to shake the foundations of the existing order, to serve notice that the times, indeed, were "a-changing." Perhaps more importantly, rock helped to shape the budding youth culture of the 1960s, unifying and homogenizing the movement until it became a truely powerful force in America. Rock in the 1970s served equally significant functions, defining and shaping the "Me Generation."

We use music as a sort of mental shorthand to help us quickly explain to our friends and peers not only what we believe, but who we are as well. People who listen to country music, for example, are not so inclined to spend an evening with Sex Pistols fans. The automatic assumption is that members of one group share much, much more than simply a like of a certain kind of music. Rather, listening to a certain kind of music becomes both a political and a cultural statement. (I have seen people mortally offended by the simple fact that I owned a certain record, as if this piece of vinyl opened some dark door to my soul.)

Not surprisingly, with the rise in importance of popular music came the growth of rock journalism. Music writing has never topped the scales in journalistic importance. At a *More* magazine journalism convention in New York City a few years back, there was a penny arcade squeeze machine designed to rate the user's journalistic weight. At the top of the scale was Investigative Reporter; at the very bottom, Rock Writer.

Modern rock journalism sprang directly from the formation of *Rolling Stone* magazine in the late 1960s. Prior to *Rolling Stone,* writing about popular music tended to be straight criticism or personal essays. The genius of *Rolling Stone*'s creator, Jann Wenner, was that he treated the music exactly as if it were an important topic of current affairs and the musicians as if they were political dignitaries. Musicians were asked not about their favorite guitar but about their feelings on the Vietnam war, and the information was dutifully transmitted to the booming rock audience.

Rock journalism's greatest triumph has been its coverage of the cutting edge of pop culture. No other form of journalism is as close to the people and events it covers, and no other form of journalism can so quickly isolate and report on a new trend. Rock journalism's major fault can be termed a case of wretched excess, or possibly a crucial shortage of adjectives to describe this year's Next Big Thing. The fact of the matter, one supposes, is that while rock is a vitally important element of today's culture, it is not nearly as important as it thinks it is.

All of which is a roundabout explanation of *Who's Who In Rock* and how it came to be written. There is certainly no shortage of rock and roll encyclopedias, and as a

music journalist, I've used most of them at one time or another. But what I wanted—
and what I thought was needed—can be summed up in the proverbial quote from Sgt.
Joe Friday in the old television series "Dragnet," "Just the facts, ma'am." The crucial
elements in rock are not so much who played with what band when, although such
elements matter quite a bit to musicologists, or what some organ player feels about
his favorite guru. Rather, I was more interested in how a person or group fits into the
overall scheme of rock. What are they famous for or best remembered for, how did
that affect the music and, ultimately, how did that affect me?

To the best of my ability, *Who's Who In Rock* addresses those questions. Where at
all possible, I've tried to add an element of perspective missing in other volumes. I've
written the encyclopedia with the layman in mind, perhaps the newspaper reporter or
student working on an article or paper on rock, and I've tried to use as much anecdotal
material as possible. After all, encyclopedias ought to be fun.

Some 25 reference books were used constantly in the preparation of *Who's Who*,
as well as numerous other one-shot books, magazine articles and literally thousands
of record company biographies. I was also lucky to have the services of a top-notch
researcher, Kenny Kertok, whose obsessive knowledge of popular music alternately
awed and scared me. A number of other first-rate music critics, including John
Morthland, Peter Guralnick, Nick Tosches, Robert Duncan, Lester Bangs, Billy Altman,
Douglas B. Green, Russ Barnard, Martha Hume and Walter Dawson, contributed their
advice, support and help, which I hope is reflected in the final work. Finally, I was lucky
enough to have as a copy editor Joe Reilly, whose strengths perfectly matched my
weaknesses and whose contributions to the final product were enormous.

Writing an encyclopedia is a traumatic experience. I still can't listen to the radio
without having a page of biographical material on the artist pop into my mind. There is
also the fact that no matter how fast one writes, rock and roll is still faster. There are
already new whos for *Who's Who*.

But that's rock and roll for ya'.

Michael Bane
February 1981

WHO'S WHO
IN ROCK

Abba Agnetha Ulvaeus (vocals), Bjorn Ulvaeus (guitar, vocals), Benny Andersson (keyboards, vocals), Anni-Frid Lyngstad-Fredriksson (vocals)—Sweden's best-known musical export, the rock foursome known as Abba (the first letter of the first name of each member) ranks second only to the Beatles in international record sales. They've reached this exalted position, moreover, without a major U.S. tour and without the unswerving loyalty of the American market.

Their secret is a clean, totally foolproof AM sound—a four-part harmony reminiscent of the early Beach Boys—with the lilting female vocals of Anni-Frid and Agnetha leading the way. Although the group was

Abba

formed in 1972—Anni-Frid from a successful television show, Agnetha from solo performing, Benny from the rock Hep-Cats and Bjorn from the folkish Hootenanny Singers—it took the 1974 Eurovision Song Contest, a uniquely European spectacle with many million dedicated—indeed, fanatical—viewers, to launch Abba into the rarified reaches of superstardom. Abba's winning song, "Waterloo," became a top European hit and made a dent (top 10) in the American charts. The group's subsequent American hits included the enormously successful "Dancing Queen," "Mamma Mia" and "Fernando."

AC/DC Angus Young (guitar), Malcolm Young (guitar), Cliff Williams (bass), Phil Rudd (drums), Brian Johnson (vocals)—Hard, hard rock from the land of the kangaroos, AC/DC was formed in Australia during the early 1970s. The group garnered nothing but bad press until a revival of heavy metal music at the close of the seventies. AC/DC scored in 1979 with the hit album *Highway To Hell* and, after the death of vocalist Bon Scott in 1980, followed up with *Back In Black*. In 1982 *For Those About To Rock* also headed up the charts, proving the heavy metal revival still in full swing and leaving aging rock critics to wonder what the next generation was coming to.

Ace, Johnny Best known for his 1955 hit, "Pledging My Love" (later recorded by Elvis Presley on his last album, *Moody Blue* in 1976), Johnny Ace (born Johnny Marshall

Alexander, Jr. on June 9, 1929 in Memphis, Tenn.) is another of that city's many contributions to popular music. His rich voice and gospel-styled delivery marked the first successes of what would become known as "soul" music in the early 1960s.

Ironically, Johnny Ace killed himself playing Russian roulette (that peculiar craze especially popular in the mid-1950s) on Christmas Day, 1954 in Houston, Tex. and "Pledging My Love" became one of the biggest hits of the new year.

Ace Phil Harris (guitar), Alan King (guitar), Paul Carrack (keyboards), Tex Comer (bass), Fran Byrne (percussion)—Formed in England during the early 1970s, the group excelled in jazzy rock arrangements, which culminated in its 1975 hit, "How Long (Has This Been Going On)." Ace has cut three moderately successful albums in addition to the hit single, *Fire-A-Side, Time For Another* and *No Strings.*

Acuff, Roy One of the true godfathers of country music, Acuff's musical influences have percolated through all forms of popular music. He was born on Sept. 15, 1903 in Maynardsville, Tenn. After his dream of becoming a big league baseball player was ended by a case of sunstroke, Acuff turned to music.

He joined the Grand Ole Opry in 1940 after appearing in minstrel shows and was soon the premier attraction with his versions of the "Wabash Cannonball," "Crash On The Highway," "Great Speckled Bird" and "Night Train To

Roy Acuff

Memphis." He became the first of a long string of singer/bandleader stars, focusing public attention on his eclectic singing voice.

With songwriter Fred Rose, Acuff launched his own publishing company, Acuff-Rose, in 1942, which grew to be one of the largest and most influential music publishers in the country. Acuff performed at the Opry through the 1970s and was elected to the prestigious Country Music Hall of Fame in 1963.

Adderley, Julian "Cannonball" Born on Sept. 15, 1928 in Tampa, Fla., Cannonball Adderley became a virtual legend among fans of the alto saxophone. Beginning his first group in 1959, he was already a star on the jazz circuit when, in 1967, his "Mercy Mercy Mercy" brought him long-overdue pop recognition. He died from a heart attack in 1975.

Aerosmith Steve Tyler (vocals), Joe Perry (guitar), Brad Whitford (guitar), Tom Hamilton (bass), Joey Kramer (drums)—One of Boston's contributions to hard rock in the mid-1970s. Aerosmith has managed to parlay a strong regional following in the New England area into a national audience, thanks largely to nonstop touring and basic, no-frills rock and roll—dismissed by some critics as no-imagination rock and roll.

The group was originally classed as a Rolling Stones sound-alike, but with its release of *Get Your Wings* in 1974 and *Toys In The Attic* in 1975, the boys from Boston firmly established themselves as hitmakers.

Akkerman, Jan A cult favorite for many years, this Dutch guitar virtuoso founded the group Focus. He has released two solo albums, and his most recent record is a collaboration with fellow countryman Kaz Lux titled *Eli.* His best-known work, recorded while he was still with Focus, is *Profile,* cut in the mid-1970s.

Alaimo, Steve Born Dec. 6, 1940 in Rochester, N.Y., Alaimo took an early interest in the blues and scored in 1963 with "Every Day I Have To Cry Some." He followed that with a lyrical version of "Cast Your Fate To The Wind" (1965) and an upbeat "When My Little Girl Is Smiling" (1971).

Albert, Morris Born in 1951 in Brazil, Morris Albert became a star early on in his home country and, eventually, throughout South and Central America. His only significant break in the American market came in 1975 with the soppy ballad "Feelings."

Alexander, Arthur Born in Sheffield, Ala., Alexander had a hit in 1962 with his own composition "You Better Move On," later recorded by the Beatles. Recently he's been making the rock revival circuit, benefiting from his earlier work.

Alexander, Willie, and the Boom Boom Band Currently billed as New Wave, Willie Alexander and the band—David McLean (drums), Billy Loosigian (guitar) and Severin Grossman (bass)—began their careers in the Boston area playing rhythm and blues. Alexander had served a brief stint with the Velvet Underground before launching the Boom Boom Band in the late 1970s.

Allanson, Susie Allanson is best known for her resurrection of Buddy Holly's "Maybe Baby," which made the country and pop charts in 1978, under the direction of producer/husband Ray Ruff—one of Holly's coproducers.

Allen, Peter Perhaps the best-known member of the New York City cabaret circuit, Allen had some radio success with his "I Go To Rio" in the late 1970s.

Allen, Rex, Jr. Son of cowboy star Rex Allen, Rex Junior is one of the "new breed" country stars prevalent in the late 1970s. His music draws heavily from pop (middle-of-the-road) music—smooth arrangements with lush strings and the like. 1980 found him one of the fastest rising stars in that field.

Allen, Rex, Sr. Nicknamed the Arizona Cowboy, he was born on Dec. 31, 1924 in Wilcox, Ariz. During the 1950s he made 32 cowboy movies for Republic Films. He wrote over 300 songs and had a million seller in 1953 with "Crying In The Chapel."

Allman Brothers Band, The
Gregg Allman (vocals, keyboards), Dickey Betts (guitar, vocals), "Jaimoe" Johanny Johanson (drums, percussion), Butch Trucks (drums, percussion), David Goldflies (bass), Dan Toler (guitar)—The Allman Brothers Band is unique on two counts: no other band has been able to synthesize so successfully the numerous musical influences of the South into such a cohesive and musically varied "groove"; and no other band has been able—indeed, has ever tried—to come back from so many personal disasters.

Formed in 1969, the band was the brainchild of Macon, Ga. based rhythm-and-blues manager Phil Walden. It centered around the brothers Allman, Duane (born on Nov. 20, 1946 in Nashville) and Gregg (born on Dec. 8, 1947 also in Nashville). Duane had caught the eye of Walden and Atlantic Records' chief Jerry Wexler while a blazing hot studio guitar picker in Muscle Shoals. Walden was launching his own record company with Atlantic handling distribution, and the Allman Brothers Band was to be the centerpiece of that label.

That is exactly what happened. Duane's dual guitar leads with Dickey Betts and Gregg's mournful blues set the tone, and the band hit the road

The Allman Brothers

with a vengeance. The formula clicked, and their 1969 album, *The Allman Brothers Band,* was met with critical acclaim. The Brothers' music was a complex blend of blues, rhythm and blues, bluegrass, country and the ubiquitous Southern bar boogie, sparked by Duane and Dickey's soaring

solos. By 1971, with the release of *Live At The Filmore East,* the Brothers were one of the biggest draws in the country.

Then Duane Allman was killed in a motorcycle accident on Oct. 29, 1971, followed one year later by bassist Berry Oakley. The band sorrowfully continued, adding jazz keyboard wizard Chuck Leavell and bassist Lamar Williams. In 1974 Gregg launched his own solo career and began his flirtations with Hollywood and heroin, eventually marrying television star Cher. The band broke up, finally, over a vicious drug scandal, with Gregg eventually testifying against his own road manager.

Then, strangely, the band re-formed in 1978, cut a critically well-received album, *Enlightened Rogues,* and began a sold-out, standing-room-only national tour. Interestingly enough, their storied career has produced only one AM hit, "Ramblin' Man," a light countryish number written by Dickey Betts.

Alpert, Herb   Along with his group, the Tijuana Brass, Alpert provided an unbroken string of hits from "The Lonely Bull" in 1962 to "Last Tango In Paris" in 1973. Born on March 31, 1935 in Los Angeles, he formed the group after attending a bullfight in Mexico. Together with Jerry Moss he also launched A&M Records—now a major company—in 1962. His string of hits included "A Taste Of Honey" (1965), "Tijuana Taxi" (1965), "The Happening" (1967) and "Last Tango In Paris" (1973). In 1979 he returned to the charts with "Rise," a disco single in the classic Herb Alpert style.

Amazing Rhythm Aces, The   Russell Smith (guitars, harmonica, vocals), Billy Earheart (keyboards), Butch McDade (drums, vocals), James Hooker (piano, vocals), Jeff Davis (bass, vocals),

Duncan Cameron (guitar)—Originally the backup band for Jesse Winchester, the Aces represent a continuing tradition of Memphis music—country, blues, a speck of jazz and a dollop of down-home craziness. They won a Grammy for Best Country Vocal Performance by a Group in 1976 for "The End Is Not In Sight" and had a major hit with "Third-Rate Romance," an absolutely perfect "cheatin' song" written by Smith.

Amboy Dukes, The   A Midwestern power group—that is, concentrating on very loud, very basic rock—from the early 1970s remembered only for providing rock-and-roll wild man Ted Nugent with a warm place to grow and for making a bizarre psychedelic rock slammer called "Journey To The Center Of The Mind."

America   Gerry Beckley (vocals, guitar), Dan Peek (vocals, guitar), Dewey Bunnell (vocals, guitar)—Although starter Dan Peek was absent on the group's later releases, America (formed by the sons of three England-based U.S. servicemen in 1969) continues as an easy listening, Crosby-Stills-Nash-Young-influenced group. The group is best known for "A Horse With No Name" (1972), "Ventura Highway" (1972), "Tin Man" (1974) and "Sister Golden Hair" (1975).

American Breed, The   Al Ciner (guitar), Charles Colbern (bass), Lee Graziano (drums), Gary Liozzo (guitar, vocals)—Formed in Chicago in the mid-1960s, the group is mainly known as the seed for the soul

group Rufus, which the American Breed eventually evolved into. The group's biggest hit came in 1967 with "Bend Me, Shape Me."

American Flyer   Craig Fuller (guitar, vocals), Steve Katz (guitar), Doug Yule (bass), Eric Kaz (drums)—Formed in 1976 from bits and pieces of the Blues Project, Blood, Sweat and Tears, the Velvet Underground and the Blues Magoos, American Flyer never quite jelled as a supergroup, although its debut album, *American Flyer,* was an FM favorite. The band broke up two years later after a second album.

Ames Brothers, The   Ed, Vic, Gene and Joe Ames produced a string of hits through the 1950s, including "Rag Mop" (1950), "Wang Wang Blues" (1951) and "Tammy" (1957). Ed Ames continued as a solo singer ("Try To Remember" and "My Cup Runneth Over") and a television personality—he played Mingo in the successful "Daniel Boone" television series. The Ames Brothers specialized in supersoft collegiate harmony.

Andersen, Eric   One of the best folk guitarists of the 1960s, though largely unsuccessful, Eric Andersen enjoyed a strong following on FM radio. Born on Feb. 14, 1943 in Pittsburgh, Pa., he was among the first "folkies" to write his own material, such as "Thirsty Boots" and "Close the Door Lightly."

Anderson, Bill   One of the most successful country

singers of the mid-1960s, "Whispering" Bill is best known for his soft whisper of a voice. In the late 1970s Anderson (born Nov. 1, 1937 in Columbia, S.C.) tried what he termed "country disco" without success.

Anderson, Ian Flamboyant lead singer and moving spirit behind the group Jethro Tull, Ian Anderson was one of the first to see the potential of the rock-and-roll flute. Born on Aug. 10, 1947 in Scotland, he studied art and worked with the John Evan Group in Blackpool, England before forming Tull, named after the 18th-century British agriculturist and inventor.

Anderson, Jon Born on Oct. 25, 1944 in England, Jon Anderson launched the tremendously successful group Yes with bassist Chris Squire in 1968. He has also served as lead singer for the cult band United Kingdom.

Anderson, Lynn Country-pop singer Lynn Anderson was born on Sept. 26, 1947 in Grand Forks, N.D. She is best known for her across-the-board hit record "Rose Garden" (1971) and her work as the token pop singer on television's "The Lawrence Welk Show." Earlier she had been quite successful as a recording artist for Chart Records, with such regional hits as "That's A No No" (1969). She followed up her "Rose Garden" hit with a series of albums and television appearances that firmly established her as a country-pop star in the early 1970s. Unfortunately the style of the music was going through a shift back to its roots, to more basic country music, and Anderson's career suffered as a result. Since the late 1970s she has been pushing for a major comeback, with the aid of substantial promotion money from her record company, but success has still eluded her. Nevertheless, Lynn Anderson remains perhaps the most articulate and outspoken female country artist on all issues from the record business to women's rights.

Angel An imitation Kiss group from Washington, D.C., Angel is best known for the introduction of three-dimensional holography in its stage show. Formed in 1975, the group and its music remain unknown to the public at large.

Angels, The Peggy Santiglia, Barbara Allbut, Phyllis "Jiggs" Allbut—Vocal group best known for their 1963 hit, "My Boyfriend's Back," the three formed in 1961 in their home town of Orange, N.J. and then moved to New York City to work as backup singers. The group still occasionally performs in oldies shows as the Angels.

Animals, The Eric Burdon (vocals), Alan Price (keyboards), Chas Chandler (bass), Hilton Valentine (guitar), John Steel (drums)—Once in a rare while a song hits the charts with such power and such overwhelming strength that it leaves a permanent mark. Such a song was the Animals' 1964 release of "House of the Rising Sun," Eric Burdon's powerful, bluesy tribute to a New Orleans bordello.

With that song the Animals—so named, the legend goes, because the locals in Newcastle, England thought the group looked like animals—rudely captured the charts from fellow Englishmen the Beatles, and there was no doubt that Britain ruled the American airwaves.

The Animals' music, particularly Burdon's gutsy vocals, was deeply rooted in American black music (*Ebony* magazine even featured the group), and it was soon taken to heart by the American audiences who, strangely, would have nothing to do with genuine black music performed by blacks. The Animals became the first—and the best—spokesmen for the budding teenage angst, with songs like "Don't Let Me Be Misunderstood" (1965), "We Gotta Get Out Of This Place" (1965) and, especially, "It's My Life" (1965), a song and arrangement later resurrected by rock superstar Bruce Springsteen.

The group fell apart in the midst of quarreling between Burdon and the Animals' original leader, Price. Burdon, retaining the group name, went on to cut several mystical San Francisco flower songs, including "Warm San Franciscan Nights" (1967). A reunion album, *Before We Were So Rudely Interrupted,* was released in 1977, with the kindest reviews stating that it wasn't as bad as expected.

Anka, Paul The prototype teenage idol, Anka was born on July 30, 1941 in Ottawa, Canada, and by the time he'd

5

Paul Anka

reached the tender age of 15, he was a star, thanks to a song called "Diana." (Ah, the agony of teenage love — he's only 15, and she's "so old," maybe even 18!) He followed up "Diana" in rapid order with "You Are My Destiny" (1958), "Lonely Boy" (1959), "Put Your Head On My Shoulder" (1959) and "Puppy Love" (1960), written for Mouseketeer dreamboat Annette Funicello, and a host of others through 1963.

While others faded into obscurity, Anka later devoted himself to songwriting, penning such classics as "My Way," first a theme song for Frank Sinatra and then Elvis Presley, and "She's A Lady," for Tom Jones. He even managed to write the theme song for Johnny Carson's "Tonight Show." Anka stormed back on the charts in 1974 with "You're Having My Baby," a huge hit that made

feminists everywhere cringe. He remains a successful recording artist and in demand on the lucrative Vegas circuit.

Annette   Annette Funicello (born on Oct. 22, 1942 in Utica, N.Y.) turned a nation of boys into avid fans of the "Walt Disney Show" when she joined as a Mouseketeer in 1955. While her songs, such as "Tall Paul" (1959), "Jo-Jo the Dog-Faced Boy" (1959) and "O Dio Mio" (1960), never set the world on fire, many men today still have fond memories of watching the little Mouseketeer grow up before their very eyes. In recent years she has appeared in TV commercials and oldies revival shows.

Ann-Margret   Hard though it may be to believe, actress Ann-Margret (*Carnal Knowledge, Magic*) took a stab at a recording career in 1961 with her release of "I Just Don't Understand," followed later by "It Does Me So Good." She has returned to singing with a slick stage act, featuring a little dance and a little song. She was born on April 28, 1941 in Stockholm, Sweden.

April Wine   Formed in the mid-1970s in Montreal, April Wine, a punkish group of rockers, gained notoriety with its *Live At The El Mocambo* album in 1979.

Arbors, The   Edward Farran (vocals), Fred Farran (vocals), Scott Herrick (vocals), Thomas Herrick (vocals) — Vocal group formed in Michigan in the mid-1960s and successful in 1967 with "A Symphony For Susan." The group still works together on vocals for radio and

television commercials but is out of pop music.

Archies, The   A footnote to the history of rock, the Archies were a Saturday morning cartoon show based on the ever-popular Archie and Jughead comics transmuted into the late 1960s. In 1969 the cartoon's theme song, "Sugar Sugar," played by a group of studio musicians masquerading as the comix kids, became one of the biggest selling singles in the history of the planet, proving once and for all that you don't have to be old enough to vote to buy records. Since it never really existed except for records, the group is still around on cartoon reruns. (See also Don Kirshner.)

Area Code 615   Less a true band than a shifting collection of players, Area Code 615 (the telephone area code for Nashville) consisted of the best musicians Nashville had to offer. Formed in 1969, the band was the first "country" group to make a strong impact on popular music — many rock musicians who had discounted Nashville as an influence found themselves in awe of the Nashville sidemen's expertise and fluid style. They cut two albums, *Area Code 615* and *Trip In The Country,* before returning to their duties as sessions players. The primary personnel were Mac Gayden (guitar, vocals), Weldon Myrick (pedal steel), Kenny Buttrey (drums), Charlie McCoy (harmonica, vocals), Bobby Thompson (banjo, guitar), Wayne Moss (guitar, bass), Buddy Spicher (fiddle, viola, cello), David Briggs

April Wine

(keyboards) and Norbert Putnam (bass, cello).

Argent   Rod Argent (keyboards, vocals), John Verity (guitar, vocals), Robert Henrit (drums), Jim Rodford (bass)—The group was formed in 1969 by Rod Argent (born on June 14, 1945 in St. Albans, England) after the breakup of his immensely more popular Zombies. Despite nine albums and two interesting hit singles, "Hold Your Head Up" (1972) and "God Gave Rock And Roll To You" (1973), the group never jelled into a single entity, and by 1976 it was disbanded.

Armatrading, Joan   Born on Dec. 9 , 1950 in the West Indies, Armatrading has been working the road since 1973, and despite predictions and some limited FM success, she remains more a potential than an accomplished fact. Her strange, almost toneless vocals have built quite a cult following in the New York City area.

Asher, Peter   One-half of the popular 1960s duo Peter and Gordon (Gordon Waller), who dominated the charts in the

mid-1960s with such hits as "World Without Love" (1964), "True Love Ways" (1965) and "Lady Godiva" (1966). More importantly, after Peter and Gordon had run their course, Peter connected with budding singer/songwriter James Taylor while working for the Beatles' Apple Records. Peter spirited James Taylor away from Apple, produced his next couple of albums—*Sweet Baby James* and *Mudslide Slim*—on Warner Brothers label and helped make him a superstar. In 1973 he performed the same trick for a folkie singer named Linda Ronstadt, easily his greatest hit, begining with *Don't Cry Now* that year.

Ashford and Simpson
Nicholas Ashford and Valerie Simpson gained recognition as songwriters for the Motown organization. (Before joining Motown they had written Ray Charles' number one R&B hit "Let's Go Get Stoned" in 1966. They wrote for and produced some of Motown's biggest acts, including Marvin Gaye and Tammi Terrell, before striking out on their own in 1973. While their best

songwriting ("Ain't No Mountain High Enough," for Terrell and Gaye in 1967, for example) and production work has been in hard-core rhythm and blues, the duo decided to stick to love ballads on their solo work. The ballad formula was successful for them in 1974, when they scored with "Anywhere."

Asleep at the Wheel
Another huge conglomeration of players—as many as 14, as few as three—who went through the psychedelic era of San Francisco and came out playing Western Swing. The band was formed in late 1970 by Ray Benson (guitar, vocals), Lucky Oceans (pedal steel) and Leroy Preston (guitar) to play country music. They were joined by Chris O'Connell, a secretary from Virginia who wanted to be a singer, and the whole group migrated to San Francisco, picking up various and sundry fiddle players, accordionists and horn men along the way. The group's music branched out from its country and Western Swing beginnings into a free-wheeling swing, and O'Connell matured into a fine big band vocalist.

The problem, according to Benson, was that with so many people touring, the band was never able to make any money.

Association, The Russ Giguere (vocals), Ted Bluechel (drums), Brian Cole (guitar, vocals, clarinet), Terry Kirkman (vocals, several instruments), Larry Ramos (guitar, vocals), Jim Yester (guitar, vocals, keyboards)—Shocked a complacent America by revealing on national television that the "Mary" in their hit song "Along Comes Mary" was actually marijuana— remember, this was 1966 and even musicians didn't admit to such things, at least not yet. Nevertheless, the group pressed on, doing penance with a string of harmless love ballads—"Cherish" (1966), "Windy" (1967) and "Never My Love" (1967)—before drifting away during the more hip seventies.

Atkins, Chet A shy, unassuming man destined to take his place as one of the most influential guitarists in history. Born on June 20, 1924 in the tiny town of Luttrell, Tenn., Atkins toured the South as a picker. In 1946 he arrived in the budding Music City of Nashville, where he became a regular at the Grand Ole Opry and a sessions musician for RCA. By 1957 he was the head of studio operations for RCA.

He is best known as the "inventor" of the Nashville Sound, that fluid, jazzy background that found its way on seemingly every record that came out of Nashville throughout the 1960s. In addition to his influence as a picker, his style of production

left country music forever more cosmopolitan— something he actually apologized for in later years. Oddly enough, he was also directly responsible, as head of RCA, for expanding Elvis Presley's appeal into a national mania. It was Atkins who suggested drums, the braying electric guitars and the backup vocal group that we remember so well.

Beginning in 1976 Atkins emerged from retirement to make two records with another legendary guitar figure, Les Paul, and the two of them actually did—and still do—a little touring, to wildly enthusiastic audiences.

Atlanta Rhythm Section Barry Bailey (guitar), Ronnie Hammond (vocals), Paul Goddard (guitar), Robert Nix (drums), J.R. Cobb (guitar) Dean Daughtry (keyboards)— One of the more successful Southern rock bands in the wake of the Allman Brothers, the members of the Atlanta Rhythm Section (ARS) got started as studio musicians at Studio One, in Doraville, Ga., a town just outside Atlanta that is celebrated in the group's first commercial success, "Doraville" (1974). Cobb and band manager Buddy Buie had been members of the Classics IV, best known for their late 1960s hits of "Spooky" and "Stormy." Of all the Southern rock bands, ARS probably owes the least to the traditional Southern blend of blues, rhythm and blues and country, sticking closer to the English pop sound of the Classics IV. Other members of the group had toured as the backup band for Roy Orbison

and played later as the Candymen. In 1978 ARS had a hit with "Imaginary Lover" and the group released a remake of "Spooky" the following year.

Atomic Rooster Primarily a showcase for Vincent Crane, author of Arthur Brown's bizarre hit "Fire" in the late 1960s, Atomic Rooster, formed in 1969, was also briefly the home of Carl Palmer, who later went on to join Emerson, Lake and Palmer. The band struggled along until 1973.

Auger, Brian Auger, born in 1939 in London, is best known for those whom he nurtured in his various bands. His Steampacket, created in 1964, featured Long John Baldry, one of the most flamboyant British blues singers; soon-to-be superstar Rod Stewart; and Julie Driscoll, formerly the secretary to Brian's manager. The result was one of the most free-wheeling British blues bands of the period, more interested in expanding the horizons of white blues than faithfully mimicking black American performers. The band lasted until 1966, finally flying apart in a spate of personality conflicts. Auger continued to tour with various new bands, but with none of the earlier success or flair—the old days are available only on record.

Auldridge, Mike Auldridge is one of the masters of the dobro, a guitar with raised strings and a metal resonator producing a sound similar to a Hawaiian guitar. He is best known for session work behind Linda Ronstadt, Emmylou

Harris and Jonathan Edwards, in addition to solo bluegrass albums.

Autry, Gene   The most successful of the singing cowboys, Autry was born on Sept. 29, 1907 in Tioga, Tex. After a successful recording career, including "Silver-Haired Daddy Of Mine" (1931), which sold over five million copies, he went to Hollywood to star in a Western science fiction serial, *The Phantom Empire.* He continued his film career in a successful series of "B" Western movies for Republic Films in the 1930s and 1940s and, more importantly, began making country and Western hit songs, including "Yellow Rose Of Texas" (1933), "The Last Roundup" (1934) and "Back In The Saddle Again" (1939). He's had three additional million-selling records: "Here Comes Santa Claus" (1947), "Peter Cottontail" (1949) and "Rudolph The Red-Nosed Reindeer" (1948), which is still making the rounds every Christmas. The rise of the singing cowboys also marked an important step in the national popularization of radio, paving the way for the wholesale acceptance of this medium in future years.

Avalon, Frankie   Frankie Avalon was one of the best-known teen heartthrobs during rock's "in-between" period in the late 1950s, the time between the cooling of the Elvis Presley phenomenon and the coming of the Beatles. Born on Sept. 18, 1940 in Philadelphia, Pa., Avalon originally wanted to be a boxer but tossed that idea aside for

the trumpet after seeing the movie *Young Man With A Horn.* By the tender age of 12, he was working with a teen band in Atlantic City, N.J. and scored appearances as a child prodigy on the television variety shows of Jackie Gleason, Paul Whiteman and Ray Anthony. He soon branched into singing and was snapped up by two local managers and songwriters, Bob Marcucci and Peter de Angelis. Nothing much happened in his career until he tried pinching his nose at a recording session to get a nasal effect. The result of the pinch was "Dede Dinah," a hit in 1958. Avalon was quickly scooped up by Dick Clark, the host of Philadelphia's "American Bandstand" television show, who was working hard to prove that all rock and rollers weren't totally degenerate. The clean-cut Avalon fit the bill perfectly, and with continuous coverage on

that show, he went on to such hits as "You Excite Me" (1958), "A Boy Without A Girl" (1959), "Why" (1959), "Just Ask Your Heart" (1959) and, of course, "Venus," his biggie, also in 1959. A comeback effort in the mid-1970s failed to generate any enthusiasm.

Average White Band   Alan Gorrie (bass, vocals), Hamish Stuart (guitar, vocals), Onnie McIntyre (guitar, vocals), Steve Ferrone (drums), Roger Ball (keyboards, sax), Malcolm Duncan (sax)—Aptly named, the Average White Band is yet another exponent of British soul, sort of the logical outgrowth of the British fascination with blues and black music in general. The group's biggest success came in 1974 with "Cut The Cake," a repetitive ditty from the netherworld between soul and disco. That success was cut short by the drug-related death of Robbie McIntosh in 1974,

Average White Band

the band's original drummer, at a chic party in Los Angeles.

Axton, Hoyt A singer and songwriter whose songs have constantly outstripped his singing. Axton's "Greenback Dollar" was a success for the Kingston Trio in 1962, and "The Pusher" became one of the great underground hits for the heavy metal group Steppenwolf in 1967. In the early 1970s his songwriting helped propel the good-time music of Three Dog Night to the top with such hits as "Joy To The World" (1970) and "Never Been To Spain" (1972). His own albums have been punctuated by clever lyrics and folksy arrangements and have seen some success on the country charts. In the late 1970s, Axton turned up in bit parts on television, perhaps signaling a change of careers.

Axton, Mae Bordon Songwriter, best known as the author of "Heartbreak Hotel," Elvis Presley's first RCA hit in 1956. She is also the mother of Hoyt Axton.

Ayers, Kevin Eclectic rock guitarist, drifting in and out of the British rock scene. His successes include an early tour with Jimi Hendrix and his *Confessions of Dr. Dream* album, released in 1974.

Ayers, Roy One of the more successful jazz-pop musicians of the 1970s and leader of Ubiquity. His music reflects a heavy Latin and rhythm-and-blues influence, more so than most of the jazz-pop players, who lean toward less funky, pop arrangements.

Aztec Two Step Rex Fowler and Neal Shulman became popular FM radio artists in the early 1970s with their debut folk-rock album; their subsequent work has been more electric and less played. They're best known for their East Coast classic "The Persecution And Restoration Of Dean Moriarty (On The Road)," one of the duo's earliest numbers.

Babys, The John Waite (vocals, bass), Wally Stocker (guitar), Mike Corby (guitar), Tony Brock (drums)—Another attempt, this one in 1971, to prove that hype is more important than public opinion. Despite a huge publicity campaign and much posturing, this Warner Brothers group has never made anything noteworthy but headlines.

Bacharach, Burt Born on May 12, 1928 in Kansas City, Mo., Bacharach is one of the best-known composers in pop music. He came to public attention in the early 1960s with a string of hits that included "Walk On By," "This Girl's In Love With You" and "I Say A Little Prayer," all done by Dionne Warwick. So great was his impact that he became as well known as his songs—a fact not hurt by his recently ended marriage to actress Angie Dickinson, possessor of one of the great pairs of legs in Hollywood.

Perhaps Bacharach's

greatest success to date has been his association with the enormously popular movie *Butch Cassidy and the Sundance Kid,* for which he received two Oscars, one for the soundtrack and another for the theme song, "Raindrops Keep Falling On My Head," which went on to become a million-selling hit for B.J. Thomas in 1969. As has been the case with the most successful Bacharach tunes, the lyrics for "Raindrops" were provided by veteran lyricist Hal David.

Bachman, Randy Randy Bachman, of the Guess Who and Bachman-Turner Overdrive, is one of Canada's few contributions to American rock. And what an unusual contribution he turned out to be! Beginning with a band called Al and the Silvertones in 1959, guitarist Bachman first achieved prominence in the Guess Who, a popular singles band of the late 1960s. The Guess Who, in fact, laid the groundwork for the plethora of hard rockers that was to follow—appeal to the younger, AM market; slam home one hit single after another and don't worry too much about FM radio and "critical" appeal. Some of the Guess Who's biggest successes were written by Bachman, notably "American Woman" (1970).

Bachman, a Mormon, grew disillusioned with the group's wild and woolly road life and left in the summer of 1970, forming a not-too-memorable country-rock ensemble called Brave Belt. He eventually settled on another teen power group called Bachman-Turner Overdrive. In 1977 he left the group to go solo, without marked success.

Bachman-Turner Overdrive Randy Bachman (vocals, guitar), Fred Turner (vocals, bass), Blair Thornton (guitar), Robbie Bachman (drums)—Viewed in retrospect, one of the classic formula bands of the mid-1970s. And the formula wasn't all that hard either: keep it simple and play *real* loud. Overdrive is an apt description.

The band was formed by Randy Bachman in 1972, after he left the successful Guess Who. Bachman-Turner Overdrive (BTO) quickly supplanted the struggling remnants of the Guess Who as Canada's top rock band, a somewhat dubious distinction, to be sure, and by 1974 were making serious inroads into the American teenybopper market with such stuttering singles as "You Ain't Seen Nothing Yet" (1974). Three years later Bachman left the group, which immediately shifted into low gear but came back strong in the late 1970s.

Back Street Crawler Terry Wilson Slessler (vocals), Paul Kossoff (guitar), Terry Wilson (bass), Tony Braunagel (drums), Mike Montgomery (keyboards)—Primarily a vehicle for firebrand guitarist Paul Kossoff, formerly of the group Free, the band lost its moving force when Kossoff died of an apparent heart attack in 1976.

Bad Company Paul Rodgers (vocals, guitar), Simon Kirke (drums), Mick Ralphs (guitar), Boz Burrell (bass)—A power rock group

Bachman-Turner Overdrive

centered around the nucleus of the band Free, Paul Rodgers and Simon Kirke. Always more successful than the other Free-spinoff, Back Street Crawler, Bad Company dominated the charts and the concert tours of the mid-1970s with such straight-ahead rock and roll as "Can't Get Enough," (1974), "Feel Like Makin' Love" (1975) and "Young Blood" (1976). After a period of inactivity, the band came back in 1979 with its tried-and-true combination of slam-bam rock, achieving

fair success in the disco-dominated market of that year.

Badfinger Pete Ham (vocals, guitar, piano), Tom Evans (vocals, bass), Mike Gibbins (drums), Joey Molland (vocals, guitar)—Casualties of the waning years of Beatlemania, Badfinger (originally an English group called the Iveys) was signed to Apple Records by the Beatles themselves in 1968. The group's first single, "Maybe Tomorrow," proved to be a monster hit. Featuring a catchy single called "Come And Get It," penned by Paul McCartney, Badfinger did the soundtrack to a bizarre Peter Sellers movie (costarring none other than Ringo Starr) entitled *The Magic Christian,* the climactic scene of which featured the Badfinger/McCartney song in all its glory while various citizens bobbed for money in a vat of animal excrement—this could only happen in the 1960s. The group backed several of the now-separate Beatles in their solo endeavors and had a striking success with "Day After Day" (1972), produced by Todd Rundgren. But a shift to Warner Brothers Records to escape the collapsing world of Apple proved disastrous, and after announcing his retirement, vocalist Ham committed suicide in 1975.

Baez, Joan   Originally a fine folksinger, Baez became the most visible "protest" singer of the 1960s. Born on Jan. 9, 1941 in New York, she began her career singing in a local choir and eventually became the runaway hit of the 1959 Newport Folk Festival, her springboard to national acclaim. She might have had her brief moment in the limelight and then joined most other folkies in obscurity had it not been for two things: her romantic involvement with Bob Dylan (beginning around 1963 and ending dramatically in 1965) and her obsession with liberal politics, from civil rights to the Vietnam war.

The early 1970s brought her most political album, *Where Are You Now, My Son,* part of

which was recorded in Hanoi during a bombing raid. Within two years, however, she did an amazing turnabout. While sticking to her ideological guns, she announced a strictly commercial album, for the money. *Diamonds And Rust,* announcements aside, gave her career a boost, and the title song, a rumination on her affair with Dylan, received strong airplay. She joined Dylan on the fabled Rolling Thunder tour, released a live album and continued her commercial ways with *Gulf Winds.*

Her staunch ideology resurfaced in 1979, when she chastized the government of Vietnam for not being the great democratic savior it had been billed as. She also criticized a host of her radical buddies for not being more vocal in their complaints.

Baker, Ginger   Best known as drummer for the seminal power rock trio Cream, Baker (born Peter Baker in 1939 in London) joined Eric Clapton on the ill-fated Blind Faith tour after the breakup of Cream and tried to put together several powerhouse groups, all with limited success.

Baldry, "Long" John   A flashy white blues singer, Baldry was born in 1940 in London. Dubbed "Long" because of his six-foot seven-inch height, he worked with Brian Auger in the Steampacket and, later, with Elton John in Bluesology. His only U.S. success was with a little number called "Don't Try To Lay No Boogie Woogie On The King Of Rock And Roll," which, with its long spoken

intro, recounted Baldry's arrest in London for singing "boo-gee woo-gee" music in the street. The song was popular on FM radio in the early 1970s.

Balin, Marty   Sometimes lead singer of the Jefferson Airplane (later, the Jefferson Starship), Balin was born on Jan. 30, 1943 in Cincinnati, Ohio and grew up in California. After starting the quasi-folk Airplane in San Francisco in 1965, Balin left the group years later because he was uncomfortable with its musical directions. He rejoined in 1975, bringing the Starship its first commercial success in years with a single called "Miracles." In the late 1970s Balin left the group again, along with lead singer Grace Slick.

Ball, Marcia   A cult country-rock singer from Austin, Tex. with a tremendous voice, Ball has had a seemingly unlimited quota of bad luck, largely the result of being slightly ahead of her time. Her theme song is "I Just Want To Be A Cowboy's Sweetheart."

Ballard, Hank   With his group the Midnighters, Ballard was one of the victims of the pop music industry's unwillingness to accept authentic black music. His tough, explicit rhythm and blues in the late 1940s ("Roll With Me Annie") set the stage for rock and roll and was a huge hit on the R&B (read, black) charts. But the music was considered too raw for the apparently more sheltered white audiences. In 1958 he had a modest hit with "Teardrops On My Letter." On the flip side of that hit was a number called "The Twist," which was heard by an aspiring rock and roller named Chubby Checker. His cover version of "The Twist" became one of the best selling singles of all time. Ballard did eventually make the charts, but it was with the watered-down lightweight pop material of the late 1950s, including "Finger-Poppin' Time" and "Let's Go Let's Go Let's Go," both in 1960. Ironically, the songs, virtually party dance records, were styled after Chubby Checker's version of "The Twist."

Band, The   Rick Danko (bass, vocals), Richard Manuel (piano, vocals), Robbie Robertson (guitar, vocals), Levon Helm (drums, vocals), Garth Hudson (organ, sax)—On Thanksgiving Day, 1976 the Band ended its enormously successful career with the same style it had shown since its formation back in 1966. After 10 years on the road, the group stepped down with a spectacular concert—called The Last Waltz—at San Francisco's Winterland, where it had debuted in 1969.

The Band was unique in pop music for its total unwillingness to compromise, despite the pressures of superstardom. The group began in the early 1960s as the backup band for a Southern hell-raiser named Ronnie Hawkins, and on those early tours its members picked up an abiding love of Southern music, from the blues to country honky-tonks. In 1966 they backed Bob Dylan on his British tour and later on the semilegendary *Basement Tapes* (recorded in Dylan's basement in 1967 and eventually released as a two-

record set in 1975). Dylan's name alone was enough to boost them from unknowns into stars, and in 1968 the Band cemented that position with the release of the album *Music From The Big Pink,* which featured the soon-to-be classic "The Weight."

As is the case with any band of this stature, critics have poured over the subsequent albums with two or three fine-toothed combs. Certainly *The Band* album was an instant classic, with such cuts as "The Night They Drove Old Dixie Down," "Rag Mama Rag," "Up On Cripple Creek," "King Harvest (Has Surely Come)" and others. But the Band's great contribution has been its assimilation of early American music and the ability to fuse its roots into the next logical step. The Band offered tiny vignettes of life, lovingly crafted and presented with a passion only love can bring.

The Winterland show was filmed by Martin Scorsese (*Taxi Driver, Mean Streets*), and the subsequent movie, *The Last Waltz,* has been hailed by critics as one of the finest rock-and-roll movies ever made—a fitting tribute to the Band.

Bandy, Moe   A Mississippi-born country singer largely responsible for the rebirth of honky-tonk country music in the late 1970s. In 1973, while country music was still concentrating on heavily orchestrated string arrangements, Bandy bucked the trend with "I Just Started Hatin' Cheating Songs Today." With the rise of the "urban cowboy" in the late 1970s, Bandy's hard-core country

music has been one of the big winners, essentially being in the right place at the right time.

Bare, Bobby   Born on April 7, 1935 in Ironton, Ohio, Bare had the second largest selling hit of 1958, "All American Boy," only to discover that he'd sold all the rights for $50. After a stretch in the Army, he came back with "Detroit City" (1963), "500 Miles Away From Home" (1963) and others, eventually establishing himself as a solid country star. His reputation in Nashville was enhanced by his use of up and coming songwriters, including Kris Kristofferson and Shel Silverstein.

Barefoot Jerry   Wayne Moss (guitar), Jim Colvard (guitar), Russ Hicks (steel guitar), Si Edwards (drums), Terry Dearmore (bass, vocals), Warren Hartman (keyboards)—Barefoot Jerry picks up where Area Code 615 left off, essentially a group of country sessions men working in a pop format. The group had modest success in the mid-1970s with the single "You Can't Get Off With Your Shoes On" and the album *Grocery.*

Bar-Kays, The   James Alexander (bass, vocals), Ben Cauley (trumpet), Larry Dodson (vocals), Winston Stewart (piano, synthesizers), Michael Beard (drums, vocals), Charles Allen (trumpet, vocals), Harvey Henderson (sax, percussion), Lloyd Smith (guitar), Frank Thompson (trombone, percussion), Mark Bynum (keyboards, vocals), Sherman Guy (percussion, vocals)—The original Bar-Kays were the house band at Stax

Records in Memphis and backed soul singer Otis Redding on the road. In 1967 they scored a hit with "Soul Finger." The same year all of the original members of the group but James Alexander and Ben Cauley were killed in the plane crash that took Redding's life. In 1968 the Bar-Kays re-formed around Alexander and went back to the studio, once again achieving preeminence as a studio group. In 1976 they returned to doing their own recording with a number of succesful soul and disco cuts. The Bar-Kays' album *Flying High On Your Love* (1977) went gold, and their popularity continues in the disco-funk mold.

Bass, Fontella Born on July 3, 1949 in St. Louis, Mo. and trained as a gospel singer, Bass worked as the pianist and vocalist in Little Milton's band before her landmark rhythm-and-blues hit "Rescue Me" (1965). Her tough, bluesy vocals soon gave way to milder material, and she vanished from the charts.

Bassey, Shirley Born on Jan. 8, 1937 in England, Bassey became an overnight household word in 1964, when she sang the classic themesong from the James Bond movie *Goldfinger.* Already an accomplished singer and performer, she parlayed the success of her "Goldfinger" recording into a Las Vegas showroom-style act that is still packing them in years later. In 1972 she had a hit with the theme to *Diamonds Are Forever,* another Bond movie.

Bay City Rollers, The Leslie McKeown (vocals), Stuart Wood (guitar), Ian Mitchell (bass), Eric Faulkner (guitar), Derek Longmuir (drums)—"The biggest thing since the Beatles." Every English band at one time or the other claims that particular phrase as its own (and its alone). Aimed at Britain's throbbing preteen market and powered by unlimited hype, the Bay City Rollers grabbed a sizable chunk of the U.K. market and achieved some success in America with "Saturday Night" in 1976. About their music, the less said the better. Suffice it to say that one of the group's original members, Alan Longmuir, left because at the age of 26 he felt he was too old for the band.

Beach Boys, The Brian Wilson (vocals), Dennis Wilson (vocals, drums), Mike Love (vocals), Al Jardine (vocals, guitar), Carl Wilson (vocals, guitar)—Take a dash of 1950s harmony, add some upbeat guitar twang and mix the whole thing up with a surfboard and you've got the Beach Boys, who came out of California in 1962 to prove to the world how wonderful the Endless Summer could be (and trigger a deluge of beach rock; including Jan and Dean, the Surfaris and the like). Formed in Los Angeles in 1961 by the brothers Wilson, the Beach Boys were really created when Dennis, a surfer, suggested to Brian, who studied music theory, that maybe there should be some songs about surfing. Just like that, Brian wrote "Surfin'," and the group formally became the Beach Boys to match the music. Their first album, *Surfin' Safari*

The Beach Boys

(1962), was any orgy of girls, beach, waves and suntan oil, including the title song; "Little Girl (You're My Miss America)"; "409," a hymn to a Chevy, the only other thing worthy of a beach boy's attention; and "Summertime Blues." From then on the group hung in the groove with such summer classics as "Fun Fun Fun" (1964), "I Get Around" (1964), "Don't Worry Baby" (1964), "When I Grow Up To Be A Man" (1964), "Help Me Rhonda" (1965), "California Girls" (1965), "Wouldn't It Be Nice" (1966), "Good Vibrations" (1966) and on and on.

In 1965 Brian suffered a nervous breakdown and left the group. The formula held for a while, but by the late-1960s it appeared that the wave had passed. In 1971, though, a swell appeared on the horizon in the form of *Surf's Up,* and from then on the band was under way again. In 1973 the group released *Holland,* including Brian Wilson's outstanding "Sail On Sailor." Since then, with Brian more or less in the fold (he returned formally in 1975), the Beach Boys have continued an erratic career. At times it seems they are haunted by their surf-and-good-times past, wishing that all of it would suffer the Big Wipe Out. During the late 1970s the group dabbled in country music, although it's still a little early to tell how successful such a cross will prove.

The early Beach Boys gave American rock a focal point in the grim years of the British Invasion (the early 1960s). The Beach Boys' distinctive harmony style, actually an updating of the harmony groups of the 1950s, can still be heard echoing through rock's most famous California groups, from the Byrds to the Eagles.

Beatles, The   Paul McCartney (bass, vocals), John Lennon (guitar, vocals), George Harrison (guitar, vocals), Ringo Starr (drums, vocals)—The Beatles, along with Elvis Presley and Bob Dylan, are the very bedrock on which today's popular music is founded. From their 1963 release of "I Want To Hold Your Hand" to their dissolution in 1971, the Beatles were the very cutting edge of rock, not only musically and lyrically, but in concepts, ideas and production as well. The group had an almost uncanny ability to sense when the times were getting ready to change, and their music always appeared at the forefront of that change.

All four of the Beatles were born in Liverpool—John Lennon on Oct. 9, 1940; Paul McCartney on June 18, 1942; George Harrison on Feb. 25, 1943; and Ringo Starr on June 7, 1940. The basic group began with Lennon and McCartney playing skiffle music, a sort of simple English folk music, and they eventually evolved into a rock band, the Quarrymen. Harrison folded his own band to join the group, which at that point included Stu Sutcliffe on bass and Pete Best on drums. Their name eventually changed from the Quarrymen to the Silver Beatles, a play on the name of Buddy Holly's band, the Crickets. With the name boiled down to the Beatles, the group began a series of tours in Hamburg, Germany, where the four began honing their stage act to a fine edge. They also picked up a new drummer, Ringo Starr, to replace Pete Best, who'd been released. Sutcliffe had resigned from the band earlier to pursue his interest in art.

After the first Hamburg tour, the Beatles hooked up with Brian Epstein, the son of a record store owner. Epstein was to play a major role in their career until his death in 1967. In 1962 he arranged a contract with EMI Records, under the production of George Martin. The first single, "Love Me Do" (1962), did well, but not spectacularly so. Number two, "Please Please Me" (1963), topped the British charts, as did "From Me To You" (1963) and "She Loves You" (1963). Number five was "I Want To Hold Your Hand" (1963). The response around the world, including the United States, was quite simply without precedent. The Beatles were swept away on a tide of Beatlemania.

The stunning success of the Beatles also triggered the "British Invasion"—the domination of the American musical charts by British acts. The reasons for the Beatles' success lie both in the exceptional quality of their work and the situation in American popular culture—the bellwether pop culture—at that time. The Beatles' work was head and shoulders above that of almost all the other rock groups working. The exceptional songwriting of Lennon and McCartney and the high production standards they set for themselves made

The Beatles

their work stand out like gems on the normally mundane charts and ultimately set whole new standards. In addition, America was flagging musically. The old rock-and-roll stars of the 1950s had lost their fires, and the music that had replaced their music was milder, to say the least. The rock-and-roll fury that had begun in the 1950s had lost its voice by the early 1960s. The time was ripe for something new. Finally, the Beatles and the subsequent British Invasion groups provided a solution to the most critical problem in American pop music—that of race. The Beatles and their

army of followers rose above the question of race music (white boys singing the blues) because they were English, foreigners.

The Beatles' extraordinary career continued unabated, through two landmark films (by Richard Lester), *A Hard Day's Night* (1964) and *Help* (1965)—a third, *Let It Be* (1970), chronicled the breakup of the group—to the brilliant *Rubber Soul* (1965) album (featuring such hits as "Norwegian Wood," "Michelle," "It's Only Love," "You Won't See Me" and "Run For Your Life" to *Sergeant Pepper's Lonely Hearts Club*

Band (1967), perhaps the single most influential album in the history of rock. That album featured a dazzling blend of styles, culminating in the climactic "A Day In The Life." Aside from being one of the first concept albums and the first album to elevate album covers into an art form, *Sergeant Pepper* pointed rock in a whole new, more introspective direction.

Subsequent releases were equally excellent (*The Beatles*, often called The White Album, most notably), but cracks were appearing in the monolith. John Lennon had married Yoko Ono, and her presence at the recording sessions grated on the band's nerves. In 1971 the Beatles went their separate ways. In 1976 their music went through a major revival, with two "new" albums, *Love Songs* and *Live At The Hollywood Bowl*, topping the charts again.

The Beatles now have more than 60 million-selling records—the number grows each year—and have sold well over 400 million records worldwide; "I Want To Hold Your Hand" alone sold 12 million. The group had over 20 number one hits in America. In addition, the songwriting duo of Lennon and McCartney is the most successful such team in the history of popular music.

Despite peer pressure, media hype, outrageous offers of money and outright begging by all manner of fans and promoters, throughout the 1970s the Beatles made no effort to re-form. The killing of John Lennon in December 1980 in New York City dashed forever hopes of a reunion of the original foursome.

Beau Brummels, The Sal Valentino (vocals), Ron Meagher (bass), Ron Elliott (guitar), John Peterson (drums), Declan Mulligan (bass, vocals)—Best known for their 1965 single "Laugh Laugh," the Beau Brummels were one of the many Beatles sound-alikes from the British Invasion years. The twist is that the Brummels were an American band, and a good one. They disbanded in the late 1960s and re-formed with minor success in 1975.

Be-Bop Deluxe Bill Nelson (guitar, vocals), Charles Tumahai (bass), Andrew Clarke (keyboards), Simon Fox (drums)—A British band that had a sizable following on American FM radio, thanks to its *Modern Music* album released in 1976.

Beck, Jeff Dubbed by one critic as an "elder statesman" of rock and by another as one of the greatest British guitarists, Beck is probably a little of both. Born in June 1944 in Surrey, England, Beck captured the public's attention around 1966, when he began a two-year stint with the Yardbirds. He had two solo hits in England after leaving the Yardbirds, "Hi Ho Silver Lining" and the middle-of-the-road "Love Is Blue."

Thereafter he began a procession of Jeff Beck Groups, which featured the likes of Ron Wood, Rod Stewart and Nicky Hopkins in one incarnation. His latest work has included touring and recording with the Jan Hammer Group and more solo work, largely in a jazz-rock mode. To be sure, he's one of the most influential blues-based British guitarists, though he still dims in the light of Eric Clapton.

Bee Gees, The Robin Gibb (guitar, vocals), Maurice Gibb (guitar, vocals), Barry Gibb (guitar, vocals)—Originally from England by way of Australia, the trio of brothers began singing together in the mid-1950s and became quite popular in Australia before returning to England and signing with budding impresario Robert Stigwood in 1967. That year they had the first of many huge hits, "New York Mining Disaster Of 1941," followed in rapid succession by "To Love Somebody" (1967), "Holiday" (1967), "Massachusetts" (1967), "Words" (1968) and "I've Got To Get A Message To You"

Jeff Beck

(1968). Despite inevitable comparisons to the Beatles, the Bee Gees were more in the mold of the old male vocal harmony groups. In fact, they were (and are) the masters of slick harmony, and from the very beginning had an excellent grasp of not only the uses of harmony, but also the blending of such harmonies with an orchestra. Despite sibling spats (Robin tried briefly for a solo career), the Bee Gees have been steady residents on the charts. In 1975 they began making serious inroads in the disco market with their *Main Course* album, featuring the hits "Jive Talkin'" and "Nights On Broadway," which established the brothers as superstars all over again. The release of the soundtrack album to *Saturday Night Fever* in 1977, a movie that captured the waning 1970s brilliantly, was another enormous success for them. That album, featuring the Bee Gees' "How Deep Is Your Love," "Night Fever" and the expressive "Stayin' Alive," became the biggest seller in the history of pop music, with some 15 million albums already under the bridge and more coming. The album was so successful, in fact, that it demanded a whole new terminology ("triple platinum") to describe it and set wild standards for future releases. The Bee Gees remain at the top, three of rock's most successful survivors.

Bell, Al Vice president and producer for Stax Records, one of the cornerstone rhythm-and-blues labels of the 1960s. A former R&B disc jockey in Washington, D.C., Bell joined the Memphis label at the suggestion of Atlantic Records president Jerry Wexler. Stax rode the very crest of the "soul man" craze with acts like Otis Redding, Sam and Dave, Booker T. and the MGs, Arthur Conley and others, only to go down in flames in a cross-fire of financial mismanagement, falsified loans and misdealings.

Bell, Archie, and the Drells In 1968 Archie Bell and the Drells (James Wise, Willie Pernell and Lee Bell) dominated the singles charts with the catchy "Tighten Up," written and produced by the crack Philadelphia team of Gamble and Huff. The popularity of that record marked the ascendancy of the Philly dance sound over the more R&B-oriented Stax and pop-styled Motown. The group scored another hit later in 1968 with "I Can't Stop Dancing."

Bell, Maggie Born on Jan. 12, 1945 in Scotland, Bell achieved a brief bit of fame as the lead singer of the cult favorite Stone the Crows. Her solo career, while critically a success, has yet to shake the world.

Bell, Thom Philadelphia producer who scored first with the Spinners in the late 1960s and early 1970s and eventually became one of the foremost proponents of the pop-disco Philadelphia Sound. In the late 1970s he began working with Elton John and was responsible for refurbishing John's flagging career with a shot of disco.

Bell, William Born on July 16, 1939 in Memphis, Tenn., William Bell became one of

that city's better known soul artists, peaking in 1969 with "I Forgot To Be Your Lover."

Bellamy Brothers, The As mindless country-pop vocalists, Howard and David Bellamy fit the bill. They are best known for their hit singles "Let Your Love Flow" in 1976 and "If I Said You Had A Beautiful Body Would You Hold It Against Me" in 1979. The duo began playing together in high school, and in 1973 brother David wrote "Spiders and Snakes," a hit for Jim Stafford.

Benatar, Pat The heir apparent to the rock-and-roll sex symbol throne vacated by Linda Ronstadt, Benatar quickly became one of the most talked-about stars of 1980. Her stance is tough, *a la* the male rock icons of the 1960s, such as Mick Jagger or Roger Daltrey; her style is pure sexual energy. Born Pat Andrzejewski in 1952 and pointed in the direction of the stage by a mother who sang opera in New York City, Benatar seemed headed for the loftier reaches of the music business. She passed on an opera career for marriage, however. After the marriage broke up, she found herself back in New York City playing the cabarets. There she adopted her hard-edged rocker stance, which was evident on her 1979 *In The Heat Of The Night* album. In 1980 her career shifted into high gear with the single "Heartbreaker," followed quickly by "Hit Me With Your Best Shot," a top 10 song in early 1981. Her *Crimes Of Passion* was also a top selling album in 1980-81.

Benson, George Born on March 2, 1943 in Pennsylvania George Benson has worked steadily as a jazz-rock fusion player, breaking onto the rock charts in 1976 with "This Masquerade," from his *Breezin* album. The song was written by rock master Leon Russell. In 1978 he did a touch-new version of "On Broadway," the Drifters' hit from 1963.

Benton, Brook Most recently remembered for his superb rendition of Tony Joe White's "Rainy Night In Georgia" (1970), Benton made the charts several times in the late fifties and early sixties. One of his biggest successes came in 1961 with a song he coauthored with writing partner Clyde Otis, "The Boll Weevil Song." Born on Sept. 19, 1931 in Camden, S.C., he toured with a gospel group before teaming up with Otis in 1958. Their best-known collaboration was probably Clyde McPhatter's "Lover's Question" in that year.

Berry, Chuck Chuck Berry's story has all the makings of legend. Born Charles Edward Berry on Oct. 18, 1926 in Wentzville (outside of St. Louis), Mo., Berry aspired to be a hairdresser or perhaps a photographer. He'd done three years in a reform school for attempted robbery and wanted to get his life on solid footing in order to support his wife and two kids. Instead, he found rock and roll.

He'd been interested in music all through high school. He formed his first group, the Chuck Berry Combo, in 1952, but nothing happened until 1955, when he sat in with blues

Chuck Berry

godfather Muddy Waters in Chicago. Waters was impressed enough to send Berry around to Leonard Chess, head of Chess Records, who gave a listen. The result was a contract and a song named "Ida Red," which Berry changed to "Maybellene."

"Maybellene" became a giant hit in 1955, both on the pop and R&B charts, and eventually passed into rock-and-roll folklore as one of the great songs of the 1950s. Then in slam-bang succession came such Berry classics as "Roll Over Beethoven" (1956), "Too Much Monkey Business" b/w "Brown Eyed Handsome Man" (1956), "School Days" (1957), "Sweet Little Sixteen" (1958), "Johnny B. Goode" (1958), "Almost Grown" (1959), "Back In The U.S.A." (1959) and others, some of which were not even released as singles during this period. As a result Berry soared into the stratosphere of the rock revolution.

Berry came to symbolize the youth rebellion of the 1950s and, moreover, became one of the first black artists to reach a young white market. In light of that, it's not surprising the roof fell in. In 1959 Berry was charged with violating the Mann Act, and after two years of litigation, he was sent to prison for two years. He returned in 1964, facing a music world he'd helped create. Amazingly, he bounced back that year with a string of three classic hits, "Nadine," "No Particular Place To Go," and "You Never Can Tell." He sprinkled the 1960s and early 1970s with fine work and had his biggest success ever in 1972 with "My Ding-A-Ling."

At this point, according to legend, Berry should spend his retirement counting his money and musing on the rock and roll he helped create. Real life is seldom so accommodating, though. In 1979 a tearful Chuck Berry was convicted of income tax evasion and served three months in jail; although he swore the time would kill

him, the judge was unrelenting. But now Berry's back on the road again.

Betts, Dickey Guitarist for the Allman Brothers Band and author of the Brothers' sole AM hit, "Rambling Man," Dickey Betts (born Richard Betts on Dec. 12, 1943 in West Palm Beach, Fla.) grew up listening to country music and bluegrass in central Florida. Those roots were clearly visible in Betts' solo album *Highway Call* in the mid-1970s and in his unsuccessful venture with his own band, Great Southern, after the breakup of the Brothers. His crystal clear, bluegrass-tinted guitar runs have spawned a million imitators, as has his dual lead guitar work with Duane Allman. The Brothers at their peak, in fact, represent some of the finest guitar work in popular music.

B-52s Kate Pierson (vocals), Cindy Wilson (vocals), Fred Schneider (vocals), Ricky Wilson (bass), Keith Strickland

B-52s

(drums)—Formed in Athens, Ga. in 1976, the B-52s quite simply defy categorization. They affect 1960s styles— miniskirts, bouffant hairdos (in fact, B-52 is a local colloquialism for the beehive hairdo) and girl group songs. The group became a favorite of the critics with songs like "Rock Lobster" from *The B-52s* album in 1979 and "Private Idaho" from the *Wild Planet* album in 1980.

Big Bopper, The   Born Jape Richardson in 1935 in Beaumont, Tex., he changed his name to J.P. Richardson when he began his professional career. His career was just taking off after his 1958 release of "Chantilly Lace" when he was killed in a plane crash with Buddy Holly and Richie Valens on Feb. 3, 1959 en route to a show in Fargo, N.D.

Big Brother and the Holding Company   Pete Albin (bass, vocals), Sam Andrew (guitar, vocals), James Gurley (guitar, vocals), David Getz (vocals), Janis Joplin (vocals)—The band itself was a casualty of the phenomenal rise of Janis Joplin. Things had been going just fine for the San Francisco group when, in 1966, a friend suggested Big Brother could use a girl singer. Joplin became a 1960s re-creation of the Judy Garland legend, and nobody could remember anything at all about the band. In 1968 Janis Joplin and Big Brother parted ways, leaving the band to record two obscure albums before fading away and Janis to follow her own path to

personal tragedy. Nevertheless they left behind one of the great white blues albums of rock, *Cheap Thrills,* recorded in 1968 and featuring Janis doing "Piece Of My Heart," "Summertime," "I Need A Man To Love" and "Ball And Chain."

Big Star   Named for a supermarket chain in Memphis, Big Star provided a brief home for Box Tops lead singer Alex Chilton. The Box Tops rode to stardom with such hits as "The Letter" (1967) and "Cry Like A Baby" (1968), but the band broke up when one of the members insisted on going to college. Chilton then worked in Big Star and eventually found his way to New York City, where he has worked regularly with his own New Wave band.

Bilk, Acker   A former blacksmith turned clarinet player, this British instrumentalist captured the charts in 1962 with his "Strangers On The Shore," spending some 21 weeks on U.S. charts and 39 weeks on British charts.

Bishop, Elvin   Southern rocker Charlie Daniels once remarked in song that Elvin Bishop "ain't good lookin', but he sure can play," which is the gospel truth. Born on Oct. 21, 1942 in Tulsa, Okla., he joined Paul Butterfield in 1960 and immediately moved to the forefront of white blues, remaining there until signing with Capricorn Records, the Macon, Ga. home of the Allman Brothers Band, in 1973. There he tempered his blues with a dose of Southern

Elvin Bishop

bar boogie and eventually got an AM hit, "Fooled Around And Fell In Love," in 1976. His sixth album on Capricorn, *Hog Heaven,* finds the Tulsa-born good ole boy to be totally assimilated into the Southern boogie train.

Bishop, Steven   Born in 1951 in San Diego, Calif., Steven Bishop did backup work for such artists as Art Garfunkel before going on his own in 1976 with *Careless,* which produced the hit "Save It For A Rainy Day." His 1977 hit, "On And On," established him as a solid seller and concert draw, much in the vocal style of Garfunkel.

Black, Bill   Best known as the bass player in Elvis Presley's original trio at Sun Records (Scotty Moore, the third member, played guitar), Black also backed Elvis on later RCA albums. In 1959 he formed the Bill Black Combo and began a string of instrumental hits, including "Smokie Part II" (1959), "White

Silver Sands" (1960) and "Don't Be Cruel" (1960). He continued with modest success until his death in October 1965.

Black, Cilla   Born Priscilla Maria Veronica White on May 27, 1943 in Liverpool, Cilla Black was a huge success in Britain during the Beatles' years of the 1960s. She was an instant smash with the Burt Bacharach/Hal David "Anyone Who Had A Heart" (1964), followed three months later by "You're My World." Beatle manager Brian Epstein persuaded her to change her name because, he said, people thought she "sounded black."

Blackmore, Ritchie   Born on April 14, 1945 in England, Blackmore is best known as one of the founding fathers of the heavy metal rock group Deep Purple. He had limited success with his own group, Ritchie Blackmore's Rainbow.

Black Oak Arkansas   Jim "Dandy" Mangrum (vocals), Stan "Goober" Knight (guitar), Ricky Reynolds (guitar, vocals), Pat Daugherty (bass, vocals), Jimmy Henderson (guitar), Tommy Aldridge (drums)— Black Oak, Arkansas was once only a place, and that's perhaps what it should have remained. As a rock group centered there, Black Oak has very little to say for itself, although Jim "Dandy" has the potential to be a great singer in the howling Memphis tradition. The group is best known for its sleazy album covers and raunchy sex lyrics, although buried in the past is a truly brilliant rock-and-roll album, done under the group's earlier

incarnation of the Knowbody Else (also the name of the album) and produced by the inimitable James Luther Dickinson of Memphis.

Black Sabbath   Ozzie Osbourne (vocals), Tony Iommi (guitar), Geezer Butler (bass), Bill Ward (drums)—

Black Sabbath

Formed in 1968, the group hit the charts with a mixture of occult mumbo-jumbo and loud noise, which powered it just fine through 1973. Black Sabbath defined a whole genre of rock that became known as heavy metal, with such hits as the *Paranoid* album in 1970 (the single of the same name was also a hit) and the *Sabbath, Bloody Sabbath* album in 1973. In 1977 the group fell victim to the rock audience's inability to be shocked anymore and turned over its following to bands

such as Kiss and Aerosmith. Surprisingly, Black Sabbath returned in 1978 with *Never Say Die,* but eventually lead singer Osbourne went solo.

Blake, Norman   Born on March 10, 1938 in Chattanooga, Tenn., Blake is a leading sessions guitarist in Nashville and consistent recorder and proponent of what he calls "mountain music."

Blakely, Ronee   Yet another folkie, Blakely was born in Idaho. Her career took a turn for the better in 1975, when she was nominated for an Academy Award for her portrayal of a haunted country singer in Robert Altman's *Nashville.* Later in 1975 she recorded an album called *Welcome,* produced by no less than Atlantic heavyweight Jerry Wexler, and then joined Bob Dylan on the Rolling Thunder tour, but no sparks seemed to fly. Since then she's returned to films.

Bland, Bobby "Blue"
Robert Calvin Bland (born on Jan. 27, 1930 in the tiny town of Rosemark, Tenn.) grew up listening to the Beale Street blues in Memphis. He sang the blues in high school and by the late 1940s found himself a member of a band called the Beale Streeters, which also boasted B.B. King, Johnny Ace and Roscoe Gordon. Through the 1950s and 1960s Bland was established in the black music market as a solid rhythm-and-blues seller, with such hits as "Call On Me" and "Farther Up The Road." In the early 1970s, however, he found his appeal shifting to a white audience, turned on to blues by white British and Southern singers. His position now seems assured, and he tours regularly with B.B. King as a one-two punch from old Beale Street.

Blind Faith   Stevie Winwood (keyboards, guitar, vocals), Eric Clapton (guitar), Ginger Baker (drums), Rich Grech (bass, violin, vocals)—The first rock supergroup, formed from the remains of Cream (Clapton and Baker), Traffic (Winwood) and the British band Family (Grech). Blind Faith debuted with a free concert in London, released a single album and began what is generally called the ill-fated U.S. tour—ill-fated because the group wasn't really a group yet, just a collection of individuals who weren't sure what was going

on. The album, *Blind Faith,* was better than critics said it was, and with a little less hype, the band might have proven to be more than a flash in the pan.

Blondie   Deborah Harry (vocals), Frank Infante (guitar), Clem Burke (drummer), Nigel Harrison (bass), Chris Stein (guitar), Jimmy Destri (keyboards)—The first New York band to break out of the city's fertile, if insular, New Wave (aka punk, generally a return to rock basics) scene, on the strength of two huge single successes—"Heart Of Glass" and "One Way Or Another," both in 1979. The secret of the band's success was blond, vampish ex-Playboy bunny Deborah Harry, an unabashed sex symbol for the cynical seventies. Despite all the protestations ("Blondie is a group not just a girl singer...."), Harry's punchy vocals and overpowering stage presence were what packed in the crowds. It is interesting to note that while Blondie's success was seen as a vindication of New Wave-punk rock, the group's 1979 hit "Heart Of Glass" was

99 and 44/100 percent disco. Nevertheless, Blondie's formula kept working, as it demonstrated in early 1981 with the album *Autoamerican* and the singles "The Tide Is High" and "Rapture" in the top 10. Harry later went solo.

Blood, Sweat and Tears
David Clayton-Thomas (vocals), Bobby Colomby (drums), Bill Tillman (sax), Ron McClure (bass), Dave Bargeron (trombone), George Wadenius (guitar), Larry Willis (keyboards)—One of the first great experiments in fusing jazz and rock, Blood, Sweat and Tears was launched in 1967 by rock icon Al Kooper, who was looking to expand the guitar-organ-drums rock axis. The first album, *Child Is Father To The Man* in 1968, was true to Kooper's vision, but Kooper wasn't hanging around for the second—visions are notoriously short-lived. The second album, bolstered by Canadian David Clayton-Thomas, was something nobody expected—a hit. *Blood, Sweat and Tears* spawned three hit singles in a row: "You Made Me So Very

Blondie

Happy" (1969), "Spinning Wheel" (1969) and "When I Die" (1969), a feat the band was never able to either match or follow up to any great extent. Although the group is still working (Clayton-Thomas left for a while to pursue a solo career that didn't happen, but he returned in 1974), little can be said for its host of later albums.

Bloom, Bobby   Originally a member of a group called the Imaginations, Bloom came to public attention in 1970 with a light, summery sounding song called "Montego Bay." He died in 1974, the victim of an accidental shooting.

Bloomfield, Mike   One of the first blues guitarists to achieve enormous success without being either black or British, Bloomfield always seemed on the verge of permanent success. As a guitarist for Paul Butterfield's Blues Band in the mid-1960s and the founder of the fine group Electric Flag in 1967 (with Buddy Miles and Nick Gravenites), Bloomfield was a college campus and FM radio stalwart. His *Super Session* album with Steve Stills and Al Kooper in 1968 was an instant classic, as was the follow-up *The Live Adventures Of Mike Bloomfield And Al Kooper*. But somehow Bloomfield failed to find a comfortable niche, and although he drifted from group to group, he did nothing to outpace his work in the 1960s.
   On Feb. 15, 1981, Bloomfield was found dead in his car.

Blue Cheer   Leigh Stephens (guitar), Dickie Peterson (bass,

vocals), Paul Whaley (drums)—Although Blue Cheer recorded six albums altogether, the group remains best known for its single hit in the summer of 1968, a pile-driver rendition of "Summertime Blues." The song captured perfectly the mania of that summer of acid-rock and miscellaneous psychedelia. The band, however, was ill-equipped to cope with the soothing seventies.

Blue Oyster Cult   Eric Bloom (vocals, guitar), Allen Lanier (keyboards), Albert Bouchard (drums, vocals), Joe Bouchard (bass, vocals), Donald Roeser (guitar, vocals)—One of the *heaviest* of the heavy metal groups, complete with bizarre, overpowering guitar duals and enough decibels to shake the fillings out of your teeth. Amazingly enough, the group got its start in 1971 at Stony Brook College on Long Island, New York. The group's basic philosophy is mirrored in the title of one of its albums—*On Your Feet Or On Your Knees* (1975)—and its lone hit single —"(Don't Fear) The Reaper" (1976). The band summed up the music of the 1970s quite nicely in its 1977 release— "This Ain't The Summer Of Love." Indeed!

Blue Swede   Djorn Skifs (vocals), Bosse Liljedahl (bass), Anders Berglund (keyboards, vocals), Thomas Berglund (trumpet), Michael Areklew (guitar), Hinke Ekestubbe (sax), Jan Guldback (drums)—Swedish group best known for its remake of B.J. Thomas' "Hooked On A

Feeling" in 1974, which featured an oddly captivating tribal chant in the background.

Blues Image, The   Dennis Correll (vocals); Joe Lala (congas, vocals); Manuel Bertematti (drums); Skip Konte (keyboards); Kent Henry (guitar); Malcolm Jones (bass); additional member, Michael Pinera (vocals)—Pioneers in the Latin-rock style, the group had a single hit, "Ride Captain Ride" in 1970.

Blues Magoos, The   Ronald Gilbert (bass), Ralph Scala (keyboards), Emil Thielhelm (guitar), Michael Esposito (guitar), Jeffrey Daking (drums)—A psychedelic group from the mid-1960s best known for the frenetic 1966 recording "We Ain't Got Nothing Yet." While the music was straight San Francisco psychedelia, the group was from the Bronx, New York City. It survived, in one form or other, into the early 1970s.

Blues Project, The   Al Kooper (keyboards), Steve Katz (guitar), Danny Kalb (guitar), Andy Kulberg (bass, flute), Roy Blumenfeld (drums)—Ah yes, the *original* Al Kooper white blues band, formed in New York City in the early 1960s. The band built its reputation playing Cafe Au Go Go in Greenwich Village and went on to become one of the best-known underground bands in America. But the mercurial Kooper couldn't be chained up in one project for long, and he soon drifted on (with Katz) to experiment with Blood, Sweat and Tears. A 1973 reunion produced one album, *Reunion In Central Park."*

Blunstone, Colin Born on June 24, 1945 in England, Blunstone is best known as a founding member of the Zombies. He is presently recording for Elton John's Rocket Records.

Bob B Soxx and the Blue Jeans Darlene Love (vocals), Fanita James (vocals), Bobby Sheen (vocals)—Originally a collection of backup singers on the West Coast, the group was created by producer Phil Spector in 1962, and its first song, "Zip-A-Dee-Doo-Dah," was a hit that year. Darlene Love went on to sing the lead on Spector's masterpiece "He's A Rebel" (with the Crystals) and later had a successful solo career, beginning in 1963 with "Today I Met The Boy I'm Gonna Marry" and "Wait 'Til My Bobby Gets Home."

Bolan, Marc Born in 1947 in London, Bolan and his group, T. Rex, enjoyed a brief fling as teenybopper heroes in 1972 with their *Slider* album. Teen hero was a strange position for Bolan, who'd begun his career sunk in a mythology of his own making, complete with wizards, miscellaneous demons and last-minute salvation via rock and roll. He had some minor fortune on the American singles chart in 1972 with "Bang A Gong," but he never achieved the kind of success in the United States that he enjoyed in England. He was killed in a car crash on Sept. 16, 1977, leaving a legacy of 16 albums.

Bond, Graham Called by some the father of the British blues movement, Bond was instrumental in the creation of the great rhythm-and-blues upheaval in England during the early 1960s. He cut his teeth on jazz saxophone and formed his first R&B band in 1963, featuring Jack Bruce and Ginger Baker (both of Cream fame) and soon-to-be superguitarist John McLaughlin. He toured extensively throughout the 1960s, playing R&B with a variety of groups under the general head of the Graham Bond Organization. But R&B innovators—both black and white—have a way of getting lost in the shuffle, and Bond was no exception. In later years he did some work with Baker's power group, Ginger Baker's Air Force, and surfaced in 1972 to do an album with Peter Brown and singer Diane Stewart called *Two Heads Are Better Than One*. Although the album was well received, Bond drifted on, becoming obsessed with the occult, forming various unsuccessful new groups and drifting in and out of drugs. In 1974 he died under the wheels of a London train.

Bonds, Gary "U.S." Gary Anderson (born on June 6, 1939 in Jacksonville, Fla.), changed his name to Gary Ulysses Samuel Bonds in 1960 and began making a series of rock-and-roll classics. His first hit was "New Orleans" in 1960, but his biggest came the next year, when technicians recorded a jam session between Bonds and a group called Daddy G. The song was called "Quarter To Three," and it swept the country in 1961. He followed that up with three more top 10 hits ("School Is Out" in 1961, "Dear Lady Twist" in 1962 and "Twist, Twist Senora" in 1962) before fading onto the oldies circuit. "Quarter To Three" was resurrected in the late 1970s by Bruce Springsteen, who used the song to close his concerts.

Bono, Sonny The lesser half of Sonny and Cher was born Salvatore Bono in Detroit on Feb. 16, 1935. He met Cher in 1963, when they were both singing backup for Phil Spector's group the Ronettes, and it was more or less love at first sight. After a quick marriage in Tijuana, they worked as Caesar and Cleo until 1965, when they dropped a bomb on the music world in the form of a single titled "I Got You Babe." Overnight the freakily dressed lovers were a sensation, to the tune of a $3 million gross for that year alone. Their total income the year before had been a paltry $3,000. For the next two years they prospered, then the pop-folkie period waned. But unlike most others of the period Sonny and Cher headed for Vegas, a move that eventually led to their enormously successful television show, with Sonny as the straight man for Cher's deadpan humor. What followed is best left to the gossip mags, but in brief: Cher emerged as the perfect talent for the seventies; the pair got divorced; and Sonny sulked, tried his own shows, was briefly reunited and was last seen playing a detective in Nashville in his own made-for-television movie. What the future holds for Sonny is anybody's guess, but it probably doesn't hold Cher.

Bonzo Dog Band Viv Stanshall (vocals, trumpet), Neil Innes (keyboards, guitar, bass, vocals), Roger Ruskin Spear (sax), Rodney Slater (sax), "Legs" Larry Smith (percussion)—A strange group, to be sure. Crazy and brilliant, the band began in 1966 as sort of a home for wayward and eccentric musicians (note the musical lineup). While other groups of the time were trying to fuse rock and rhythm and blues (or something similar), the Dogs were trying to fuse ragtime and surrealism. Their first album, *Gorilla*, included such ditties as "I'm Bored," "Look Out, There's A Monster Coming" and "I Left My Heart In San Francisco." They followed that up with *I'm The Urban Spaceman* in 1969, produced by none other than Paul McCartney (under the name of Apollo C. Vermouth) and featuring such cuts as "Can Blue Men Sing The Whites," "My Pink Half Of The Drainpipe" and the ever-popular "We Are All Normal." Innes went on to join the insane comedy troop Monty Python, while Rodney Slater went into politics.

Booker T. and the MGs Booker T. Jones (keyboards), Steve Cropper (guitar), Al Jackson (drums), Donald "Duck" Dunn (bass)—The personification of the clean, cool Memphis Sound of the 1960s, Booker T. Jones and the MGs (short for "Memphis Group") were actually studio musicians at Stax Records in Memphis. Jones and Jackson were black, Dunn and Cropper white; among them they produced some of the finest

soul music ever made. They played behind Wilson Pickett, Rufus and Carla Thomas and Otis Redding, as well as making their own recordings. In 1962 they cut a song written by Jones, Cropper and Jackson called "Green Onions," and within weeks they were international stars. Their sporadic string of hits continued until 1971, when Jones married Priscilla Coolidge, sister of singer Rita Coolidge, and left to work full time on her career. In 1975 Jackson was stabbed to death at his home by an intruder, and Stax Records was in decline. Cropper and Dunn later joined "Saturday Night Live" regulars John Belushi and Dan Ackroyd as part of the Blues Brothers, a sort of loving spoof—or not-so-loving spoof, depending on your point of view—on the music of the fifties and sixties and R&B in general.

Boomtown Rats, The Irish punk band led by vocalist Bob Geldof, the group was billed by the English press in the late 1970s as "the new Rolling Stones." Since then the Boomtown Rats have backed off a bit from their tougher-than-thou stance, but they remain one of the few winners in the New Wave sweepstakes. Of their two albums, *Boomtown Rats* (1978) and *A Tonic For The Troops* (1979), *Boomtown Rats* is probably the best.

Boone, Debby Daughter of the white-bucked Pat, Debby Boone came out of nowhere in 1977 with "You Light Up My Life," an across-the-board hit that spent more time at the top of the charts than any other

song in the last 23 years. The song and Debby also picked up two Grammies and one Academy Award (it was the theme song for the dreadful Joe Brooks movie of the same name) and a bunch of other minor awards as well. While the song intimates a relationship between a man and a woman, Boone revealed that she was singing the song for Jesus, which explained its transcendent quality. She was born on Sept. 22, 1956 in Los Angeles, Calif.

Boone, Pat No Who's Who would be complete without him. He was born on June 1, 1934 in Nashville, Tenn. and his recording career began there in the early 1950s. Things really didn't click, however, until 1955, when he recorded "Ain't That A Shame," an old Fats Domino number. After that he provided, albeit unwittingly, a strange service for rock and roll. All through the 1950s and into the next decade, while he was cutting cover after cover of rock hits—"Tutti Frutti" (1956), "Long Tall Sally" (1956), "Why Baby Why" (1957), "Good Rockin' Tonight" (1959)—he was legitimizing the new music with the Frank Sinatra generation and providing much-needed royalty money to such rock pioneers as Fats Domino and Little Richard, whose songs Boone copied with such great success.

Boston Tom Scholz (guitar, keyboards), Bradley Delp (vocals, guitar), Barry Goudreau (guitar), Fran Sheehan (bass), Sib Hashian (drums)—Since its debut in

Boston

until the album *Ziggy Stardust And The Spiders From Mars* in 1972 that ripples were first felt in America. Despite (or perhaps because of) his predilection for wearing dresses, dying his hair orange and other such mannerisms, his American fame grew.

The real break came in 1974 with his standing-room-only Diamond Dogs tour of the U.S. and album of the same name, with Bowie riding the crest of science fiction rock across the country. Seizing on the sci-fi theme, he starred in Nicolas Roeg's haunting film *The Man Who Fell to Earth,* about a

David Bowie

1976, Boston has sold around seven million albums, which should qualify the group as some kind of phenomenon. Boston's secret is straight-ahead rock and roll, "progressive" enough to make it on FM radio but tight and catchy enough to grab those big AM radio audiences (and bucks).

The real phenomenon, though, is Scholz, who literally invented Boston in his home-built basement recording studio. With a master's from MIT, Scholz is hardly the prototypical rock-and-roll hero. By day he was a senior product designer for Poloroid, by night the mad artiste of the studio, producing demos and circulating them to record companies. In 1976, after a couple of tough turndowns, Epic Records bit, and Scholz

hustled around to find a band that sounded like the demos. Its members named the band after where they lived, and their debut album, named after the band and the city, sold half a million copies in 11 weeks. The second album, *Don't Look Back,* came in 1978, and while it didn't duplicate the incredible success of the first, it did well.

Bowie, David   A clear case of talent winning out over weirdness, Bowie was born David Jones in London in 1947, but he changed his name in 1963 to avoid being confused with David Jones the Monkee—arguably a fate worse than death for a rock star. He worked with his own band and, later, with a mime troupe before gaining a following in England with his first two albums. But it wasn't

26

spaceman who literally fell to earth and was trapped on this backward planet.

During the late 1970s he worked as a producer for Brian Eno, and his bizarre visions of the future have lost none of their power, as evidenced by a live double album released in 1979, *Stage,* and his 1980 release, *Scary Monsters.*

Boxtops, The   Alex Chilton (vocals), Billy Cunningham (bass), Gary Talley (guitar), Danny Smythe (drums), John Evans (guitar, organ)— Described by one critic as the blackest sounding white group in ages, the Boxtops grabbed the top of the charts in 1967 with "The Letter," produced by veteran Memphis producer Chips Moman. They kept turning out their black-white music until 1970, when they drifted away to other pursuits, such as college. The group also produced a classic ode to groupies called "Sweet Cream Ladies Forward March."

Bramblett, Randall   Born in Jesup, Ga., Randall Bramblett first came to attention as a sessions keyboard and saxaphone man in Muscle Shoals, Ala. and Macon, Ga. He toured with Gregg Allman, garnering rave reviews for his work, before launching his recording career in 1976 with *That Other Mile.* The album quickly established him as an FM favorite, which he remains today.

Bread   David Gates (vocals, guitar, keyboards), James Griffin (vocals, guitar), Larry Knechtel (keyboards), Mike Botts (drums)—A very soft rock ensemble formed in 1969. The group's first big success came the next year with "Make It With You," followed by "It Don't Matter To Me" (1970), "If" (1971), "Baby I'm A Want You" (1971) and others. Lead singer Gates played in a high school band in Tulsa, Okla. with Leon Russell, backed such greats as Chuck Berry, Carl Perkins and Johnny Burnette and worked with Elvis Presley in a film. Griffin had worked for Buddy Holly's Crickets and Burnette and had won an Academy Award for his songwriting (under the name of Arthur James) for "For All We Know" from the film *Lovers and Other Strangers.* Like so many other groups, Bread broke up to allow its members to find fame as solo acts, only to re-form in 1976 when that fame wasn't forthcoming; they are now known as David Gates and Bread.

Brewer, Teresa   Basically a high-pitched country-styled crooner, Brewer (born on May 7, 1931 in Toledo, Ohio) is best remembered for songs like "A Tear Fell" (1956), her biggest hit, and for her cover versions of such rhythm-and-blues standards as Johnny Ace's "Pledging My Love" (1955).

Brewer and Shipley
Michael Brewer and Thomas Shipley got together in the late 1960s in Los Angeles after several years of solo folk work. In 1971 they released a sort of doper's national anthem, "One Toke Over The Line," their only major hit.

Brinsley Schwarz   Brinsley Schwarz (guitar, vocals), Nick Lowe (bass, vocals), Billy Rankin (drums), Bob Andrews (keyboards), Ian Gomm (guitar)—Launched in 1970 with one of the largest hype campaigns (i.e., for that time— hype campaigns tend to get bigger each year, sort of like the national debt), Brinsley Schwarz managed to survive by becoming an extremely competent bar band, eventually building a cult following in the United States. Actually, the band is better known now for its New Wave alumni—Nick Lowe has found a lucrative solo career and works sometimes with his band, Rockpile; Andrews and Schwarz play with Graham Parker's band, the Rumour; and Ian Gomm recently launched his solo career with a U.S. tour.

Bromberg, David   Born in September 1945 in Philadelphia, Pa., folklorist/ sessions player David Bromberg made his mark on Bob Dylan's *New Morning* album. Although he's made several solo albums, including *Midnight On The Water* in 1975 and *How Late'll Ya Play 'Til?* in 1976, which feature a blend of jazz, folk and blues, he remains best known to a small clique of fans.

Brooklyn Bridge, The   Johnny Maestro (vocals), Fred Ferrara (vocals), Mike Gregorio (vocals), Les Cauchi (vocals), Tom Sullivan (arrangements), Carolyn Woods (organ), Jim Rosica (bass), Jim Macioce (guitar), Artie Cantanzarita (drums), Shelly Davis (trumpet), Joe Ruvio (sax)—Formed in New York City in 1968 from the remnants of two groups (the

Del-Satins and the Rhythm Method), the Brooklyn Bridge gained a national audience in 1968 with the Jim Webb-penned "The Worst That Could Happen" and a string of similar songs, although none equaled the success of the first. The lead singer, Johnny Maestro, whose real name was Johnny Mastrangelo, had been lead singer for a late-1950s group called the Crests.

Broonzy, Big Bill Born in June 1893 in Scott, Miss., Big Bill Broonzy began playing the blues in Chicago during the 1920s and eventually came to dominate the blues scene in that city. During the early 1950s (after the death of Leadbelly) Broonzy toured Europe extensively, building on Leadbelly's foundation and establishing American blues as something of a European mania. Broonzy died in 1958.

Brown, Arthur One of rock's more bizarre exponents, Arthur Brown (born in 1944 in Yorkshire, England) was a philosophy student before he turned into the Crazy World of Arthur Brown, one of rock's first outrageous stage acts. In one variation Brown, dressed in enough feathers for several Indian tribes, would be lowered onto stage with a crane; he ended his performance by setting various and sundry items on fire. Other times he hung himself on a cross. His single American hit came in 1968 with "Fire," an obsessive little ditty that opened with references to a god of Hell Fire and went on from there. Although he continued working through the 1970s (including a bit part in the

movie *Tommy*), the capacity of audiences to be shocked was noticeably dulled in later years.

Brown, Clarence "Gatemouth"
Contemporary bluesman Clarence "Gatemouth" Brown is best known for his work with country singer and instrumentalist Roy Clark, who has worked steadily to bring Brown to public attention. Brown's jazzy blues are augmented by his use of the electric fiddle.

Brown, James The self-proclaimed Godfather of Soul, Minister of the New New Super Heavy Funk and Soul Brother

Number One was born on May 3, 1933 in Augusta, Ga. and, from a childhood of picking cotton, shining shoes and washing cars for a living, went on to become, hyperbole aside, the most important black artist in America. Beginning with such rhythm-and-blues hits as "Please, Please, Please" (1956), "Try Me" (1958) and "Night Train" (1962) and a dynamic stage show, Brown quickly established himself as the top R&B performer in the country. Almost a decade later, however, he shifted directions—Brown saw the beginnings of the British Invasion and realized what he

James Brown

was seeing was repackaged American black music. He assembled a huge entourage of singers, dancers and his own backup group, the Famous Flames, and went out to give the white kids a taste of the real thing. The result was two million-sellers in 1965, at the very height of the Beatles' influence, including the classic "Papa's Got A Brand New Bag." From then on he concentrated on the black and white market with such hits as "It's A Man's Man's Man's World" (1966), "Cold Sweat" (1967) and "I Got The Feelin'" (1968). That year, after the assassination of Dr. Martin Luther King, Brown went on national television with a plea for peace—a plea that is credited with defusing riots across the country and that earned Brown a commendation from the White House. Brown's hit for 1968 was, appropriately, "Say It Loud (I'm Black And I'm Proud)." Yet Brown never forgot the roots of his music— you could always dance to James Brown music—and when the trend turned to disco dance music in the mid-1970s, he was already there with such classics as "Hot Pants" (1971) and his 1976 *Body Heat* album, which went on to become one of the biggest sellers of his career. As recently as 1975, Brown was still working 300 nights a year, a killing regimen that he clung to for over 20 years. In addition to his music, he owns a publishing company, a record production company and several radio stations and has extensive real estate holdings. If there is a secret to his music, it is the incredible intensity with

which he approaches every song. True to his gospel background James Brown is a believer, both in his music and in his audience—a James Brown concert is an experience that one seldom forgets, with all the features of a tent revival meeting, political rally and 24-hour dance party. In short, James Brown is an American original, and all of popular music today is in his debt.

Brown, Ruth Born on Jan. 30, 1928 in Portsmouth, Va., rhythm-and-blues singer Ruth Brown was one of the cornerstones of Atlantic Records' domination of black music in the early 1950s. Such songs as "Five, Ten, Fifteen Hours" (1952) and "Mama, He Treats Your Daughter Mean" (1953), both million sellers on Atlantic, helped establish that label as a force in black music and paved the way for the coming of rock in the mid-1950s. Brown herself benefited from that coming, crossing onto the pop charts in 1957 with "Lucky Lips." She began her career singing in the church, but was soon swayed by the more secular music of such jazz singers as Billie Holiday. Her career almost ended before it got off the ground when she was injured in an automobile accident on her way to her debut at the Apollo Theater in New York City. Brown was hospitalized for almost a year, but she came back strong after her release.

Browne, Jackson The prime practitioner of Los Angeles angst was born on Oct. 9, 1948 in West Germany and raised in the City of

Jackson Browne

Angels. His early career was highlighted by his songwriting for such a diverse group as Nico, Joe Cocker, the Nitty Gritty Dirt Band and Tom Rush. In 1971 he debuted with an album of his own, *Jackson Browne,* featuring "Doctor My Eyes" and "Rock Me On The Water." He soon established himself as the most literate of the L.A. country-rock axis (featuring, most notably, the Eagles and Linda Ronstadt). In 1976 his wife, Phyllis Major, committed suicide, and the event so ruptured Browne's life that he began an introspective odyssey into the laid-back world of southern California. The result was an album titled *The Pretender,* released later that year, which proved to be his masterpiece—especially the title track. It took a bitter look at the attitudes and life- styles of the mellow world of southern California—as well as the rest of the country—and remains one of the most eloquent documents of the waning decade.

Brownsville Station
Michael "Cub" Koda (guitar, vocals), Michael Lutz (bass), T. J. Cronley (drums), Anthony Driggins (bass)—Formed during the late 1960s in Ann Arbor, Mich., Brownsville Station developed a reputation for being "punk," then meaning junior high snotty, before scoring big in 1973 with "Smokin' In The Boys Room," which dominated AM radio for a whole summer. The group is now "punk" in the sense of New Wave, or basic rock, music.

Bruce, Jack   Born on May 14, 1943 in Scotland, bassist Jack Bruce is best known for his work with the supergroup trio Cream (with Eric Clapton and Ginger Baker). After the demise of Cream, Bruce released a couple of solo albums (including the well-received *Songs For A Tailor*) before drifting closer and closer to jazz, forming several groups that fell apart and eventually taking a brief retirement. He returned to recording in 1977 with *How's Tricks*.

Bryant, Anita   Born on March 25, 1940 in Tulsa, Okla., the former "Orange Juice Queen" is best remembered for her string of ballads in the late 1950s, including "Til There Was You" (1959), her first hit, and "Paper Roses" (1960), her best-known song. She was a second runner-up to Miss America in 1958. In 1980 Bryant divorced her husband.

B.T. Express, The   William Risbrook (sax, flute), Louis Risbrook (bass), Richard Thompson (guitar), Barbara Joyce Lomas (vocals), Olando Terrell Woods (drums), Carlos Ward (sax), Dennis Rowe (percussion), Michael Jones (organ)—Formed in the mid-1970s by producer King Davis to cash in on the budding disco boom. And cash in they did, with such hits as "Do It (Til You're Satisfied)" (1974) and "Express" (1975). Pioneers of formula funk.

Buchanan, Roy   Guitarist Roy Buchanan (born in Arkansas) worked as a master guitarist behind literally hundreds of bands from 1959 until 1972, when he launched a solo career with *Roy Buchanan.* The album received considerable FM play, and since then he has had a moderately successful career.

Buckingham, Nicks   The husband/wife duo of Lindsey Buckingham and Stevie Nicks released a single album, *Buckingham/Nicks,* in 1973 before joining the enormously successful Fleetwood Mac. Their songwriting, arranging and melodic contributions galvanized Fleetwood Mac and were largely responsible for that group's tremendous surge in popularity. Unfortunately it also broke the duo up. As for *Buckingham/Nicks,* it is best remembered for its cover, which features Ms. Nicks and Mr. Buckingham nude.

Buckinghams, The   Denny Tufano (vocals), Carl Giamarese (guitar), Jon Paulos (drums), Nick Fortune (bass,) Marty Grebb (organ)—

Extremely popular, extremely commercial singles band from the mid-1960s, launched in Chicago in 1965. The band began moving in 1966 with "Kind Of A Drag," followed by "Don't You Care" (1967), "Mercy Mercy Mercy" (1967), "Hey /Baby (They're Playing Our Song)" (1967), "Susan" (1968) and "Kind Of A Drag" again in 1969. About then the band totally ran out of steam as the full effects of the San Francisco underground sound began to be felt.

Buckley, Lord   Born in 1905 in Stockton, Calif., Richard "Lord" Buckley was one of the first humorists to make extensive use of street language and humor. Jimmy Buffett recorded a rollicking version of Buckley's classic "God's Own Drunk" in 1974.

Buckley, Tim   Folksinger Tim Buckley (born on Feb. 14, 1947 in Washington, D.C.) spent much of his time building up a cult following with one album, then dashing their hopes with the follow-up. From folk he drifted toward jazz and, after a brief layoff, toward straight commercial rock. In all, he produced nine albums before his untimely death in 1975 of a drug overdose. His best-known albums include *Goodbye And Hello, Happy/Sad* and *Blue Afternoon.*

Buffalo Springfield
Stephen Stills (guitar, vocals); Richie Furay (guitar, vocals); Neil Young (guitar, vocals); Dewey Martin (drums, vocals); Bruce Palmer (bass), later replaced by Jim Messina—In retrospect, *the* group of the

mid-1960s. In three albums the Buffalo Springfield (named for a brand of earth-moving equipment) defined what was to become known as the West Coast Sound—a little bit of folk, a little bit of country, a whole bunch of harmonies. The Springfield was launched in 1966, the brainchild of Stephen Stills, who'd been working in New York with Richie Furay in a group called the Au Go Go Singers. Neil Young was a Canadian folk singer Stills had met earlier; according to the legend, Stills and Furay spotted him one day in an L.A. traffic jam and the Buffalo Springfield was formed. The group's debut album, *Buffalo Springfield,* in 1966 featured all Stills and Young original compositions, such as "Burned," "Nowdays Clancy Can't Even Sing" (an excellent song that was refused airplay because the lyrics included the word "damn") and the band's first hit, "For What It's Worth," a mini-masterpiece by Stills. The Buffalo Springfield toured as the opening act for the Beach Boys, and the band's success seemed assured. It cemented that feeling with a second, more polished album, *Buffalo Springfield Again,* released in 1968, including such classic compositions as "Rock And Roll Woman," "Bluebird," "Mr. Soul," "Expecting To Fly" and "Broken Arrow." But in the meanwhile personal pressures, especially the much-publicized bitterness between Stills and Young, were tearing the group apart. The split finally came in the middle of a third album, *Last Time Around,* with Jim Messina replacing Palmer. By 1968 everybody had gone on

to bigger and better things— Stills and Young, eventually, to Crosby, Stills, Nash and Young; Furay and Messina to Poco; Martin to successful sessions work.

Jimmy Buffett

Buffett, Jimmy   One of the finest good-time singer/ songwriters to emerge in the 1970s, Buffett was born on Dec. 25, 1946 in Mobile, Ala. After earning a degree in journalism, he went to Nashville to be a country singer, a career that, thanks to Nashville's then straitlaced ways, was stillborn. Buffett retreated to Key West and produced the offbeat *A White Sport Coat And A Pink Crustacean* album. It was uphill from there. Beginning with the next album, *Living And Dying in 3/4 Time,* which featured the hit "Come Monday," Buffett began building an ever-larger cult following that finally burst into the open with his huge 1977

hit "Margaritaville." Buffett's songwriting exhibits a journalist's eye, turning brief incidences into wry little stories with titles like "The Great Filling Station Holdup," "My Head Hurts, My Feet Stink And I Don't Love Jesus" and the infamous "Why Don't We Get Drunk (And Screw)." On stage he is hopelessly likable, with his permananet Key West tan and his tightly arranged rock and roll. As more than one critic has commented, it's good to see at least one nice guy win once in a while.

Burdon, Eric   Born on May 11, 1941 in England, Burdon is best known as the gravel-throated vocalist for the Animals, one of the better English rhythm-and-blues groups to emerge in the mid-1960s. After the Animals, Burdon (who supposedly discovered R&B from a merchant seaman living in the apartment below his) drifted with the times, emerging, strangely, in the late 1960s as something of a flower child; his "Warm San Franciscan Nights" and epic antiwar opus "Sky Pilot" were quite successful. In 1970 he joined up with War, an all-black rock group, and turned out a hit, the odd "Spill The Wine." That partnership lasted two years, and since then Burdon has drifted from one project to another, including working with blues great Jimmy Witherspoon and a brief reunion of the Animals. He is a mercurial talent, at his best interpreting rhythm and blues. In fact, along with Joe Cocker, Eric Burdon is one of the best rhythm-and-blues singers to come out of Great Britain.

Burgess, Sonny Born in 1931 in Newport, Ark., Burgess was reputedly the wildest, most frenetic stage performer in the Sun Records' stable during the 1950s. His songs, such as "Red-Headed Woman" and "Ain't Got A Thing," established him as a regional rockabilly success, as well as the rockabilly artist with the greatest appreciation of his rhythm-and-blues roots.

Burke, Solomon Born in 1935 in Philadelphia, Pa., Burke began as a child evangelist, "the Wonder-Boy Preacher," before going "secular" in 1960. He produced a string of modest soul hits throughout the 1960s—including "Just Out Of Reach" (1961), "If You Need Me" (1963), "Tonight's The Night" (1965) and "Proud Mary" (1969)—but was overshadowed by the more flamboyant soul men coming after him, such as Wilson Pickett and Otis Redding, who were more willing to "let go" in their vocal delivery than the smooth, slickly produced Burke. Recently he has been touring with an all-soul revue.

Burnette, Johnny and Dorsey Johnny Burnette (born on March 25, 1934) and his brother, Dorsey (born on Dec. 28, 1932), attended high school with Elvis Presley in Memphis and even worked with him at the same electrical supply company. In 1956 the two brothers, along with Paul Burlison, formed the Johnny Burnette Trio, which proceeded to win the "Ted Mack Amateur Hour" competitions in New York. Johnny's hits didn't begin

coming until he left the trio in 1960 and recorded "Dreamin'," followed by "You're Sixteen" (1960), "Little Boy Sad" (1961) and "God, Country And My Baby" (1961). He died in 1964.

Brother Dorsey also began recording in 1960, producing two rock-and-roll classics, "Tall Oak Tree" and "Hey Little One," before fading into obscurity. In the late 1970s Dorsey began a comeback attempt in country music, which ended abruptly with his death in 1979.

Burton, James The hottest rock guitarist of the late 1970s, Burton was first heard in 1957 behind Dale Hawkins on "Suzie Q." In the 1970s he began working with the many country-rock groups getting started on the West Coast (including Gram Parsons, the godfather of the whole scene), where he eventually came to the attention of Elvis Presley, who invited Burton to join his band. He stayed with Presley until 1975, when he toured with Emmylou Harris as a member of the Hot Band, leaving after a year to return to Presley. Some of his finest recent work appears on Jerry Lee Lewis' first Elektra album, *Jerry Lee Lewis* (1979). He is a fine guitarist, with a heavy leaning toward almost rockabilly riffs.

Butler, Jerry Born on Dec. 8, 1939 in Sunflower, Miss., Butler was raised in Chicago, where he worked as a gospel singer before linking up with Curtis Mayfield to form the Impressions. That group's first hit, "For Your Precious Love" (1958), was erroneously credited to "Jerry Butler and

the Impressions," and the subsequent hard feelings forced Butler to go on his own. He worked steadily as a balladeer in the 1960s and 1970s, with hits ranging from his outstanding interpretation of "Moon River" (1961) to the more soul-oriented "Only the Strong Survive" (1969). In fact, during the late 1960s Butler had his most successful string, including, in addition to the aforementioned hit, "Never Give You Up" and "Hey Western Union Man" in 1968 and "What's The Use In Breaking Up" in 1969.

Butterfield, Paul One of the original white blues kids, Paul Butterfield (along with such soulmates as Michael Bloomfield and Nick Gravenites) pioneered the blues explosion that was to shape rock music in the mid-1960s. Butterfield (born on Dec. 17, 1942) grew up in Chicago, and unlike most of the other white kids, he eagerly ventured down to the city's tough South Side to see such blues greats as "Little Walter" Jacobs, Muddy Waters, James Cotton, Junior Wells and Buddy Guy. But Butterfield wasn't content to just listen. He learned the blues harp and soon formed his own band (with Elvin Bishop, Jerome Arnold and Sam Lay)—the Butterfield Blues Band—and began playing electric blues. Butterfield and his band became local heroes around the University of Chicago campus, which bordered the South Side, and Butterfield was soon welcomed in the South Side clubs. His virtuosity and depth of knowledge about the blues and the men who played it endeared him to both blacks and whites. In 1965 the Butterfield Blues Band (including guitar wiz Bloomfield) shook the Newport Folk Festival to its acoustic core, becoming the first electric band to play at the festival and backing Bob Dylan on his first electric set. The *Butterfield Blues Band* album, cut in 1965, quickly became a cult classic, but the band itself was too far ahead of its time to be really successful. Butterfield kept producing albums, drifting from blues to soul music and back to blues, but he never seemed to come to grips with the public ho-hum. In 1976 he appeared on the Band's *Last Waltz* album and in the movie of the same name, rendering a stunning version of Junior Parker's (and Elvis Presley's) "Mystery Train." He later joined former Band member Rick Danko on tour. His importance, though, centers not so much on his musical output, but on the success shared by the white blues kids in bringing black blues back into rock and roll. The blues shaped rock in the late 1960s, as it had shaped the original music in the 1950s.

Byrds, The Roger McGuinn (guitar, vocals), David Crosby (guitar, vocals), Gene Clark (vocals), Chris Hillman (bass, vocals), Michael Clarke (drums)—One of the most important groups in American popular music, the Byrds were the first group to do what today seems painfully obvious— combine folk music with rock music. When the band was formed (by McGuinn, Crosby and Clark) in 1964, that idea

The Byrds

seemed a revelation, and, as the band's initial hit of Bob Dylan's "Mr. Tambourine Man" in 1965 clearly showed, the public was ready. At one point the Byrds were touted as America's answer to the Beatles—rock and roll for the thinking person. And their subsequent hits were amazingly (for the times) literate and musically accomplished; "I'll Feel A Whole Lot Better" (1965), "Turn Turn Turn" (1965) and even "Eight Miles High" (1966) were rock and roll you could take home to your mother (at least until "Eight Miles High" started getting banned as one of the first dope songs). Things began coming apart in 1966 when Gene Clark left. As a quartet the Byrds pressed on with such bittersweet classics as "So You Wanna Be A Rock And Roll Star" and "My Back Pages" (both 1967). In 1968 Crosby left and Gram Parsons joined the group, which led to the Byrds' second great contribution—country rock, embodied in their *Sweetheart Of The Rodeo* album in 1968. Then everybody but McGuinn left, and the group began to run out of inspiration, its last

gasp being the theme song for the ultimate 1960s movie *Easy Rider*. The Byrds' six albums since *Sweetheart* do provide some excellent moments, most notably the aforementioned theme "Ballad of Easy Rider" (1969), "Wasn't Born To Follow" (1969), "Lover Of The Bayou" (1970) and "Chestnut Mare" (1970). Yet the spirit that moved the group in the past had clearly departed, leaving, in its wake, Roger McGuinn to a solo career; Crosby to Crosby, Stills, Nash and Young; Chris Hillman and Gram Parsons to the Flying Burrito Brothers; and the listening public to a country-rock boom that continues today.

Cactus Carmine Appice (drums), Tim Bogert (bass), Rusty Day (vocals, harmonica), Jim McCarty (guitar)—A short-lived ensemble formed in 1969 from the wreckage of the very heavy metal Vanilla Fudge ("You Keep Me Hanging On,"

cut in 1967), in the persons of Appice and Bogert; Mytch Ryder's Detroit Wheels; and the Amboy Dukes. Cactus' biggest success, if it can be called that, came in the summer of 1970, when the group hit virtually every outdoor festival in the country, trying its best to cash in on the post-Woodstock get-drunk-and-boogie syndrome. By 1972 the group was ready to hang up the guitars, only to be reborn in 1973 and disappear again.

Cale, J.J. A buddy of Leon Russell, the pair grew up in Tulsa, Okla. and knocked around the local honky-tonks for a number of years. Cale came to national attention in 1970 as the author of Eric Clapton's hit single "After Midnight" and later found a comfortable niche as a country singer and songwriter.

Cale, John The spiritual force behind the Velvet Underground, New York's greatest cult band, and its most famous alumnus, Lou Reed. Cale was willing to push his classical training to the very extreme, which resulted in the formation of a sort of decadent New York avant garde. While Cale's solo work has been less than well received outside of the New York womb, his work as a producer has helped shape the acceptance of the New York fringe element nationwide. His production of Patti Smith's first album, *Horses* in 1975, was a masterpiece of powerful rock and roll, almost haunting in its understatement. In late 1979 he remained a fixture in the New York scene with his own record label, Spy, which

worked with local New Wave acts and occasionally released a record.

Campbell, Glen Became in the mid-1970s the very symbol of what country music wanted to grow up to be—flashy, trendy, chic and wildly successful. Glen Campbell was born on April 22, 1938 in the tiny town of Delight, Ark. and rose to fame in the late 1960s as the forerunner of the "new" country music, riding such compositions as "Gentle On My Mind" (1967), "Wichita Lineman" (1968) and "Galveston" (1969) and his own television series to huge success. His seemingly meteoric rise obscured the fact that he was and is one of the finest modern guitarists, an outstanding picker with an almost uncanny gift for choosing his material (he is primarily an interpreter of other songwriters' work). He even served as a part-time Beach Boy in the mid-1960s subbing whenever the group was in transition.

He has the rare ability to come back after periods of seeming decline, as he did in 1975 with the wildly successful "Rhinestone Cowboy" and again in 1979 with the simply arranged "Fool." The top of the charts seems to be his whenever he chooses to reach for them.

Canned Heat Bob "the Bear" Hite (vocals), Alan "Blind Owl" Wilson (guitar, vocals), Adolfo de la Parra (drums), Larry Taylor (bass), Henry Vestine (guitar) and others—A group of white boys who fell in love with the blues and actually managed to play them right.

And what an assembly—Hite started singing while a bag boy in a supermarket; Wilson, one of the leading authorities on the blues, was a music major from Boston University; Taylor, at the tender age of 14, was already backing rockabilly madman Jerry Lee Lewis; and Vestine had played sessions all over the country. What they shared was an abiding love of the blues, a love that is reflected in their best music: "On The Road Again" (1968), "Going Up The Country" (1968) and their albums *Livin' The Blues* (1968) and *Cookbook* (1969). Formed in 1966, the group really took off after the 1967 Monterey Pop Festival, only to have its soul fall apart in 1970 when "Blind Owl" Wilson died. Although the group continued to work with numerous other musicians, Canned Heat was never even a shadow of its former self.

Bob Hite died in April 1981.

Cannibal and the Headhunters Frankie "Cannibal" Garcia, Robert Jaramillo, Joe Jaramillo, Richard Lopez—Organized in Los Angeles in the mid-1960s, the Latin rock group became moderately famous in 1963 for "Land Of 1000 Dances," a bar band standard. The song was successfully rereleased in 1965 and was a big hit for Wilson Pickett in 1966.

Cannon, Ace Memphis sax player. Born in 1934 in Mississippi, Ace Cannon is best known for his hit "Cottonfields" (1963).

Cannon, Freddy Born Fredrick Anthony Picariello on Dec. 4, 1940 in Revere, Mass., he was rechristened "Boom Boom" Cannon in 1959 with the release of a song written by his mother. The song was "Tallahassee Lassie," and although one critic called it the single worst rock-and-roll song ever written, it catapulted "Boom Boom" into stardom. He was a fixture on the rock shows from Philadelphia, the home of his record company, Swan, and in 1962 he scored again with "Palisades Park," which has since become something of a rock and roll standard on the revival circuit.

Cannon, Gus   Born in 1883 in Red Banks, Miss., Gus Cannon was the leader of the greatest of the Memphis "jug bands," those blues ensembles featuring guitar, banjo and the ever present jug—Cannon played banjo and jug. He might have joined the numerous other blues singers and musicians in obscurity had the Rooftop Singers, a white folk group, not chosen to record what they thought was a traditional ballad—"Walk Right In"—in 1963. The song became a hit, and the real author, Gus Cannon, then 79 years old, was found working as a yardman in Memphis. He wrote "Walk Right In" in 1930 and rerecorded it for Stax Records in 1963, after the Rooftop Singers' success; it too was a hit. Gus Cannon lived quietly in Memphis off his royalties until his death in 1980.

Capaldi, Jim   Helped found the landmark British group Traffic in 1967 with Stevie Winwood, Dave Mason and Chris Wood. Capaldi has also worked as a solo act, but the

demand for superstar drummers is small.

Capricorn Records
Launched in 1969 by Phil Walden, the white Georgia fraternity boy who had parlayed a love for black music and a personal friendship with Otis Redding into a budding R&B empire, Capricorn is best known as the home of the Allman Brothers Band and a base for Southern rock.

From its headquarters in Macon, Ga., Capricorn spread the gospel of Southern rock—a peculiar fusion of rhythm and blues, country and three-chord rock and roll born on the grueling circuit of bars throughout the South—nationwide with bands like the Allman Brothers, the Marshall Tucker Band from South Carolina, guitar flash Elvin Bishop and others. Capricorn also remained one of the few independent record labels to survive in an era of conglomerates, contracting with the major labels to distribute its product.

As of 1981 the future of Capricorn is uncertain, although it appears finished. The on-again, off-again Allman Brothers and a changing record market cut deep into Capricorn's once phenomenal

profits, and the phones in the office have recently been disconnected, while rumors of an overseas sale persist. All in all a sad ending for the company that pioneered Southern rock, which proved to be one of the most durable and loved trends of the 1970s.

Captain and Tenille, The
Fresh-faced and wholesome, Toni Tenille and Daryl Dragon (he was dubbed "Captain Keyboard" by Beach Boy Mike Love) won a Grammy in 1975 for "Love Will Keep Us Together," a tuneful Neil Sedaka ditty. The husband and wife team could best be described as Sonny and Cher without tears, right on down to their own television show, although their most recent album covers revealed a vast amount of Toni Tenille leg and their recent release, "Do It To Me One More Time," was, well, suggestive. Toni Tenille is sure to remain a favorite of the easy listening set.

Captain Beefheart   Born Don Van Vliet in 1941 in Glendale, Calif., the soon-to-be Beefheart fell in with bad

Captain Beefheart & The Magic Band

companions in high school—most notably Frank Zappa. The two played together in a band, and then Van Vliet, assuming *nom de guerre* of Beefheart, formed his own Magic Band in 1964. Beefheart made a couple of avant-garde country-blues albums (the style was old; the treatment was new), but it wasn't until *Trout Mask Replica* in 1968, done in conjunction with Zappa, that Beefheart hit his stride. In 1971 Zappa and Beefheart parted ways, a split that would last for several years. In 1978 he produced *Shiny Beast/Bat Chain Puller,* probably his best album.

Carmen, Eric The former lead singer of the tremendously successful bubblegum group the Raspberries ("Go All The Way" in 1972), Carmen was born on Aug. 11, 1949 in Cleveland, Ohio. The Raspberries were a calculated imitation of British pop bands that worked surprisingly well. In 1976 Carmen went solo, determined to forsake imitation. The result was "All By Myself," another tremendous hit that sounded uncannily like those by Barry Manilow.

Carnes, Kim Born in 1948 in Los Angeles, Carnes dominated the 1981 charts with her hit single "Bette Davis Eyes." She began her career with the New Christy Minstrels in the 1960s and eventually became a success as a songwriter for such stars as Frank Sinatra, Barbra Streisand and Anne Murray. Her performing career was given a boost by her duet with Kenny Rogers ("Don't Fall In

Love With A Dreamer" from the *Gideon* album) in 1980. Her voice has been described as that of "a mentholated Rod Stewart."

Carpenters, The If a single word had to be used to describe the brother-sister duo of Richard and Karen Carpenter, that word would be "nice." So nice, in fact, that they've managed to sell some 30 million records worldwide, garnered three Grammy Awards and had 17 gold records while staying the most wholesome pair this side of Donny and Marie Osmond.

The secret is harmony, learned, according to brother Richard, from the Beatles, the Beach Boys and Burt Bacharach. Both were born in New Haven, Conn.—Richard in 1945, Karen in 1950. Richard immersed himself in music, first at Yale and later at Cal State, while Karen learned the drums and honed her magnificent voice. They formed a jazz instrumental trio with friend Wes Jacobs and even managed to win the Hollywood Bowl Battle of the Bands before Richard decided vocal harmonies were the way. That way lead to Herb Alpert at A&M Records, who knew a monster when he saw one. The first salvo was the million-selling "Close To You" in 1970, penned by the time-honored team of Burt Bacharach and Hal David. That was quickly followed by "We've Only Just Begun" (1970), "For All We Know" (1971), "Rainy Days And Mondays" (1971), "Superstar" (1971) and on and on and on. One particular high point was a remake of "Please Mr. Postman" in 1974, and

their 1973 album of greatest hits remains one of the largest selling albums of all time.

Cars, The Ric Ocasek (vocals, guitar), Benjamin Orr (vocals, bass), Elliot Easton (guitar), Greg Hawkes (keyboards), David Robinson (drums)—The most critically acclaimed group of 1978, the Cars, formed in Boston the previous year, returned a very basic element to the charts—simple pop music. The success of their singles "Just What I Needed" and "My Best Friend's Girl" as well as the subsequent debut album, *The Cars,* brought back a nearly Beatlesque pop simplicity to a music scene almost totally dominated by disco music. The next album, *Candy-O* (1979), also fared well, and the 1980 release, *Panorama,* cracked the top five. Despite some grousing among the critics about too much simple pop music, the group remains popular, scoring in 1982 with "Shake It Up."

Carter, Carlene Granddaughter of "Mother" Maybelle Carter, eldest daughter of country singer June Carter, stepdaughter of Johnny Cash—nobody figured Carlene Carter for a punk rocker, but that's what she is (punk country?). She's even married to English New Wave producer Nick Lowe. She first toured America with fellow New Waver Graham Parker's band, the Rumour, and is still trying to generate the steam her record company says she's capable of. But not to worry,

The Cars

she's only 23 years old. There's still time.

Carter, Clarence   Once a gospel singer, Clarence Carter became one of the staple soul singers of the late 1960s. Working with Rick Hall and his acclaimed (and well-integrated) rhythm section in Muscle Shoals, Ala., the professionally trained blind singer and composer first hit the charts with "Slip Away" and "Too Weak To Fight" in 1968. His powerful "Patches" was a number one hit in 1970.

Carter, "Mother" Maybelle
One of the original members of the Carter Family, "Mother" Maybelle inspired a whole generation of folk singers in the early 1960s. She also

appeared on the Nitty Gritty Dirt Band's *Will The Circle Be Unbroken* album in 1971, one of the very first attempts to refuse the sundered elements of old-time country and modern pop music. She died in 1978.

Carter Family, The   One of the most important influences in country—and modern—music, the Carter Family originally consisted of Alvin Pleasant "A.P." Carter, born in 1860 in Maces Spring, Va., Sara Carter, born in 1899 in Wise County, Va., and Maybelle Carter, born in 1909 in Nickelsville, Va. The Carters came out of the Virginia mountains on Aug. 1, 1927 to record for RCA Victor talent scout Ralph Peer in a house in Bristol, Tenn. That same day another country singer named

Jimmie Rodgers also recorded.

The Carters gave America the traditions and ballads of the mountains and, along with Rodgers, were responsible for popularizing what would later be called country music. A portion of the Carters' body of work includes "Wildwood Flowers," "Keep On The Sunny Side," "Worried Man Blues," "I Shall Not Be Moved," "You Are My Flower," "Wabash Cannonball," "I'm Thinking Tonight Of My Blue Eyes" and others. That body of work has been recycled constantly into popular music. A.P. Carter died in 1960, "Mother" Maybelle in 1978, but the Carter ballad style remains a living thing. June Carter Cash—wife of country superstar Johnny Cash—and Anita and Helen

Carter still sing together as the Carter Family.

Cash, Johnny   When Johnny Cash began rocking at Sun Records in Memphis in the 1950s, right along with Elvis Presley, Carl Perkins and Jerry Lee Lewis, no one would ever have suspected that he would eventually become the Grand Old Man of Country Music. He was born on Feb. 26, 1932 in Dyess, Ark. and raised a strict Baptist in a dirt-poor sharecropping family. In 1955 he signed with Sun, and his first million seller came a year later with "I Walk The Line." The hits just kept on coming for the next couple of years— "Guess Things Happen That Way" (1958), "Ballad Of A Teenage Queen" (1958) and the first incarnation of "Folsom Prison Blues."

With the turn of the decade, however, things began to go sour. Cash still had hits, notably "Ring Of Fire" (1963), but a serious addiction to pills began taking its toll. Arrests and near death from an overdose brought him to the brink, where, in a story that might only happen in a country song, he was saved by the love of a good woman. June Carter, daughter of "Mother" Maybelle Carter and author of "Ring Of Fire," stepped into Cash's life and pulled him out of a tailspin, and by the late 1960s Cash was an institution. His television series and work with Bob Dylan did more to bring country and rock closer together than anything else, and he became a genuine household word with a second "Folsom Prison Blues" from the album *At Folsom Prison* in 1968 and a Shel Silverstein

Johnny Cash

song titled "A Boy Named Sue" from the album *At San Quentin* in 1969.

Lately, Cash has returned to veteran Sun producer Jack Clement, and the quality of his record releases has increased dramatically. He appears regularly in various television specials and remains deeply religious.

Cassidy, David   Born on April 12, 1950 in New York the son of actor Jack Cassidy and actress Evelyn Ward, Cassidy became a number one teenage heartthrob as Keith Partridge in the popular television series "The Partridge Family." Out of the show came a hit song, "I Think I Love You" (1970), and a slew of similar songs for the next three years, along with several Cassidy solo efforts. He left the show in

1974 and since then has concentrated on a solo career with limited success.

Cassidy, Shaun   A David Cassidy clone, Shaun followed his half-brother's method of success, parlaying a regular gig as one of television's "Hardy Boys" into a singing career. Born on Sept. 27, 1958 the son of actress Shirley Jones and actor Jack Cassidy, Shaun had a few European hit records before landing the role of Joe Hardy. Then wham bam, his first two albums go platinum and every girl under the age of 12 is in love with him. That's rock and roll. Remember him for his covers of old rock classics, including "Da Doo Ron Ron" (1977) and "Do You Believe In Magic" (1978).

Cat Mother and the All-Night Newsboys   Bob Smith (vocals, keyboards), Roy Michaels (guitar, bass), Michael Equine (vocals, percussion), Charlie Chin (guitar, banjo), Larry Packer (guitar, violin, banjo)—Trendy New York City band produced by Jimi Hendrix in 1969. The band made four albums and one good single, "Can You Dance To It" (1969), before fading away.

Cate Brothers, The   Twin brothers born on Dec. 26, 1942 in Arkansas, Ernie and Earl Cate never seemed to get off the ground, despite a superb production job by former Stax ace Steve Cropper and wildly enthusiastic reviews. They played very bluesy Southern rock, and there are three good albums, *Cate Brothers, Cate Brothers Band*

and *In One Eye And Out The Other,* lying around cut-out bins.

Chad and Jeremy   Chad Stuart and Jeremy Clyde rode in with fellow Englishmen the Beatles during the mid-1960s with their soft, folkish songs— "Summer Song" (1964), "Willow Weep For Me" (1965) and "Before And After" (1965). In 1967 Jeremy left to pursue an acting career, and Chad eventually became a comedy writer.

Chambers Brothers, The George and Joe Chambers began as a gospel group in their home state of Mississippi in 1961, turned to secular music in 1965 and electrified the budding FM radio scene in 1967 with their supercharged "Time Has Come Today." The song, which ran upwards of 30 minutes, was a cross between a gospel shout and the psychedelic music of the times, and it was as powerful as it was popular. Unfortunately none of their subsequent work could match it.

Chandler, Gene   Born on July 6, 1937 in Chicago, Ill., Chandler recorded one of the greatest cult favorites of all time, "Duke of Earl" in 1962. His next biggest hit came eight years later with "Groovy Situation."

Chantays, The   Brian Carman, Bob Marshall, Warren Waters, Bob Spickard, Bob Welch—They produced a single hit, the great instrumental "Pipeline" (1963).

Chantels   Arlene Smith (vocals), Sonia Goring (vocals),

Lois Harris (vocals), Jackie Landry (vocals), Reene Minus (vocals)—Girl group formed in the Bronx during the mid-1950s and best known for its hits "Maybe" (1958) and "Look In My Eyes" (1961). Centered around the superb vocal lead of Arlene Smith, the Chantels were forerunners of many of the 1960s girl groups.

Chapin Harry   Born on Dec. 7, 1942, Chapin was raised in America's hotbed of folk music, Greenwich Village, and, not surprisingly, he chose that idiom to express himself. After a brief stint as a filmmaker (he wrote, directed and edited a documentary titled *Legendary Champions,* which was nominated for an Academy Award in 1964) and as a member of a folk group with his two brothers and father, he set out on his own in 1971. His music had evolved from folk into a series of melodramatic story songs, such as his first success, "Taxi" (1972), which won him widespread acceptance as a "literate" rock and roller. He retained that title with such follow-up hits as "WOLD" (1973) and "Cat's In The Cradle" (1974), his biggest success. Chapin devoted much of his time, energy and money to the cause of relieving world hunger before his death in a car accident on July 16, 1981.

Charles, Bobby   The man who wrote "Walkin' To New Orleans" and "See You Later Alligator" recorded for Chess Records in the 1950s but could never match the success of the songs he wrote. Charles cut one album for Bearsville

Records in the 1970s and was last seen (for the first time in 20 years) at the Band's Last Waltz farewell concert in 1976.

Charles, Ray   Once in a very rare while a performer comes along who makes the whole idea of musical "labels" seem small and childish. Ray Charles is just such a performer. His music ranges from gospel roots through pop to country and Western, and he is, quite simply, one of the most influential people in the history of rock and roll.
   Born Ray Charles Robinson on Sept. 23, 1930 in Albany, Ga., he contracted an illness that left him permanently blind at the age of six. Orphaned at 15, he began making his way as a singer two years later. In 1957 Ahmet Ertegun brought him to Atlantic Records, and in no time he was Atlantic's biggest moneymaker ever. Songs like "What'd I Say" (1959) made his gospel-fired piano a national mania and laid the groundwork for the soul music that would become one of the dominant forces in the 1960s. He released several hits following "What'd I Say," such as "Georgia On My Mind" (1960), "One Mint Julep" (1961), "Hit The Road Jack" (1961) and "Unchain My Heart" (1962), before turning the music world upside down by announcing he would record an album of country music. What Ray Charles realized, of course, was that country and black music had always been close in spirit, and he turned that knowledge into an unprecedented string of hits, including Hank Williams' "I Can't Stop Loving You" (1962) and "Your Cheatin'

Heart" (1962).

Yet despite the success, Charles was a victim of the musicians' disease—drug abuse. He was able to kick heroin while in a sanatorium during the mid-1960s. Since then he has revitalized his career through a series of personal appearances (including acting as guest host on the popular TV comedy show "Saturday Night Live") and his own record label, Crossover—a music industry term meaning that a song has crossed over onto a different chart, such as when an R&B song becomes a country hit. In 1975 he won a Grammy for his version of Stevie Wonder's "Living In The City." His concerts are still classified as bonafide events.

Cheap Trick   Rick Nielsen (guitar), Robin Zander (vocals), Bun E. Carlos (drums), Tom Petersson (bass)—Launched in Illinois in 1977, Cheap Trick successfully treads the narrow ground between put-on and pretense, backed up with surprisingly powerful rock and roll and strong, melodic songs. In 1979 the group moved into the reaches of stardom with "Surrender," a live cut that combined the band's antic weirdness (its members dress like clones) with a driving rock song.

Checker, Chubby   Born Ernest Evans on Oct. 3, 1941 in Philadelphia, Pa., Chubby Checker began his career as a singing chicken plucker at a poultry shop. His name was a play on the name of his favorite artist, Fats Domino, given to him by Mrs. Dick Clark after she caught Ernest Evans on

her husband's "American Bandstand" show.

Checker's claim to fame came in 1960 with a song called "The Twist," first recorded by popular R&B artist Hank Ballard. For three years America twisted, and Checker was the hottest artist in the country. He cut numerous other dance records, including "Pony Time" (1961), "Let's Twist Again" (1961), "The Fly" (1961), "Slow Twistin' " (1962), "Limbo Rock" (1962), "Twist It Up" (1963) and on and on and on.

"The Twist" was important because it revived the flagging tradition of dance music.

Cheech and Chong   The strange crossing of a Mexican-American from California, Richard "Cheech" Marin, and a Chinese-Canadian from Alberta, Thomas Chong, first happened in a comedy improvisation group during the early 1970s. They eventually signed with Ode Records in 1971 as sort of drug culture comedians. Their album *Big*

Cheech and Chong

Bambu in 1972 went gold, as did *Los Cochinos* a year later, but after that their dope humor

("Oh wow, man! I am so-o-o-o stoned!") seemed to wear thin. Then, in what has to be one of the record combacks of all time, Cheech and Chong resurfaced in 1978 with a movie, *Up In Smoke,* which two years later was *still* making the drive-in circuit. Amazingly, after five years of relative obscurity, the two comedians rebuilt their career on virtually the same material.

Chenier, Clifton   The master of the Louisiana Cajun accordian, Chenier has made a career of touring the tiny dance halls and honky-tonks of the bayou country of Louisiana and southern Texas. He records for Arhoolie Records, a small folk and blues label, and in the late 1970s received his first national attention.

Cher   The great American chanteuse, the better half of Sonny and Cher, given to skimpy outfits and possessing unbelievably long legs—what else is to be said about Cher? Born Cherilyn Sakisian on May 20, 1946 in El Centro, Calif.; married Sonny Bono in 1964, creating one of the biggest pop-folk duos of the time; divorced Sonny; married Gregg Allman of the Allman Brothers Band; divorced Gregg (apparently several times); continued to make albums and television specials.

She is, in short, one of those strange creatures known as celebrities, whose mere existence is enough to set tongues wagging and fill the front page of every tabloid between Los Angeles and Australia. Neither her looks nor her singing are particularly spectacular, although her recent disco music was quite decent and her much-publicized "breast-lift" has also helped.

The likelihood of her simply fading away is slim. Ditto for the likelihood of her ever making a great contribution to music or the popular arts.

Chess Records   One of the greatest rhythm-and-blues labels of the 1950s, Chess grew out of a number of "after hours" jazz clubs owned by Leonard Chess in Chicago dating way back to 1938. In 1950 the sporadic Aristocrat Records formally changed its name to Chess, under the direction of Leonard and brother Phil Chess. One of the first signings was bluesman Muddy Waters, and soon Chess was off and running, with Leonard scouring the South for black talent.

Chess became a national success in 1955, thanks to one Chuck Berry, who walked into the Chess offices more or less out of the blue. The company added Bo Diddley, The Moonglows and a host of others, and soon Chess rivaled Sun Records in Memphis, from

which Chess had once leased tapes.

But despite numerous hits, Chess fell victim to a changing marketplace and eventually joined the other independent labels in oblivion after being sold to GRC during the late 1960s. There remains the remote possibility of a revival by Tomato Records, which now owns the tapes.

Chic   Norma Jean (vocals), Claire Bethe (vocals), Nile Rodgers (guitar), Bernard Edwards (bass), Tony Thompson (drums), Andy Schwartz (keyboards), Kenny Lehman (woodwinds)—One of the big winners in the disco boom of the late 1970s, Chic was originally a backup group working the New York City recording studios when, in 1977, the group decided to record on its own. That year's "Dance, Dance, Dance" launched the group onto the dance floor, but it was 1978's "Le Freak" that turned them into superstars. Of the seemingly billions of disco groups, Chic seems closer to R&B roots then most of the others

Chicago   Robert Lamm (keyboards, vocals), Terry Kath (guitar, vocals), Pete Cetera (bass, vocals), James Pankow (trombone), Lee Loughnane (trumpet), Walter Parazaider (reeds), Daniel Seraphine (drums), Laudir De Oliveira (percussion)—The phenomenally successful godfathers of the whole pop-jazz craze of the mid-1970s began their career in Chicago in 1968, where nobody wanted to hear a band that didn't play the hits. Undeterred, the group,

then called the Chicago Transit Authority, moved to Los Angeles to work with producer James Guercio.

The result was the odd fusion of a standard rock rhythm section with a brass section, a first album titled *Chicago Transit Authority* and an incredible procession of hit songs that is still going on today—without altering the formula one iota. The hits have included "Questions 67 & 68" (1969), "Make Me Smile" (1970) and "Color My World" (1971).

That formula depends as much on vocal harmonies as the rock-jazz angle and might be compared to a "soft," Beach Boys sound, with lilting melodies floating over the horn section. The group's continued success baffles critics. Guitarist Kath died on Jan. 23, 1978 of an accidental gunshot wound.

Chiffons, The   Judy Craig (vocals), Barbara Lee (vocals), Patricia Bennett (vocals), Sylvia Peterson (vocals)—From the Bronx, New York City, this group, though formed in 1960, had its first hit in 1963 with "He's So Fine." They continued releasing records through 1966, with modest success—notably "Sweet Talkin' Guy" (1966). The Chiffons still perform at oldies shows.

Chi-Lites, The   Marshall Thompson (vocals), Creadel Jones (vocals), Eugene Record (vocals), Robert Lester (vocals)—Formed in 1961 in Chicago—hence the name—the Chi-Lites burst on the charts in the early 1970s with the stirring "(For God's Sake) Give More Power To The

People." Their biggest success came in 1972 with the soft, 1950s-sounding "Have You Seen Her?" They followed that song with a number of hits.

Christie, Lou   Born on Feb. 19, 1943 in Glen Willard, Pa., Christie recorded in Pittsburgh until 1963, when his "The Gypsy Cried," featuring his high falsetto voice, became a national hit. He is best known for "Lightnin' Strikes" in 1965.

Clanton, Jimmy   In the summer of 1958, Clanton burst on the scene with "Just A Dream." He was born on Sept. 2, 1940 in Baton Rouge, La. and played locally with a group called the Rockets. In 1962 he recorded what was to become another classic, "Venus In Bluejeans."

Clapton, Eric   One of the greatest rock guitarists of all time, Clapton was born on March 30, 1945 in Surrey, England. Like many of his English contemporaries, he was deeply influenced by American black music, especially that of Muddy Waters and Chuck Berry. He began learning blues licks at the age of 17, and his first band came in 1963 (the Roosters). He occasionally played pubs as a substitute for the better-known Mick Jagger.

In 1963 Clapton joined the Yardbirds and remained for a couple of years—long enough to play on their 1965 smash "For Your Love"—finally departing because he felt the band was ignoring the artistic end of things in its drive for commercial success. Ironically, after a brief stint with English bluesman John Mayall,

Clapton went on to form one of the great legendary—read, commercial—rock bands of all time, Cream, with Jack Bruce and Ginger Baker. Cream's *Disraeli Gears* album (1967), featuring the hit single "Sunshine of Your Love," is considered one of the high points of 1960s rock. The band came apart at the seams in 1968, with Clapton leaving to form yet another superstar group, Blind Faith, which produced a single album and tour and a lot of internal animosity. By 1969 Blind Faith was no more.

What followed was a series of guest appearances, which, if anything, established Clapton as a musical genius. He worked with Leon Russell, Delaney and Bonnie, Stephen Stills, George Harrison and others, producing some of the finest music of the period. Yet Clapton was obsessed with escaping from his reputation. His next group, he decided, wouldn't even have his name on it. That group was Derek and the Dominos, featuring Clapton and Allman Brothers' guitarist Duane Allman. In 1970 they recorded an album called *Layla,* which, containing the classic title track, still stands as a monument to rock and roll. Perversely, the record didn't sell until after the group had broken up. A decade later it's still selling.

The failure of *Layla* and the death of Duane Allman, a close personal friend of Clapton, combined to send him into seclusion for several years, sinking him into drugs and depression. Fortunately, he fought his way back and made a series of modestly tuneful records beginning with his *461*

Ocean Boulevard album in 1974 and continuing into the 1980s. Clapton has worked extensively with country artist Don Williams, whose soft, simple harmonies have found their way into his music. In recent years Clapton has finally been recognized for his important contributions to pop music.

Clark, Claudine   Born on April 26, 1941 in Macon Ga., Claudine Clark flared briefly in 1962 with her self-composed "Party Lights," then faded away.

Clark, Dave, Five   See Dave Clark Five.

Clark, Dick—Originally the host of Philadelphia's "American Bandstand," Bronxville, N.Y.-born (Nov. 30, 1929) Dick Clark dominated the fallow rock years between the enlistment of Elvis in the Army and the coming of the Beatles. "American Bandstand" generated hits like they were going out of style, most notably "The Twist," elevating Chubby Checker into a national idol. While he was touched briefly by the payola scandals in the early 1960s, Clark emerged as rock's cleanest supporter and has since continued parlaying that image into a rock empire. One of his many TV efforts during the 1970s was a made-for-television movie in 1978 on the life of Elvis Presley; it told "the King's" story brilliantly. Clark followed that in 1979 with a similar, but less successful, story about the Beatles.

Clark, Gene   Born in 1941 in Tipton, Mo., Gene Clark joined with Roger McGuinn and David Crosby in 1964 to form the original Byrds. He left the Byrds in 1966, stating that he was afraid to fly to the band's dates, and has since pursued a solo career on the ground.

Clark, Petula   A star since the tender age of nine, Petula Clark was born on Nov. 15, 1932 in Surrey, England. Between the ages of 11 and 18, she made some 20 films and even managed to win an award in 1950 for her television acting. She began recording in 1955 and scored several major English and European hits in the early 1960s. She didn't become a household word in the United States until her 1964 release of "Downtown," which went on to become her fourth million-selling record worldwide and a number one hit in the U.S. Her hits, including "I Know A Place" (1965), "Sign of the Times" (1966), "Color My World" (1967) and "Kiss Me Goodbye" (1968), continued with the regularity of clockwork through the 1960s, while the 1970s saw her star in decline.

Clark, Roy   Billed as the man who brought country music to Las Vegas, Roy Clark (born on April 15, 1933 in Meherrin, Va.) is perhaps best known as the star of the unsinkable "Hee Haw" television series. A virtuoso on guitar and banjo, Clark has been a consistent country and pop artist with his melodramatic renditions of such songs as "Yesterday When I Was Young" (1969) and his more upbeat pop material like "If I Had To Do It All Over Again" (1974). Under the tutelage of country impresario Jim Halsey, Clark has indeed become a staple performer on the lucrative

The Clash

Vegas circuit and is a regular host of Johnny Carson's "Tonight" show.

Clash, The   Mick Jones (guitar), Nicky Headon (drums), Paul Simonon (bass), Joe Strummer (vocals)—One of the most hyped and best received of the English New Wave bands, the Clash formed in 1976 in the working-class pubs of London. Unlike the Sex Pistols, with whom the Clash has been constantly compared, the group seems uninterested in punk shock tactics, concentrating instead on giving voice to England's latest generation of rebels without a cause. Nevertheless, the group's music does show an ironic sense of what rock and roll is all about and features a surprising amount of gallows humor—songs like "White Riot" (1978) and "Last Gang In Town" (1978) touch on the central subjects of the 1970s: apathy and "intramural infighting."

Clayton-Thomas, David   Born in 1944 in London, David Clayton-Thomas is best known for his powerful, ragged vocals

with the group Blood, Sweat and Tears in the late 1960s. He left the group in 1972 to pursue a solo career, to no avail, and eventually returned to the fold.

Cleftones, The   Herbie Cox (vocals), Berman Patterson (vocals), Warren Corbin (vocals), Charles James (vocals), William McClain (vocals)—As the Silvertones, they were the "house band" at Jamaica High School in Queens, New York City. Starting in 1956 the Cleftones recorded a string of regional N.Y. hits that included "You Baby You," "Little Girl Of Mine" and "Can't We Be Sweethearts," riding on the new popularity of rock and roll. It was not until 1961, however, that the group scored a national hit with "Heart And Soul," which lasted on the charts for a week. The Cleftones still appear at fifties revival shows.

Clements, Vassar   Perhaps the best-known and certainly one of the most-respected fiddle players in the country, Clements was born in Kinard, S.C. in 1928. From the relative obscurity of a sessions player in Nashville, Clements has moved into a more rock-oriented style in the early 1970s and now tours on his own.

Jimmy Cliff

Cliff, Jimmy   Born in 1948 in St. Catherine, Jamaica, Cliff has brushed with fame as the star of the reggae epic movie *The Harder They Come* and with the modest hit "Wonderful World, Beautiful People" (1969). His problem is twofold: first, reggae, that strangely rhythmic, lilting Jamaican music, has never found the widespread acceptance in America that most critics predicted; and second, Cliff himself is more interested in classic American soul music than serving as reggae's ambassador. If there is a way out of Cliff's particular trap, he hasn't come near to finding it yet.

Climax Blues Band, The   Peter Haycock (vocals, guitar), Richard Jones (keyboards), John Cuffley (drums), Colin Cooper (vocals, guitar, sax), Derek Holt (vocals, bass)—Yet another British blues band from the late 1960s, albeit one of the more successful ones. The band successfully released albums (without a single hit) until 1974, when it disbanded. In 1975 original founder Richard Jones re-formed the band, and in 1977 the group had its first U.S. hit, "Couldn't Get It Right."

Clovers, The   John "Buddy" Bailey (vocals), Harold Jerome Winley (vocals), Harold Lucas (vocals), Mathew McQuater (vocals), Bill Harris (vocals)—Formed in Washington, D.C., the Clovers landed two songs on the R&B charts in 1951, "Don't You Know I Love You" and "Fool, Fool, Fool," both of which were blendings of gospel and rhythm-and-blues styles. They continued to dominate those charts throughout the early 1950s, cutting "Blue Velvet" in 1955 and "Devil Or Angel" in 1956, which became big hits in the early 1960s for Bobby Vinton and Bobby Vee respectively. The Clovers had a minor pop hit with "Love Love Love" (1956) but are best known for "Love Potion Number Nine" (1959), written by Leiber and Stoller.

Coasters, The   Carl Gardner (vocals); Billy Guy (vocals); Leon Hughes (vocals); Bobby Nunn (vocals); and others, including Young Jessie, Cornell Gunter, Earl "Speedo" Carroll, Will "Dub" Jones, Ronnie Bright, Adolph Jacobs—Virtually defined pop music in the late 1950s—in fact, when people discuss fifties nostalgia and start naming favorite songs, it usually sounds like a Coasters' greatest hit album—"One Kiss Led To Another" (1956), "Young Blood" (1957), "Searchin'" (1957), "Yakety Yak" (1958), "Charlie Brown" (1959), "Along Came Jones" (1959), "Poison Ivy" (1959) and many others. These were among the funniest rock-and-roll records ever made, but the group was also capable of excellent straight rhythm and blues like "Zing Went The Strings Of My Heart." The Coasters were an outlet for the phenomenal songwriting team of Jerry Leiber and Mike Stoller, who put the group together from an earlier incarnation, the Robins. Leiber and Stoller were white, the Coasters black, but the songwriters had an almost uncanny feel for rhythm and blues, which translated into the Coasters greatest songs. In 1971 the group (or various pieces of the group, as it were) cut "Love Potion #9" (a hit for the Clovers in 1959), a refreshing change from that year's particular obsession with bubblegum music. They still tour all over the country. The current lineup is Ronnie Bright, Earl Carroll, Thomas Palmer and Carl Gardner, the group's founder and lead singer.

Cochran, Eddie   One of the most accomplished of the rockabilly rebels, Cochran was born on Oct. 3, 1938 in Minnesota. At the time of his death in April 1960, in a car crash in England, he was already a recording star, with "Summertime Blues" (1958), "C'mon Everybody" (1959) and "Somethin' Else" (1959), and a successful actor, appearing in *The Girl Can't Help It*. Cochran was on his way to the airport in London

Eddie Cochran

after a whirlwind tour with fellow rocker Gene Vincent when he was killed. He was a more competent performer than some of the other first-generation rockers from the South—certainly a better guitar player—without losing any of the raw power.

Cocker, Joe   Perhaps the finest rhythm-and-blues singer to come out of England, Cocker's career has been punctuated by a series of personal disasters undermining his professional success. Born on May 20, 1944 in Sheffield, he discovered Ray Charles' music at the age of 14 and started his own band the next year. His musical career was strictly an off-again, on-again proposition until 1969, when an appearance at the Windsor Jazz and Blues Festival and a hit recording of the Beatles' song "With A Little Help From My Friends" placed him permanently in the limelight. An American tour followed (with his Grease Band), and a second tour was scheduled in 1970. On the first tour Cocker had met Leon Russell, who helped produce the *Joe Cocker* album and contributed Cocker's next hit, "Delta Lady." Cocker arrived in America for the second tour having already released his band and intending to cancel the whole thing, but Russell interceded, assembling an entourage of some 40 people, a camera crew and various groupies and hangers-on, all of which were set in motion across America. The tour was called *Mad Dogs and Englishmen*, and the results were threefold—a brilliant movie of the same name, a brilliant double record set, also of the same name, and the almost total disintegration of Joe Cocker.

Since then Cocker basically has been trying—without

Joe Cocker

success—to put himself back together again. He toured again in 1972, in even worse shape; retired for a couple of years; and tried comebacks in 1974 (with a hit single, "You Are So Beautiful") and in 1977, both to no avail. His spastic, wildman delivery style has become a source of derision, parodied on late night television, and Joe Cocker is still trying to find the pieces of his life.

Coe, David Allan   One of the more bizarre personalities of modern country music, Coe reportedly did time on death row in Ohio for killing another inmate—at least Coe says he did. He has a striking voice and is an outstanding songwriter ("Will You Lay With Me [In A Field Of Stone]" was a hit for nubile singer Tanya Tucker in 1974; "Take This Job And Shove It," as recorded by Johnny Paycheck, was the biggest country hit of 1978). His own success has been limited. After a good start with Steve Goodman's "You Never Even Called Me By Name" (1975), Coe seemed to fall by the wayside. He still releases albums, but with none of the fanfare of his work a few years back.

Cohen, Leonard   The heartthrob of college girls everywhere, Cohen was born in 1934 in Montreal, Canada. Initially he became known as a poet, an image that changed in 1966, when Judy Collins recorded his "Suzanne." Cohen's songs have a haunting, lilting quality, especially when he delivers them in his flat, almost atonal voice. His first album, *The Songs Of Leonard Cohen,* was released in 1968. After a period of less activity, he has been recording again, including an interesting 1977 album with the king of the 1960s Wall of Sound rock, Phil Spector. The film *McCabe and Mrs. Miller,* with Warren Beatty and Julie Christie in the title roles, was conceived by Robert Altman after he listened to Cohen's first album. The movie, which features several of the album's songs, remains the absolute best way to hear Leonard Cohen.

Cole, Nat "King" Nat "King" Cole began his recording career in 1944 with "Straighten Up And Fly Right," and he managed to sustain that career right up until his death in 1965. Cole was born on March 17, 1919 in Montgomery, Ala., the son of a minister. His soft crooner's voice figured prominently in the development of soul music and he served as an inspiration for any number of singers. Among Cole's numerous hits his best-known songs include "Mona Lisa" (1950) and, of course, "Ramblin' Rose" (1962).

Cole, Natalie Daughter of Nat "King" Cole, Natalie Cole won two Grammy awards in 1976 as the best new artist of the year, based on her debut album, *Inseparable.* Born in 1950 in Los Angeles, she continues her successful career, although she has not repeated her overwhelming achievements of 1976.

Collins, Judy Born on May 1, 1939 in Denver, Colo., Collins began as a very earnest, scrub-faced folk singer (*A*

The Coasters

Maid of Constant Sorrow in 1962). She moved from folk to protest (*Judy Collins No. 3* in 1963)—becoming one of the first folkies to make the transition successfully—from protest to unabashed romanticism (*In My Life* in 1966 and *Wildflowers* in 1967) and from romanticism to singing duets with humpback whales ("Fairwell

Judy Collins

To Tarwathie," an old whaling song with the voices of the whales overdubbed, from her 1971 *Whales and Nightingales* album). "Fairwell To Tarwathie," in fact, remains one of the eeriest evocations ever placed on vinyl.

And she shows not even the slightest sign of slowing down. In 1975 she had a hit recording with "Send In The Clowns," from Stephen Sondheim's musical *A Little Night Music.* The year before, she'd been nominated for an Oscar for her documentary film entitled *Antonia: A Portrait of the Woman,* about her former classical piano teacher Antonia Brico.

Her secret, perhaps, is an absolute willingness to take chances (and a stunning voice doesn't hurt)—the cover for her recent album *Hard Times For Lovers* (1979) features a nude portrait of her by photographer Francesco Scavullo. When questioned about the photo, her reply was, more or less, that she'd never done it before, so why not?

Commander Cody and His Lost Planet Airmen "Commander Cody"—George Frayne (vocals, piano), Andy Stein (fiddle, horns), Bobby Black (pedal steel), Bill Kirchen (guitar, vocals), Bruce Barlow (bass, vocals), Lance Dickerson (drums, vocals), Norton Buffalo (harp, vocals, trombone), Rick Higginbotham (guitar)—Founded in Detroit in the mid-1960s and transplanted to the more fertile ground of San Francisco in 1969, Commander Cody specialized in a bizarre blend of truckers' music, country, rock, Cajun and whatever else was handy. While the group had a dedicated following, it's recording career never got off the ground. It's two biggest albums were *Lost In The Ozone* (1971), the title track of which became something of a theme song, and *Hot Licks, Cold Steel And Truckers' Favorites* (1972). The group disbanded in 1976, although Commander Cody is still touring and releasing albums. The group is best remembered as the primary subject of a book on the seamier aspects of the music business titled *Star-Maker Machinery*. Written by *Village Voice* writer Geoffrey Stokes, the book chronicled, in some detail, how the group failed to become a household word.

Commodores, The Lionel Richie (sax), Thomas McClary (guitar), William King (trumpet), Milan Williams (keyboards, drums, guitar), Ronald LaPread (bass, trumpet), Walter "Clyde" Orange (drums, vocals)—Motown group first formed in Alabama. The Commodores

(original name, the Jays) began as the opening act for the enormously popular Jackson Five. Their albums routinely go platinum, cashing in on the current rage for disco. However, their slow, soft single "Once, Twice, Three Times a Lady" (1978) has become practically an anthem.

Conlee, John One of the more successful up and coming country-pop singers, Conlee worked as an undertaker and county coroner for six years before his success with "Rose-Colored Glasses" (1978).

Conley, Arthur Born on Jan. 14, 1946 in Atlanta, Ga., Conley's career really began in 1965 when he met and impressed soul king Otis Redding. In 1967 Redding produced Conley's first and only major hit, "Sweet Soul Music," a song written earlier by Redding, Conley and Sam Cooke. The song remains one of the finest examples of mid-1960s soul music, Memphis style.

Contours, The Huey Davis, Billy Gordon, Joe Billingslea, Sylvester Potts, Hubert Johnson, Billy Hoggs—One of the early vocal groups (1962) on Berry Gordy's Gordy label, a subsidiary of Motown. The Contours are best known for their hit "Do You Love Me" in 1962. The song was written by Gordy.

Cooder, Ry Born on March 15, 1947 in Los Angeles, Cooder has found a unique way to pay tribute to his favorite forms of music, including blues, Hawaiian, big band and early rock: he cuts superbly

constructed, immaculately arranged albums incorporating them. He began working as a sessions man in the early 1960s, waiting almost 10 years before embarking on his own career. *Chicken Skin Music* (1976) and *Bop Til You Drop* (1978) have enhanced his reputation, but he remains a limited—if skillful—cult artist.

Cooke, Sam Born in Chicago on Jan. 22, 1935, Cooke began his career as a gospel singer, starting in his father's church and working up through a number of gospel quartets. After a year of experimentation, Cooke released his first pop song, "You Send Me," in 1957 and was instantly established as America's top soul singer. His soft, soulful delivery sparkled on such hits as "Everybody Likes To Cha Cha Cha" (1959), "Only Sixteen" (1959), "Wonderful World" (1960), "Chain Gang" (1960), "Twistin' The Night Away" (1962), "Having A Party" (1962), "Another Saturday Night" (1963), "Little Red Rooster" (1963) and many others. On Dec. 11, 1964 he was shot to death by a woman in a motel in Los Angeles, where he'd gone for Christmas.

He remained—and still remains—one of the most influential black singers of the period. His music forms a bridge between the hard rocking rhythm and blues of the 1950s and the softer, more melodious Motown sound of the mid- and late-1960s.

Cookies, The Dorothy Jones (vocals), Margaret Ross (vocals), Earljean McCree (vocals)—Originally from

Brooklyn, New York City, the Cookies worked as backup singers for artists like Carole King and Neil Sedaka and backed Little Eva on her classic "Locomotion". They are best remembered for their hit single "Chains" (1962), written by Carole King and Gerry Goffin.

Coolidge, Rita   Born in 1944 in Nashville, Tenn., Rita Coolidge is yet another of Delaney and Bonnie's "friends," who joined them on their many tours in the 1960s. Her success has been mixed, from being a regional star around Memphis in the mid-1960s to her recent hits with softer, disco-styled material— "We're All Alone" and "Higher and Higher" (both 1977). In addition, she is the wife of singer/actor Kris Kristofferson, although as of 1979 the marriage was apparently on the rocks.

Cooper, Alice   Vincent Furnier—aka Alice himself (vocals, harp); Michael Bruce (guitar, keyboards); Glen Vuxton (guitar); Neal Smith (drums); Dennis Dunaway (bass); and others, including Richard Wagner (guitar), Jozeff Chirowski (keyboards), Steven Hunter (guitar), Pentti Olan (drums), Prakash John (bass)—Rock-and-roll weirdness at its zenith (or nadir, if you prefer) complete with live boa constrictors, attacks by tooth creatures, S&M fantasies, chopped-up baby dolls, mock electric chairs and even a little music on the side. At the center of it all was Vincent Furnier, the son of a Protestant minister, and his canny manager/publicity man, Shep

Alice Cooper

Gordon. Furnier had been in several rock ensembles before linking up with Gordon in 1968. Nothing much happened until 1970, when *Love It To Death,* featuring the superb teen anthem "I'm 18," hit the charts (as did the equally good 1972 album *School's Out,* featuring the hit title track). From then on it was gangbusters, with hit singles, hit albums and unlimited hype. In 1975 Furnier, who by now was known to the world as Alice, had dumped the original band and gone on to weirder and weirder (as well as more expensive) stage shows. The hype seemed to have a dual-edged effect on Alice, who on the one hand tried to keep upstaging himself, while on the other tried to prove how "normal" he really was (favorite sport: golf; favorite comedian: Bob Hope). Alice still slugs on, with some 60 million records under his belt, but weirdness has been ebbing of late, relegating him to the position of the Grand Old Man of Rubber Chickens (Rock and Roll Branch).

Corea, Chick Your basic pop-jazz (or jazz-pop) fusion player, Corea became a much sought-after sessions piano man (including stints with Herbie Mann and Miles Davis) before setting out on his own. Born in Chelsea, Mass., he grew up listening to his father's Dixieland band and gained an abiding love for all forms of music. In the mid-1970s he formed the instrumental group Return to Forever (with Anthony Braxton, Barry Altschul and Dave Holland) to begin his assault on pop strongholds, which he continues with moderate success today.

Coryell, Larry Born on April 2, 1943 in Galveston, Tex., Coryell grew up listening to the guitar music of Chet Atkins, Chuck Berry and Django Reinhardt. He studied journalism in college, but his heart was set on jazz. In 1965 he formed the Free Spirits (with Jim Pepper, Bob Moses, Chris Hill and Chip Baker), one of the first jazz-pop fusion groups; the band lasted for one album, *Out Of Sight And Sound*. Coryell was then in demand as a sessions guitarist, as well as working with the Gary Burton Quartet. In 1974 he formed the Eleventh House, a reference to his own embracing of the Eastern teachings of guru Sri Chinmoy (as had such other heavyweight musicians as John McLaughlin and Carlos Santana). Coryell, in continuing his musical experimentation, is currently working with European avant-garde jazz guitarist Philip Catherine (*Twin House* in 1977 and *Splendid* in 1979).

Elvis Costello

Costello, Elvis Born Declan MacManus in England, Elvis Costello has soared to the top of the charts both as a songwriter and performer. His songs are the toughest, most alienated music since Pete Townshend wrote "My Generation"—songs like "Watching The Detectives" (1977), a demonic ballad about a girl entranced with a television cop show; "This Year's Girl" (1978), about the annual reigning sex symbol; and "Radio Radio" (1978), a devastatingly accurate picture of popular radio. As a performer, he is both electrifying and unsatisfying— he is as distant and bitter as his music, at times vitriolic and hostile to both fans and press alike (in one celebrated instance he was decked by former Ikette Bonnie Bramlett for referring to Ray Charles as a "nigger"). When his record company announced that both Linda Ronstadt and country legend George Jones would cut Costello songs, his reported reply was that he was honored by George Jones and he needed the money from Ronstadt. Controversy aside, he is one of the unique talents in today's music, with the rare ability to transcend hype by sheer talent alone. His 1979 *Armed Forces* album was further demonstration of his abilities.

Count Five, The John Michalski (guitar), Sean Byrne (guitar), Roy Chaney (bass), Kenn Ellner (vocals)— California psychedelic group from the mid-1960s, best known for "Psychotic Reaction" (1966), its only hit.

Cowsills, The When Chief Petty Officer Bud Cowsill retired from the Navy in 1963 after 20 years of service, he decided to do something entirely out of the ordinary—he put the wife and kids on the road. Bud and wife Barbara, six sons—Bill (born 1948), Bob (born 1949), Barry (born 1954), John (born 1956), Dick (born 1950), Paul (born 1952)—and daughter Susan (born 1959), collectively known as the Cowsills, went off to become stars. Pretty soon they were $100,000 in debt, and the legend has them burning the furniture in their Rhode Island home to keep warm. Well, maybe. But in 1967 the family met Artie Kornfield, a producer looking for a wholesome act. The result was "The Rain, The Park And Other Things" (1967), followed by "Indian Lake" (1968) and "Hair" (1969), their biggest hit, a cleaned-up version of the title song to the hit Broadway musical. Then they went on to television. They've since faded from public view entirely.

Cramer, Floyd   A premier Nashville pianist, Cramer played on most of the biggest hits in country music throughout the 1950s and 1960s, including Elvis Presley's "Heartbreak Hotel" (1956). He was born on Oct. 27, 1933 in Shreveport, La. and came to Nashville in 1955 at the behest of Chet Atkins. He is perhaps best known for "Last Date," his solo hit in 1960.

Crawler (formerly Back Street Crawler)   Paul Kossoff (guitar), Terry Wilson Slesser (vocals), Terry Wilson (bass), Tony Braunagel (drums), Mike Montgomery (keyboards)—Originally Back Street Crawler, the band was launched in 1975 by guitarist Paul Kossoff of Free. Kossoff died in 1976, and the band reformed under the name of Crawler, sticking to the Kossoff formula of straight-ahead rock, heavy on the guitars. Present members also include Geoff Whitehorn (guitar) and John Bundrick (keyboards).

Crazy Horse   Billy Talbot (bass), Ralph Molina (drums), Frank Sampedro (guitar)—Originally a West Coast group called the Rockets, the group (less Sampedro, but with Danny Whitten on drums and vocals) backed up Neil Young on his landmark solo album *Everybody Knows This Is Nowhere* (1969). The band went solo in 1971 with its critically well-received *Crazy Horse* album, featuring Jack Nitzsche and Nils Lofgren, and a second album the next year entitled *Loose.* The group disbanded in 1972 after the drug-related death of Whitten. Young revived the group in 1975, which—as Crazy Horse,

with Sampedro added— backed Young on his haunting *Tonight's The Night* album, dedicated to Whitten and featuring the powerful song "The Needle And The Damage Done." After touring with Young the band released another solo album, *Crazy Moon,* again to critical acclaim.

Creach, Papa John   Born on May 17, 1917 in Beaver Falls, Pa., Papa John Creach may hold the record for being the oldest rock and roller. He took it up at the tender age of

Papa John Creach

53, joining, of all people, the Jefferson Airplane as a fiddle player. He's also played for Hot Tuna and has several solo albums to his credit. He joined the Airplane after a chance meeting with soon-to-be Airplane drummer Joey Covington in 1967 over a bulletin board at the local musicians' union hall. His fiddle has added a different dimension to the groups he's played with, bringing in the dance music of the 1930s and

1940s as well as his hard rock licks. Creach is a most unusual rock-and-roll star.

Cream   Eric Clapton (guitar, vocals), Jack Bruce (bass, vocals), Ginger Baker (drums)—The original slam-bang blues-rock power group, which Clapton always claimed was supposed to be a blues trio. What Cream did was take blues standards, such as "Crossroads" or "I'm So Glad," update them with Clapton's powerful R&B-based guitar and play them *real* loud and *real*

long. The formula was a smashing success.
   Clapton was already a star when Cream was formed in 1966, and the group was an instant success. Cream's 1967 debut album, *Fresh Cream,* went gold, as did the subsequent *Disraeli Gears, Wheels Of Fire* and *Goodbye.* Recorded in 1968 and released in 1969, *Goodbye* signaled exactly what the title said—the band broke up, unable to stand the pressures demanded of a

supergroup.

Creedence Clearwater Revival

John Fogerty (guitar, vocals), Tom Fogerty (guitar), Stu Cook (bass), Doug "Cosmo" Clifford (drums)—In 1968, while the rest of the rock world was looking for profundity, Creedence Clearwater Revival—CCR for short—was looking for hit singles. And did the group ever find them! "Suzie Q" (1968), "Proud Mary" (1969), "Bad Moon Rising" (1969), "Green River" (1969), "Fortunate Son" (1969), "Down On The Corner" (1969), "Travelin' Band" (1970), "Who'll Stop The Rain" (1970), "Up Around The Bend" (1970), "Run Through The Jungle" (1970), "Long As I Can See The Light" (1970), "Looking Out My Back Door" (1970), "Hey Tonight" (1971) and "Sweet Hitch-Hiker" (1971). The secret weapon for this assault on AM radio was John Fogerty, whose gravel voice and uncanny ability to write hit singles made CCR the best thing on AM for four years. Fogerty had the rare knack of writing songs with an air of instant authenticity—he might have never lived in the South (he was born in California), but he understood the rhythm and blues of the area, and he never betrayed the spirit of that music in his writing. "Proud Mary," later recorded by the very Southern Ike and Tina Turner, is a case in point. While the band broke up in 1972, its legacy lives on in three-chord bar bands everywhere.

Crewe, Bob

Best known for his "Music To Watch Girls By" (1966), Crewe (born on Nov. 12, 1931 in Belleville, N.J.) has contributed his share of hit songs for other artists, including the Rays' "Silhouettes" (1957), written with Frank Slay, and such hits for the Four Seasons as "Big Girls Don't Cry" (1962) and "Walk Like A Man" (1963), written with Bob Gaudio, a member of the group. He is presently a producer and manager in Los Angeles.

Crickets, The

Buddy Holly (vocals), Jerry Allison (drums), Niki Sullivan (guitar), Joe Mauldin (bass)—Buddy Holly's first four hits—"That'll Be The Day," "Oh Boy" and "Maybe Baby" (all 1957) and "Think It Over" (1958)—were credited to the Crickets. He formed the group in his home town of Lubbock, Tex. in 1957, the name coming, according to the cinematic legend, from a noisy cricket in Holly's garage rehearsal studio. Sullivan left in early 1958, and later that year Holly was married and the group cooled decidedly, resulting in Holly's departure to pursue a solo career. That career lasted until Feb. 3, 1959, when Holly was killed in a plane crash. Again, according to the legend, Holly was set to rejoin the group at the time of his death.

The Crickets continued on their own with various changes in membership and are presently riding a high after the release of the extremely successful movie *The Buddy Holly Story* in 1978.

Creedence Clearwater Revival

Croce, Jim Born in 1942 in Philadelphia, Croce's career was just gathering steam when he was killed in a plane crash in Louisiana on Sept. 20, 1973. He is best remembered as a balladeer ("Bad, Bad Leroy Brown" in 1973 and his posthumous album and single hit *I Got A Name,* released in late 1973) with a wry sense of humor and a special affinity for the working man.

Cropper, Steve One of the staples of Stax Records in Memphis, Cropper was born in Missouri on Oct. 21, 1942. After moving to Memphis, he formed the group the Mar-Keys, with Donald "Duck" Dunn, while still in high school and then moved to Booker T. and the MGs—short for Memphis Group.

He is a guitarist, composer (Wilson Pickett's "In The Midnight Hour," Otis Redding's "Sitting On The Dock Of The Bay") and producer (Jeff Beck, the Cate Brothers) and has played in numerous sessions and on special albums. He presently works as a producer and composer in Los Angeles and tours with John Belushi and Dan Ackroyd as part of the Blues Brothers.

Crosby, Bing Born on May 2, 1904 in Tacoma, Wash., Bing Crosby had some 22 million-selling records at the time of his death in 1977. His first million seller came in 1937 with "Sweet Leilani"; his last was "True Love," with Grace Kelly, from the film *High Society* in 1956. Then of course there was "White Christmas," first recorded in 1942 and still selling. By 1970 "White Christmas" had sold some 68 million copies,

helping make Bing Crosby the largest record seller of all time—with collective sales amounting to 400 million albums.

Crosby, David The perennial folkie, David Crosby first gained recognition in 1964 as one of the original Byrds. He was born on Aug. 14, 1941 in Los Angeles and worked as a solo folkie until meeting Gene Clark and Roger McGuinn and forming the nucleus of the Byrds. His biggest contribution was his excellent vocal harmonies; his songwriting was a mixed blessing— eventually breaking up the group, in fact, when the Byrds refused to perform Crosby's "Triad," a rather lovely ballad about a *menage a trois,* later recorded by the Jefferson Airplane and Crosby, Stills and Nash.

Beginning in 1968 he joined with Steve Stills and Graham Nash to form Crosby, Stills and Nash (CSN), later adding Neil Young. Their music, which continues off and on and in various permutations—Crosby and Nash, CSN re-formed etc.—set the tone for the mellow revolution of the West Coast Sound, slick harmonies and all. After over 10 years those harmonies still sound great.

Crosby, Stills, Nash and Young David Crosby (vocals, guitar), Stephen Stills (vocals, guitar), Graham Nash (vocals, guitar), Neil Young (vocals, guitar)—CSN&Y were formed in the summer of 1968 by David Crosby from the Byrds, Stephen Stills from the Buffalo Springfield and Graham Nash from the Hollies, with Canadian folksinger Neil Young, also from the Buffalo Springfield, added for the second album.

The first album, *Crosby, Stills and Nash,* yielded two hits, Stephen Stills' epic to Judy Collins, his then-girlfriend, titled "Suite: Judy Blue Eyes" and Nash's "Marrakesh Express." With Young they cut one of the classic rock albums of all time, *Deja Vu,* which virtually defined the laid-back L.A. sound for the next decade. Immediately after *Deja Vu* in 1970, the band began coming apart, with the members wanting to go in similar but not identical directions. A mediocre live album, *Four Way Street,* follwed, featuring a live rendition of "Ohio," Young's bitter anthem to the student shootings by the National Guard at Kent State University, and "Find The Cost Of Freedom," Stills' runner-up theme for the movie *Easy Rider.* In 1972 the band split, with each member following a fairly successful solo career. In the mid-1970s, though, various members began drifting back together—Stills and Young; Nash and Crosby; Crosby, Stills and Nash—but a complete reunion never materialized. CS&N are presently active in the antinuke movement.

Cross, Christopher Born in 1949 in San Antonio, Cross became the musical phenomenon of 1980 with his hit album *Christopher Cross.* The folk-rock sounds of such singles as "Sailing" and "Ride Like The Wind" won him a handful of Grammies and airplay on stations across the board. He got his start in an Austin bar band called Flash, playing everyone else's hits.

Crowell, Rodney Born and raised in Texas, Crowell

Crosby, Stills & Nash (Without Young)

became known as a member of Emmylou Harris' Hot Band before making a name for himself as a songwriter. Harris has recorded a number of Crowell's songs, including "Amarillo" and "Leaving Louisiana In The Broad Daylight," both moderate successes in the late 1970s.

Crudup, Arthur "Big Boy"   Bluesman, born in 1905 in Forest, Miss. He worked as a waterboy, logger, levee worker and truck driver and at other occupations before moving to Chicago to sing blues. For a while, he lived in a wooden crate beneath an elevated subway station and played his guitar for dimes. He is best remembered as the author of a tune called "That's All Right Mama," which so fascinated a young white

singer named Elvis Presley that he sang it for his first recording session on June 6, 1954. It was Presley's first release on Sun Records.

Crusaders, The   Wilton Felder (bass, sax), Robert Popwell (bass), Joe Sample (keyboards), Larry Carlton (guitar), Nesbert "Stix" Hooper (drums, percussion)—Yet another jazz-rock fusion group (once called the Jazz Crusaders), the Crusaders lean closer to rock than to jazz. They are best known for backing Joan Baez on her acclaimed *Diamonds And Rust* album (1975) and their own 1975 *Chain Reaction* album.

Crystals, The   Mary Thomas (vocals), Lala Brooks (vocals), Barbara Alston (vocals), Pat Wright (vocals), Dee Dee

Kenniebrew (vocals)—Another group of Brooklyn girls, but this particular group fell in with superstar rock producer Phil Spector in 1961. The payoff came in 1962 with a song written by Gene Pitney—"He's A Rebel" (with Darlene Love singing lead). The song was an overnight classic, and the group followed it up with a couple of more—"Da Doo Ron Ron" (1963) and "Then He Kised Me" (1963); all three were great Phil Spector-produced performances.

Curtis, King   During the 1950s Curtis was a sessions saxaphone player in New York City known especially for his work on Atlantic/Atco records, such as those by the Coasters. In the 1960s he distinguished himself as a soul saxaphonist and bandleader, evidenced by his *Live At The Fillmore West,* with Curtis fronting a powerful band that includes Cornell Dupree and Bernard Purdie.

He was stabbed to death in front of his apartment house in New York City in 1971.

Cyrkle, The   Tom Dawes (guitar, vocals, banjo), Don Dannemann (piano, guitar), Marty Fried (drums), Earl Pickens (organ)—A retread of the Rondells, the Cyrkle got its strange name from a suggestion by Beatles' manager Brian Epstein; the spelling was John Lennon's idea. The group's initial release, "Red Rubber Ball" (1966), written by Paul Simon (of Simon and Garfunkel) and Bruce Woodley (of the Seekers), was a huge hit, and the group toured with the Beatles in 1966. The Cyrkle managed to have one other hit that year, "Turn Down Day," then sank without a trace the following year.

Dakotas, The   Billy J. Kramer (vocals), Mike Maxfield (guitar), Robin McDonald (guitar), Tony Mansfield (drums), Raymond Jones (bass)—Properly named Billy J. Kramer and the Dakotas, this English group was another project of Beatles' manager Brian Epstein in the early 1960s. The group hit in 1963 with the Lennon and McCartney composition of "Bad To Me," followed the next year by "Little Children."

Although they sounded enough like the Beatles to keep them around, the Dakotas had only a couple of more English hits before joining several other Epstein projects in oblivion.

Daltrey, Roger   Flamboyant lead singer of the Who, Daltrey (born on March 1, 1944 in England) has found time to cut three successful solo albums on his own and star in two Ken Russell movies, including the title role of the movie based on *Tommy,* the Who's best-known work. His most successful solo effort has been his first solo album, *Daltrey* (1973), which featured the works of Leo Sayer.

Damned, The   Dave Vanian (vocals); Brian James (guitar, vocals); Captain Sensible, aka Ray Burns (bass, vocals); Rat Scabies (drums, vocals)—One of the first English New Wave bands, formed in 1975. Unlike such bands as the Clash and the Sex Pistols, the Damned's political urgings lie more toward the wallet than smashing the Queen.

Daniels, Charlie   One of the true godfathers of the Southern rock movement, Daniels was born in 1937 in Wilmington, N.C. He came to Nashville in 1967 as a sessions player (mostly fiddle and guitar) and backed such artists as Bob Dylan, Ringo Starr and Leonard Cohen before launching his own career with a novelty tune, "Uneasy Rider" (1973), which played on the us-versus-them, rednecks-versus-hippy mentality of the times. Yet Daniels repudiated the sentiments of "Uneasy Rider" almost immediately, moving to

Mt. Juliet, Tenn. with his band, which now included Joel "Taz" DiGregorio (keyboards), Fred Edwards (drums), Don Murray (percussion), Tom "Bigfoot" Crain (guitar, vocals) and Charlie Hatward (bass)—and began a successful series of albums, keying on tight rhythms, double guitar leads and Daniels' high nasal vocals. He has stuck to that formula through the years, breaking into the disco-oriented 1979 charts with one of the biggest hits of that summer, "The Devil Went Down To Georgia." He is also known for his annual Volunteer Jams, a huge jam session of Southern bands held in Tennessee each January.

Darin, Bobby   The name came out of the phonebook and the kid, Walden Robert Cassotto, born on May 14, 1936, came out of the Bronx. Since he didn't want to be a street tough and was crummy at sports, he decided on show business. For two years Darin tried without success and then one afternoon in 1958 he sat down and wrote "Splish Splash" in 10 minutes—from that moment he was on his way to being a teen idol. He became a hit singer, with such songs as "Mack The Knife" (1959) and "You Must Have Been A Beautiful Baby" (1961); a movie star, beginning with *Come September* in 1960; and the husband of another teen idol, Sandra Dee. His career slowed and his marriage ended in divorce. In the late 1960s he had a hit with a folk-type ballad entitled "If I Were A Carpenter." He died in 1973 during heart surgery in Los Angeles.

The Charlie Daniels Band

Dave Clark Five, The   Dave Clark (drums), Lenny Davidson (guitar), Rick Huxley (guitar, banjo), Denis Payton (guitar, reeds, sax), Mike Smith (vocals, keyboards, vibes)—Essentially a Beatles imitation, the Dave Clark Five burst on the American scene in 1964 with "Do You Love Me" and "Glad All Over." They continued doing competent, though not inspired, singles work until 1973.

Davies, Cyril   Born in 1932 in England, Davies is best known as one of the fathers of English rhythm and blues, joining Alexis Korner in the early 1960s to form Blues Incorporated. That band featured, at various times, Mick Jagger, Charlie Watts, Brian Jones, Jack Bruce and Ginger Baker. Davies died of leukemia on Jan. 7, 1964.

Davis, Clive   As the head of the powerful CBS Records, Clive Davis was responsible for many of that company's biggest catches, including Bob Dylan and Janis Joplin. After a brief, apparently overblown monetary scandal, Davis stepped down, eventually taking over as the head of the fledgling Arista Records. Although Arista has yet to duplicate CBS' huge success, it has become a solid label with such Davis' finds as Patti Smith and the Outlaws. He was born on April 4, 1932.

Davis, Mac   Along with Glen Campbell and, most recently, Kenny Rogers, one of the best-known country-pop singers, Mac Davis was born in Lubbock, Tex. on Jan. 21, 1942. He first hit in 1972 with "Baby Don't Get Hooked On Me," a pop and country hit, and has been a staple on the country charts ever since. He is the author of Elvis Presley's hit "In The Ghetto" (1969) and has had his own television variety show. In 1979 he made his acting debut in the movie *North Dallas Forty* and, much to the shock of film critics everywhere, was good at that too.

Davis, Miles   Best known as one of the greatest jazz trumpet players of the late 1940s and early 1950s, Miles Davis provided a solid center for the numerous jazz players interested in experimenting with the new phenomenon of rock. In 1969 and 1970 Davis advanced the jazz-rock movement by light years with his release of two albums, *In A Silent Way* (1969) and *Bitches Brew* (1970), both heavily influencd by the hard rock prevalent at the time. He has also served as a way station for a number of fusion musicians, including Herbie Hancock, Chick Corea and John McLaughlin. Oddly, although so many musicians of such talent have labored to produce the jazz-rock fusion, the sum has proved to be far less than any of its parts.

The Dead Boys

Davis, Reverend Gary
Bluesman Blind Gary Davis (born in 1896 in South Carolina) worked as a street singer with the guitar and the harp in South Carolina until 1935, when he rejected the blues for gospel. For a while he toured the South with Sonny Terry and worked as a street singer in Harlem. He tutored several pop artists, including David Bromberg, before his death in 1972.

Davis, Sammy, Jr. An American institution, Sammy Davis, Jr. shows up once every decade with a hit pop song out of left field. In 1962, right in the middle of all that rock and roll, it was "What Kind Of Fool Am I?"; in 1972, in the midst of all that hard rock, "Candy Man." He should be due again in a couple of years. Davis was born on Dec. 8, 1925 in New York City. In 1956 he played the lead in the Broadway show *Mr. Wonderful* and went on to stardom in Hollywood, Las Vegas and TV appearances. He hasn't slowed down since, joining with knockaround buddies Frank Sinatra, Dean Martin and Peter Lawford in one of the better known rogues' galleries ever.

Davis, Spencer Leader of a tough English pub group, the Spencer Davis Group (which included teenaged Stevie Winwood), Spencer Davis distinguished himself with a series of hard driving singles, including "Gimme Some Lovin'" (1967) and the group's anthem, "I'm A Man" (1967). The Spencer Davis Group broke up in 1969. Davis was born on July 17, 1942 in England. (See also Spencer Davis Group, The.)

Day, Bobby Born in 1934 in Los Angeles, Bobby Day wrote and recorded a rock classic in 1957 called "Little Bitty Pretty One," only to have all the glory stolen by a cover version done by Thurston Harris. But the next year Day came back with "Rockin' Robin" and "Over and Over."

Day, Doris The most wholesome girl in the world—at least all through the 1950s—Doris Day was born Doris Kappelhoff on April 3, 1924 in Cincinnati, Ohio. She is remembered for "Secret Love" in 1954, the same year that Elvis Presley went into a recording studio for the first time.

Dead Boys, The Cheetah Chrome (guitar), Stiv Bators (vocals), Johnny Blitz (drums), Jimmy Zero (guitar), Jeff Magnum (bass)—Don't let the names fool you, folks, these guys are from Cleveland, Ohio. They got their first taste of success in the New York New Wave scene in 1976, and despite their decidedly weird appearance, they've got a pretty good grip on rock and roll. Their album titles tell it all—*Young, Loud And Snotty* and *We Have Come For Your Children* (produced, incidentally, by rock veteran Felix Pappalardi). "It's the old philosophy," said Stiv Bators recently, "if I'm too loud for you, you're too old for me."

Dean, Jimmy Born on Aug. 10, 1928 in Plainview, Tex., Dean became one of the most successful pop singers of the mid-1950s, managing to coexist with the budding rock-and-roll frenzy with such songs as "Deep Blue Sea" (1957), "Little Sandy Sleighfoot" (1957) and the classic "Big Bad John" (1961), his most famous performance. Since then he has moved effortlessly to a career in television.

Dee, Joey, and the Starlighters Joey Dee (vocals), Carlton Latimor (organ), Willie Davis (drums), Larry Vernieri (vocals), David Brigati (vocals)—In a case of blind luck, the Starlighters were working as the house band at the Peppermint Lounge on

West 45th Street in New York City when the twist suddenly became a national mania. The Peppermint Lounge, thanks to media exposure, became Mecca for twist-o-philes, and the Starlighters' own "Peppermint Twist" became *the* song for 1961.

Dee, Kiki An English blues singer who found her groove with Elton John, Kiki Dee was born Pauline Matthews in 1947. Although she began her professional career in 1964 and six years later signed with Tamla/Motown (the company's only white British girl singer, by the way), she didn't find success, however, until joining John's Rocket Records in 1973. She hit in 1975 with "I've Got The Music In Me" and the next year with a duet with Elton John titled "Don't Go Breaking My Heart." Her recent album *Stay With Me* (1978) was only moderately successful.

Deep Purple Rod Evans (vocals); Jon Lord (keyboards); Nick Simper (bass); Ritchie Blackmore (guitar); Ian Paice (drums); and others, including Tommy Bolin (guitar), Ian Gillan (vocals), Roger Glover (bass), David Cloverdale (vocals), Glenn Hughes (bass, vocals)—Beginning in Germany in 1968 as sort of a mystical heavy rock ensemble (exemplified by the *Book of Taliesyn* album in 1968), the group chucked the mystical stuff (and members Simper and Evans) to concentrate on eardrum-busting heavy metal rock in the 1970s. The personnel changed on a daily basis, with at least one drug-related death (Bolin, in 1975). Deep Purple reached a peak in 1973 with the hit single "Smoke On The Water" and were gone by 1976.

Delaney and Bonnie
Another sad rock-and-roll story. Delaney Bramlett was a Shindog, one-half of the popular duo on television's "Shindig" show, and Bonnie Lynn was a hell-bent-for-leather white blues singer in Memphis, the first white Ikette, part of the Ike and Tina Turner revue. They met in 1967 and married after a courtship lasting exactly seven days. They then became the first white group to sign with Stax Records in Memphis and immediately cut *Down Home,* with Booker T. and the MGs backing them up.

In 1969 they went on the road with their "friends," which amounted to anyone who could make it and included, at various times, Leon Russell, Eric Clapton, Duane Allman, Bobby Whitlock, Rita Coolidge, Dave Mason and, once or twice, George Harrison. The result from that year was the brilliant album *Accept No Substitute—The Original Delaney And Bonnie,* a fusion of soul, Southern bar boogie, gospel and country, with Bonnie's incredible voice topping it off. But the energy couldn't hold, and the ensemble drifted apart—many to Joe Cocker's version of blue-eyed soul, the Mad Dogs and Englishmen tour.

The duo broke up in the early 1970s, and since then both have tried for solo success without avail. Bonnie joined the Allman Brothers on their reunion tour in 1979, and she also grabbed a few headlines by punching out English New Waver Elvis Costello in a brawl over his allegedly using the word "nigger" in a disparaging way.

Delfonics, The A trio from Pennsylvania, the Delfonics became prime movers of

Deep Purple

The Dells

Thom Bell's Philly Sound, a soft, syrupy sound closer to the black groups of the early 1950s than the soul singers of the 1960s. Wilbert and William Hart and Randy Cain had been singing together since 1961, when "La La Means I Love You" became a hit in 1968. In 1970 the group won a Grammy for best rhythm-and-blues performance for "Didn't I Blow Your Mind This Time."

Dells, The   Marvin Junior (vocals), Johnny Carter (vocals), Verne Allison (vocals), Mickey McGill (vocals), Chuck Barksdale (vocals)—The Dells began as a street corner a capella group in Chicago (they're all from Harvey, Ill., where they all still live) some 23 years ago. They hit the charts for the first time in 1956 with "Oh, What A Night." The same song was a hit again in 1969. Their most recent hit was "Give Your Baby A Standing Ovation" in 1973, and the group continues to record for Mercury/ Phonogram.

Denny, Sandy   Lead singer for the English groups the

Strawbs (1968) and Fairport Convention (1969), Denny left the latter to pursue a career of her own. She died on April 28, 1978.

Denver, John   John Denver (born Dec. 31, 1943) used to be John Henry Deutschendorf, an Air Force brat who wanted to be a folk singer. He later worked as one of the Chad Mitchell Trio and wrote "Leaving On A Jet Plane" for Peter, Paul and Mary. Denver is the quintessential star, his every move faithfully recorded in *People* magazine, while critics damn his easy listening music that the public can't seem to get enough of.

To be sure, what he does, he does well. From his first album, *Rhymes And Reasons* (1969), Denver has kept a constant finger on the pulse of much of America, providing folk music without protest, country music without honky-tonk angst. "Take Me Home, Country Roads" (1971) and "Rocky Mountain High" (1973) are indeed masterpieces of the easy listening mold. When he was honored by the Country Music Association in 1975, an

act that enraged country music fans and critics, some of Nashville's biggest stars stepped forward and pointed out that "Back Home Again" (1974) happened to be a very good song, even if it *was* written and sung by Denver, who might not know country music from whatever.

Recently Denver has embarked on a film career (receiving good reviews in *Oh, God* [1978], with George Burns in the title role) and has appeared in television specials and late night talk shows. He regularly works Lake Tahoe on a double bill with Frank Sinatra, and the two recently shared a television special. His latest 1979 album, *John Denver,* was essentially more of the same. Why change a winning formula?

John Denver

De Paul, Lynsey Successful as a singer and songwriter in England, 25-year-old Lynsey De Paul made her American debut in 1975 with the album *Love Bomb,* which saw limited success with the single "Sugar Shuffle," as icky-sweet as its title.

Derek & the Dominos

Derek and the Dominos Eric Clapton (guitar, vocals), Bobby Whitlock (keyboards, vocals, guitar), Jim Gordon (drums, piano), Carl Radle (bass, percussion), Duane Allman (guitar)—The greatest lost group in rock-and-roll history, Derek and the Dominos was formed by Eric Clapton, ace British guitarist, in 1971. Clapton joined Duane Allman of the Allman Brothers Band, already on his way to becoming America's premier rock guitarist, to produce *Layla And Other Assorted Love Songs* (1971). The double-record album is a masterpiece, a slick blending of Clapton's British interpretations of blues and Allman's more visceral Southern rhythm and blues. Amazingly, it was a total commercial failure—1971

marked a lull in rock, with only the Rolling Stones bucking the trend to softer material. Clapton was stunned at the record's failure and more so by the death of Duane Allman later that year. A second recording session never really got off the ground. A single live album was released in 1973, a year after the band's total dissolution by a despondent Clapton. Ironically, "Layla," released in 1972 as a single, became a hit and is still heard on FM radio today.

Derringer, Rick Best known as the producer of Texas bluesmen Johnny and Edgar Winter, Derringer has had a string of successes since his days in Union City, Ind. as a member of the McCoys, where he played the guitar, sang and wrote the group's 1965 hit "Hang On Sloopy" at the tender age of 18. He remains in demand as a guitarist (mainly with one of the Winters) and works with his own band, Derringer.

DeShannon, Jackie Something of a renaissance woman, DeShannon has

worked as an actress (television's *My Three Sons, The Wild, Wild West* and *The Name of the Game*), a songwriter (beginning with Brenda Lee's recording of her "Dum Dum" in 1961) and a singer—in fact, she had her own radio show at the age of six. Her two biggest hits were the Burt Bacharach/Hal David "What The World Needs Now," nominated for four Grammys in 1965, and her own "Put A Little Love In Your Heart" in 1969. In 1975 she made *New Arrangement* and followed two years later with *You're The Only Dancer.*

Devo Jerry Casale (bass), Bob Casale (guitar), Mark Mothersbaugh (keyboards, guitar), Bob Mothersbaugh (guitar), Alan Meyers (drums)—Akron, Ohio's contribution to rock-and-roll dementia, Devo (short for de-evolution) plays rock and roll for the mechanical future—precise, machine- (i.e., synthesizer-) oriented revisions of what has come before (such as the group's cover of the Rolling Stones' "Satisfaction"). *Q: Are We Not Men? A: We Are Devo,* released in 1978, showed the group in fine form (aluminum jumpsuits and all).

Diamond, Neil Born on Jan. 24, 1941 in Brooklyn, New York City, Diamond began his career in the mid-1960s writing for the television pop group the Monkees. His solo career started with "Solitary Man" (1965) and continued through "Cherry, Cherry" (1966), "Girl, You'll Be A Woman Soon" (1967), "Brooklyn Roads" (1968), "Sweet Caroline" (1969), "Holly Holy" (1969),

"Cracklin' Rosie" (1970) and so on. In 1979 Diamond teamed up with Barbra Streisand to cut a best selling single, "You Don't Send Me Flowers." Although he has continually courted the rock crowd, it has remained beyond his grasp, even while his audience boomed. He remains a powerful singer and an extraordinary songwriter, one of the few who can transcend the label of easy listening to make a permanent mark.

Dick and Dee Dee   Dick St. John Gosting and Dee Dee Sperling, both from Los Angeles, got together in 1961 as writing partners, with Dee Dee singing only when a female voice was needed for a demo record. The flip side of one demo turned out to be "The Mountain's High," a million seller in 1961.

Dickinson, James Luther
A Memphis-trained piano player and producer, Dickinson played keyboards for the Rolling Stones and worked with the Dixie Flyers in Miami during the early 1970s. He produced Ry Cooder before returning to Memphis in the late 1970s and made one solo album, *James Luther Dickinson,* in the mid-1970s, a masterpiece of rockabilly/funk/rock and roll.

Dictators, The
"Handsome" Dick Manitoba (vocals), Ross "the Boss" (guitar), Top Ten (guitar), Adny Shernoff (keyboards, vocals), Ritchie Teeter (drums, vocals), Mark "the Animal" Mendoza (bass)—Launched in 1975 as "the only Jewish heavy metal band," the Dictators predated

punk with perhaps one of the most genuinely bizarre albums in rock, *The Dictators Go Girl Crazy,* featuring such gems as "I Got You Babe, "Back To Africa," "Master Race Rock" and "I Live For Cars And Girls." The really odd thing is that they were *good,* not the least bit caught up in the pretension that would drag punk down. Their most recent album was *Manifest Destiny* (1977).

Diddley, Bo   Bo Diddley was born Otha Ellas Bates on Dec. 30, 1928 in McComb, Miss. He was later adopted by the McDaniel family and he became Ellas McDaniel. Growing up in the fertile world of Chicago blues, he decided to learn the guitar (at the age of 10) when he heard John Lee Hooker's "Boogie Children." In the early 1950s he began playing at Chicago's 708 Club, where he came to the attention

of Leonard and Phil Chess, who signed him to a contract with Chess Records in 1955. In one of the great pieces of cheek in rock, Bo Diddley's first song was one he had written all about himself, titled (not surprisingly) "Bo Diddley." "Bo Diddley" was released in 1955, right along with Chuck Berry's "Maybellene," and it became an instant classic. He followed with the howling electric rhythms of "Say Man" (1959) and "Who Do You Love" (1959).

What he brought to rock and roll was a wildness and a willingness to experiment with strange rhythms and almost hypnotic repetition—"the Bo Beat"—something that has influenced almost every rock performer since.

Dillards, The   A collective name given to the various permutations of the groups

Bo Diddley

headed by Doug and Rodney Dillard, who are best known for their eclectic and innovative approach to bluegrass music. Their greatest influence has been on West Coast musicians, where the Dillards' form of lighthearted, semi-countrified bluegrass has found a permanent home in the country-rock sound of people like the Eagles, Jackson Browne and Linda Ronstadt.

Dion With "A Teenager In Love" in 1959, Dion DiMucci and his group, the Belmonts, from the Bronx, New York City, established a major fact—that America was in love with a teenager. Well, ex-teenager really, since Dion was born July 18, 1939. He was, however, one of the hottest artists of the late 1950s and early 1960s. Dion and the Belmonts had two big hits—"Teenager In Love" (1959) and "Where Or When" (1960). In 1960 Dion broke off from the Belmonts and started churning out hits on his own, such as "Lonely Teenager" (1960), "Runaround Sue" (1961) and "The Wanderer" (1961). Without Dion the Belmonts— Fred Milano, Carlo Mastangelo and Angelo D'Aleo—scored a national hit in 1961 with "Tell Me Why," before falling into obscurity. As Dion DiMucci, Dion made the charts twice in 1963 with "Donna The Prima Donna" and "Drip Drop." After drifting away in the mid-1960s (with a vicious drug habit), he returned—clean—in 1968 with the folkish "Abraham, Martin And John," written about the assassinations of Martin Luther King, Jr. and the Kennedys. He then rode the wave of rock-and-roll revivals into the 1970s,

culminating in a reunion with the Belmonts at Madison Square Garden in 1972. In recent years he has turned out two albums, *Streetheart* and *Lifesong* (1978), which contained the single "I Used To Be A Brooklyn Dodger."

Dire Straits Mark Knopfler (guitar, vocals), David Knopfler (guitar), John Illsley (bass), Pick Withers (drums)—This

Dire Straits

English band, formed in 1977, burst on the American scene with "Sultans Of Swing" (1978), a polished guitar-backed single that turned the group into real contenders and led to work with Bob Dylan. The band's album *Dire Straits*, containing that single, was a best seller in 1979, and a year later it released *Making Movies.* The band is heavy on the guitar work and leans on Mark Knopfler's hoarse vocals.

Dixie Cups, The Barbara Ann Hawkins, Rose Lee Hawkins, Joan Marie Johnson—A discovery by Mike Stoller and Jerry Leiber, who signed them to their Red Bird label. Their biggest hit was

"Chapel of Love" (1964), written by Phil Spector, Jeff Barry and Ellie Greenwich.

Dixiebells, The Shirley Thomas (vocals), Mary Hunt (vocals), Mildred Pratcher (vocals)—A Memphis vocal group, the Dixiebells are best known for their two infectious hits, "Down At Papa Joe's" (1963) and "Southtown U.S.A." (1964).

Dixon, "Big" Willie Blues bass player and composer for Muddy Waters and others in Chicago, Dixon also served as the talent scout for Leonard and Phil Chess of Chess Records in the late 1940s, funneling such blues masters as Muddy Waters to the two brothers.

Dixon, Floyd Texas bluesman who moved to the West Coast in the mid-1940s and contributed to the increasing sophistication of the blues there. A pianist, he worked extensively with "Ivory" Joe Hunter.

Dr. Hook Ray Sawyer (vocals, guitar, percussion),

Dennis Locorriere (vocals, guitar), Bill Francis (keyboards, vocals), Rik Elswit (guitar, vocals), Jance Garfat (bass, vocals), John Wolters (drums, vocals), Bob "Willard" Henke (guitars, vocals)—Genuine rock-and-roll survivors, Dr. Hook (formerly Dr. Hook and the Medicine Show) began in 1972 as a novelty act for *Playboy* cartoonist and songwriter Shel Silverstein (who wrote the group's first hits, "Sylvia's Mother" and "The Cover Of The Rolling Stone"), moved into boogie and rock, went bankrupt, decided they were really country singers and ultimately came out singing disco in 1979 ("Better Love Next Time," their most recent hit). They continue to live and record in Nashville and tour worldwide with their outrageous (and never dull, to be sure) stage show. Their secret, aside from the astute management of Ron Haffkine, who met the group with Silverstein in the early 1970s, is that their interest in music isn't the slightest bit bound by certain categories, nor are they worried about being "labeled" as a country, rock or disco act. It makes perfect sense to Dr. Hook to shift from a country weeper about dying children to Sam Cooke's "Only Sixteen," to the rockish "Sharing The Night Together" or the disco sound of "When You're In Love With A Beautiful Woman," all hits for the group. They are, incidently, the only group to get on the cover of *Rolling Stone* magazine by simply singing about it.

Dr. John   Born in 1941 in New Orleans, Mac Rebennack

grew up in the recording studios of that famous city, listening to the likes of Professor Longhair and Fats Domino, and by 1956 he was already working sessions. His fame as a sessions man spread, and when he made the move to Los Angeles in the mid-1960s, he had as much work as he wanted for people like Sam Cooke, Sonny and Cher and Phil Spector. In 1968 he surfaced on his own as Dr. John "the Night Tripper" (his answer to the Beatles' "Day Tripper") with *Gris Gris*, a powerful blend of rhythm and blues, rock, Cajun music and voodoo chants. He added to the effect of his songs by appearing on stage in robes and feathered headdresses. The formula worked right up through the mid-1970s and even resulted in a hit single, "Right Place Wrong Time" (1973). But the edge wore off, and the mysterious man of voodoo became just another rocker.

Domino, Fats   Antoine "Fats" Domino was always a rock and roller: he just had to wait around a few years for rock to start. Born on Feb. 26, 1928 in New Orleans, he was playing the piano by the time he was 10. Domino's first million seller came with "The Fat Man" (1948), his first release. He really hit his stride, though, in the mid-1950s, when rock got rolling. Songs like "Ain't That A Shame" (1955), "Blueberry Hill" (1956), "I'm Walkin'" (1957) and, of course, "Walking To New Orleans" (1960) show the Fat Man in complete control, his thick voice rolling like molasses. Like so many others

his career waned in the hard rock sixties, picking up again in the rock revival years. Over the years he has sold some 65 million records.

Dominoes, The   Clyde McPhatter (vocals), Charlie White (vocals), Joe Lamont (vocals), Bill Brown (vocals), Billy Ward (piano)—Formed in 1950 as a gospel ensemble by Billy Ward, the group is best remembered—ironically—for its earthy 1951 recording of "Sixty Minute Man." The Dominoes had another hit on the R&B charts with "Have Mercy Baby" a year later. In 1953 McPhatter left the group, which was now billed as Billy Ward and His Dominoes, after a dispute with Ward and formed the Drifters. He was replaced by Jackie Wilson, who, after singing lead on additional mid-1950s hits for the group, eventually departed and became a hit solo act in 1957.

Donegan, Lonnie   Born in 1931 in Scotland, Donegan enjoyed tremendous success as a balladeer and folk singer in England from 1956 to 1962 (in fact, *none* of his single releases failed to become a hit). Many of his hits were cover versions of material from the United States ("Battle of New Orleans" in 1959 and "Tom Dooley" the year before, for example). His only successes in the U.S. came in 1956 with "Rock Island Line" and in 1961 with "Does Your Chewing Gum Lose It's Flavor (On The Bedpost Overnight)."

Donovan   Perhaps the prototypical flower child, Scotsman Donovan Leitch was born May 10, 1946, became an instant star on English television in 1965 and managed to fade away by the end of the decade. At the height of psychedelia, he was in there with the best of them, writing and recording "Catch The Wind" (1965), "Sunshine Superman" (1966) and "Mellow Yellow" (1966). His downfall began with the hugely pretentious *Gift From A Flower To A Garden* album in 1967, when he took himself and his message a bit more seriously than the rest of the world. He did, however, come up with the mini-classic "Atlantis" in 1968. In 1976, on the unsuccessful comeback trail, he released a single titled "A Well-Known Has-Been."

Doobie Brothers, The Pat Simmons (guitar, vocals), Jeff "Skunk" Baxter (guitar, vocals), John Hartman (percussion), Michael McDonald (keyboards, vocals), Tiran Porter (bass), Keith Knudsen (drums)—A band that could only happen in the musically mercurial 1970s, the Doobies started the decade as hard rockers, *a la* the Allman Brothers; drifted to heavily arranged, almost gospel-flavored material; returned to rock and finally settled on disco-oriented rhythm and blues in the closing minutes of the decade. The band was brought together by ex-Moby Grape, ex-Jefferson Airplane drummer Skip Spence in 1969 in San Jose, Calif. In 1972, after a hard rock premier album the year before, the Doobies released *Toulouse Street,* a gold album, featuring the huge hit "Listen To The Music." They repeated the trick the following year with *The Captain And Me,* another gold album highlighted by another huge hit, the gospel-tinted "Long Train Running." Next year the same thing: *What Were Once Vices Are Now Habits* sold like hot cakes and included the superb single "Black Water," which sounded like nothing the Doobies had ever done before—heavy on flowing rhythms, white soul vocals and an excellent a capella finish. With added Steely Dan members Jeff "Skunk" Baxter and Michael McDonald, the next two years marked a return to straight-ahead rock on *Stampede* (1975) and *Takin' It To The Streets* (1976), both of which went gold, then platinum (representing one million sales). The following year's *Livin' On The Fault Line* contained two exceptional cuts—"Nothin' But A Heartache" and "Echoes Of Love." Their 1977 *Best Of The Doobies* album has to date sold some three million copies. In 1978 the group released *Minute By Minute* (heavy on the rhythm and blues and disco rhythms), which became another giant success. The title track and "What A Fool Believes," with McDonald playing keyboards and singing lead, were national hits in 1979, and the album and "What A Fool Believes" each won the group a Grammy. The Doobies, in fact, are exemplary of 1970s music—shunning the labels that divided music in the 1960s and showing a willingness to go straight for the commercial, without sacrificing quality. And what worked for them in the seventies was still working as they began the next decade, scoring in 1980 with another hit single, "One Step Closer."

The Doobie Brothers

The Doors

Doors, The Jim Morrison (vocals), Ray Manzarek (keyboards), Robby Krieger (guitar), John Densmore (drums)—Perhaps the most charismatic figure—certainly one of the most literate—rock has ever produced is that of James Douglas Morrison (born on Dec. 8, 1943 in Melbourne, Fla.), and a decade after his death the legend and the music are still going strong. The music of the Doors (the name is from William Blake), with its heavy imagery of violence and death, reflected Morrison's own preoccupations. But it also perfectly captured some of the spirits of the times, the forces building and shaping in the late 1960s.

The band got together in 1965, when Morrison met Manzarek in Los Angeles and decided to form a group. Manzarek, a classically trained musician with an abiding interest in black music, found the remainder of the Doors working in a band called the Psychedelic Rangers. The first Doors album, *The Doors,* came in 1967, and much to everyone's surprise it was a monster hit, not only on trendy FM radio, but "Light My Fire" (the short version) was an instant classic and AM radio hit. Strangely, the continuing AM success of the Doors— with "Crystal Ship" (1967), "We Could Be So Good Together" (1968), "Touch Me" (1969) and "Riders On The Storm" (1971)—hurt the band's credibility, i.e., nothing that successful could be really *good.* The continued critical carping hit Morrison hard. His music was all about living on the edge, and more and more he began to live his songs. There were arrests in 1967 (obscenity and inciting to riot for mentioning his arrest on stage) and in 1969 (lewd and lascivious behavior on stage in Miami, including allegedly exposing himself). At the height of his popularity in 1971, Morrison quit. He went to Paris to rest and on July 3, 1971 he died there of a heart attack. The band went on, but its heart had been cut out. The Door's *L.A. Woman* (1971), featuring the title cut and "Riders On The Storm," remains one of the greatest rock albums ever, a tribute to the man who conceived it.

Dovells, The Len Barry, Jerry Summers, Mike Dennis, Arnie Satin, Danny Brooks—A vocal group from Philadelphia, Pa., best known for its 1961 recording of "Bristol Stomp," riding that year's craze for dance music, especially from Philly. Barry later went on to a moderately successful solo career with "1-2-3" (1965) and "Like A Baby" (1966).

Dowd, Tom Best known as an outstanding producer for such artists as Otis Redding

(*Saturday Night At The Apollo*), Eric Clapton (*461 Ocean Boulevard*), Rod Stewart (*Atlantic Crossing*), and Lynyrd Skynyrd (*Gimme Back My Bullets, One More From The Road*). He originally began work for Atlantic Records in the late 1940s.

Drifters, The 1953-58: Clyde McPhatter, Gerhart Thrasher, Andrew Thrasher, Bill Pinckney, Jimmy Oliver. McPhatter was replaced as lead singer in 1954 by David Baughan, who was replaced by Johnny Moore in 1955, who was replaced by Bobby Hendricks in 1957. Additional personnel included Tommy Evans. 1959-66: Ben E. King, Charley Thomas, Doc Green, Elsberry Hobbs. King was replaced as lead singer in 1961 by Rudy Lewis, who was replaced in 1964 by veteran Johnny Moore. Less a coherent group than an experimental "sound," the Drifters (so named because the members "drifted" from group to group) were more or less created by Ahmet Ertegun of Atlantic Records as a vehicle for Clyde McPhatter. With McPhatter the Drifters recorded one R&B classic, "Money Honey" (1953), and three other rhythm-and-blues successes—"Such A Night" (1954), "Honey Love" (1954) and "White Christmas" (1954). Following McPhatter's departure the group had additional hits, such as "Soldier Of Fortune" (1956). The Drifters' second incarnation was engineered by manager George Treadwell in 1958, who turned a group called the Five Crowns into the new Drifters and immediately

had a hit in 1959 with the Ben E. King composition "There Goes My Baby." King also sang on two of the group's most famous songs in 1960, "This Magic Moment" and "Save The Last Dance For Me" (written by the ace team of Mort Shuman and Doc Pomus)—the latter being the group's only number one hit. King's successor, Rudy Lewis, sang lead on two of the best-remembered hits, "Up On The Roof" (1963) and "On Broadway" (1963). In the mid-1960s, with Johnny Moore once again at the helm, the Drifters did "Under The Boardwalk" (1964) and "Saturday Night At The Movies" (1964).

Dury, Ian Sort of a New Wave college professor, Dury was a university instructor in England when the bug bit him. In 1973 he formed his first band, Kilborn, and enjoyed moderate success in 1977 riding the New Wave wave. His American release of *New Boots And Panties* in the late 1970s found fans in the New Wave quarter but failed to achieve major commercial success.

Dylan, Bob Robert Allen Zimmerman was born on May 24, 1941 in Duluth, Minn. He changed his name to Dylan, in honor of poet Dylan Thomas, while in college during the late 1950s. In 1961 he turned up in New York City, where he began singing almost immediately in the folk clubs of Greenwich Village.

And that is where the Bob Dylan story really begins. Dylan's music was seminal to the early 1960s, giving rock

and roll a political focus it had lacked up until then. Dylan also fueled the fires of the folk music explosion, which in turn would fuel the fires of rock and roll. While his first album in 1962, *Bob Dylan,* established hs credentials as a folk singer, it was his second album, *Freewheelin' Bob Dylan,* the next year that featured such classics as "Blowin' In The Wind," "I Shall Be Free," "Master Of War" and "Talking World War III Blues." Within a couple of years, though, Dylan was turning away from politics. By *Bringin' It All Back Home* in 1965, Dylan was not only depoliticized but gone rock-and-roll electric as well. His folkie fans hated him for it, but the next album, *Highway 61 Revisited,* produced a bonafide hit, "Like A Rolling Stone," and Dylan became a household word. While riding high on the charts (with his backup group, the Hawks, who later became the Band), he was severely injured in 1966 in a motorcycle accident, causing a two-year layoff, during which he recorded the celebrated *Basement Tapes,* eventually

Bob Dylan

released in 1975, with the Hawks (the Band). In 1968 he resurfaced with *John Wesley Harding,* recorded in Nashville, which he followed with his landmark *Nashville Skyline* album in 1969. That album represented one of the first attempts to rejoin the sundered traditions of rock and country (Dylan had corresponded with Johnny Cash and later appeared on his television show), and the album itself was a masterpiece, producing such classic hits as "Lay Lady Lay" and "Tonight I'll Be Staying Here With You." All the fans who had gotten comfortable with the rock-and-roll Dylan were shaken by the new country gentleman. They were even more shaken when he followed that album with the self-indulgent *Self Portrait.* Since then his career has been musically erratic, although still very successful. He returned to touring in the mid-1970s with his famed Rolling Thunder Revue, featuring the Band and a host of others. He starred in a Sam Peckinpah movie titled *Pat Garrett and Billy the Kid;* made his own movie, the painfully lonely *Renaldo and Clara,* which stiffed; and finally emerged in 1979 as a born-again Christian. Despite the twists and changes, his overall influence on today's music is tremendous.

Dyson, Ronnie   Born in Washington, D.C. on June 5, 1950, Dyson launched his career as one of the leads in the rock musical "Hair" and reached his peak in 1970 with his tour-de-force vocal performance on "(If You Let Me Make Love To You Then) Why Can't I Touch You."

Eagles, The   Don Henley (drums), Glenn Frey (guitar), Timothy B. Schmit (bass), Don Felder (guitar), Joe Walsh (guitar)—The Eagles represent the logical conclusion of the move toward country rock among West Coast groups beginning with the Byrds and the Buffalo Springfield. Which is not to say that the Eagles aren't good—they are, exceptionally so. They have carved out such a niche that "Eagles" is practically synonymous with "laid back."

The group was organized in 1971 out of the wreckage of Linda Ronstadt's backup group. Don Henley and Glenn Frey recruited former Poco member Randy Meisner and Flying Burrito Brother Bernie Leadon, and the Eagles were off. Working with soulmate Jackson Browne, Glenn Frey penned "Take It Easy," a huge hit in 1972, which the Eagles followed up with a couple of more big hits, "Witchy Woman" and "Peaceful Easy Feeling." From that point on the Eagles were well established as hitmakers, adding such other smash singles as "The Best Of My Love" (1974), "One Of These Nights" (1975) and "Lying Eyes" (1975). A major

The Eagles

reshuffling in 1975 added Don Felder as the fifth member and Timothy Schmit as a replacement for Meisner. The next year Leadon quit and was replaced by eclectic guitarist Joe Walsh, who added immensely to *Hotel California* in 1976, which showed the Eagles parodying their own laid-back style to everybody's advantage and spawning a whole bunch of non-Eagle sounding hits, including the title cut, "New Kid In Town" and "Life In The Fast Lane." They waited three years before releasing the next album, *The Long Run,* which mixed some excellent cuts with more than a dab of overindulgence.

Earth, Wind and Fire
Maurice White (vocals, drums), Verdine White (vocals, bass), Philip Bailey (vocals, bass), Larry Dunn (piano, synthesizer), Al McKay (guitar), Ralf Johnson (drums), Fred White (drums), Johnny Graham (guitar), Andrew Woolfolk (sax), Donald Murick (sax), Louis Satterfield (trombone), Michael Harris (trumpet)—Formed in 1971 by ex-Memphian Maurice White, a drummer with the Ramsey Lewis Trio, Earth, Wind and Fire first broke through in 1975 with *The Way Of The World*, a brassy collection of jazz/rock/soul with an almost danceable beat and featuring the hit single "Shining Star." The album is representative of the group's music up to that point and through today. Its stage shows, while less spectacular than such wildly visual groups as P-Funk, are nothing to be sneezed at, and the group's message remains one of good cheer and boogie.

One of the first black rock-soul bands to cross over into a white market, Earth, Wind and Fire rose to superstar status in the late 1970s, helped by the popularization of disco music.

Eastwood, Clint   Stone-faced actor Clint Eastwood, star of numerous "spaghetti" Westerns and *Dirty Harry* movies, actually tried his hand at singing in the 1950s (he released one single, a song titled "Burning Bridges") before wisely returning to a career in acting. In the mid-1960s he attempted another shot, singing in the movie version of *Paint Your Wagon,* before again giving up to become a screen hero. In 1980 he tried once more, this time in a duet with country superstar Merle Haggard in the movie *Bronco Billy.* As a singer, he's a great actor.

Easybeats, The   George Young (guitar, vocals), Gordon "Snowy" Fleet (drums, vocals), Dick Diamonde (bass, vocals), Harry Vanda (guitar, vocals), "Little" Stevie Wright (drums, guitar, vocals)—Once Australia's most popular band (the Easybeats caused riots when they played), this quintet leaped out of the world's car radio in 1966 with "Friday On My Mind," written by Young and Vanda. While nothing else the group cut ever amounted to much, "Friday On My Mind" remains one of the greatest songs to listen to while driving.

Eddie and the Hot Rods
Barrie Masters (vocals), Dave Higgs (guitar), Paul Gray (bass), Steve Nicol (drums)— Formed in England in 1975, the Hot Rods are sort of an

English version of the Ramones, three-chord rock and roll played very, very fast, very loud and with enough energy to power London for weeks. The group is best known for its wild (and very quick) version of Bob Seger's "Get Out Of Denver" (1976).

Eddy, Duane   Born on April 26, 1938 in Phoenix Ariz., Eddy began developing his "twangy" guitar style at the age of 15. In 1958 he recorded "Rebel Rouser," the first of a long line of guitar hits. In the late 1970s he tried briefly for a comeback, cutting a record with country star Waylon Jennings and Jessi Colter, now married to Jennings and the former wife of Eddy. The song, "You Are My Sunshine," was a hit, but nothing further came of Eddy's attempted return.

Edison Lighthouse
Basically an ensemble of studio musicians formed in England in the early 1970s around songwriters Tony Burrows and Tony MacAuley. The group's big hit came in February 1970 with "Love Grows (Where My Rosemary Goes)."

Edmunds, Dave   English rockabilly guitarist Dave Edmunds achieved a spectacular success in 1970 with a remake of the 1950s standard "I Hear You Knocking." Since then he has worked steadily in England and recently, with the widespread acceptance of New Wave music in America, he has been a success touring with Nick Lowe's on-again, off-again band, Rockpile. He is a dynamic, slam-bang guitarist and has an unswerving dedication to hardcore rock and roll. He was born on April 15, 1944 in Wales.

Edwards, Jonathan   Best known for his 1971 hit single, "Sunshine," Jonathan Edwards has had some other limited success as a country-flavored vocalist.

Edwards, Tommy   Born in 1922, Edwards scored a hit in 1958 with an up-tempo version of "It's All In The Game," a band standard written by Gen. Charles Gates Dawes, a Chicago banker and Vice President of the United States under Calvin Coolidge. Edwards died in Virginia in 1969.

Electric Flag, The   Mike Bloomfield (guitar), Nick Gravenites (vocals), Buddy Miles (drums), Barry Goldberg (organ), Harvey Brooks (bass), Peter Strazza (sax), Marcus Doubleday (trumpet), Herbie Rich (guitar)—Best known for the virtuosity of its players, the Electric Flag was formed in 1967 by Michael Bloomfield after his rip with the Paul Butterfield Blues Band. The Electric Flag was also the first rock ensemble to use horns, a harbinger of things to come. A 1974 reunion failed, but two albums from the group's heyday remain: *A Long Time Comin'* and *An American Music Band,* both from 1968.

Electric Light Orchestra   Jeff Lynne (vocals, guitar), Bev Bevan (drums), Kelly Groucutt (bass), Hugh McDowell (cello), Melvyn Gale (cello), Mik Kaminski (violin), Richard Tandy (keyboards)—Electric Light Orchestra (ELO) was originally launched in 1971 by Jeff Lynne, Bev Bevan and Roy Wood as part of Wood's preoccupation with orchestral rock, such as the Beatles' "Strawberry Fields Forever." Woods dropped out early on, leaving the band to follow its own more eclectic leanings. So far the group has covered everything from the Creation (*On The Third Day* in 1973) to "Roll Over Beethoven" (1973), gathering a huge following along the way. At times ELO's music sounds as if a symphony orchestra were being made to play rock and roll at gunpoint, and if they didn't get it exactly right, they'd all be shot.

Electric Prunes, The   Ron Morgan (guitar), Mark Kincaid (guitar, vocals), Richard Whetstone (drums, guitar, vocals), Brett Wade (bass, flute, vocals)—A southern California band, the Electric Prunes are remembered for a fantastic psychedelic single titled "I Had Too Much To Dream Last Night" (1967).

Elliman, Yvonne   Born in Hawaii, Elliman got her first break in the musical *Jesus Christ Superstar,* in which she played Mary Magdalene in the London and Broadway versions. She works as vocalist with Eric Clapton and has had several modest hits ("Hello Stranger," "Love Me," both in 1977) on her own.

Emerson, Lake and Palmer   Keith Emerson (keyboards), Greg Lake (bass, guitar, vocals), Carl Palmer (drums)—The bastard

Keith Emerson of Emerson, Lake and Palmer

offspring of computer science and rock showmanship, Emerson, Lake and Palmer (ELP) gathered together three rock veterans in 1969 (Emerson from the group Nice, Lake from King Crimson and Palmer from Atomic Rooster). At present their blend of classical music and pretentious Wall of Sound— the overpowering background of instruments pioneered by Phil Spector—rock combined with all manner of flashy theatrics (Emerson is rather fond of knife throwing) is extremely popular. They are still riding the crest of their 1977 *Works* and its single "Fanfare For The Common Man." In 1974 the band's *triple* record set, *Welcome Back, My Friends, To The Show That Never Ends,* shipped platinum—one million copies right off the bat.

England Dan and John Ford Coley   Two Texans, Danny Wayland Seals and John Edward Coley became international stars in the early 1970s with their easy listening country rock, only to retire from the road after two albums. In 1976 the duo staged a very impressive comeback with "I'd Really Love To See You Tonight," a top hit song, and remains successful with the same mellow formula.

Eno, Brian One of rock's premier electronic experimenters, Brian Eno's

Brian Eno

commercial efforts have always fallen short of widespread acceptance. After a stint with the avant-garde band Portsmouth Sinfonia, Eno launched Roxy Music with Brian Ferry in 1971. He lasted two years with Roxy Music, the dissension between Eno and Ferry over the band's direction eventually leading Eno to opt for a solo career in 1973. His first solo album, *Here Come*

The Warm Jets (1974), flopped, and he began a series of projects with similarly minded musicians (Robert Fripp, John Cale, Phil Manzanera). In 1977 he began working with the then-waning David Bowie on his *Low* album. The results, spread over the next three albums (*Low, Heroes* and *Lodger*), helped to revitalize Bowie's career and bring Brian Eno's musical visions to a much larger audience. He was born in 1948 in Woodbridge, England.

Entwistle, John Bass player for the Who, Entwistle has found the time for a number of solo albums (including one in 1975 with his own band, Ox, called *Mad Dog*). He produced the excellent Who compilation *Odds 'n' Sods* (1974) and in general has kept the Who away from the rock-and-roll pretension that has affected so many other long standing groups.

Epstein, Brian The Man Who Managed the Beatles was born on Sept. 19, 1934 in Liverpool, England. He first heard of the group that was to be his destiny in 1961, when he was asked for one of the Beatles' early German records while working at his father's record shop. It was Epstein who cleaned up the Fab Four and hustled them all over England, drumming up work and, eventually, a recording contract.

He was moderately successful with other acts, including Billy J. Kramer and the Dakotas and Cilla Black, and soon spread out to his own performance hall and other

interests. He died on Aug. 27, 1967, the victim of drugs.

Ertegun, Ahmet President and founder of Atlantic Records, one of the most influential and important record labels of the 1950s and 1960s. Beginning in 1947, Ertegun, along with Jerry Wexler, raised Atlantic from a blues label to a force in pop music with such acts as the Drifters, Clyde McPhatter and Ruth Brown. More importantly, it was Atlantic Records that in the early 1950s began relentlessly canvassing the South for talent, an action that has reaped everything from Professor Longhair in New Orleans to the Allman Brothers Band in Georgia. Atlantic was instrumental in finding and encouraging Southern acts, especially through Stax Records in Memphis and the various Muscle Shoals recording studios. Atlantic, both on its own and through its distributorship of Stax, was responsible for much of the soul music of the 1960s.

Essex, David Born on July 23, 1947 in London, Essex got to be a rock star by playing the movie role of a rock star in the cult film hits *That'll Be The Day* and its sequel, *Stardust*. The role of rock singer Jim McLaine catapulted Essex, who'd unsuccessfully tried for a career earlier, into an international star, a status he cemented with the hit single "Rock On" (1973). But strangely enough, that's where it ended. He seems torn between the hard rock of his movie protagonist and yearnings to the softer pop side of things, and the result is a career at a standstill.

Estes, Sleepy John
Memphis bluesman, Estes was born in 1904 in Brownsville, Tenn. and died in 1978 in Memphis. He and harp player Hammie Nixon, who joined with Estes in 1927 when only 12 years old, worked the South for decades—Estes' crying voice matched by Nixon's harmonica. In the 1930s Estes recorded in Chicago, then returned to Memphis, later becoming fully blind and totally destitute. His lot did improve some, thanks to blues revivals, by the time of his death. He is best remembered for his composition of "Corrina, Corrina," a hit song for numerous people through the years.

Everett, Betty Born in 1939 in Mississippi, Everett recorded the original of "You're No Good" (later made famous by Linda Ronstadt) in 1963. She is best known, however, for her follow-up, "The Shoop Shoop Song (It's In His Kiss)," a top 10 hit in 1964. Singing with Jerry Butler, she had two other national hits that same year, "Let It Be Me" and "Smile."

Everly Brothers, The Phil and Don Everly (Phil, born on Jan. 19, 1938; Don, born on Feb. 1, 1937—both in Brownie, Ky.) set the standard for harmonies, laying the groundwork for the countless country-rock groups today. Their high, youthful harmonies were and are fun to listen to— quintessential teen music. The sons of country singers, they came to Nashville in 1956 and began working with Chet Atkins. They also met the husband/wife writing team of

Boudleaux and Felice Bryant, who were to supply many of the Everly Brothers' standards. In 1957 they were off and running with two Bryant compositions, "Bye Bye Love" and "Wake Up Little Susie" (initially controversial because Susie and her date were "sleeping" at the movie). They continued on with "All I Have To Do Is Dream" (1958), "Devoted To You" (1958), "(Til) I Kissed You" (1959), "When Will I Be Loved" (1960), "Cathy's Clown" (1960) and several others. The two, despite a nervous breakdown by Don in 1963 and a stint in the Marine Corps, actually stayed together until 1973 and both Don and Phil released solo albums. They remain one of the most influential groups in the history of popular music, for their harmonies as well as their songs.

Every Mother's Son Lary Larden (vocals, guitar), Dennis Larden (vocals, guitar), Bruce Milner (keyboards), Christopher Augustine (drums, percussion), Schuyler Larden (bass)—Formed in the mid-1960s around the folksinging duo of the brothers Lary and Dennis Larden, the group scored its only hit in 1967 with "Come On Down To My Boat."

Exciters, The Brenda Reid (vocals), Carol Johnson (vocals), Lilian Walker (vocals), Herbert Rooney (vocals)— Formed in the early 1960s while the members were in high school in Queens, New York City, the Exciters produced one of the classic hits of the early 1960s, "Tell Him" (1962). Their additional releases continued until 1966, but nothing matched their first hit.

Don & Phil Everly

Fabulous Poodles Richie C. Robertson, Tony de Meur, Bryn B. Burrows, Bobby Valentino—Yet another rock-and-roll footnote, the Fabulous Poodles surfaced in late 1978 at the height of the New Wave frenzy. Given to bizarre costumes and rather basic music, the Poodles are doing just fine providing a sort of comic relief in the grim business of New Wave rock.

the Faces, with superstar Rod Stewart at the forefront, represented the peak of boozy English pub music—hard driving, good time, but with a tendency to fall offstage in an alcoholic stupor. Originally the Small Faces ("Itchycoo Park" in 1967), they dropped the "Small" in 1969 with the departure of Steve Marriott (to Humble Pie) and the addition of Stewart and Wood (from the Jeff Beck Group). Their albums (the best being numbers two and three, *Long Player* in 1971 and *A Nod's As Good As A Wink* in 1972)

representative of the band and its work. It was downhill from there, with increasing personality problems pulling the group apart. Stewart, by this time a huge international star on his own, grumbled about the band's choice of material. Lane left in 1973, eventually finding status for himself. Wood left in 1975 to join the Rolling Stones, and Stewart himself gave up his association in 1976. The next year the band began working on a reunion of the Small Faces, which was greeted with a shrug.

Fahey, John Best known as the founder of the small independent record label Takoma (most famous artist: Leo Kottke), Fahey (born on Feb. 28, 1939 in Takoma Park, Md.) is an accomplished and influential acoustic guitarist and the author of a biography of bluesman Charley Patton.

Fairport Convention Dave Swarbrick (violin, vocals), Simon Nicol (guitar, vocals), Dave Pegg (bass), Bruce Rowlands (drums)—Originally launched by Ian Matthews in London in 1967, the band achieved a large cult following in the United States as a sort of English Jefferson Airplane. It's best album was *Leige And Lief* in 1969, featuring Sandy Denny as lead vocalist.

Faith, Adam Born on June 23, 1940 in London, England, Faith, along with Cliff Richard, was one of the great English teenage idols of the early 1960s. He turned to producing (Leo Sayer and, later, Lonnie Donegan) and to acting (*Stardust*). (See also David Essex.)

The Fabulous Poodles

Faces, The Rod Stewart (vocals), Ron Wood (guitar), Ronnie Lane (bass), Kenny Jones (drums), Ian McLagan (keyboards)—Collectively the Dean Martin of rock and roll,

were like their reputation—occasionally exhilarating, usually uneven and great fun to listen to. Their peak came in 1971 with the hit single "Stay With Me," which is completely

Marianne Faithfull

Faithfull, Marianne "My first move was to get a Rolling Stone as a boyfriend," Marianne Faithfull told an English rock paper in 1974. "I slept with three and decided the lead singer was the best bet." Less known for her singing ("As Tears Go By" in 1964, "Come And Stay With Me" in 1965) than her tortuous affair with Rolling Stone Mick Jagger, Faithfull was born the daughter of an Austrian baroness in England. From 1965 to 1969 she was Jagger's constant companion and even got busted once with Jagger and Keith Richards for possession of drugs. She spent the first six years of the 1970s trying to shake Jagger and drugs and eventually staged a critically successful comeback as a punk rocker in the late 1970s.

Falcons, The Eddie Floyd (vocals), Joe Stubbs (vocals),

Bonny Rice (vocals), Willie Schoefield (vocals), Lance Finnie (guitar)—A Detroit group that provided a starting ground for Stax soul singer Eddie Floyd ("Knock On Wood" in 1966) and, briefly, soul singer Wilson Pickett, who sang lead on the group's 1962 hit, "I Found A Love." They are best remembered, however, for their classic "You're So Fine" in 1959.

Fame, Georgie At one point, around 1965, it looked like Georgie Fame (born on June 26, 1943 in England) and his Blue Flames might give the Beatles a run for their money, when "Yeh, Yeh" knocked the Beatles off the top of the chart. His more rhythm-and-blues and jazzy music couldn't keep up the popular appeal, however, although in 1968 he had a hit in the U.S. with "The Ballad Of Bonnie And Clyde."

Family Roger Chapman (vocals), Charlie Whitney (guitar, vocals), Rob Townsend (drums), Tony Ashton (keyboards, vocals), Jim Cregan (bass, guitar)— Formed in England in the mid-1960s, Family is best known for the album *Music In A Doll's House* (1968), one of the high points of English progressive rock. The band knocked around with numerous personnel changes until 1973, when it disbanded after a very successful goodbye tour.

Fanny June Millington (guitar, vocals), Jean Millington (bass, vocals), Nicole Barclay (keyboards), Alice DeBuhr (drums)—Launched in 1970 as the first all female rock group, Fanny's first three albums—produced by Richard Perry—were critical, if not commercial, successes. A fourth album (*Mother's Pride* in 1973), this time produced by Todd Rundgren, seemed to cement the band's place as an ongoing critics' delight. Once cemented, however, the band immediately began to fall apart, producing one mediocre album, ironically titled *Rock And Roll Survivors,* before breaking up in 1976.

Farina, Richard and Mimi Richard Farina (born in 1937), the underground novelist who wrote *Been Down So Long It Looks Like Up To Me,* and his wife, Mimi (born on May 1, 1945), younger sister of Joan Baez, were the toasts of the New York folkie scene in the mid-1960s. In addition to being a novelist and songwriter, Richard Farina fought briefly with the IRA in Ireland, went to

Cuba and returned to New York as a dashing, Hemingwayesque figure. With Mimi, an excellent singer and songwriter herself, he cut two near-brilliant albums, *Celebrations For A Grey Day* and *Reflections In A Crystal Wind.* Richard Farina was killed in a motorcycle accident in 1966, on the way to a party for his *Down So Long* novel. Mimi Farina gave up performing until 1971, when she linked up with Tom Jans for a simple, vastly underrated album titled *Take Heart.* In 1979 she staged a "folkie reunion," which featured many of the greats from the Greenwich Village years, including her big sister.

Farlowe, Chris An English rhythm-and-blues singer, Farlowe is best known for his work with Mick Jagger in the mid-1960s, which resulted in the hit "Out Of Time," written by Jagger and Keith Richards, in 1966. He has also worked with guitar flash Albert Lee and Carl Palmer of Emerson, Lake and Palmer.

Farner, Mark Lead singer and guitarist for the heavy metal group Grand Funk Railroad, Farner (born on Sept. 29, 1948 in Flint, Mich.) was castigated for his flashy, not-particularly-polished guitar style with Grand Funk. Throughout the 1970s the critics made fun of him, while his fans made him rich. Eventually he got respectable and poor.

Feathers, Charlie
Rockabilly legend Charlie Feathers was born on June 12, 1932 in Holly Springs, Miss. He began his career in Memphis, cutting a series of frenetic rockabilly records beginning with "Defrost Your Heart" in 1954. He later recorded for King Records in Cincinnati and through the years built up a huge underground following. To this day he claims that had the breaks gone his way, he would have beaten out Elvis Presley, and the rock-and-roll story would be different.

Feliciano, Jose Born on Sept. 8, 1945 in Puerto Rico and blind since birth, Feliciano is best known for his slow, soulful rendition of the Doors' hit "Light My Fire" in 1968. He was discovered at Folk City, a famous Greenwich Village folkie hangout, in 1963, when a record company executive came to see another act. The executive was so impressed with Feliciano that the other act was totally forgotten. He is a virtuoso on guitar, banjo, organ, mandolin, harmonica and piano, as well as being able to sing in seven languages.

Felts, Narvel One of the many 1950s rockers to find his home in country music, *a la* Johnny Cash and Conway Twitty, Felts began his career singing "Blue Suede Shoes" in a high school talent contest in 1956. He so impressed the disc jockeys at the local station in Bernie, Mo. that they put out a call for him to come in. He ended up at Sun Records in Memphis and eventually released two modest hits, "Honey Love" and "3000 Miles." In the 1970s he went to Nashville and was quite successful as a country artist, beginning with a country cover of the Dobie Gray hit "Drift Away" in 1973. As a country singer Felts has helped pioneer something of a rockabilly revival in Nashville with such songs as "Reconsider Me" (1975) and others. He was born in 1939 in Missouri.

Fender, Freddy Born in 1937 in the border town of San Benito, Tex., Freddy Fender (aka Baldemar Huerta) was once considered the Elvis of the border country, touring the honky-tonks and bars of both sides of the border with his Tex-Mex rockabilly blend throughout the late 1950s. His "Wasted Days And Wasted Nights" (1960) was a huge local hit, and his future looked sure, but later in the year he was busted for possession of a tiny amount of marijuana and sentenced to five years, of which he served three. A condition of his parole (arranged by Louisiana Gov. Jimmie "You Are My Sunshine" Davis) was that Fender give up the entertainment business, which he never seriously tried to do. In 1974 Fender met rhythm-and-blues producer Huey P. Meaux, who figured that by adding one Tex-Mex rockabilly singer and one rhythm-and-blues producer, he ought to be able to come up with one country singer. That is exactly what happened. On the strength of two songs— "Before The Last Teardrop Falls" and a remake of "Wasted Days And Wasted Nights"—Fender's career was successfully relaunched. Still going strong, his powerful, emotional voice is a definite plus for country music.

Fender, Leo The designer of the solid body electric guitar, without which none of this would have been possible. The guitar was designed in Fender's garage in the 1940s, originally with a section of planking as the body of the guitar.

Ferguson, Jay Born on May 10, 1947 in California, Ferguson and friend Mark Andes teamed up with Randy California, Ed Cassidy and John Locke to form the group Spirit in the mid-1960s, with Ferguson handling most of the songwriting chores. In 1971 Ferguson and Andes left Spirit to form a rock-and-roll band called Jo Jo Gunne, which initially hit with "Run Run Run" (1972). The usual reasons—personnel conflicts and changes, management changes, differences of opinion on direction—kept the band out of the limelight, and after four albums it disbanded in 1975. Ferguson's solo career has been building (rather slowly). In 1979 he released an album titled *Real Life Ain't This Way*.

Ferry, Brian Born on Sept. 26, 1945 in England, Ferry established a reputation as the guiding force (after the departure of Brian Eno) for the art-rock group Roxy Music. In the mid-1970s he left Roxy Music (after a series of critically well-received and commercially successful albums) to pursue a solo career, which to date has exhibited neither the vision nor the virtuosity of Roxy Music at its best.

Fifth Dimension, The
Marilyn McCoo (vocals), Billy Davis, Jr. (vocals), Ron Townson (vocals), Lamonte McLemore (vocals), Florence LaRue (vocals)—The Fifth Dimension originally began as a blues group (first the Versatiles, then the Hi-Fis) and even toured with Ray Charles, before returning to their home in Los Angeles to make their fortune with soft, Mamas and Papas-type harmonies. Their first hit came in 1967 with "Go Where You Wanna Go" (written by Papa John Phillips), followed by such smashes as "Up, Up And Away" (1967), which began their lucrative association with then-unknown songwriter Jim Webb; "Stoned Soul Picnic" (1968); and "Aquarius/Let The Sun Shine In" (1969), the theme from the Broadway musical *Hair* and one of their biggest hits ever. They continued into the 1970s, relying on the vocal talents of McCoo and LaRue on such numbers as "(Last Night) I Didn't Get To Sleep At All" (1972) and "If I Could Reach You" (1972), until changing tastes brought an end to their successes. Husband/wife team Billy Davis, Jr. and Marilyn McCoo readily adapted to the soft strains of disco and in 1976 returned to the top with *I Hope We Get To Love In Time*, featuring the hit single "You Don't Have To Be Star."

Firefall Rick Roberts (vocals, guitar), Jock Bartley (vocals, guitar), Larry Burnett (vocals, guitar), Mark Andes (vocals, bass), Michael Clarke (drums)—Formed in Denver in 1975 to cash in on the mellow California Sound, Firefall had a quick hit the next year with "You Are The Woman," then, inexplicably, released the violently misogynic "Cinderella," which put a cramp in the band's rise. Still, Firefall overcame its critics and continued charting modest hits.

Five Keys Maryland Pierce, Rudy West, Dickie Smith, Ripley Ingram, Bernie West, Joe Jones—R&B harmony group from the early 1950s, formed in Newport News, Va., and best known for such hits as "Close Your Eyes" (1955) "Wisdom Of A Fool" (1956), "Out Of Sight, Out Of Mind" (1956) and "Let There Be You" (1957).

Five Royales, The Lowman Pauling (vocals), Clarence Pauling (vocals), Johnny Tanner (vocals), Johnny Moore (vocals), Obediah Carter (vocals)—Originally a gospel group, the Five Royales had two of 1953's top 10 rhythm-and-blues hits: "Baby, Don't It" and "Help Me Somebody." Five years later they cut "Dedicated To The One I Love," a hit for the Shirelles in 1961. The Five Royales were among the first harmony groups to successfully blend gospel and blues vocal styles.

Five Satins Fred Parris (vocals); Rich Freeman (vocals); West Forbes (vocals); Lewis Peeples (vocals); Sy Hopkins (vocals); additional member: Bill Baker—R&B harmony group best known for its classic 1956 hit, "In The Still Of The Night," ironically the B side of the release, written by Fred Parris while he was in the Army. The A side, "The Jones Girl," sank without a trace, except among doo-wop worshippers, who still revere it.

Five Stairsteps, The The Five Stairsteps consisted of the five children of Chicagoan Clarence Burke—Clarence Jr., James, Aloha, Kenny and Dennis. In the mid-1960s Burke entered the children in a talent contest in Chicago—they not only won the contest, but were spotted by Curtis Mayfield, then lead singer for the Impressions and local record producer. The group produced a series of R&B hits, culminating in 1970 with "Ooh Child," a soft, heavily instrumented arrangement. That style of R&B (rhythm and blues without the rhythm or the blues, sniffed one critic) would soon become known as the Philadelphia Sound and find a welcome home on the disco floor.

Flack, Roberta Flack was first signed in 1967, but her career remained stalled until her "First Time Ever I Saw Your Face" was featured in the Clint Eastwood movie *Play Misty for Me* in 1972. She continued on with "Killing Me Softly" (1973), written for singer Don McLean, "Feel Like Making Love" (1975) and others. By the end of the 1970s, her career was languishing and she was singing commercials on television. She was born on Feb. 10, 1939 in Ashville, N.C.

Flamin' Groovies, The Cyril Jordon (guitar), George Alexander (bass), Chris Wilson (vocals), James Farrell (guitar), David Wright (drums)—A strange case—the Groovies were a mid-1960s San Francisco band who refused to get psychedelicized, preferring instead to play plain three-chord old-time rock and roll *a la* Chuck Berry. To say the Groovies were unpopular would be a vast understatement. Yet the band remained together, through busts and broken contracts, and the pendulum has swung back toward it. At the beginning of the 1980s, the Groovies were still hard at work, still playing the same old rocking music, this time in the more fertile New Wave era.

Flamingos, The Nathan Nelson (vocals), John Carter (vocals), Terry Johnson (vocals), Ezekiel Carey (vocals), Paul Wilson (vocals), Jacob Carey (vocals), Sollie McElroy (vocals)—Chicago vocal group formed in 1952. Despite their popularity with rhythm-and-blues audiences, their sole national hit was "I Only Have Eyes For You" in 1959. They can still be heard at oldies shows, although the original line up is not the same.

Flatt, Lester Along with five-string banjo picker Earl Scruggs, Flatt was tremendously influential in shaping modern bluegrass music and in the popularization of modern country music. Flatt (born on June 19, 1914 in Tennessee) and Scruggs began working together in the late 1940s, when both left Bill Monroe's band. Flatt gave Scruggs full range to experiment with the banjo while following along on lead guitar. In 1949 they recorded a tune called "Foggy Mountain Breakdown," which went on to become perhaps the best-known bluegrass number in the world, thanks to its use in the movie *Bonnie and Clyde* as background music for one of the great car chases. Through the 1950s they toured the South, eventually linking up with the budding folk scene, which recognized them as two of America's most important folk artists. In 1962 they became national stars playing the theme for "The Beverly Hillbillies" television show. Their numerous appearances on television helped spark a renewed interest in country music. The duo broke up in 1969, with Flatt sticking to a more traditional form of music while Scruggs set out to experiment in more popular directions. Flatt died in 1979.

Fleetwood Mac Mick Fleetwood (drums); John McVie (bass); Christine McVie (keyboards, vocals); Stevie Nicks (vocals); Lindsey Buckingham (guitar, vocals); and others, including Peter Green, Jeremy Spencer, Danny Kirwan, Bob Welch, Bob Weston, Dave Walker—Since 1975 Fleetwood Mac has been well on the way to becoming a couple of household words, rock and roll for grown-ups. It is one of the few bands that has been able to change with the times without losing sight of either its identity or its roots. Originally launched in 1967 in England as a hard-core blues band by Peter Green, John McVie and Mick Fleetwood, alumni of John Mayall's Bluesbreakers, Fleetwood Mac soon developed a devoted following of its own. Initially, the group stuck to the proven British blues formulas, but within a couple of records it began to experiment more and more. The band was shaken in 1969

Fleetwood Mac

by a major change of personnel, founder Green retiring and Jeremy Spencer running off to join a religious cult, the Children of God. The group retrenched, added Christine McVie and Bob Welch and pressed on, drifting farther away from the blues of the original axis to a more mellow sound. Nothing seemed to go right for Fleetwood Mac, however, culminating in the early 1970s when the band's former manager put another group on the road with the name Fleetwood Mac. The ensuing court case tied the real band up for a year. In 1974, on the eve of stardom, Fleetwood Mac came back strong with *Heroes Are Hard To Find,* an FM favorite. With the band's typical luck, Bob Welch departed, but

it smartly added the duo of Lindsey Buckingham and Stevie Nicks, who'd recorded one unsuccessful album on their own. The next album was titled *Fleetwood Mac* (as was the original group's debut album in 1968), and it was hugely successful, spawning two hits, "Over My Head" and "Rhiannon." *Rumours,* the follow-up in 1977, became the second biggest selling album of all time, trailing only the *Saturday Night Fever* soundtrack. The work on *Rumours* was both lyrically sophisticated and hard rocking, proving that the band hadn't forgotten from whence it came. The long-awaited *Tusk* (1979) lacked the across-the-board appeal of *Rumours* but featured some outstanding work.

Fleetwoods, The   Gary Troxel, Barbara Ellis, Gretchen Christopher—The pride of Washington State, the trio met while in high school there in 1958, originally calling themselves Two Girls and a Guy. Retitled the Fleetwoods (after the telephone exchange of their record producer), they released "Come Softly To Me" in 1959, followed by "Mr. Blue" the next year.

Flo and Eddie   Former Turtles Marc Volman and Howard Kaylan were metamorphosed into Flo (short for the Phlorescent Leech) and Eddie after a stint with Frank Zappa and the Mothers of Invention. In 1972 they went out on their own, only there was some question as to where they were going—

satire or straight rock. Three albums later, including the aptly titled *Immoral Illegal And Fattening,* we're still wondering. As the spiritual inspirations for the Turtles, however, they produced some of the great singles of the mid-1960s, including "It Ain't Me Babe" (1965), "Happy Together" (1967) and "Elenore" (1968).

Floyd, Eddie   One of the staple soul singers of the 1960s at Stax Records in Memphis, Floyd helped define the Memphis Sound with his first hit, "Knock On Wood" (1967), followed by "Bring It On Home To Me" (1968). He was born on June 25, 1935 in Montgomery, Ala.

Floyd, Harmonica Frank
Born in 1908 in Toccopola, Miss., Harmonica Frank recorded for Sam Phillips at Sun Records in Memphis—the home of Elvis Presley and much of early rockabilly—in 1951 and was perhaps the first white man who sang like a black and got recorded. Later, Phillips would describe Harmonica Frank as the first step in trying to find the fusion between country music and the blues that eventually became rock with the advent of Elvis. Today Harmonica Frank lives in Cincinnati and still claims that the mantle of the first rocker rightfully belongs to him, not Elvis.

Flying Burrito Brothers, The   Chris Hillman (guitar, vocals); Gram Parsons (guitar, vocals); Chris Ethridge (bass); "Sneaky Pete" Kleinow (pedal steel); and others, including

Bernie Leadon (guitar, vocals), Rick Roberts (guitar, vocals), Al Perkins (steel guitar), Byron Berline (fiddle), Kenny Wertz (guitar), Roger Bush (bass), Erick Dalton (drums), Don Beck (steel guitar), Alan Munde (guitar), Gib Guilbeau (guitar, fiddle), Gene Parsons (drums), Joel Scott Hill (guitar), Skip Battin (bass)—The ins and outs of this group could take up a whole volume, but the reason the Burritos were important is: they were the first group to try seriously to incorporate country music into a rock-and-roll format. All the so-called country-rock or soft country or West Coast-Sound groups (including the Eagles, whose Bernie Leadon did his time with the Burritos) have sprung from the original grouping of ex-Byrds Parsons and Hillman, steel guitar ace "Sneaky Pete" and sessions bassist Ethridge. The band was actually the brainchild of Mississippi visionary Gram Parsons, who truly believed that the rock audience would love country music if they ever got a chance to hear it. He was right of course, although it wasn't the Burritos who proved it—it was more like Bob Dylan with *Nashville Skyline* (1969) and Linda Ronstadt's huge success, followed by that of her backup band, the Eagles. Various incarnations of the Burritos are still kicking around, but the thrill is clearly gone, despite a fluke hit in 1976—"Bon Soir Blues." Better to remember them for *The Gilded Palace Of Sin* (1969), *Burrito Deluxe* (1970) and *The Flying Burrito Brothers* (1971), featuring one of the great road songs of all time, "White Line Fever."

Focus   Thijs van Leer (keyboards, flute, vocals), Bert Ruiter (bass, vocals), David Kemper (drums), Philip Catherine (guitar); and others, including Martin Dresden (bass), Hans Clever (drums)—Originally formed in Holland in 1969 as the backup band for the Dutch version of the rock musical *Hair,* Focus went on to delve into experimental music, reaching their peak around 1973 with flamboyant guitarist Jan Akkerman. They are best remembered for such instrumental efforts as "Hocus Pocus" (1971) and "Sylvia" (1973).

Dan Fogelberg

Fogelberg, Dan   Born on Aug. 13, 1951 in Peoria, Ill., balladeer Dan Fogelberg broke out in 1974 with a hit album titled *Souvenirs,* one of that year's most popular FM products, including the hit singles "There's A Place In The World For A Gambler" and "Part Of The Plan." More recently Fogelberg has been working with flutist and ace musician Tim Weisberg (*Twin Sons Of Different Mothers* in 1978), leaning more on instrumental improvisation than on Fogelberg's lilting voice.

Fogerty, John   Born on May 28, 1945 in Berkeley, Calif., Fogerty is best known as the creative genius behind Creedence Clearwater Revival, one of the greatest singles bands ever. In 1972, when Creedence broke up, Fogerty formed the Blue Ridge Rangers—a vehicle for his songs, singing, instumental virtuosity and arrangements. Their first album yielded two hits, Hank Williams' "Jambalaya" and "Hearts Of Stone," both in 1973. A solo album, *John Fogerty,* appeared in 1975, and he provided the music for the movie *Who'll Stop The Rain* (from the title of a Creedence song) in 1978.

Foghat   "Lonesome" Dave Peverett (guitar, vocals), Roger Earl (drums), Rod Price (guitar), Craig MacGregor (bass)—An expatriot English band cloned from the similarly boogie-minded Savoy Brown in 1971, Foghat stepped out of relative obscurity in 1977 with the album *Foghat Live,* which quickly went gold, then platinum—superseding the group's successful 1975 release of *Fool For The City.* The band's music is undistinguished, relying on the straight-ahead British rhythm-

and-blues formula—guitars, extended solos, long songs and, above all, volume!

Fontana, Wayne, and the Mindbenders   Wayne Fontana (vocals), Michael Eric Stewart, Jr. (guitar), Robert F. Lang (bass), Ric Rothwell (drums)—One of the British Invasion groups of the early 1960s, Wayne Fontana and the Mindbenders was formed when an English bar band singer named Glyn Geoffrey Ellis auditioned with Fontana Records in 1963. Only one member of his group, Robert Lang, showed up for the audition and Ellis had to use a couple of other local musicians. Surprise! Fontana Records signed him up, and he changed his name to Wayne Fontana and named his new group after a film showing at the time. In 1965 all the gimmicks paid off with a huge hit, "The Game Of Love." Fontana soon drifted off on his own, and the Mindbenders scored again in 1966 with what has become something of a syrupy classic, "A Groovy Kind Of Love."

Foreigner   Lou Gramm (vocals), Mick Jones (guitar, vocals), Ian McDonald (guitar, keyboards, vocals), Al Greenwood (keyboards, synthesizer), Dennis Eliott (drums)—Another bonafide rock phenomenon, the English band Foreigner appeared in 1977 with a debut album entitled *Foreigner* and a monster hit single called "Feels Like The First Time." The group's next album, *Double Vision* (1978) with its hit single by the same name, established Foreigner's

Lou Graham & Mick Jones of Foreigner

enormous popularity. The music is formula British, mind-rending volume and standard rhythm-and-blues riffs, with Gramm's wailing vocals on the side. Most of the members are survivors from similar rock outfits—Gramm from Black Sheep, Eliott from If, Jones from Spooky Tooth, McDonald from King Crimson.

Fortunes,The   Barry Pritchard, Glen Dale, Rod Allen, David Carr, Andrew Brown—British Invasion vocal group who scored in 1965 with the excellent "You've Got Your Troubles." Although the group maintained its popularity in

England, it wasn't until 1971's "Here Comes That Rainy Day Feeling Again" that the group had another American hit. Unfortunately, that was also their last hit, and thereafter the group faded.

Four Freshmen, The Bob Flanigan (vocals); Ross Barbour (vocals); Hal Kratzch (vocals); Don Barbour (vocals); and others, including Bill Comstock, Ray Brown, Ken Albers, Ken Errair—Formed in 1947 in Indianapolis, Ind., the group actually had only four hits "It's A Blue World" (1952), "Day By Day" (1955), "Charmaine" (1955) and "Graduation Day" (1956). What makes the Four Freshmen special is that they just kept right on working, singing the same type harmonies while the world changed around them. By ignoring the rest of the world, they've had some 34 hit albums and are still together and in demand.

Four Lads, The Frank Busseri (vocals), Bernard Toorish (vocals), James Arnold (vocals), Connie Codarini (vocals)—This Canadian foursome got their start as choirboys and eventually became backup singers. In 1952 the four went on their own with "The Mockingbird," but their big success wasn't until 1955, when they recorded "Moments To Remember," followed the next year by "No, Not Much," insuring the group's place in pop music history.

Four Preps, The Bruce Bellard (vocals), Glen Larson (vocals), Ed Cobb (vocals),

Marv Ingram (vocals)—The most clean-cut of the 1950s vocal groups (hence the name), these Californians sent a message to the Beatles in 1964 (appropriately titled "Message To The Beatles") that they didn't approve of all that long-hair stuff. Their only million seller was "26 Miles," released in late 1957. Perhaps their most memorable song, though, was "Big Man" in 1958.

Four Seasons, The Frankie Valli, Tommy DeVito, Bob Gaudio, Joe Long—First launched in Newark, N.J. in 1956 as the Four Lovers (with an original lineup of Frankie Valli, Tommy DeVito, Nick DeVito and Hank Majewski), the group got its name and start around 1959—the name from a bowling alley, the start from producer Bob Crewe. In 1962 the Four Seasons (Valli, Tommy DeVito, Nick Massi

and promising songwriter Bob Gaudio) came out swinging with "Sherry" and haven't stopped since—"Big Girls Don't Cry" (1962), "Walk Like A Man" (1963), "Candy Girl" (1963), "Stay" (1964), "Dawn" (1964), "Rag Doll" (1964), "Let's Hang On" (1965), "Working My Way Back To You" (1966), "C'Mon Marianne" (1967), "Who Loves You" (1975). In fact, the Four Seasons survived not only the Beatles, but the psychedelic sixties, heavy metal, the West Coast Sound and disco. (Their "December 1963 Oh, What A Night" and "Who Loves You" were also disco hits in 1975.) The secret, aside from Valli's falsetto, is that the band represents the very best of American music—perhaps the ultimate synthesis of 1950s music—music that gets under your skin and insanely catchy lyrics, most written by Gaudio. Although the band has

Frankie Valli & the Four Seasons–1980

floundered on occasion (its 1969 "heavy" album, *Genuine Imitation Life Gazette,* and an abortive stint with Motown Records in the early 1970s), it has constantly held to basic Four Seasons music, no frills. And it's worked. Valli does occasionally pursue his own career, hitting with "My Eyes Adored You" (1975) and with the title song of the movie *Grease* (1978).

Four Tops   Levi Stubbs, Renaldo "Obie" Benson, Abdul "Duke" Fakir, Lawrence Payton—Along with the Supremes, the Four Tops became the best-known purveyors of the Motown Sound in the 1960s. Although the group got together in Detroit in 1954, the Tops didn't come into their own until 10 years later with "Baby, I Need Your Loving." The highpoint was from 1965 to 1967, when the group turned out such hits as "I Can't Help Myself," "It's The Same Old Song," "Reach Out (I'll Be There)," "Standing In The Shadows Of Love," "Bernadette" and "Seven Rooms Of Gloom." Most of the Tops' hits came from the crack Motown songwriting team of Brian Holland-Lamont Dozier-Eddie Holland (see Holland-Dozier-Holland), and with these hits they defined the slick Motown vocal group approach to soul (as opposed to the soul men of Stax Records in Memphis). While their career waned in the 1970s, the victim of changing tastes, the Four Tops staged a moderately successful comeback in 1972 with "Keeper Of The Castle," following that with the tough soul song "Are You Man Enough" in 1973.

Four Tunes, The   William Best (vocals), James Nabbie (vocals), James Gordon (vocals), Danny Owens (vocals)—An R&B vocal group from the late 1940s, the Four Tunes scored a pop hit in 1953 with the enormously successful "Marie."

Fowley, Kim   Every business needs at least one Kim Fowley—instigator, visionary and free-lance madman. He first made his mark in the music business in 1960 as the organizer of the Hollywood Argyles and their great hit song, "Alley Oop." He went on to produce B. Bumble and the Stingers ("Nut Rocker" in 1962) the Murmaids ("Popsicles And Icicles" in 1963) and other such notables until the mid-1960s, when he decided that what the world needed then was flower power. He became flower power's biggest exporter, organizing love-ins, cutting solo albums and acting in a few movies here and there. He later worked as producer on Jonathan Richman's wacked-out album *Jonathan Richman And The Modern Lovers* (released in 1976) and recruited an all-girl, all-sleaze punk band, the Runaways, from magazine ads.

Frampton, Peter   A classic example of easy come, easy go, Frampton came out of nowhere (actually, from Humble Pie) in 1976 with his live *Frampton Comes Alive* album, which immediately went gold, then platinum, and established the English guitarist as an international superstar. The album went on to become one of the biggest selling records of all time, and

Peter Frampton

the next year's *I'm In You* repeated the trick. Frampton (born on April 22, 1950 in Kent, England) first got a taste of stardom as the lead singer for the Herd, a popular English singles band. He joined Humble Pie in 1968 but left in 1971 to find his own career. To be sure, Frampton did establish himself as a fine guitarist, but most critics (and even some fans) were at a loss to explain his wild success in 1976. That success more or less came to an end in 1979, when he fell victim to the quixotic tastes of his audience. In fact, rumor had at least one major Frampton concert canceled in 1980 due to lack of advance ticket sales, and the general response seems to be, "Peter who?"

Francis, Connie   Born Constance Franconero on Dec. 12, 1938 in Belleville, N.J., Connie Francis began playing the accordian at age four and hit the road professionally at 11. In 1958 she recorded "Who's Sorry Now," one of her father's favorite songs, which proved to be one of *everybody's* favorite songs. She followed that up with "Stupid Cupid" (1958), "Lipstick On Your Collar" (1959), "Everybody's Somebody's Fool" (1960), "Where The Boys Are" (1961) and a string of others until 1967. She is best remembered for the catch in her voice, sort of a rock-and-roll Tammy Wynette.

Franklin, Aretha   Born on March 25, 1942 in Detroit, Mich., Aretha Franklin grew up in the church and with its music. Her father, the Reverend C.L. Franklin, had released some 70-odd gospel albums on Chess Records, and by the age of 14 she was already touring with him nationwide. In 1960 she signed with Columbia Records, but it wasn't until her association with Atlantic Records and Jerry Wexler in 1966 that she really came into her own. Wexler correctly realized that the only place where Aretha's gospel-fired music would blossom was in the South, where she could be surrounded by sidemen who understood the music and its roots. Together they went to Muscle Shoals, Ala. and turned out "I Never Loved A Man (The Way I Love You)" (1967), "Respect" (1967), "Natural Woman" (1967), "Chain Of Fools" (1967), "The House That Jack

Built" (1968) and on and on until the turn of the decade, when personal problems slowed her down and for a while returned her to the church. In the late 1970s she returned to performing and recording, although with a greater emphasis on heavily orchestrated arrangements.

Aretha Franklin, along with the soul men from Stax Records in Memphis, practically defined soul music, one of the major influences of the 1960s. Not since the 1920s and 1930s had a woman singer (particularly a black woman singer) had such a galvanizing effect on pop music.

Michael Franks

Franks, Michael   Billed as the "thinking man's rock and roller," Franks is best known for his album *The Art Of Tea* (1976), which demonstrated his heavily jazz-influenced rock. Two subsequent albums showed him still thinking along the same lines. His doctoral dissertation at UCLA was entitled "Contemporary Songwriting and How It Relates to Society."

Freddie and the Dreamers
Freddie Garrity and his Dreamers (Derek Quinn, Roy Crewdson, Pete Birrell and Bernie Dwyer) burst off BBC Television's "Let's Go!" show in the early 1960s, digging their way into the teenybopper hall of fame in 1963 with "I'm Telling You Now" and "You Were Made For Me." They went on to become one of the largest selling groups of the time—especially in 1965, when Freddie went on American television and introduced his dance—"the Freddie"—which featured a series of Frankenstein-like moves and windmill flailing of the arms. They were immediately hailed as the biggest thing since the Beatles (something invariably proclaimed every year since 1964), and dance floors were a decidedly more dangerous place to be for a while.

Free   Paul Rodgers (vocals), Paul Kossoff (guitar), Andy Fraser (bass), Simon Kirke (drums)—Launched as a pub band in the British rhythm-and-blues mode in 1968, Free soon established itself as *the* English band of the 1970s. Its music was clean and dynamic, with Rodgers swaggering vocals and Kossoff's slick guitar work leading the way. Free's second album, *Free,* released in 1970, established the group as a cult favorite in the United States, while a third album, *Fire And Ice,* released the same year, provided a major hit single, "All Right Now." The title, however, was not prophetic, because things were definitely not all right with Free. Basically, the band came apart, first "for good," then re-forming with various different members (including John "Rabbit" Bundrick and Tetsu Yamauchi). The members of Free regrouped in 1972 and 1973 before finally splitting to go their separate ways. To date, Free definitely remains greater than any of its parts.

Freed, Alan   According to legend, the man who first called the new music rock and roll. Alan Freed was born in Pennsylvania in 1922. In 1952 he was working as a disc jockey for WJW in Cleveland, Ohio when he discovered that white kids were actually buying "race" records, records aimed exclusively at the black rhythm-and-blues market. He started playing what the kids wanted to hear, only he couldn't call it "Negro" music, so he grabbed a new term—rock and roll— from some rhythm-and-blues songs. In March 1952, Freed, who called himself "Moondog," sponsored a "Moondog Ball" in Cleveland that attracted so many people, both black and white, it had to be canceled. Yet the cancellation clearly demonstrated the power of the new music. Later at WINS in New York City, Freed pushed as hard as he could for rock and roll. He staged numerous rock-and-roll shows, showcasing the top rock stars of the period. He was also credited as a coauthor of such hits as "Sincerely" (1955) by the Moonglows. Freed helped to spread the musical craze until 1960, when he was indicted in the payola scandal. He did time and died a broken man in 1965.

Friedman, Kinky   The clown prince of country music and organizer of the world's greatest touring band, the Texas Jewboys, Friedman was born into a perfectly normal home in Texas. His wild, irreverent (some say irrelevant) material, such as "They Ain't Making Jews Like Jesus Anymore" and "She's Still Carrying The Torch For You," a ballad about the Statue of Liberty, has seldom enjoyed any radio play, but Kinky has achieved a national reputation of sorts, even touring with Bob Dylan's Rolling Thunder Revue for a while. At present he makes his home on the range at New York City's Lone Star Club, where he is the resident weirdo.

Fugs, The   Ed Sanders (vocals) Ken Weaver (vocals, drums), Tuli Kupferberg (vocals), Ken Pine (guitar, vocals), Charles Larkey (bass), Bob Mason (drums)—The group who made offensiveness fashionable and trendy, the Fugs began their life as poets in Greenwich Village during the mid-1960s (where anything is not only possible, but probable). Insane times were brewing, and only poets could realize just how insane, so they banded together to form a band that even today is best defined by its songs: "Slum Goddess," "Boobs A Lot," "My Baby Done Left Me," "Coca-Cola Douche," "Life Is Strange," "I Couldn't Get High" and "I Saw The Best Minds Of My Generation Rot." By 1969, mission accomplished, the Fugs disappeared, leaving the door open for a world full of whackos waiting in the wings.

Funkadelic   George Clinton (vocals), Bernie Worrell (keyboards), William "Bootsy" Collins (bass), Tiki Fulwood (drums), and others—More properly Parliament-Funkadelic, or P-Funk as the group is known, Funkadelic is the creation of George Clinton, the main man of funk. His outrageous attire and surreal road show, which features a horn section and a full chorus, has made his two groups (Parliament and Funkadelic were conceived as separate groups of the same musicians)

Funkadelic

one of the biggest touring attractions in the country. The music is sort of disco rhythm and blues with lyrics all about flying saucers. Parliament was, oddly enough, originally a 1950s doo-wop group called the Parliaments, featuring Clinton. In the late 1960s the group began its schizoid existence.

Furay, Richie   Born in Ohio, Furay first came to public attention as a member of the Buffalo Springfield. When that group came apart in 1968, Furay launched Poco (a group he originally wanted to call Pogo, after the comic strip, but Walt Kelly refused to give permission). The first Poco album, *Pickin' Up The Pieces,* in 1969 was a landmark country-rock record, which at that time practically doomed it to failure (see the Flying Burrito Brothers). After five years with Poco, Furay went solo, with a brief digression to the "superstar" Souther-Hillman-Furay Band (John David Souther, a singer/songwriter for numerous California folks, including Linda Ronstadt; Chris Hillman of the Byrds; and Furay), which released two albums to tepid reaction. Furay struck out on his own in earnest. So far, after three albums he still has yet to find a groove as exuberant as Poco.

Gabriel, Peter   Born on May 13, 1950 in England, Gabriel

Peter Gabriel

developed a substantial following as the lead singer for the group Genesis. He went solo in 1975, but it wasn't until 1977 and his *Peter Gabriel* album that he found a measure of the success he had had with Genesis.

Gallagher, Rory   Guitar virtuoso Rory Gallagher was born in Ireland and bought his first "real" guitar when he was nine. He began his solo career in 1971, after the collapse of his moderately successful band Taste, playing R&B-influenced rock to enthusiastic audience reception. While his records have yet to catch on, he is one of the better concert draws.

Gallagher and Lyle   Benny Gallagher and Graham Lyle were an English acoustic guitar duo, popular for their *Breakaway* album in 1976—the title song was eventually recorded by Art Garfunkel.

Gantry, Chris   Best known as the eclectic author of "Dreams Of An Everyday Housewife," a hit in the mid-1960s for Glen Campbell and, later, Wayne Newton.

Garcia, Jerry   One of the few performers in rock who can successfully carry the adjective "beloved," Garcia was born on Aug. 1, 1942 in San Francisco, Calif., where he returned after leaving the Army in 1959. His interests were in American musical forms—the blues, bluegrass and country—and he eventually formed a bluegrass band with what was to be the nucleus of the Grateful Dead. The band (with Bill Kreutzmann and Ron "Pigpen" McKernan), called the Zodiacs, then the Hart Valley Drifters, won the Monterey Folk Festival in 1963 and eventually evolved into Mother McCree's Uptown Jug Champions. When jug band music was discovered to be some 50 years out of fashion, the Jug Champions transmuted into a bluesy rock band called the Warlocks, who fell right smack into the Ken Kesey acid explosion of the mid-1960s. In 1966 Garcia's band formally became the Grateful Dead.

Garcia released his first solo album in 1972 (*Garcia*), which showed him retaining the same love for American down-home music, as did his later *Reflections.* In 1977 the Dead re-formed in earnest, and solo albums went on the back burner.

Garcia's love for American music helped lay the groundwork for the acceptance of Southern rock and country music in the

1970s, since the Dead had in a sense "legitimized" those forms in the group's San Francisco acid music.

Garfunkel, Art Born on Oct. 13, 1941 in New York City, Garfunkel is best known as half (some say the lesser half) of sixties heroes Simon and Garfunkel. The duo split in 1970, with Garfunkel heading for the movies. His first two films, *Catch 22* (1969) and *Carnal Knowledge* (1970), garnered respectable reviews, and after a layoff he continued his film career in 1980 with *Bad Timing*. In 1973 he surfaced with a solo album, *Angel Claire,* a lavishly produced middle-of-the-road effort. Two years lapsed before *Breakaway,* which yielded the single "I Only Have Eyes For You," a remake of the Flamingos 1959 classic that was a modest hit for Garfunkel.

Garnett, Gale Born on July 17, 1942 in New Zealand, Garnett was an accomplished actress on the stage (*The Drunkard, Guys and Dolls, The World of Suzie Wong*) and on television ("Hawaiian Eye," "77 Sunset Strip," "Bonanza") when, almost as a lark, she tried recording. Her self-penned "We'll Sing In The Sunshine" was a major hit in 1964 and won her a Grammy award as well. The song is best remembered for its decidedly emancipated viewpoint—that women can and should have lives of their own—almost a decade before such a viewpoint became common.

Garrett, Leif Born on Nov. 8, 1961 in Hollywood, Calif., Garrett shifted from being a

child star to a teeny heartthrob, apparently without effort, sticking to remakes of old standards (his first was "Surfin' USA" in 1977) and guest shots on television. His best movie role to date was as the son of Buford Pusser (played by Joe Don Baker) in *Walking Tall.*

Gates, David Born on Dec. 11, 1940 in Tulsa, Okla., Gates has been the leading force behind the group Bread. The trio broke up in the early 1970s, only to re-form several years later. Gates has released three solo albums, including the soundtrack album for the Neil Simon movie *The Goodbye Girl* (1977). He is an excellent arranger, as exemplified by such Bread hits as "Baby, I'm A Want You" (1971) and "Guitar Man" (1972).

Gaye, Marvin One of the mainstays of the Motown Sound, Gaye was born on Oct. 13, 1941 in Washington, D.C. The son of a minister, he began singing in church and eventually moved through a string of vocal groups in the early 1960s. While working with a newly organized version of the Moonglows, Gaye met Berry Gordy of Tamla/Motown Records in Detroit during the late 1950s, and Gordy persuaded Gaye to quit the group and go solo, offering him a contract with Motown as an added inducement. In 1963, after several moderately successful singles, he cut "Can I Get A Witness," one of the most powerful soul incantations ever. (The song was later covered by the Rolling Stones on their first album and thus helped

introduce Gaye to a white audience.) From then on Gaye (sometimes in a duet with Mary Wells and, later, with Tammi Terrell) was a consistent hitmaker, one of the few soul men from Motown rather than Stax. In 1968 Gaye recorded what was to become another soul standard, "I Heard It Through The Grapevine," an overnight number one song that remained at the top for seven weeks. At the height of success, however, Gaye stepped out of the limelight to reevaluate his career and his life. That reevaluation didn't bear fruit until 1971, when he released *What's Going On* (featuring the hit single of the same name), a soft indictment of many American ills that catapulted Gaye to even greater heights and became one of the biggest selling records in Motown history. Two years later Gaye changed directions again—after the church, politics and pop music, the only thing left was sex. *Let's Get It On* proved to be the biggest record ever for Motown—the single sold two million copies within six weeks. Since then Gaye has returned to recording sporadically; in 1977 he made one of the best disco songs, "Got To Give It Up." All in all, he is one of the most important stylists of the 1970s and one of the most influential black singers in the history of popular music.

Gayle, Crystal Born Brenda Gayle Webb in 1951 in Paintsville, Ky., Crystal Gayle—the younger sister of country superstar Loretta Lynn—became a major country-pop artist in 1977 with the tremendous hit "Don't It Make

My Brown Eyes Blue," which won her country music and pop awards. Unlike her older sister, Gayle has forsaken hard country ballads for the smooth pop production of manager/mentor Allen Reynolds, yet another veteran of Sun Records in Memphis. Since the success of "Brown Eyes" Gayle, who came to Nashville in 1970 after touring briefly with her sister, has concentrated on a strictly pop audience; her songs have become major country music hits almost unintentionally.

Gaynor, Gloria   Born on Sept. 7, 1949 in Newark, N. J., Gaynor had worked as an effective rhythm-and-blues singer until turning to disco in 1974 with her can-you-dance-to-it treatment of "Never Can Say Goodbye." Her string of successes culminated in the late 1970s with "I Will Survive," a tough R&B treatment of a disco song that won her acclaim. Her Queen of the Discos title, however, soon passed to superstar Donna Summer, whose fast rising career quickly swamped the less-torchy Gaynor's.

Geffen, David   Superstar manager and founder of Asylum Records, Geffen (born in 1944) is renowned for his association with the heaviest West Coast rockers, including Linda Ronstadt, the Eagles and Jackson Browne. Asylum Records (now merged with Elektra) is one of the most powerful and successful modern record companies—largely based on its total domination of West Coast acts, including the aforementioned Big Three and others, such as

Joni Mitchell (who was managed by Geffen before Asylum), Tom Waits and David Gates.

Geils, J., Band   See J. Geils Band.

Genesis   Phil Collins (drums, vocals), Steve Hackett (guitar), Tony Banks (keyboards), Michael Rutherford (bass), Chester Thompson (drums)—Your basic art-rock group, Genesis was originally formed by Peter Gabriel as a vehicle for his flashy stage show. The band knocked around England from the late 1960s until 1972, when it began reaching a mass market with the album *Foxtrot.* Its largest success, though, didn't come until after the departure of Gabriel in 1975. In 1976 Genesis released *Trick Of The Tail,* which established the group in the American market.

Gentle Giant   Derek Shulman (guitar, vocals), Ray Shulman (bass, violin, guitar), Kerry Minnear (keyboards), Gary Green (guitar), John Weathers (drums)—English progressive—i.e., heavy on classical and jazz influences—rock group formed in 1970, Gentle Giant eventually achieved success in 1974 with *The Power And The Glory* and in 1976 (perhaps the peak of progressive rock) with *Interview.* The group broke up at the end of 1980.

Gentry, Bobbie   Born Roberta Streeter on July 27, 1944 in Chicasaw County, Miss., Bobbie Gentry wrote and sang a little ditty called "Ode To Billy Joe," concerning the events that transpired one hot

afternoon on the Tallahatchie Bridge (there are a whole bunch of them in northeastern Mississippi) between the singer and one Billy Joe McAllister. The song was one of the biggest hits of 1967, spawned a perfectly awful movie 10 years later and to this day provides Gentry with a steady income as a Las Vegas casino act. She had another hit song, "Fancy," in 1969—a story song about a budding young prostitute, which led one critic to dub her the William Faulkner of pop music.

Gentrys, The   Larry Raspberry (guitar, vocals), Larry Wall (drums), Jimmy Johnson (trumpet, organ), Bobby Fisher (piano), Pat Neal (bass), Bruce Bowles (vocals), Jimmy Hart (vocals)—Influential Memphis pop group formed as a local dance band in 1963, the Gentrys hit the top 10 in 1965 with "Keep On Dancing," marked by fine vocals and slick horn background rhythms. The success of the Gentrys marked another phase in Memphis' contribution to popular music, this time as a production center for pop music.

George, Lowell   George launched his career at the tender age of six on the "Ted Mack Amateur Hour," where he and his brother Hampton and their harmonica duet finished second to a team of Hungarian acrobats. He worked with Frank Zappa before forming his own group, Little Feat, in 1971. The group was a tremendous critical success, becoming one of the greatest underground groups of the 1970s, and George's

Lowell George

own "Willin'," one of the best trucking anthems ever written, was recorded by Linda Ronstadt. In 1979 he released his first solo album, *Thanks, I'll Eat It Here,* which met with immediate critical raves, seemingly cementing his career. But while touring to boost the album that year, George died of an apparent heart attack.

Gerry and the Pacemakers
Gerry Marsden (vocals, guitar, piano), Leslie Maguire (piano), John Chadwick (guitar, bass), Freddy Marsden (drums)— Formed in Liverpool in 1959, Gerry and the Pacemakers often worked the local pubs with another group of home boys, the Beatles, and eventually joined them under the banner of manager Brian Epstein in 1962. In 1964, riding the wave of the British invasion, they had their biggest hit, "Don't Let The Sun Catch You Crying."

Gibb, Andy   The younger brother of the famed Gibb brothers—better known as the Bee Gees—began his own career in 1977 with "I Just Want To Be Your Everything," produced by brother Barry. In

1978 he scored a huge hit with the disco-styled "Shadow Dancing." He was born on March 5, 1958 in Brisbane, Australia.

Gilder, Nick   English singer Nick Gilder originally worked in the Canadian ensemble Sweeney Todd, named for the demon barber of London, before going solo and scoring one of the biggest hits of 1978 (and well into 1979), "Hot Child In The City."

Gillett, Charlie   British rock critic, author and, briefly, head of his own record label, which released a collection of Cajun music in 1974. Gillett is best known for *The Sound of the City* (1970), a book on the evolution of rock, and *Making Tracks* (1975), a history of Atlantic Records.

Gilley, Mickey   A legend in Texas as the owner of Gilley's Club in Houston, billed as the world's largest honky-tonk (seating 2,100, with standing room for 4,500). Gilley has been a persistent seller on country charts, with piano pounding similar to that of his cousin Jerry Lee Lewis, with whom he grew up. His strongly rockabilly-influenced hits have included "Lawdy Miss Clawdy" and "Don't The Girls All Get Prettier At Closing Time." Gilley's Club was the scene of much of the filming of *Urban Cowboy,* featuring John Travolta in the lead role.

Gilmer, Jimmy, and the Fireballs   Born in Texas in 1940, Gilmer met the Fireballs in New Mexico. The Fireballs had been recording with some success when they asked

Gilmer to join up in 1963. The result was the classic "Sugar Shack." As simply the Fireballs (Gilmer, George Tomsco, Stan Lark and Eric Budd), the group came thundering back in 1967 with one of the most rip-roaring drinking songs of all time, "Bottle Of Wine."

Tompall Glaser

Glaser, Tompall   Glaser is best known as one of Nashville's "outlaws," that group of country musicians and singers who revolutionized country music in the mid-1970s with their blend of country, rock and rockabilly. The music of the outlaws, including the mid-1970s Glaser/Waylon Jennings/Willie Nelson landmark album appropriately titled *The Outlaws,* paved the way for country music's major intrusion into the rock market late in the decade. Glaser is also well known for his work with his brothers, Chuck and Jim, in the early 1960s as a folkie sounding trio doing such offbeat hits as "California Girl (And The Tennessee Square)" as well as more conventional material, such as "The Last Thing On My Mind." The Glaser Brothers announced their re-formation in mid-1980.

Glitter, Gary Paul Gadd (born on May 8, 1944 in Oxfordshire, England) worked steadily as a rocker in England throughout the 1960s, having his biggest success in the musical *Jesus Christ Superstar*. That success, however, wasn't enough to make him a household name, so in the early 1970s he changed his name to Gary Glitter and in 1972 scored a top 10 U.S. hit with "Rock And Roll, Pt. II." He then quickly faded back to Mother England, where he continued to make hits until 1974.

Goffin, Louise Born on March 23, 1960 in Brooklyn, N.Y., Goffin is yet another in the long line of collaborations between Gerry Goffin and Carole King, and something from the crack songwriting team must have rubbed off on their daughter—in her debut album in 1979, *Kid Blue,* Goffin wrote or cowrote seven of her 10 songs. The album received critical approval.

Gold, Andrew Born on Aug. 2, 1951 in Burbank, Calif., Gold worked for three years as a member of Linda Ronstadt's band before striking out on his own in 1975. The next year he managed a hit single—"Lonely Boy"—from his second album, which confirmed his strong West Coast, Ronstadt/Eagles bias. A third album in 1978 was only a modest success. He

occasionally tours with Ronstadt as a guitarist and arranger.

Golden Earring George Kooymans (guitar, vocals), Rinus Gerritsen (bass, keyboards), Barry Hay (vocals, sax, flute), Cesar Zuiderwijk (drums), Robert Jan Stips (keyboards)—Dutch rock bands are few and far between—at least, ones that have ever been heard in America. Golden Earring had hung together as Holland's top rock band since 1964. In the early 1970s it finally made a dent in the American charts with "Radar Love." That was, however, the band's only dent.

Goldsboro, Bobby Born on Jan. 15, 1941 in Maryanna, Fla., Goldsboro enjoyed a successful career from the mid-1960s into the early 1970s with a series of soft, sacharine ballads, beginning with "See The Funny Little Clown" in 1964 and culminating in "Honey," a ballad about a young wife who is dying, in 1968.

Goodman, Dickie Best known for his gold single "Mr. Jaws" (1975), which capitalized on the national obsession with the horror movie *Jaws*. He had earlier been successful with a recording called "Flying Saucer" (another obsession) in 1956. Dickie Goodman was born in New York on April 19, 1934.

Goodman, Steve One of the more inventive and irreverent songwriters in rock, Goodman was born on July 25, 1948 in Chicago, Ill., where

he still lives. In 1971 Goodman, then a local folksinger, was "discovered" by Kris Kristofferson, and the next year Arlo Guthrie scored a major hit with Goodman's "City Of New Orleans." Goodman has produced a number of albums, but he has never achieved the success that other artists have doing his material (particularly Jimmy Buffett with "Door Number Three" and David Allan Coe with "You Never Even Called Me By My Name").

Gordon, Robert Born in 1947 in Washington, D.C., Gordon might be described as a punk rocker who saw the light. Although he played with numerous bands in the New York scene during the early 1970s, in 1977 he showed his true colors—a genuine rockabilly. Because of his pegged pants and motorcycle boots, the tendency was to

Robert Gordon

dismiss him, even though his debut album with rock-and-roll legend Link Wray featured a superb rendition of "Sea Cruise." A third album in 1978, *Rock Billy Boogie,* established Gordon as a serious and accomplished practitioner of rockabilly, a field he appears to have pretty much to himself. He even had a modest country music hit with "It's Only Make Believe," a remake of the Conway Twitty smash from the 1950s.

Gore, Leslie   Born on May 2, 1946 in Tenafly, N.J., Gore had perhaps the most famous party in recording history—"It's My Party" in 1963, where she loses her boyfriend, and "Judy's Turn To Cry" later that year, where said boyfriend comes back. Gore was discovered by Quincy Jones, who produced the "Party" songs and her string of hits through 1967, including "She's A Fool" (1963), "Sunshine, Lollipops And Rainbows" (1965) and "Young Love" (1966). She later worked with Bob Crewe and Motown Records without success.

Graham, Bill   Perhaps the most important rock promoter ever—certainly on the West Coast—Graham was born in 1931 in Berlin and grew up in France and Germany. In 1965 he took over operation of a crumbling theater in San Francisco's ghetto, which he renamed the Fillmore Auditorium. The Fillmore became the incubator and later the home of dozens of Bay Area bands in the psychedelic sixties. He eventually expanded to larger quarters and opened a branch, the Fillmore East, in

New York City. Graham closed the Fillmores in 1971 to concentrate on promoting some of the largest and best-remembered concerts in rock history—Dylan's 1974 tour; the Band's farewell concert (the Last Waltz) and others. His most recent project has been as manager of country singer Bobby Bare (Graham once managed the Jefferson Airplane).

Graham Central Station
Larry Graham (bass, keyboards, vocals), Gail Muldrow (guitar, keyboards, vocals), Hershall Kennedy (keyboards, trumpet, vocals), Robert Sam (keyboards, vocals), David Vega (guitar, vocals), Gaylord Birch (drums)—Formed in 1973 from an earlier Graham band (he had his first band when he was 12) called Hot Chocolate, Graham Central Station started out running with the 1974 hit "Can You Handle It." The band began in the vein of Sly and the Family Stone, for whom Graham had played, but moved to more inventive, jazzier arrangements during the mid-1970s.

Grand Funk Railroad   Mark Farner (guitar, vocals), Mel Schacher (bass), Don Brewer (drums), Craig Frost (organ)—Grand Funk Railroad is the first rock band to be declared totally and irrevocably "hype," all sound and fury, signifying nothing. Ironically, however, at the time all the critics were decrying their vacuousness, Grand Funk was the most popular band in the country. Grand Funk Railroad surfaced in Flint, Mich. during the late 1960s. It consisted of Farner,

Schacher, Brewer and Terry Knight, a Detroit disc jockey who joined the original Funk conglomeration, called the Pack, as lead singer. Knight eventually left for greener pastures, but he came back to hear the group, which had meantime dubbed itself Grand Funk Railroad. Knight saw gold and took over, for all intents and purposes, as the group's collective voice. He got a slot for Grand Funk in the 1969 Atlanta Pop Festival, *sans* pay, and the rest is history. The crowd went bonkers, and the record companies started calling. Grand Funk knocked out six gold albums in a row and, at its pinnacle, sold out New York City's cavernous Shea Stadium—not once, but twice—with its ultrabasic, heavy metal, superloud music (Rod Stewart once described them as the all-time loud white noise). In 1971 Knight and the boys squabbled and ended up in court. Knight lost, but it was the band's popularity that suffered. It was downhill from there, except for a brief uplift in 1973 from the hit song "American Band," produced by Todd Rundgren. The harder the group tried for artistic acceptance, the fewer records it sold.

Grass Roots, The   Warren Entner (guitar, vocals, piano), Rob Grill (bass, vocals), Rickey Coonce (drums), Creed Bratton (guitar, banjo, sitar)—The group was formed in 1966 when Entner and Bratton, both folk singers, met while traveling in Israel. The Grass Roots had a powerful, driving sound, set off by the joint lead vocals of Entner and Grill. The group's first hit came in 1967 with

"Let's Live For Today," followed by "Midnight Confessions" (1968), "I'd Wait A Million Years" (1969) and "Temptation Eyes" (1971).

Grateful Dead, The   Jerry Garcia (guitar); Bob Weir (guitar); Phil Lesh (bass); Mickey Hart (percussion); Bill Kreutzmann (drums); and others, including Ron "Pig-Pen" McKernan, Keith Godchaux, Donna Godchaux—The greatest San Francisco band of them all, the Grateful Dead have survived not only the waning of the electric 1960s, but the 1970s as well, with their legions of "Deadhead" fans intact. The Dead grew out of the musical cauldron of San Francisco in the early 1960s, where folk, rock, blues, country and all manner of musical influences were getting ready to come together, fueled by LSD. The immediate pre-Dead group was the Warlocks, formed from an earlier Jerry Garcia group called Mother McCree's Uptown Jug Band. Since jug bands were not in demand, the Warlocks played electric blues. As the 1960s dragged on, though, the Warlocks fell in with the proverbial bad company—Ken Kesey's Merry Pranksters and their chemical enlightenment. It was under that enlightenment that the Warlocks changed into the Grateful Dead, and in this new guise the Dead became immediate heroes of San Francisco's burgeoning underground. The group began recording in 1967 with *The Grateful Dead* album, which hardly even scratched the surface of the strange fusion the Dead was working toward. In fact, it wasn't until 1970 with *Workingman's Dead* that the group really flowered on record. *Workingman's Dead* harkened back to Garcia's love of country music (evidenced by his many bluegrass and jug bands prior to the Dead), and the formula worked stupendously. The group followed that with *American Beauty,* featuring the Dead anthem "Truckin'." The band's next album went gold, and for the first time the Grateful Dead were financially in the black. In 1973 "Pig-Pen" McKernan died of a chronic liver ailment, and Keith and Donna Godchaux were added to the band (they departed in the late 1970s). Since then the Dead's work has never captured the magic of *Workingman's Dead* or *American Beauty.* In recent years the band has once again been pulling back together after myriad solo projects that never seemed to work as well as the Dead.

Gray, Dobie   Best known for his two classics, "The In Crowd" (1965) and "Drift Away" (1973), Gray (born in 1942 in Texas) has never been able to put together a consistent winning combination. In addition to those hits, he has produced numerous excellent albums (the most recent while working with Troy Seals in Nashville for Capricorn Records), which are widely admired in the business

The Grateful Dead

Dobie Gray

but largely unsold. He began his career by answering an ad in the paper for a singer, which put him in touch with Sonny Bono around 1964. In addition to his recording career, he also spent two years in the cast of the musical *Hair*.

Grease Band, The   Henry McCullough (guitar), Neil Hubbard (guitar, vocals), Alan Spenner (bass), Bruce Rowlands (drums)—Best known as the backup band for Joe Cocker, the Grease Band was formed around Cocker in 1964, with whom it enjoyed its greatest successes. In 1971 the band went it alone, releasing a competent album entitled *The Grease Band* without a little help from friend Cocker. But Cocker proved to be the glue that had held the Grease together, and without him, despite the successful album and two good tours, the band began to come apart. By the end of 1971 it was degreased.

Greaves, R.B.   Born on Nov. 28, 1944 in British Guiana,

South America, R.B. Greaves was one of the last soul singers of the 1960s, surfacing in 1969 with "Take A Letter Maria," a very pop-influenced soul song. He followed that up the next year with "Always Something There To Remind Me," an even more pop arrangement. Since then he has faded.

Green, Al   Born on April 13, 1946 in Forrest City, Ark., Green toured with various gospel groups until 1967, when he recorded his moderately successful "Back Up Train." In 1969 Green met Willie Mitchell of Hi Records in Memphis. Mitchell, struck with Green's soulful delivery, offered him a contract and promised to make him a star in 18 months. While most such promises are little better than a bad joke, Mitchell kept his. "Tired Of Being Alone" and "Let's Stay Together" (both 1971) made Green a superstar, the top soul singer in America.

By 1973 the Green-Mitchell-Al Jackson (a sessions man at Stax and an important figure in Green's career) formula had paid off handsomely, to the tune of 20 million records. The end of 1973 marked the peak, however. Though he kept releasing albums (*Living For You* in 1974, *Explores Your Mind* in 1974, *Al Green Is Love* in 1975, *Full Of Fire* in 1976), the product, mostly a rehash of his hits, was waning. In 1974 Green was injured in his home by a woman friend who poured boiling grits over him and then shot herself. In 1975 Al Jackson was murdered. The events caused a major reevaluation of the singer's life, and in 1976 Al Green, billed by some as the

sexiest of the soul men, returned to the church. He bought a small church in Memphis, and since then his music has stayed within the realms of religion. For secular music, it is a tremendous loss.

Grinderswitch   Dru Lombar (guitar, vocals), Larry Howard (guitar), Joe Dan Petty (bass), Rick Burnett (drums), Stephen Miller (keyboards)—Launched in 1972 as yet another Allman Brothers Southern rock spinoff, the band established a good following for its live music in tours with the Brothers, Marshall Tucker and Wet Willie. Despite several well-crafted albums, however, the band failed to make a dent in a market drifting steadily away from good-time Southern bar music.

Gross, Henry   Originally a guitarist for the nostalgia group Sha Na Na, Gross (born in 1950 in Brooklyn, New York City) struck out on his own in the early 1970s but scored big in 1976 with "Shannon," which sounded more like the Beach Boys than Sha Na Na.

Grossman, Albert Originally the manager of Bob Dylan in the early days, Grossman later managed the Band and Janis Joplin before founding Bearsville Records in Woodstock, N.Y. during the early 1970s. Bearsville has featured such artists as Todd Rundgren and Jesse Winchester. Grossman was born in 1926 in Chicago, where he established himself as a blues impresario. He later managed the Newport Folk Festivals.

Guess Who, The Burton Cummings (keyboards, vocals), Billy Wallace (bass), Domenic Troiano (guitar), Don McDougall (guitar), Garry Paterson (drums)—Formed in the late 1960s in Canada by Cummings and Randy Bachman, who left after two years to form the nucleus of Bachman-Turner Overdrive, the Guess Who was yet another band that suffered critical castigation because it had hit singles. The group already had a solid reputation in Canada, where it even had its own weekly television show, before the 1969 breakthrough success of "These Eyes," from the debut *Wheatfield Soul* album. That was followed by "Laughing" (1969), "No Time" (1970) and the huge hit "American Woman" (1970). Without Bachman the band soldiered on, dipping into social criticism (hoping, one supposes, for the elusive acceptance of the "hip" market) with "Hand-Me-Down World" and "Share The Land," both in 1970, before the hits just stopped coming. The band continued with various and sundry personnel changes until 1975, when they formally called it quits.

Guitar Slim A popular rhythm-and-blues singer from the early 1950s, Eddie "Guitar Slim" Jones enjoyed a million seller in 1953, "The Things I Used To Do," a rarity for any R&B singer at that time.

Guthrie, Arlo There are still mixed opinions about Arlo Guthrie, son of folksinging legend Woody Guthrie and, lo, after all these years still best remembered for "Alice's Restaurant." The younger Guthrie was born on Jan. 12, 1947 in Coney Island, N.Y. His career really began at the Newport Folk Festival in 1967, when he recounted the sad story of why he didn't get drafted the year before—he was a criminal, convicted of illegally disposing of garbage. "Alice's Restaurant" became one of the most memorable songs of a memorable period and in 1970 was turned into a memorable movie of the same name. Since then Guthrie has had some modest hits, notably Steve Goodman's "City Of New Orleans" (1972), but for the most part he seems a misplaced angel of the 1960s, waiting for the issue to arise so that he can give it voice.

Arlo Guthrie

Guthrie, Woody America's preeminent folksinger and folklorist, Woodie Guthrie was born on July 14, 1912 in Okemah, Okla. and left home in his early teens to travel the country. He saw America at its best and worst, in good times and bad, and he translated those times into music—"This Land Is Your Land," "This Train Is Bound For Glory," "Pretty Boy Floyd" and many others. Guthrie spent the last 15 years of his life in a hospital, the victim of Huntington's Disease. He was visited there by such rock luminaries as Bob Dylan, who found much in the Guthrie style to emulate. He died on Oct. 3, 1967.

Haley, Bill As lead singer of the Saddlemen in the early 1950s, Haley (born in 1927 in Detroit, Mich.) noticed that white kids were beginning to seek out black rhythm-and-blues records for their danceable beat, so he added a little of that beat to the Saddlemen's show. In 1951 the Saddlemen released "Rock The Joint," and Haley knew for sure he was on to something. He also knew that "the Saddlemen" just didn't make it, so the next year the Saddlemen (John Grande, Billy Williamson, Al Rex, Rudy Pompelli, Francis Beecher and Don Raymond) hung up their spurs, and the newly christened Comets began shooting across the charts with "Crazy Man Crazy" (1953), from a phrase Haley knew was popular with the kids, and "Shake, Rattle And Roll" (1954), a sanitized version of Joe Turner's rhythm-and-blues classic. Haley said he played rock-and-roll music, a phrase coined by disc jockey Alan Freed supposedly when he

Bill Haley

heard one of Haley's songs, "Rock-A-Beatin' Boogie."

In 1955 came "Rock Around The Clock," selected for the movie *Blackboard Jungle,* which went on to become one of the largest selling records ever, boosting Haley into the top 10 record sellers of all time. But Haley—unlike his contemporary Elvis Presley—was never completely comfortable with the monster he had unleashed. He was a singer, not a believer, and the image of rock and roll quickly shifted away from Haley's clean-cut looks to the leather-jacketed rock-and-roll fury that was beginning to catch fire in the South.

Haley died on Feb. 9, 1981.

Hall, Tom T. Long considered one of the most literate of the country music songwriters, Hall was born in 1936 in Kentucky and first came to public attention with the across-the-board success

of his "Harper Valley PTA," recorded by Jeannie C. Riley in 1968. His story songs, many based on his experiences growing up in rural Kentucky,

such as "A Week In A Country Jail" (1969), "The Year That Clayton Delany Died" (1971) and "Old Dogs, Children And Watermelon Wine" (1973), have made him a country superstar.

Hall and Oates Daryl Hall and John Oates worked together for almost a decade before finding the right combination in 1975 with "Sara Smile." That combination was soft soul, a heavily orchestrated rhythm-and-blues groove that reflected Hall's classical training and backup singing for such soul groups as the Temptations and Oates' songwriting abilities. The two met in Philadelphia in 1967 and had several abortive starts before finding the "Sara Smile" formula. Their other hits include "She's Gone" (1974 and rereleased in 1976) and "Rich Girl"(1977). They

Daryl Hall & John Oates

achieved considerable success in 1981-82 with the albums *Voices* and *Private Eyes* (particularly the hit single "I Can't Go For That" from the latter), displaying their R&B skills.

Hamilton, George, IV　Born on July 19, 1937 in North Carolina, George Hamilton, IV became an unwitting pop star in 1956 with "A Rose And A Baby Ruth," which landed him on Alan Freed's rock-and-roll show with the likes of Buddy Holly, Gene Vincent and the Everly Brothers. By 1963 he was back to the more secure ground of his first love, country music, with "Abilene" and a regular spot at the Grand Ole Opry.

Hamilton, Roy　Born on April 16, 1929 in Leesburg, Ga., Hamilton began singing in the church and had his first hit in 1954 with "You'll Never Walk Alone." He then made a series of classic performances in a genre that would later be called soul music. The songs included "Ebb Tide" (1954), "Unchained Melody" (1955), "Don't Let Go" (1958) and "You Can Have Her." He died of a stroke on July 20, 1969.

Hammer, Jan　European composer and keyboard wizard Jan Hammer was born on April 17, 1948 in Czechoslovakia and began playing the piano at four. After coming to the United States in 1968, he toured with singer Sarah Vaughan, worked with John McLaughlin's jazz-rock Mahavishnu Orchestra and turned to solo work in 1975 with *The First Seven Days*. His *Black Sheep* in 1979 showed

him totally in control of the jazz-rock fusion—a virtuoso.

Hammond, John　The man with the golden ear. Hammond (born in 1910) is best known as the man who brought Bob Dylan to Columbia Records— and that's not to mention Pete Seeger, Aretha Franklin and, in the 1970s, rock icon Bruce Springsteen. Hammond began his association with Columbia in the 1930s, eventually bringing such jazz greats as Billie Holiday under the corporate wing. His son, John, Jr., has achieved a substantial reputation as a blues guitarist and singer.

Hancock, Herbie　Born on April 12, 1940 in Chicago, Ill., Hancock made his reputation as a member of Miles Davis' great jazz band in the mid-1960s, all the while maintaining a solo career that began in the 1950s. Hancock worked at composing everything from advertising jingles to movie soundtracks before his 1968 *Mwandishi* album moved him from jazz to the jazz-rock fusion area and established him as one of the fusion's premier stars. He consolidated his position with *Head Hunters* (1973) and *Man-Child* (1975), and he continues his exploration into the jazz-rock-electronic music area today.

Hardin, Tim　Born in 1940 in Oregon, Hardin was best known as a songwriter, although he had worked since the early 1960s as a folk singer. His most famous songs are "If I Were A Carpenter" (recorded by Bobby Darin, Johnny Cash and the Four Tops), "The Lady

Came From Baltimore" (recorded by Johnny Cash) and "Every Picture Tells A Story" (recorded by Rod Stewart). Hardin was found dead in his Los Angeles apartment in December 1980.

Harper, Roy　Born June 12, 1941 in England, Harper is best known for a tribute paid him by Led Zeppelin, which recorded "Hat's Off To Harper" on its third album. He has turned out some 10 albums over the years, making him the best recorded of England's folkie poets.

Harris, Emmylou　Born in 1947 in Birmingham, Ala., Emmylou Harris went through the almost typical career ups and downs before a chance meeting with Gram Parsons in 1971 pointed her in the right direction. She shared Parsons' love of country music and joined him on his *GP* and *Grevious Angel* albums. His death in 1973 left her temporarily unable to continue, and she returned to her parents' home in Washington,

Emmylou Harris

D.C. to try and put things back together. She found the best therapy was her music, and in 1974 she began work on *Pieces Of The Sky.* The album, released in 1975, is a country-rock classic, featuring everything from works by Dolly Parton ("Coat Of Many Colors") and Merle Haggard ("Tonight The Bottle Let Me Down") to her own composition ("Boulder To Birmingham"). It was an instant success. She backed the album up with a tour, featuring the Hot Band (including such heavyweights as James Burton, Alvin Lee, Glen D. Hardin and Hank DiVito), that heightened her success. A second album, *Elite Hotel* (1976), produced three hit singles, "Together Again," "Sweet Dreams" and "One Of These Days." The next two albums drifted more toward rock and pop, perhaps with the influence of producer (and soon to be husband) Brian Ahern. But in 1976 she returned to the idiom she knows best—country music—with *Blue Kentucky Girl,* featuring a superb (and successful) arrangement of the Doc Pomus/Mort Shuman classic "Save The Last Dance For Me." In addition to her solo work, she has joined Linda Ronstadt and Dolly Parton in vocals on numerous occasions, including a complete album that was never released (rumor said the album was "too" country).

Harris, Richard   Born on Oct. 1, 1933 in Ireland, Richard Harris is far better known as an actor (*This Sporting Life, Camelot* and, more recently,

The Wild Geese) than as a singer. In 1968, however, he recorded a full album of songs by songwriter Jim Webb titled *A Tramp Shining,* which featured the long, very melodramatic "MacArthur Park." Against all odds, "MacArthur Park" (a park off Wilshire Boulevard in Los Angeles) became a hit and even won a Grammy. The song later garnered another Grammy as a country hit by "outlaw" Waylon Jennings and came back yet a third time in a 1978 version by disco queen Donna Summer.

Harris, Rolf   Born on March

30, 1930 in Perth, Australia, Rolf Harris, not satisfied with being a cabaret performer and television personality, actually aspired to be a painter. In 1958 he had the good fortune to place one of his oil paintings, done on a piece of Masonite board, on an oil heater to dry. The board, predictably, got too hot, and holding it gingerly by the edge, Rolf wobbled it back and forth to cool it. It made a funny noise, sort of an odd twangy sound, and an idea came into Rolf's head. The noise was perfect for a song he'd been wanting to record, a song about kangaroos. "Tie Me Kangaroo Down Sport," wobbles and all, was a

George Harrison

worldwide hit in 1960 and a tremendous boon for the Masonite company. Rolf had the biggest seller in Britain in 1969 with a song called "Two Little Boys," originally written in 1903.

Harris, Thurston Best remembered for his cover recording of "Little Bitty Pretty One" (1957), a song written by Robert Byrd, better known as Bobby Day, singer of "Rockin' Robin."

Harrison, George Beatle George Harrison (born Feb. 25, 1943 in Liverpool) found his interests drifting away from the group even before the celebrated 1971 breakup. After the Beatles, Harrison cemented his stature as a solo artist with the triple album *All Things Must Pass*, a tremendous seller produced by rock legend Phil Spector. The album also featured Eric Clapton, Ginger Baker, Dave Mason, Pete Drake, Ringo Starr, Billy Preston and others. It sold 1.5 million units in one week and produced a huge hit single, "My Sweet Lord" (which, it was alleged, sounded enough like "He's So Fine" that Harrison was taken to court over it). He followed that album with the celebrated concert for Bangladesh and the live album from the concert, featuring some of rock's biggest stars in a benefit for that stricken country in 1971. Since then Harrison's work has sunk deeper and deeper into his spiritual obsessions, usually to the detriment of the music.

Harrison, Wilbert Born on Jan. 6, 1929 in Charlotte, N.C.,

Harrison was working as a one-man band when he cut a song called "K.C. Lovin' " in 30 minutes one afternoon in 1959. The song, a Mike Stoller and Jerry Leiber composition, retitled "Kansas City" quickly became a huge hit. Even more quickly, the song, the singer and the songwriters ended up in court, since none of the standard "niceties," such as contracts, royalties and what-have-you, had been observed.

Hartford, John Born Dec. 30, 1937 in New York City, Hartford first came to public attention as a songwriter and instrumentalist on the "Smothers Brothers Comedy Hour" television show in the mid-1960s. He landed a spot on Glen Campbell's television show (Hartford had written one of Campbell's biggest hits, "Gentle On My Mind" in 1967), which made his bluegrass banjo and good-natured cynicism quite famous. Since then he's been a regular guest on numerous shows and has found the time to record 12 albums. His 1976 *Mark Twang* won a Grammy in the ethnic-traditional music category. Lately Hartford has been spending as much time as possible on riverboats, his first love, plying the Mississippi River and playing his music.

Hartley, Keef English rhythm-and-blues drummer Keef Hartley (born in 1944 in England) has always been on the verge of making it big, achieving critical success in 1971 (*Little Big Band*), 1972 (*Seventy Second Brave* and *Lancashire Hustler*) and 1975 (*Dog Soldier*) without the attendant commercial success.

He remains a fine, if erratic, drummer.

Hathaway, Donny Born on Oct. 1, 1945 in Chicago, Hathaway hit the road at the tender age of three as "The Nation's Youngest Gospel Singer!" Despite such a nonsecular beginning, Hathaway carved a niche for himself as a producer and arranger for the Impressions, the Staple Singers and Roberta Flack. He also maintained a moderately successful solo singing career; his biggest hit was titled "Where Is The Love," a duet he sang with Roberta Flack in 1972.

Havens, Richie Another performer who owed his career to the Woodstock Festival in 1969, Havens had worked for years as a folk singer and artist in Greenwich Village until Woodstock made him a star. He is probably best known for his soulful interpretations of Lennon and McCartney hits, especially "Eleanor Rigby" (1968) and "Here Comes The Sun" (1971), his biggest hit. He simply lacked the versatility to continue his booming career after Woodstock—a not too uncommon problem— although he remains popular on college campuses around the country.

Hawkins, Ronnie Born on Jan. 10, 1935 in Huntsville, Ark., Ronnie Hawkins is best remembered, unfortunately, for his band, the Hawks. Later the Hawks changed their name to the Band and went on to become famous, while Hawkins faded into obscurity on his ranch in Canada. Basically, Hawkins was one of the last of the rockabilly breed, born a bit too late to catch the initial fury of the fifties and a little too early for the post-British Invasion rock of the sixties. He was a rock-and-roll wild man—his early tours through the South are still the subject of legend. On record he is best remembered for an uncanny, manic version of Bo Diddley's "Who Do You Love" in 1963, which he reprised at the Band's farewell concert, The Last Waltz, in 1976.

Hawkins, "Screamin'" Jay Born on July 18, 1929 in Cleveland, Ohio, he might have remained just plain Jay Hawkins had it not been for a concert in Atlantic City, N. J. A woman in the audience kept yelling for him to "scream the songs," and after a while he did exactly that. From then on he was "Screamin'" Jay. In 1956 he was all set to record "I Put A Spell On You" when he and the boys decided to have one or two drinks to get in the mood. The result was one of the wildest records of the period, which, because it was a hit, dictated his stage show thereafter. His only other song was a Mike Stoller and Jerry Leiber composition called "Alligator Wine" in 1958.

Hawks, The Originally the Hawks were the backup group for Ronnie Hawkins. They backed Dylan in the mid-1960s and became the Band in the late 1960s.

Hawkwind David Brock (guitar, vocals), Adrian Shaw (bass), Simon House (synthesizer), Robert Calvert (vocals), Simon King (drums)—Launched in the late 1960s, Hawkwind became England's leading psychedelic band, known more for the spirit of its playing than the virtuosity of its music. The band survived the waning of psychedelia, however, by immersing itself in science fiction, keying on the more spacey aspects of the last decade's music to keep afloat. And the group still is, barely, working at becoming, as one of its most recent albums put it, *Masters Of The Universe.*

Hayes, Isaac Seldom has an album title been as descriptive as that of Isaac Hayes' 1969 release *Hot Buttered Soul,* because that phrase perfectly summed up the artist's approach to soul music. Hayes (born on Aug. 20, 1943 in Covington, Tenn.) had built his reputation as a writer for Stax Records in Memphis during its heyday in the mid-1960s. Working with David Porter, he wrote such hits as "Soul Man," "You Don't Know Like I Know," "Hold On, I'm Coming" and "I Thank You" (all recorded by Sam and Dave); "Love Have Mercy" (by Otis Redding) and many others. *Hot Buttered Soul* featured Hayes' orchestral arrangements of pop hits overlaid with his silky smooth voice, apparently coming direct from his bedroom. His superlong version of Dionne Warwick's "Walk On By" became something of an underground hit, and *Hot Buttered Soul* went platinum, as did his next five albums. Hayes' biggest triumph, however, came in 1971, when he agreed to score a Gordon Parks movie called *Shaft,* about a black private eye named John Shaft. In addition to winning an Academy Award for Hayes, the "Theme From *Shaft*" went gold in three weeks and platinum in two months, garnered a Grammy Award (and got Hayes a long, long standing ovation at the awards ceremony) and became a number one song on the rock, rhythm-and-blues and jazz charts. The "Theme From *Shaft*" quite literally set the tone for soul music in the 1970s, ironically leaning away from Stax' hard rocking soul men toward the softer, Motown/Philadelphia soul with its heavily orchestrated backgrounds. More importantly perhaps, the *Shaft* theme ushered in a whole new generation of dance music, legitimizing the budding disco movement. Although Hayes was one of the godfathers of disco, it wasn't until 1979 that he was able to profit from the music he had helped create with "Don't Let Go."

Hazlewood, Lee Los Angeles record producer Lee Hazlewood had a series of duet hits with Nancy Sinatra in the late 1960s, including "Jackson" (1967) and "Lady Bird" (1967).

Heart Ann Wilson (vocals, flute, guitar), Nancy Wilson (guitar, mandolin), Roger Fisher (guitar), Howard Leese (keyboards), Steve Fossen (bass), Mike Derosier (drums)—One of the more popular questions (right after "Can a white man sing the blues?") has been, "Can women really rock?" Surprising as it sounds, women have seldom ventured beyond the vocal end of rock, but Heart is a major (and successful) exception. Formed

Heart

in Canada in the mid-1970s around Nancy and Ann Wilson, Heart is a tough, no-nonsense rock band, with the two Wilsons handling the guitar chores. In 1976 the band scored a hit with "Magic Man," consolidating its position with the album *Little Queen* a year later, *Dog And Butterfly* in 1979 and an album recorded earlier titled *Magazine.* The next year, though, the group really took off with its *Bebe Le Strange* album, which made it into the top 10 and established the sisters Wilson as one of rock's top acts.

Hendrix, Jimi The legend of Jimi Hendrix is one that has both inspired and haunted rock since Hendrix' death from drugs in 1970. Hendrix (born on Nov. 27, 1942 in Seattle, Wash.) remains rock's most influential guitarist. He managed to expand the horizons of rock by taking the blues-based music he grew up

playing and pushing it into psychedelia and harder and harder rock veins, without ever losing sight of its roots. Hendrix began his career along

Jimi Hendrix

traditional rhythm-and-blues lines—after a discharge from the military in 1963, he hit the road playing guitar for such artists as Little Richard, Wilson Pickett and Jackie Wilson. He even briefly backed up his childhood idol B.B. King before going to New York City to make it on his own. While playing in Greenwich Village, he was "discovered" by Chas Chandler, a former member of the Animals turned manager and producer. Chandler bundled Hendrix off to England and put together a rhythm section consisting of Mitch Mitchell on drums and Noel Redding on bass. Dubbed the Jimi Hendrix Experience, the group was an immediate success with "Hey Joe" in 1966, followed by "Purple Haze" a year later. Hendrix was the quintessential soon-to-be superstar—an imposing, seemingly mythical figure,

fraught with imagined significance and with a weakness for the lyrics of Bob Dylan. The Jimi Hendrix Experience came to America in 1967 to appear at the legendary Monterey Pop Festival (which also launched Janis Joplin and Otis Redding), an event arranged by Beatle Paul McCartney. The performance, recorded on film, remains one of the most powerful in rock history.

Hendrix' three subsequent albums—*Are You Experienced?, Axis: Bold As Love* and *Electric Ladyland,* with a cover featuring nude women that was intended to capitalize (rather overtly) on his sexual star imagery—became big sellers. Ironically, Hendrix came under pressure from both his audience, which was almost entirely white, and the musical establishment to disband the Experience, which was white, and form an all-black band, which he did in 1969—the Band of Gypsies, featuring Buddy Miles (drums) and Billy Cox (bass). In August 1969 he appeared at Woodstock and delivered a stunning version of "The Star-Spangled Banner," but the rest was downhill. In just over a year he was dead.

Henry, Clarence "Frogman"
Born in 1937 in Louisiana, Henry got christened "Frogman" because people claimed that one of the three voices he used on his first hit, "Ain't Got No Home" (1956), sounded like a frog. Five years later he turned out another rock classic, "I Don't Know Why I Love You, But I Do."

Hicks, Dan, and His Hot Licks
Dan Hicks (vocals, guitar); Bill Douglas (bass); David Laflamme (electric violin); Misty Douglas (vocals); Patti Urban (vocals); and others, including Jaime Leopold (bass), John Weber (guitar), Sid Page (electric violin), Sherry Snow (vocals), Tina Gancher (vocals)—A shifting group of musicians who performed jug band material interspersed with raunchy lines and rhythm-and-blues lyrics. The group was formed in San Francisco in 1968 and reconstituted a year later when David Laflamme left to start It's a Beautiful Day. Hicks and His Hot Licks made four albums, starting with *The Original Recording* in 1969. Their final album was *Last Train to Hicksville* in 1973.

Hillman, Chris
Best known as a member of the Byrds and, later, the Flying Burrito Brothers, Hillman was working as a bluegrass mandolin player when he got together with Roger McQuinn, David Crosby and Gene Clark to form the Byrds in 1964. In 1969 he and Gram Parsons left the group to form the Burritos. He later went on to join Stephen Stills' sometimes backup group, Manassas, hooked up with John David Souther and Richie Furay (the Souther-Hillman-Furay Band) for two albums and turned to solo work.

Holland-Dozier-Holland
Crack Motown songwriting team featuring the brothers Eddie and Brian Holland and Lamont Dozier. Although Eddie Holland was successful as a singles artist for Berry Gordy at Motown ("Jamie" in 1962), his success was nothing compared to that of such Holland-Dozier-Holland hits as the Four Tops' "Baby, I Need Your Loving" (1964), "I Can't Help Myself" (1965) and "It's the Same Old Song" (1965); the Supremes' "Come See About Me" (1964), "Stop In The Name Of Love" (1964) and "You Keep Me Hangin' On" (1966) and many others. The three eventually formed their own label, Invictus, in 1970.

Hollies, The
Graham Nash (guitar, vocals), Eric Haydock (bass), Allan Clarke (vocals), Tony Hicks (guitar, vocals), Bobby Elliott (drums)—This original lineup was launched in 1963 in England, where the Hollies were consistent hitmakers. Their first break in the United States came in 1966 with "Bus Stop," which they followed with the classic "Stop Stop Stop" (1966), a risque song for its time, "On A Carousel" (1967), "Carrie Anne" (1967) and others. The secret to the early success was the one-two punch of Clarke's lead vocals and Nash's impeccable harmonies. The band began shuffling members in 1968, and a new ensemble emerged in 1970 with "He Ain't Heavy, He's My Brother." After disappearing for a while, the Hollies reemerged in 1973 with different members and a new sound, highlighted by "Long Cool Woman In A Black Dress," featuring Clarke again as lead vocalist. The group has continued since then with moderate success, a 1970s version of a 1960s harmony group.

Holly, Buddy The short, amazingly influential career of Charles Harden Holly (born on Sept. 7, 1936 in Lubbock, Tex.) has recently enjoyed a major revival, thanks to an excellent movie version of his life (*The Buddy Holly Story* in 1978) and a recognition of his contribution to the music. Holly's upbeat pop music, such as "That'll Be The Day," "Peggy Sue," "Oh Boy," "Maybe Baby" and "Not Fade Away" in 1957-58, was the link between the raw, powerful rockabilly of the Sun Records axis and the more sophisticated pop music that would follow. In fact, it's almost impossible to hear a song on the charts today that doesn't owe something to Buddy Holly. He began his career in the mid-1950s singing country music over radio station KDAV in Lubbock and envisioned himself as a country singer. His work in Nashville with his band, the Crickets—Jerry Allison (drums), Niki Sullivan (guitar) and Joe Maudlin (bass)—never quite meshed, and it wasn't until he linked up with producer Norman Petty in Clovis, N.M. that the Holly legend began to perk. In June 1957 "That'll Be The Day" was released and became virtually an overnight hit for Holly, who quickly rivaled Elvis Presley in the popularity polls. In February 1959 Holly chartered a plane after an engagement in Clear Lake, Iowa. The plane crashed, killing Holly, the Big Bopper and Richie Valens. Holly's legacy seems to grow more important with each passing year, and his songs are regularly recycled on the pop and country charts with great success.

Holman, Eddie Best known for his soulful recycling of the Ruby and the Romantics' hit "Hey There Lonely Boy" (1963) into "Hey There Lonely Girl," one of the biggest soul songs of 1970. He was born in 1946 in Norfolk, Va.

Holy Modal Rounders Formed in the late 1960s around the weird axis of Steve Weber and ex-Fug Peter Stampfel, the group produced one of the better songs in the movie *Easy Rider* called "Bird Song" and continued to perpetrate such all-time classics as "Boobs-A-Lot" and "My Mind Capsized."

Hombres, The Gary Wayne McEwen (guitar), Jerry Lee Masters (bass), B.B. Cunningham (organ), John Hunter, (drums)—Yet another group from Memphis, the Hombres, led by guitarist Gary Wayne McEwen, had one of the truly bizarre hits of the 1960s, "Let It All Hang Out" (1967). The song featured chanted lyrics that were, depending on one's point of view, either totally profound or utterly nonsensical. Actually, the song was a wry satire on the pseudo-profound lyricism of the San Francisco/psychedelic school of rock.

Hooker, John Lee Born on Aug. 22, 1917 in Clarksdale, Miss., bluesman John Lee Hooker worked odd jobs along Beale Street in Memphis before moving to Detroit in the 1940s, where his career really got under way. His 1948 cut of "I'm In The Mood" boosted him to the top of the rhythm-and-blues charts and became one of the biggest R&B sellers in the country. He recorded for numerous small labels under several false names, his bosses not wanting to "glut the market" with Hooker material. In the early 1960s he came back (actually he'd never gone away), based on the strength of his following in England, with his third million seller, "Dimples."

Hopkin, Mary Born on May 3, 1950 in South Wales, Hopkin was signed to the Beatles' Apple label by Paul McCartney upon the recommendation of emaciated model and culture hero Twiggy. Hopkin's first two hits were her biggest—"Those Were The Days" (1968) and the Lennon/McCartney song "Goodbye" (1969).

Hopkins, Lightnin' Texas bluesman Sam "Lightnin'" Hopkins was born around 1912 in Centerville, Tex. and left home as a child to wander the South with his brother Joel and bluesman Blind Lemon Jefferson. His nickname didn't come until years later, when he recorded in Los Angeles with Wilson "Thunder" Smith and was dubbed Lightnin' by one of the recording engineers. Returning to Houston, Hopkins personified the down-home style of blues, eventually enjoying a bit of success with the blues revivals of the 1960s and 1970s. He died on Jan. 31, 1982.

Hopkins, Nicky Britain's nearly legendary rock pianist was born on Feb. 24, 1944 in London and played in one of that country's seminal rhythm-and-blues groups, Cyril Davies' All Stars, before bad health forced an early retirement in

1963. As a sessions player he later backed the Beatles ("Revolution"), the Who (*My Generation*), Jeff Beck (*Truth*), the Jefferson Airplane (*Volunteers*) and the Rolling Stones (*Their Satanic Majesties Request*). He joined Quicksilver Messenger Service in the late 1960s and settled in California. He released his first solo album in 1973, *The Tin Man Was A Dreamer*. In 1974 Hopkins returned to England, in frail health.

Horslips   Charles O'Connor (fiddle, mandolin, vocals), Jim Lockhart (flute), Barry Devlin (bass, vocals), Eamon Carr (drums), Johnny Fean (guitar, banjo, vocals)—This Irish rock band launched in the early 1970s utilizes native Irish music and folklore in a rock format.

Horton, Johnny   Born on April 30, 1927 in Tyler, Tex., Horton is best remembered for his string of story songs, beginning in 1959 with the immensely popular "Battle Of New Orleans" and continuing through "Sink The Bismarck" (1960) and "North To Alaska" (1960), from the John Wayne movie of the same name. He was killed on Nov. 5, 1960 in an auto accident near Austin, Tex. after a successful engagement there.

Hot Chocolate   Errol Brown (vocals), Patrice Olive (bass), Larry Ferguson (keyboards), Tony Connor (drums), Harvey Hinsley (guitar)—Best known in the United States for "You Sexy Thing" in 1975, Hot Chocolate was launched by Errol Brown in 1970 and was successful in England for a

number of years before the group's U.S. breakthrough. Hot Chocolate's subsequent music remains close to the "Sexy Thing" vein—funky disco.

Hot Tuna   Jorma Kaukonen (guitar, vocals), Jack Casady (bass), Bob Steeler (drums)—Splintered from the Jefferson Airplane around 1969, Hot Tuna was originally titled Hot Shit, which sent record company execs into a frenzy. The group debuted with *Hot Tuna* in 1970. John Sherman joined Kaukonen, Casady and Steeler for the 1975 *Yellow Fever* album, which was followed the next year by *Hoppkorv*. The group never did find a groove, however, vacillating from acoustic to electric to hard rock to anything else that caught Casady and Kaukonen, and hence had limited commercial success. Since the breakup of the group, Kaukonen has pursued a solo career.

Howlin' Wolf   Born Chester Arthur Burnett on June 10, 1910 near Aberdeen, Miss., Howlin' Wolf—so named because of his distinctive howl in his music—became perhaps the greatest of the bluesmen and, ultimately, a bridge between the blues of the 1940s and the rock of the 1950s. He came to West Memphis in 1948 and put together a band that featured James Cotton and Little Junior Parker, and it was there that he was "discovered" by Ike Turner (later of Ike and Tina Turner), a talent scout for Sam Phillips' Sun Records. Phillips leased the tapes of Howlin' Wolf to Chess, and finally Leonard Chess himself came to

Memphis to take the Wolf back to Chicago—largely to protect his investment. He was a walking encyclopedia of the blues and stamped the music with his own individualistic, intense delivery, becoming a hero to such groups as the Rolling Stones and other white rhythm-and-blues artists.

Hubbard, Ray Wylie   Texas country-rock composer best known for his early 1970s composition of "(Up Against The Wall) Redneck Mother," as recorded by Jerry Jeff Walker.

Hues Corporation, The
St. Clair Lee (vocals), Tommy Brown (vocals), H. Ann Kelly (vocals)—Best known for the huge hit "Rock The Boat" (1974). That stylish soul number with its catchy rhythm clearly pointed the way black music was headed at the time, although the Hues Corp. never returned to collect on its insight.

Humble Pie   Steve Marriott (guitar, vocals), Greg Ridley (bass, vocals), Jerry Shirley (drums), Dave Clempson (guitar, vocals)—Originally launched in the late 1960s during the mania for "supergroups," Humble Pie came out of the chute and immediately stumbled. The problem was the same as with so many of the other "supergroups"—a hopeless lack of direction. The group's original members—Steve Marriott from the Small Faces, Peter Frampton from the Herd and Greg Ridley and Jerry Shirley from Spooky Tooth, all seemed to be pulling in opposite directions—they couldn't decide whether they wanted to be the English version of the Band, a melodic pop group (the Frampton direction) or a collection of hard rock rangers (Marriott's pleasure). The problem was almost solved in 1969 when the group's record company folded, but surprisingly, the band emerged in 1970 with *Humble Pie,* a hard rocking sound that immediately established them as a hit group. Such singles as "I Don't Need No Doctor" (1971) and "Hot And Nasty" (1972) established the group's direction solidly, culminating in the *Smokin'* album in 1972. Immediately thereafter, however, Humble Pie stopped smokin' and disbanded in 1975.

Humperdinck, Engelbert
If you said "Tom Jones *sans* sex," you'd come close to defining Engelbert Humperdinck, born with the more modest name of Arnold George Dorsey on May 2, 1936 in Madras, India. He knocked around England for years before hooking up with Tom Jones' manager, Gordon Mills, who suggested he take the name of the famous German composer and carefully follow Mills' instructions. The result was that suddenly in 1967 Humperdinck was *everywhere,* releasing in machine-gun procession "Release Me," "There's Goes My Everything" and "The Last Waltz," all monster hits. But the formula began misfiring, and although it was unlikely that he would starve—the dinner club Las Vegas circuit would see to that—he was waning as a pop threat. He did come back

strong in 1976 with a touch more of the Tom Jones formula: sex, in this case a song called "After The Loving." But since then the man with the unwieldy name has stuck with what he does best, playing the big-money Vegas circuit.

Hunter, Ian   Born on June 3, 1946 in England, Ian Hunter is best known as the lead vocalist and guiding light of the group Mott the Hoople. He went solo in 1975, and his career is still at the "getting ready to take off" stage. He is one of the most literate rock composers.

Hunter, "Ivory" Joe   Born in 1911 in Kirbyville, Tex., Ivory Joe Hunter recorded his first record, "Blues At Sunrise," in 1943 (although he had been recorded for the Library of Congress by folk researcher Alan Lomax 10 years earlier). After an extremely successful career as a rhythm-and-blues artist, Hunter elected to go pop in 1950, immediately breaking onto the charts with "I Almost Lost My Mind." In 1956 he had a knockout hit with his own "Since I Met You Baby." He was one of the first R&B singers to record country material, cutting Hank Williams' songs 10 years before Ray Charles would make it respectable. After a brief comeback in 1971, Hunter died on Nov. 8, 1974.

Hunter, Tab   Your basic 1950s teenage heartthrob, Tab Hunter (born Arthur Kelm on July 11, 1931 in New York City) made his career in television and the movies, breaking into recording in 1957 with "Young Love," number one for six weeks.

Hurt, Mississippi John
Born in 1895 in Teoc, Miss., bluesman Mississippi John Hurt recorded briefly in 1928 (including a rendition of the "Stack 'O' Lee Blues"), then was heard from no more until the blues revivals of the early 1960s, when he became extremely popular. His repertoire contained a number of ragtime "dance" tunes, unusual for a bluesman of that period but not surprising for a man who made his living with a guitar. He died in 1966.

Husky, Ferlin   Born Dec. 3, 1927 in St. Louis, Mo., Husky gave up working as a disc jockey to become a country singer. His 1957 recording of "Gone" went on to become a pop hit as well as a country hit, as did his "Wings Of A Dove" in 1960. He retains a strong following in country music and has had some bit parts in the movies.

Hyland, Brian   Born on Nov. 12, 1943 in Woodhaven, N.Y., Hyland was a sophomore in high school when he decided to record a novelty tune he'd heard that cashed in on the latest fad in beach wear. In 1960 his "Itsy Bitsy Teenie Weenie Yellow Polka Dot Bikini" did more for that bathing suit (and dedicated girl watchers everywhere) than a photo layout in *Look,* and his career was in high gear. He made a number of pop classics in the 1960s, including "Sealed With A Kiss" (1962) and "Tragedy" (1969). In 1970 he had a million-selling hit with "Gypsy Woman," written by composer Curtis Mayfield and originally a hit for the Impressions in 1961.

Ian, Janis Born on May 7, 1951 in New York City, Ian was a regular in the Greenwich Village folk scene when, at the age of 16, she recorded one of her own compositions titled "Society's Child." That song, about the romance of a white girl and a black boy, was an instant hit—and instantly controversial, far beyond its rather mild statement. The song was banned in many cities, and Janis Ian became a *cause celebre* in liberal drawing rooms across the country. But the angry young

Janis Ian

crusader image wore off fast, and by 1971 Ian chucked the whole thing to retire to Philadelphia and get married at the ripe old age of 20. Eventually she drifted back to her first love, music, and 1974 found her releasing a new album, *Stars*. That album introduced a new Janis Ian, an introspective balladeer, gently cynical about the trappings of success. It became an FM hit, virtually by word of mouth, as did a second album, *Between The Lines* (1975), which featured "At Seventeen," her first hit since "Society's Child," and the superbly crafted "When The Party's Over." Since then she has plied the college campus circuit with wholesale success, reminding each first-year college woman that she's not alone.

Ikettes, The A generic name for the shifting group of women singers (and dancers) who backed up the Ike and Tina Turner Revue in the 1960s. One incarnation—Alice Faye, Robbie Johnson and Josse Armstead—recorded several hits of its own in the 1960s ("I'm Blue" in 1962, "Peaches 'N' Cream" in 1965, "I'm So Thankful" in 1965), while a second included white soul singer Bonnie Bramlett— the first white Ikette.

Impressions, The Sam Gooden, Fred Cash, Ralph Johnson, Reggie Torian— Originally formed by Curtis Mayfield and Jerry Butler in 1956 in Chicago, the Impressions have gone on to become one of the most durable and influential black vocal groups ever. The first hit came in 1958 with "For Your

Precious Love," which through a foul-up was released as Jerry Butler and the Impressions— helping launch Butler's career and causing his departure from the group. Things really got going again in 1961 with the Mayfield-penned "Gypsy Woman." At first, the group stuck to straight rhythm and blues—"Talking About My Baby" (1964), "It's All Right" (1964)—but beginning with "Keep On Pushing" (1964), "Amen" (1964) and "People Get Ready" (1965), Mayfield and the Impressions moved to the forefront of the budding black consciousness in America. The Impressions somehow managed to bridge the gap between gospel music and the rhetoric of black power, culminating in 1969 with their powerful incantation "Choice of Colors"—one of the most profound songs dealing with the issue of race ever. In 1970 Mayfield left to pursue his own career, but within a few years the Impressions were back on top with *Finally Got Myself Together* (1974).

Incredible String Band, The Robin Williamson (vocals, guitar, other instruments), Mike Heron (vocals, guitar, other instruments)—Essentially a vehicle for the multitalented Robin Williamson and Mike Heron, the band was launched in Scotland in 1966 and became an immediate sensation on the folk circuit. Later the group was adopted by the budding flower power movement in Britain, which it barely survived. It eventually folded in 1974.

Ingram, Luther Born in 1950 in Jackson, Tenn.,

Ingram worked as a soul singer around the country before really hitting it big in the film *Wattstax,* a concert film of the best of the Watts-Stax soul artists. In 1972 he sang "If Loving You Is Wrong (I Don't Want To Be Right)," which became his biggest hit ever.

Ink-Spots, The   One of the most successful black vocal groups of the 1940s, the Ink-Spots (so named for their color, by the way) were a sensation in postwar America with "To Each His Own" and "Gypsy Woman," both in 1946. There are still at least two groups touring today as the Ink-Spots, both claiming the rights to the name. The Ink-Spots' biggest contribution to rock was providing the prototype (and the inspiration) for the hundreds of black harmony groups that would follow them. Eventually the black harmony craze was labeled "doo-wop," for the nonsense syllables used as the harmony parts in many of the most famous songs.

International Submarine Band, The   Gram Parsons (vocals), John Nuese (guitar), Ian Dunlop (bass), Mickey Gauvin (drums)—Launched by a young Gram Parsons (18 years old) while at Harvard University in 1964, the band cut one album, *Safe At Home,* which is considered by many critics to be the first country-rock album—a style that would come to dominate the early years of the 1970s.

Intruders, The   Sam Brown (vocals), Phillip Terry (vocals), Robert Edwards (vocals),

Eugene Daughtry (vocals)—One of the earliest Philadelphia Sound groups, the Intruders' success came in 1968 with "Cowboys To Girls," the first million seller for Kenny Gamble and Leon Huff's Gamble label in Philly.

Iron Butterfly   Doug Ingle (keyboards, vocals); Ron Bushy (drums); Jerry Penrod (guitar); Danny Weiss (guitar); Darryl DeLoach (bass); and others, including Lee Dorman (bass), Erik Braunn (guitar), Larry Reinhardt (guitar), Mike Pinera (guitar), Phil Kramer (bass), Bill DeMartines (keyboards)—The first of the supersuccessful heavy metal groups, Iron Butterfly took off from San Diego, Calif. in 1968 with the album *Heavy,* but it wasn't until later that year that the album *In A-Gadda-Da-Vida,* with its 17-minute title track, boosted the group to previously unknown heights. "In A-Gadda-Da-Vida" was the longest single ever recorded (at that time) and featured an unprecedented (and apparently endless) extended drum solo smack in the middle of the song (in concert, the rest of the band wandered offstage for a break while the drummer earned his pay). Virtually overnight Iron Butterfly was the hottest group in America, and the *In A-Gadda-Da-Vida* album became the first ever to go platinum. After *In A-Gadda-Da-Vida* (which was supposed to mean "In The Garden Of Life"), there seemed to be nothing the group could do for an encore. Following several more modest hits, group reorganizations and comeback attempts, the Butterfly finally returned to its cocoon.

Isley Brothers, The   Ronald Isley (vocals), Rudolph Isley (vocals), Kelly Isley (vocals), Ernie Isley (guitar, drums), Marvin Isley (bass), Chris Jasper (keyboards)—The three original Isley Brothers (Ronald, Rudolph and Kelly) launched their career in 1959 with "Shout," joined the twist bandwagon in 1962 with the hit version of "Twist And Shout" and eventually drifted to Motown in 1965, where they enjoyed a string of softer (up-tempo) hits, such as "This Old Heart Of Mine" (1966) and "I Guess I'll Always Love You" (1969). (Along the way they briefly employed a new guitarist named Jimi Hendrix, whose playing affected their later sojourns into rock.) In 1969 the group (with its own label) returned to hard funk with "It's Your Thing," a million seller that set the tone for the Isleys' future releases. The group continued in the funky-rock vein with "That Lady" (1973), a tremendous hit, and the next few albums, including the million-selling *Harvest For The World* (1976) and *Go For Your Guns* (1977).

It's A Beautiful Day   David Laflamme (electric violin), Val Fuentes (drums), Pattie Santos (vocals), Bill Gregory (guitar), Tom Fowler (bass)—Launched in San Francisco during the halcyon flower power days of the late 1960s, It's a Beautiful Day broke nationwide in 1969 with a debut album of the same name, featuring the cut "White Bird," which became *de rigueur* for hip FM programming around the country. After one other album the group folded, but

Laflamme and his electric fiddle surfaced in 1976 with another rendition of "White Bird" on his solo album of that name. It was still a spookily beautiful song.

Ives, Burl Born on June 14, 1909 in Hunt City, Ill., Ives worked as a successful movie actor (he won an Academy Award for *The Big Country*) and as an anthologist of American folk music while pursuing his own singing career, which he began in 1949 with "Riders In The Sky." He is best remembered for "A Little Bitty Tear," his biggest hit, in 1962 and his rollicking rendition of Bob Dylan's "I'll Be Your Baby Tonight" in the late 1960s.

Jackson, Chuck Born on July 22, 1937 in South Carolina, Chuck Jackson is best known for his rendition of Burt Bacharach's "Any Day Now" in 1962, although he has sustained his modest recording career since the late 1950s, when he toured with Jackie Wilson.

Jackson, Millie Born in 1944 in Georgia and raised in a strictly religious home, Millie Jackson has emerged as one of the toughest, sexiest rhythm-and-blues singers of the 1970s. Refusing a move to the safer confines of disco, Jackson has followed her 1972 hit of "My Man Is A Sweet Man" with a

series of "other woman" type songs and such R&B classics as "If Loving You Is Wrong (I Don't Want To Be Right)," a big hit for Luther Ingram.

Jackson, Wanda The Queen of Rockabilly was born on Oct. 20, 1937 in Oklahoma City, Okla. and by the age of 13 had her own radio show there. In 1954, while a junior in high school, she began recording with swing star Hank Thompson and two years later she discovered rockabilly. From 1956 to 1961 Wanda Jackson was the Queen of Rockabilly, cutting such hits as "Honey Bop," "Mean, Mean Man" and "Riot in Cell Block #9," shocking the staid music world of the late 1950s with her unabashed sexuality and angry delivery. She toured with Elvis Presley and remained a tough rocker until 1962, when she retreated (as did many of the Memphis crowd) to the relative safety of country music, eventually returning to the church and gospel music.

Jacksons, The Michael Jackson, Marlon Jackson, Jackie Jackson, Tito Jackson, Jermaine Jackson—Originally called the Jackson Five and considered a sort of black Osmond Family, the Jacksons—all the sons of Joe and Kathy Jackson—established a following for themselves in the early 1970s with their energetic teenybopper soul music, such as "ABC" (1970) and "Never Can Say Goodbye" (1971). The elder Jackson, formerly with a group called the Falcons, encouraged his kids to play and helped land them a contract with Motown Records, which produced the bulk of the group's successes. In 1975 the group moved to Epic Records (and changed its name to the Jacksons to avoid contract hassles) and the production of Kenny Gamble and Leon Huff (the kings of the Philadelphia Sound). The result was the million-selling "Enjoy Yourself" (1977), but the music was, predictably, lacking the old

The Jacksons

soul fire. Jermaine Jackson had elected to remain with Motown (an earlier solo effort, the excellent "Daddy's Home," had been a hit for him in 1973). Michael Jackson has also been quite successful as a solo artist, including a 1972 number one song, "Ben," the theme from the movie by the same name. (Ben, incidentally, was a trained rat.) In recent years the group has returned to its earlier preeminence, and Michael Jackson has gone on to an extremely successful solo career.

Jacobs, Walter   See Little Walter.

Jam, The   Rick Buckler (drums), Paul Weller (guitar, vocals), Bruce Foxton (bass, vocals)—British New Wave group launched in 1976 as sort of the 1970s answer to the Who (at least that's what the press releases said). The Jam's first album, *In The City* (1977), and a successful American tour proved the band to be much better than its press releases had indicated.

James, Etta   In recent years James (born in 1938 in Los Angeles) has staged something of a comeback, working the clubs around New York City. She is best known as the singer of "Roll With Me Henry," released as "The Wallflower," the bawdy answer to Hank Ballard and the Midnighters' "Work With Me Annie" and "Annie Had A Baby" from the early 1950s. "Roll With Me Henry" was written by white bandleader Johnny Otis, who discovered James and hoped to write her

a hit. Although the original was thought too risque for the times (1955), the song became a national hit in a "cleaned-up" version—"Dance With Me Henry" by Georgia Gibbs.

James, Skip   Born in 1902 in Mississippi, Skip James was one of the true pioneers of the blues. Early on he mastered both the piano and the guitar and went on to record in 1931. The Depression ended his recording career (as it did for many of the bluesmen), and he eventually went to Texas, where his influence spread further. In 1964 he was "rediscovered" and returned to the stage at the Newport Folk Festival that year. He recorded two albums before his death in 1969. (See also John Mayall.)

James, Sonny   Born on March 1, 1929 in Hackleburg, Ala., Sonny James came out rocking in 1956 with "Young Love" but quickly retreated to the safety of country music, where he remains today. He emerged briefly in 1969 with the hit "Running Bear."

James, Tommy, and the Shondells   Tommy James (vocals), Joseph Kessler (guitar), Ronald Rosman (keyboards), Michael Vale (bass), Vincent Pietropaoli (drums), George Magura (bass, sax, organ)—Tommy James and the Shondells emerged in one of the most fertile periods of rock music, the mid-1960s. Ironically the song that launched the group, "Hanky Panky" in 1966, had been recorded much earlier by

James for regional distribution. It was picked up by a Pittsburgh record store owner who was looking for oldies. "Hanky Panky" was such a success that James formed a new version of the Shondells and hit the road. He also produced an impressive string of hits, including "I Think We're Alone Now" (1967), "Mony, Mony" (1968) and "Crystal Blue Persuasion" (1969). In 1970 Tommy James became a solo act and a year later scored with a Shondell-styled hit, "Draggin' The Line." The success of Tommy James and the Shondells points up the powerful national longing for basic AM radio pop songs, despite whatever trends are prevalent at the time.

James Gang, The   Joe Walsh (guitar); Tom Kriss (bass); Jimmy Fox (drums); and others, including Dale Peters (bass, vocals), Richard Shack (guitar), Bubba Keith (guitar, vocals)—Launched in Cleveland in 1968, the star of the group was always Joe Walsh (now with the Eagles), one of the best rock guitarists around. The band opened for the Who—Peter Townshend admired Walsh's work—and made some excellent albums, notably *Rides Again* (1970) and *Thirds* (1971), before Walsh rode off into the sunset looking for a solo career. With Walsh gone, the band muddled on bravely, but the creative center was destroyed. The James Gang folded in 1974, re-formed in 1975 and, hopefully, is now gone for good.

Jan and Dean   Jan Berry and Dean Torrence met in the

late 1950s on their high school football team. They decided to make records and started recording in a garage. The records were wonderful—"Baby Talk" in 1959; "Surf City" in 1963; "Drag City," "Dead Man's Curve," "Ride The Wild Surf" and "Little Old Lady From Pasadena," all in 1964. They celebrated the great American institutions—cars, the beach and girls in bathing suits—and they made you feel *good*, maybe even better than the Beach Boys (close friends of theirs, incidentally) because the music of the Beach Boys always hinted there was something else, that summer must ultimately end. Jan and Dean would have no part of that. In 1966 Jan Berry, a fast car nut, totaled his Corvette on Whittier Boulevard in Los Angeles. He was paralyzed for almost a full year, with severe mental and physical damage. Dean eventually turned to a new career as a graphic artist. The two have since gotten together occasionally on stage and did some limited tours in 1980.

Jarrett, Keith   Born on May 8, 1945 in Allentown, Pa., Jarrett began playing the piano at the age of three and in the mid-1960s toured with some of the biggest names in jazz. Running against the grain of the jazz-rock fusion people of the 1970s, Jarrett stuck with an acoustic piano and traditional jazz instrumentation, which ironically led to his greater success with the young rock audience than that of most of the fusion players. In the late 1970s he established himself as one of the top jazz

performers (so named by such magazines as *Rolling Stone* and *Downbeat*) without as much as a bow to the fusion end of the business.

Jay and the Americans   Jay Black (vocals), Kenny Vance (vocals), Sandy Dean (vocals), Marty Sanders (guitar)— Formed in Brooklyn, New York City, the group originally wanted to be known as Binky Jones and the Americans, although, thankfully, cooler heads prevailed. In 1962 the group had a hit with "She Cried," only to lose the lead singer, Jay Traynor. David Black was eventually hired to fill the slot and changed his name to "Jay" to keep the group's credibility. The real turning point came the next year, when the group heard a song recorded by the Drifters called "Only In America." Atlantic Records was unwilling to release it because the lead singer not only aspired to get the girl, but also implied he could even become President, a goal that did not sit well with the folks at the record company. Jay and the Americans, being the right color, ended up with the song, which became a huge hit, and they followed up with the classic "Come A Little Bit Closer" in 1964. In the late 1970s the group tried to stage a comeback with little success. Jay and the Americans can still be heard at oldies shows, however.

Jay and the Techniques
Jay Proctor, Karl Landis, Ronald Goodly, John Walsh, George Lloyd, Charles Crowl, Dante Dancho—Formed in Philadelphia during the mid-

1960s, Jay and the Techniques produced a string of upbeat soul hits, including "Apples, Peaches, Pumpkin Pie" (1967) and "Keep The Ball Rolling" (1967), their biggest hit.

Jayhawks, The   James Johnson, Carl Fisher, Dave Govan, Carver Bunkum, Richard Owens—A Los Angeles group, the Jayhawks made the original version of "Stranded In The Jungle," a novelty number that became a national hit for the Cadets in 1956. In 1961 they had two hits under different names—"The Watusi" as the Vibrations and the classic "Peanut Butter" as the Marathons.

Jefferson Starship/ Jefferson Airplane
Originally formed in San Francisco in the mid-1960s, the Jefferson Airplane became the most famous psychedelic band from that city, combining drug-saturated lyrics (such as the hit single "White Rabbit") with superb musicianship and outstanding choice of material. Amazingly the flower-powered Airplane survived the transition into the revolutionary rhetoric of the Starship fairly easily. In turn, the revolutionary rhetoric gave way to love songs and, most recently, hard rock. The Airplane was originally formed in 1965 by Marty Balin and Paul Kantner (with vocalist Signe Anderson, Jorma Kaukonen, Jack Casady and Skip Spence). The break didn't really come until vocalist Anderson was replaced by the lead singer for the Great Society, an ex-model named Grace Slick. With Slick's soaring vocals, Balin's excellent songwriting and

Jefferson Starship with both Grace Slick & Marty Balin

Kantner's musicianship, the band prospered. As the decade wore on, the band became politicized—causing the nonpolitical Balin to split—and produced a series of radical, up-against-the-wall albums that, while hardly profound, were certainly inspiring. In 1973 the Airplane, floundering, became the Starship, with Slick and Kantner joining David Freiberg, Pete Sears, Craig Chaquico and John Barbata and Marty Balin returning to the fold. The results were a

whole series of new Starship hits, including the very successful "Miracles" in 1975. Eventually, both Balin and Slick left. Most people expected the group to fold. Instead, Kantner tightened up the group and came back strong in 1979 with *Freedom At Point Zero.*

Jeffreys, Garland One of New York City's contibutions to modern rock, Jeffreys mixes the varied styles of the big city—rock, R&B, a touch of

reggae—into a smooth blend. He became an FM favorite in 1977 with his *Ghost Writer* album, including the pounding rocker "Wild In The Streets" and the next year's "One-Eyed Jack."

Jennings, Waylon The most important and influential country artist to emerge in the 1970s, Jennings (born in 1937 in Littlefield, Tex.) toured with Buddy Holly as his bass player in 1959—in fact, he gave up his seat on Holly's ill-fated plane trip to J.P. Richardson, the Big Bopper. He came to Nashville in 1965 at the invitation of RCA studio head Chet Atkins and immediately started making waves. The central problem was that Jennings was unwilling to mold himself to the prevailing fad in Nashville, *de rigueur* for a country artist at that time. Jennings demanded artistic independence (something that went almost without saying for rock artists), and after years of bitter infighting, he got it. He turned to writers such as Billy Joe Shaver, who wrote the bulk of Jennings' watershed *Honky Tonk Heroes* album in 1973, and friend Willie Nelson to forge what became known as "outlaw" country music— essentially country shorn of its soppy strings and with a trace of rockabilly (*a la* Buddy Holly) returned. Jennings, Nelson, Tompall Glaser and the other "outlaws" were spectacularly successful, bridging the gap between country and the younger, rock-oriented music and permanently changing the dynamics of country music. In 1976 Jennings began working with veteran Memphis producer Chips Moman, who

107

has provided him with a string of monster hits starting with "Luchenbach Texas," the biggest selling single in the history of country music and a crossover pop hit.

Jethro Tull   Ian Anderson (flute, guitar, vocals), Martin Barre (guitar), John Evan (keyboards), Barriemore Barlow (drums), John Glascock (bass)—Launched in 1968 in England and called one of the premier bands in that country's progressive rock movement, Jethro Tull nonetheless achieved huge success in the United States by satisfying the need for "heavy" music. Tull (the name comes from the 18th century British agriculturist and inventor) started its career in the United States with the 1971 concept album *Aqualung,* which dealt with sick bums and religion— hardly subjects for the pop culture. But with Anderson's leering presence, standing on one leg like a maniacal stork and playing the flute, Jethro Tull really took off. While critics lambasted the group's overplayed, pretentious music, Tull's success continued through *Thick As A Brick* (1972) and *Passion Play* (1973), and, surprisingly, the music has worn well today, thanks largely to Anderson's distinctive vocals. The band continued on with some singles hits "Bungle In The Jungle" in 1975 until the mid-1970s, when it appeared to disband. But it returned a few years later to strong audience approval and is still going strong.

Jewels, The   The first rhythm-and-blues group to record "Hearts Of Stone" (1954). The song returned for an encore several times, including versions by the Fontaine Sisters and Otis Williams and the Charms and, later, the Rolling Stones and Bruce Springsteen.

J. Geils Band   J. Geils (guitar), Peter Wolf (vocals), Danny Klein (bass), Seth Justman (keyboards), Stephen Bladd (percussion), "Magic Dick" (harp)—Formed in Boston in 1969, the height of the psychedelic sixties, J. Geils stuck to the basic formula of white man's rhythm and blues. For a while the band's members dressed as fifties greasers, slicked-back hair and black leather jackets, which worked particularly well with Wolf's manic vocals. They produced nine high-energy albums, particularly *Ladies Invited* (1973) and *Blow Your Face Out* (1976), before the thrill started to run out along about 1978, roughly the same time vocalist Wolf began his short-lived marriage to actress Faye Dunaway, proving, perhaps, that it's hard to be trendy and sing the blues.

Since the Wolf/Dunaway breakup, the band has been rebuilding steam, and in 1980 its *Love Stinks,* including the title track, was well received.

Jive Five, The   Eugene Pitt, Richard Harris, Norman Johnson, Billy Prophet, Jerome Hanna—Launched in Brooklyn, New York City in 1959, the Jive Five broke big in 1961 with "My True Story" and continue working together today.

Joel, Billy   One of the very few superstars to emerge in the latter part of the 1970s, Joel was born on May 9, 1949 on Long Island, N.Y. and first made a name for himself in the mid-1960s as a member of a local gang and rock band called the Echoes. After years of piano lessons, his professional break came in 1972, when a Philadelphia radio station picked up his "Captain Jack," a ballad of suburban angst, which eventually led to his first successful album, *Piano Man* (1974). The single by the same name, an autobiographical study of Joel's years playing for nickels and dimes in a piano bar, was a hit, as well as "Travelin' Prayer" and the suburban soap opera "Captain Jack," recut on the album. In 1975 Joel, who had been living in California, returned to New York City both to live and to record. The result was the

Billy Joel

1976 album *Turnstiles,* with "New York State Of Mind," "Say Goodbye To Hollywood" (later recorded by Ronnie Spector backed by Bruce Springsteen's "E" Street Band) and "Miami 2017 (Seen The Lights Go Out On Broadway)." The album established Joel as a major artist and songwriter and kicked off a series of nationwide standing-room-only tours. His next two albums, *The Stranger* (1977) and *52nd Street* (1979), were even greater successes, featuring the hits "Just The Way You Are," which won Joel a Grammy, and "Only The Good Die Young" on *The Stranger* and the brilliant satire "Big Shot" on *52nd Street,* which earned him another Grammy. His *Glass Houses* album in 1980 continued his string of successes, both the album and the single "It's All Rock And Roll To Me" from the album made the charts. Joel retains a sense of the street that's unusual in an artist with his success, and his songwriting seems to get better with each album.

John, Elton Dubbed the Liberace of the 1970s, Elton John is one of the few stars to be confined entirely to that decade. For a period in the mid-1970s, he was the largest selling entertainer in the world, doted on by the press and adored by his legions of fans. And he has produced—along with lyricist Bernie Taupin— some of that decade's most striking songs: "Tiny Dancer," "Rocket Man," "Crocodile Rock," "Saturday Night's All Right For Fighting," "Philadelphia Freedom," "Island Girl" and "Bennie And

Elton John

The Jets," to name just a few. John was born Reginald Kenneth Dwight on March 25, 1947 in Middlesex, England. He had always sought a career in the entertainment business and at one time held down three jobs—messenger for a music publishing company, member of the group Bluesology and piano player at a local pub, where he regaled the crowd with such standards as "Roll Out The Barrel." As soon as he got enough money

to purchase an electric piano of his own, he began working seriously with Bluesology, which at that time had managed to become a backup group for touring soul musicians. Ultimately, Bluesology came to the attention of R&B hero Long John Baldry, who recruited the group to back him in 1967. Along about then Reg Dwight decided he could use a bit better name, so he borrowed the first from the band's saxophone player, Elton Dean, and the last from Long John himself—Elton John. Baldry eventually found a home on the bar curcuit, and Bluesology found themselves unemployed. John answered an ad for "New Talent" in the *New Musical Express.* When John showed up to audition, the only catch was that he'd never sung while in Bluesology. The result apparently was a music executive's nightmare, with John crooning out soupy Jim Reeves' country ballads. Since he could write music, however, they pointed him in the direction of another new talent, a lyricist named Bernie Taupin. John didn't meet Taupin for six months, but they eventually landed a job as a songwriting team, writing top 40 hits for such artists as Cilla Black. It wasn't until the late 1960s, in fact, that John and Taupin conceived a project of their own.

The first Elton John single, "Lady Samantha," came in 1969 and the first album, *Empty Sky,* came in June of that year, but it wasn't until the release of the album *Elton John,* containing the hit single "Your Song," the following year that his career really took off. By 1971 John was a huge American success, his albums quickly going gold there and around the world. His biggest hits were in the mid-1970s (those listed above), and his concert triumphs became legion. In 1973 he started his own record company, Rocket, and had successes with Kiki Dee (with whom he recorded the hit "Don't Go Breaking My Heart" in 1976) and old-time rocker Neil Sedaka, who

staged a remarkable comeback. By the late 1970s John's work was on the wane, partly a result of sheer exhaustion and partly the victim of changing musical tastes. In 1979, after a brief absence for the first time since the beginning of the decade, John returned to the charts with a song from an album produced by Thom Bell, the master of the Philadelphia Sound. That song was "Mama Can't Buy You Love," pointing a new direction—sans Taupin—for the 1980s, although it remains to be seen whether John can ever duplicate his phenomenal successes of the 1970s.

John, Robert   Born in 1946 in Brooklyn, New York City, John worked steadily throughout the 1950s and 1960s as a singer until 1971, when he had his only major hit with a remake of "The Lion Sleeps Tonight," a 1961 hit for the Tokens. The song is actually a reworking of a Zulu song called "Mbube," which was first recorded in South Africa in the 1930s.

Johnny and the Hurricanes   Johnny Paris (sax), Paul Tesluk (organ), Dave Yorko (guitar), Butch Mattice (bass), Tony Kaye (drums)—An instrumental group from the late 1950s, Johnny and the Hurricanes got started in 1959 with "Crossfire" and cut the classic "Beatnik Fly" the next year. Their only top 10 hit came later in 1959 with "Red River Rock."

Johnson, Robert   One of the most famous and most influential of the Delta blues

singers, Johnson remains, some 40 years after his death, a mysterious figure. He was born around 1910 and was murdered 28 years later; some say stabbed, some say poisoned, some even hint at "darker things." One thing is certain, Johnson produced one of the most important bodies of work ever—songs such as "Love In Vain," "Ramblin' On My Mind" and "Crossroads Blues" are staples in rock, performed by people like the Rolling Stones, Cream and many, many others. Johnson is one of the major influences on rock today, as seen by the depth of his impact on Mick Jagger, Eric Clapton, Duane Allman and literally hundreds of others. Johnson's music was dark music, with the Devil very real and breathing down his back. Pleasure—especially sexual pleasure—was something to be grabbed on the run, something to deaden the pain of an evil world, and the road was the only place to go. There is an element of terror in Johnson's music, made worse by the never-forgotten fact that there was no way out, no way to ever win the race. He remains a leading figure in the history of American music.

Jo Jo Gunne   Jay Ferguson (vocals, keyboards), Matthew Andes (vocals, guitar), Mark Andes (bass, vocals), Curly Smith (drums, vocals)—Formed from the successful California group Spirit, Jo Jo Gunne was off to a good start in 1972 with the single hit "Run Run Run." A series of swift personnel changes and the band seemed to stumble, eventually falling apart in 1974 with the appropriately titled album *So... Where's The Show?* The Andes brothers re-formed Spirit in 1976 with critical, if not commercial, success, while Ferguson moved on to a successful solo career.

Jones, George   Born on Sept. 12, 1931, in Saratoga, Tex., George Jones is one of the greatest country singers ever. He began his career in 1955 with the classic "Why Baby Why," an uptempo, rocking country number, and continued through "White Lightning" (1959), "She Thinks I Still Care" (1962) and "The Race Is On" (1964). Jones' personal life resembles the songs he sings. A marriage to country songstress Tammy Wynette proved a classic disaster, as did the relentless effects of the bottle. In recent years he's had serious personal problems, such as being charged by the police with taking a shot at his bass player, not showing at engagements and failing to finish recording work. A no-show at New York City's prestigious Bottom Line club, where he was to be debuted to a crowd of heavyweight rock critics, cost his record company a rumored $20,000, while a recent album, featuring duets with everyone from rock queen Linda Ronstadt to New Wave English rocker Elvis Costello, lay around for almost a year before Jones got to the studio. Amazingly, even as his friends were writing obits for him, Jones turned his career around with "He Stopped Loving Her Today" (1980) and a series of stunning performances, including one in New York City,

where he was joined by Linda Ronstadt. Jones is a living link to country music's past, where the boundaries between rock and country were not nearly so strong. It is fitting that not only country musicians, but the cream of rock and roll as well are giving Jones his just due.

Jones, Rickie Lee   Perhaps the most successful of a spate of women singers who launched their careers in the late 1970s, Rickie Lee Jones

had a hit single with "Chuck E's In Love" from her 1979 debut *Rickie Lee Jones* album, which also made the charts. Jones, living in Los Angeles, worked with musician/cult hero Tom Waits, which shows in her jazzy arrangements and stylish delivery.

Jones, Tom   Of all the whites who sang black music, none— with the exception of Elvis Presley—has been quite so

Tom Jones

successful as Tom Jones, born on June 7, 1942 in Wales, the son of a miner. Jones formed his own group, the Playboys, in 1962 and was very successful locally and, later, in England. The basis of his success was rooted in his love of American rhythm and blues and rockabilly—Solomon Burke and Jerry Lee Lewis were special favorites. He incorporated elements of that music into his own routine—his deep, soulful voice lent itself perfectly to the almost-gospel black delivery, and his overt sexuality was well suited to wild on-stage gyrations. In 1965 he put it all together with "It's Not Unusual" and his rollicking rendition of the theme from the movie *What's New Pussycat?* From then on he was an international star. In 1966 he followed the lead of Ray Charles and dipped into country music (as Charles had done so successfully) for "The Green Green Grass Of Home," an earlier country hit for Porter Wagoner but now permanently associated with Jones. *Fever Zone*, a landmark album issued in 1968, marked Jones at his best with such R&B hits as "Don't Fight It" (Wilson Pickett), "Hold On, I'm Coming" (Sam and Dave) and his own huge smash "Delilah." In 1969 he swept away all attendance records in Las Vegas and dominated the charts with hit singles and albums. Through it all, though, Jones was vilified by the critics, essentially for being too successful—the sight of women throwing various and sundry pieces of underwear on stage in Vegas was simply too much for an audience weened on the Rolling Stones. But

Jones remains one of the biggest stars in the world (although his music has drifted, predictably, toward the disco end of black music) and one of the most underrated.

Joplin, Janis   One of the brightest stars rock has ever produced, Joplin was a legend before she was 25 years old and dead before she was 30, the victim of heroin. Born on Jan. 19, 1943 in Port Arthur, Tex., nobody told Janis Joplin that you had to be black to sing the blues—indeed, the blues were as much a part of life for white Texans as black, and Joplin early on discovered the works of Leadbelly and Odetta to point the direction. She worked around Austin, Tex. and San Francisco through the early 1960s, singing her bluesy folk music. But things didn't begin to happen until 1966, when, back in San Francisco, she connected with a budding Bay Area cult band, Big Brother and the Holding Company (Sam Andrew, James Gurley, Pete Albin and David Getz). To front for an electric rock band, she had to shuck the last vestiges of her folkie training, open her mouth and *sing*. And after good local response, she walked out on stage at the 1967 Monterey Pop Festival and did just that, walking off stage with a Columbia Records contract and acclaim as a superstar, one of the greats. Big Brother cut one album for Columbia, *Cheap Thrills*, featuring Joplin's interpretation of Willie Mae "Big Mama" Thornton's "Ball And Chain" and a simply stunning rendition of "Piece Of My Heart." But Big Brother fell apart—largely under the larger-

than-life success of the band's lead singer—and Joplin went solo for *I Got Dem Ol' Kozmic Blues Again, Mama* (1969), a not-quite-as-satisfying effort. But by late 1969 Joplin seemed to have shaken off the demons that plagued her. She formed a new band, the Full Tilt Boogie Band (John Till, Brad Campbell, Richard Bell and Clark Pierson), and began working on a new album, *Pearl*. The album was almost completed when, on Oct. 4, 1970, she was found dead in a Hollywood hotel room from an overdose of heroin. *Pearl*, a masterpiece, was released early the next year. A third album, *In Concert*, was released in 1972. Joplin remains perhaps the greatest white blues singer, and her hard living, heavy boozing, little-girl-lost persona is now part of rock-and-roll legend.

Journey   Neal Schon (guitar), Gregg Rolie (keyboards), Aynsley Dunbar (drums), Ross Valory (bass), Steve Perry (vocals)—Formed in the early 1970s in San Francisco by former Santana members Neal Schon and Gregg Rolie, Journey has grown into an excellent, straightforward rock-and-roll band, finally breaking out of the West Coast in 1979 with "Touching, Feeling." That stunning Motown-sounding performance proved to be one of the most rousing rock records of the year and introduced Journey as a band to watch in the 1980s. Drummer Dunbar was replaced by Steve Smith after the hit.

Joy of Cooking   Toni Brown (vocals, keyboards), Terry

Garthwaite (vocals, guitar), Ron Wilson (harp, drums), Fritz Kasten (drums), David Garthwaite (bass)—Popular cult band from California in the late 1960s that, despite rave reviews for its premier album, *Joy Of Cooking* in 1970, never got beyond the cult status. Both Terry Garthwaite and Tony Brown have pursued solo careers in recent years (the band broke up in 1973), with Garthwaite enjoying moderate success.

Justis, Bill   Born on Oct. 14, 1926 in Birmingham, Ala., Justis got his start working as a sessions man at Sun Records in Memphis. In 1957 he cut his biggest hit, an instrumental called "Raunchy." He returned to work as a sessions man and, eventually, as a producer and arranger in Nashville.

Kansas   Kerry Livgren (guitar, piano, synthesizers), Steve Walsh (keyboards, synthesizers, vocals), Phil Ehart (drums, percussion), Rich Williams (guitar), Robby Steinhardt (vocals, violin), Dave Hope (bass)—Originally formed in Topeka, Kan., the group really got going in 1975 with a debut album titled *Kansas,* followed by *Song For America* later the same year. The group had a hit single in 1977 with "Point Of No Return," followed by "Dust In The Wind," from the album *Point Of No Return.* Like the Allman Brothers, Kansas' reputation rests on near-

constant touring. The group is also one of the few rock bands to do its recording in Nashville.

KC and the Sunshine Band   Harry Wayne (H.W.) Casey (keyboards), Rick Finch (bass), Jerome Smith (guitar), Robert Johnson (drums), Oliver Brown (congas), Ronnie Smith (trumpet), Denvil Liptrot (sax), James Weaver (trumpet), Charles Williams (trombone)—Launched in 1973 by H.W. Casey—better known as KC—and Rick Finch at TK Studios in Miami, the band really took off in 1975 with two huge disco hits "Get Down Tonight" and "That's The Way I Like It." Although there was much talk at the time of the "Miami Sound" (based on KC and his production of George McCrae and "Rock Your Baby"), the music has not fulfilled its earlier promise—despite several million sellers by the band. The basic problem appears to be a simple glut of the disco market and the inability of most of the disco groups to establish a solid identity beyond the dance floor.

Kershaw, Doug   Cajun fiddler Doug Kershaw, born on Jan. 24, 1936 in Tiel Ridge, La., is best known for his classic Cajun songs "Louisiana Man" and "Diggy Diggy Lo." An outstanding performer, Kershaw has yet to really break into the upper levels of rock stardom, although he is an extremely popular concert draw (thanks to his nonstop touring) and a regular on national television.

KGB   Mike Bloomfield (guitar), Rick Grech (bass), Ray

Kennedy (vocals), Carmine Appice (drums), Barry Goldberg (keyboards)—Another chapter in the apparently endless procession of "supergroups"—groups put together to showcase one or several big name stars—this one formed in 1975 as a showcase for Mike Bloomfield and Rick Grech. The debut album, however, failed to generate either audience or critical excitement, and as such groups tend to do, the band went to pieces, with Bloomfield and Grech beating a hasty exit.

King, Albert   Albert King (born on April 25, 1923 in the South) worked steadily as a rhythm-and-blues artist in the 1950s in Chicago with limited success. Eventually King made connection with Stax Records in Memphis, which turned his career around and made him one of the most visible blues-based guitarists. King's "Born Under A Bad Sign" became a standard for such white rock groups as Cream, and he continues to be one of the most successful practitioners of the blues today.

King, B.B.   If any man ever deserved the title of King of the Blues, that man is Riley "B.B." King, born on Sept. 16, 1925 in the tiny town of Itta Bena, Miss. and trained as a gospel singer. After World War II he came to Memphis, hanging out along that city's famous Beale Street, the Home of the Blues, and soaking up the music. He got a job as a disc jockey for WDIA, the city's only black radio station, and was given the name "Blues Boy," abbreviated to "B.B." In addition to playing the blues on

B.B. King

the radio, he began his performing career, scoring his first million seller in 1955 with the song that was to become his trademark—"Every Day (I Have The Blues)." He might have safely continued as the biggest blues artist ever (he had already been accepted by musicians as one of the all-time greats), but in 1968 he decided to try something novel and extremely risky—working with whites. A year later he began recording with such sidemen as Al Kooper and

Herbie Lovelle. The results were electrifying, and for perhaps the first time, a mass white audience responded enthusiastically to authentic blues instead of white interpretations. "The Thrill Is Gone," his 1970 classic with its slow, sensual opening, was an immediate hit and won King a Grammy. He also appeared before some 6,000 people at Albert Hall in London and received a wildly enthusiastic response. Since then King has carried on the message of the

blues to a whole new generation, and the legacy of Beale Street lives on.

King, Ben E.   A onetime lead singer for the Drifters, Ben E. King was born on Sept. 28, 1938 in Henderson, N.C. He left the Drifters in 1961 (after singing lead on that group's only number one hit, "Save The Last Dance For Me" in 1960) and launched his own career with the hit "Spanish Harlem" that year. He had his biggest success later in 1961 with the Mike Leiber/Jerry Stoller composition "Stand By Me," justifiably a rock-and-roll classic.

King, Carole   Carole King and her former husband Gerry Goffin were the best-known and most successful songwriting team of the early 1960s. Born on Feb. 9, 1942 in Brooklyn, New York, King formed her own rock group in the late 1950s, when she produced perfectly awful songs with names like "Baby Sittin'" and "Queen of the Beach" (her greatest hit, so to speak, was that Neil Sedaka dedicated his song "Oh, Carol" to her). In 1958 she married Gerry Goffin. With King writing the music and Goffin the lyrics, their first hit came in 1960 with the Shirelles' "Will You Still Love Me Tomorrow," which was followed by such classics as "Up On The Roof" (for the Drifters), "Loco-motion" (for their babysitter, Little Eva), "Go Away Little Girl" (for Steve Lawrence), "Take Good Care Of My Baby" (for Bobby Vee), "Don't Bring Me Down" (for the Animals), "Wasn't Born To Follow" (for the Byrds) and literally hundreds of others,

114

out-writing everyone except John Lennon and Paul McCartney.

In 1971, after returning to performing with her *Writer* album the previous year, she released *Tapestry,* which went on to become one of the biggest selling albums of all time. (It was knocked out of the top slot by the glut of huge sellers, led by the *Saturday Night Fever* movie soundtrack, in the late 1970s.) The music was soft and intimate, perfect for the times, and King became an instant superstar. Her recent albums have tended to be more and more self-indulgent, although her 1980 remake of her own "One Fine Day" (originally cut by the Chiffons in 1963) got her back on the charts. *Tapestry,* with its "You've Got A Friend," "Will You Still Love Me Tomorrow" and "It's Too Late," remains one of rock's most eloquent statements.

King, Freddie   Born on Sept. 30, 1934 in Longview, Tex., Freddie King turned away from rhythm and blues when the success of bluesman B.B. King made straight blues commercially viable. He worked steadily with white musicians, especially Eric Clapton, building a substantial body of work (*Burglar* and *Larger Than Life* were his last two albums). He died on Dec. 27, 1976 in Dallas, Tex., apparently of heart failure.

King Crimson   Robert Fripp (guitar, mellotron), Ian McDonald (reeds, keyboards), Greg Lake (bass, vocals), Mike Giles (drums), Pete Sinfield (synthesizer)—One of the best-known and most successful of

the English "art-rock" bands of the late 1960s, King Crimson was essentially the brainchild of eclectic musician Robert Fripp, who put the group together in 1969. The music was a bizarre conglomeration of rock, jazz, classical and electronic, with a healthy dose of fantasy and science fiction on the side. The first and most successful album, titled *In The Court Of The Crimson King,* came in 1969. The album was widely hailed as a masterpiece, obscure, melodic rock and roll that found an immediate home on underground FM stations everywhere. The problem seemed to be following up an underground classic, and King Crimson spent its remaining five years trying to do just that. Fripp ran through dozens of musicians (including at one point a piano player named Elton John) while producing eight other albums, none of which came close to the haunting power of *The Crimson King.* In 1974 Fripp threw in the towel and left to pursue his own career. In addition to its (at times) brilliant music, King Crimson also served as home for some of England's finest rock musicians, including Fripp, Greg Lake (Emerson, Lake and Palmer), Boz Burrell (Bad Company), Bill Bruford (Yes) and John Wetton (Family).

Kingfish   Bob Weir (guitar, vocals), Dave Torbert (bass, vocals), Matthew Kelly (guitar, harp, vocals), Robby Hoddinott (guitar), Chris Herold (drums)—Formed by Bob Weir of the Grateful Dead and Dave Torbert of the New Riders of the Purple Sage in 1976, Kingfish never quite jelled,

despite an excellent debut album, *Kingfish,* and a good follow-up, *Live 'N' Kicking.* The debut album, by the way, features an outstanding cut of Marty Robbins' cowboy epic "Big Iron," probably the only existing example of a rock-and-roll shootout song.

Kingsmen, The   Lynn Easton (vocals, sax), Gary Abbott (drums), Don Gallucci (organ), Mike Mitchell (guitar), Norman Sundholm (guitar, bass)—Launched in Portland, Ore. in 1957 by high school freshman Lynn Easton, the Kingsmen worked as one of the Northwest's best bar bands before their huge hit "Louie Louie" in 1963. The song is remembered not for its fine rhythm-and-blues delivery, but rather for the terrific controversy, which continues to this day, over its "dirty lyrics." Easton's growled vocals were not even remotely understandable (one of the song's greatest appeals), and a wildfire rumor swept the country that the growling covered some explicitly sexual images. Knowing the *real* lyrics of "Louie Louie" was the key to instant success in high schools across the country, and copies of the dirty stuff were actually offered for sale here and there. Alas, the real lyrics proved to be rather tame, but even today, when the song is played (as in the very successful movie *Animal House*), there's still lots of snickering going on.

Kingston Trio, The   Bob Shane, Nick Reynolds, Dave Guard—One of the best known of the folk groups of the late 1950s, the Kingston Trio was formed in 1957 in California and made a reputation on the San Francisco coffeehouse circuit before launching a recording career in 1958 with "Scarlet Ribbons." The Trio continued with a string of hits; some of the most famous include "Tom Dooley" (1958), "A Worried Man" (1959), "Where Have All The Flowers Gone" (1962), "Greenback Dollar" (1963) and "The Reverend Mr. Black" (1963). The group broke up in the late 1960s.

Kinks, The   Ray Davies (vocals, guitar); Dave Davies (guitar, vocals); Mick Avory (drums); Peter Quaife (bass, vocals); and others, including John Dalton (bass), Alan Holmes (sax), Laurie Brown (trumpet), John Beecham (trombone), John Gosling (keyboards)—Best known as the promulgators of Ray

Davies' bizarre world view, the Kinks began life in the early 1960s as just another English rock-and-roll band, hitting the charts with "You Really Got Me" (1964), "All Day And All Of The Night" (1964) and "Tired Of Waiting For You" (1965). The next year, though, the group began to turn weird with Davies' "Dedicated Follower Of Fashion" and the wry "Sunny Afternoon." The metamorphosis was completed in 1970, when, after a long cold period, the Kinks emerged with "Lola," an inspired song about a boy who was a girl, or something like that. From then on the Kinks were the acknowledged kings of wry rock, music with a decided edge and perhaps the very best example of the rock artist as social satirist. Their approach is at times overblown (*Soap Opera* in 1974), at times

brilliantly introspective ("Celluloid Heroes" in 1976), but mostly just plain good. A 1979 single titled "(Don't Wanna Spend My Life) Living In A Rock And Roll Fantasy" said more about the current state of popular music than 500 pounds of *Rolling Stone* magazine.

Kirshner, Don   Rock impresario Don Kirshner is perhaps best known for the syndicated television show "Don Kirshner's Rock Concert," a staple of late-night television and one of the landmarks of rock presentation on the tube. He is also the man who invented the Monkees, television's answer to the Beatles in the mid-1960s. The ploy worked spectacularly, and in no time at all the Monkees were the hottest selling group of all time. Unfortunately for

The Kinks

Kiss

Kirshner, the Monkees wanted to expand beyond the constraints of their almost cartoon character roles, and Kirshner was forced to start over. He learned his lesson, though. In his next venture there would be no people at all. The members of the band would be cartoon characters for real, with their own animated Saturday morning TV show, and the music would be provided by sessions musicians. The result was the Archies, and their "Sugar, Sugar" was one of the biggest selling records in the history of the business. It does give one pause to think. . . .

Kirshner, who began his career as a music publisher, became the head of Aldon Music in New York City's Brill Building and nurtured some of the finest talent in the business, including the songwriting team of Carole King and Gerry Goffin. He is presently a producer (Kansas) and has his own Kirshner label.

Kiss Ace Frehley (guitar), Paul Stanley (guitar), Gene Simmons (bass, vocals), Peter Criss (drums)—Cartoon rock and roll at its peak, Kiss, launched in New York City in 1973, is a bizarre collection of Kabuki makeup, science fiction theatrics (a fire-breathing bass player, for instance) and barely passable playing. Kiss became the most popular band in America, Japan and many other nations in the late 1970s. What one can expect from Kiss is explosions, flame, simulated mayhem, grotesque greasepaint and numbing volume, all very exciting if you happen to be under 14 years old—which most diehard Kiss fans tend to be. Perhaps the group's best quality (aside from Kiss' superhero comic book style) is the fact that its members don't take themselves any more seriously than their fans do, which, in these times of insufferably pretentious punk bands and strutting lords of disco, is something to be thankful for. The best Kiss album was

Destroyer in 1976, featuring the hit "Beth" and the vastly underrated "Shout It Out Loud," a real rock-and-roll song. In 1979 the group made a brief stab at disco, which caused diehard Kiss fans great pain.

Klaatu A group of Canadian sessions players got together in 1976 and put out an album, dubbed *Klaatu,* which should have died without further ado. In one of those odd quirks, a rock critic wondered in print if this mysterious group was not in fact the Beatles reunited, and the album took off. When the hoax was exposed, Klaatu managed to choke out one more album, *Hope,* before fading into well-deserved obscurity.

Knight, Gladys, and the Pips Born in 1944 in Atlanta, Ga.,Gladys Knight has been performing—successfully—for most of her life—she made her first public singing appearance at the age of four and won the "Ted Mack Amateur Hour" when she was seven. The Pips were formed in 1958 with brother Merald (Bubba) Knight and two cousins, William Guest and Edward Patten. (The name Pips comes from the nickname of yet another cousin, James Wood, who acted as the group's manager.) Success was not long in coming—in 1961 the group had its first million seller with "Every Beat Of My Heart," a Johnny Otis song. Personal factors and problems with their record company (Vee Jay) hindered the Pips until they joined the booming Motown organization in 1967. The move led to their biggest hit up to that time, "I

Heard It Through The Grapevine" (1961)—also one of the biggest songs in Motown history. But the Pips felt they were being slighted by Motown, whose concentration seemed to be on such better known artists as Marvin Gaye, the Supremes and the Four Tops. In 1973 they moved to Buddah Records—leaving behind a number one song at Motown, "Neither One Of Us (Wants To Say Goodbye)"— and began a phenomenal string of hits starting with "Midnight Train To Georgia," a classic. Since then the Pips have become something of an institution, with their flashy stage show and tight choreography (at one point they were regulars in Garry Trudeau's "Doonesbury" comic strip). While Knight's recent material has leaned toward softer ballads, she is still more than capable of the old gospel fire, her first and strongest influence.

Knox, Buddy Born on April 14, 1933 in Happy, Tex., producer Buddy Knox began his career in the mid-1950s as a member of the Rhythm Orchids with Jimmy Bowen (now head of Elektra Records' country division in Nashville). In 1957 he released a song that he and Bowen had written called "Party Doll," and it was an instant smash. A second Knox hit in 1960 became something of a classic— "Lovey Dovey."

Kooper, Al Al Kooper's name and reputation winds through rock music like a minor refrain, beginning somewhat ignobly with the novelty hit "Short Shorts" (by

the Royal Teens) in 1958 and advancing through numerous phases of pop and rock. He launched his underground genius reputation as the organist on Bob Dylan's landmark "Like A Rolling Stone" single and the album *Blonde On Blonde* (1965-66). From there he went on to form the Blues Project, which he abandoned for Blood, Sweat and Tears in 1968. He only stayed there long enough for one album (many critics say the group's best album), *Child Is Father To The Man,* before moving on to become a superstar in his own right with his *Super Session* album in 1968, featuring Mike Bloomfield (the Paul Butterfield Blues Band; Electric Flag) and Stephen Stills (Buffalo Springfield; Crosby, Stills, Nash and Young). In the 1970s he worked as a sessions man (for Dylan, the Rolling Stones, Jimi Hendrix and B.B. King), a producer (for Lynyrd Skynyrd, the Tubes, Nils Lofgren and Kooper's own Sounds of the South label) and as a solo artist, ironically his least successful venture.

Kossoff, Paul Born on Sept. 14, 1950 in London, Kossoff first sprang to public attention in 1968 as the guitarist for the group Free. His fluid, flamboyant guitar style earned him a huge following, but problems with drugs and a recurring heart ailment (that would ultimately cause his death) forced an early retirement in 1973. He returned in 1975, assembled a group, which he named after his 1973 album, *Back Street Crawler,* and produced a second album, *The Band Plays On.* A tour slated to boost the album was postponed when Kossoff suffered a serious heart attack. He refused to be daunted, however, and a second tour was scheduled for early 1976, after he had played briefly with the band at the end of the previous year. But on March 19, 1976 Kossoff died, a victim of the heart ailment he'd struggled to overcome.

Kottke, Leo   Born in Athens, Ga., guitarist Leo Kottke has built a powerful following for his mild acoustical music— definitely running against the tide in the rock years. He first became well known working for John Fahey's Takoma Records in the early 1970s (*Six And Twelve String Guitar*) in 1971 and went on to gather an even larger following on Chrysalis Records in the late 1970s (*Leo Kottke* in 1976). He is one of the few acoustical guitarists—indeed, if not the *only*—to continue building a career in a heavily electric rock market.

Kraftwerk   Ralf Hutter (vocals, keyboards, various other instruments, electronics), Florian Schneider (vocals, keyboards, various other instruments, electronics)—To date the ultimate in electronic music. The German group Kraftwerk got its beginnings, appropriately, in the superindustrialized Duesseldorf complex in the late 1960s. The group's music is repetitive in the extreme— almost hypnotic, in fact—as *Autobahn,* Kraftwerk's 1974 FM hit album and single, clearly showed. The next two

albums, *Radio-Activity* and *Trans-Europe Express,* revealed the band still enamored with the gadgetry and sounds possible from its electronic machines, although Kraftwerk has yet to duplicate its earlier success.

Kramer, Billy J.   Born on Aug. 19, 1943 in Liverpool, England, Kramer worked as an engineering apprentice on the British railway system before linking up with Beatles manager Brian Epstein in 1963. The result was a string of hits, including "Do You Want To Know A Secret" (1963), "Bad To Me" (1964), "Little Children" (1964) and others, before Kramer faded away as the British Invasion ebbed.

Krekel, Tim   Born in 1950 in Louisville, Krekel is one of the best rockabilly-styled sessions guitarists working today. He has also toured with Billy Swan and Jimmy Buffett. Krekel released a solo album in 1979 but it was quickly caught up in the apparent collapse of his label, Capricorn Records.

Kristofferson, Kris   Born on June 22, 1936 in Brownsville, Tex., Kristofferson has almost single-handedly brought Nashville into modern times with his expressive, explicit— and extremely commercial— songwriting. A Rhodes scholar and an Army helicopter pilot, he came to Nashville in 1965 and took a job as the janitor at Columbia Studios. His break came when Roger Miller recorded his "Me And Bobby McGee" (which would become a major hit for fellow Texan Janis Joplin in 1971) in the late 1960s, followed by Johnny

Kris Kristofferson

Cash's recording of his "Sunday Morning Coming Down." Kristofferson followed with a series of hit songs, both for himself and other artists, including "Help Me Make It Through The Night," "Why Me Lord," "For The Good Times," "Jesus Was A Capricorn" and "Stranger." He has lately gone wholeheartedly into movies, especially since his marriage to singer Rita Coolidge appears on the rocks. His work in films has included major roles in *Alice Doesn't Live Here Anymore, The Sailor Who Fell from Grace with the Sea, A Star Is Born* and, most recently, *Convoy,* a tremendous failure based on the country song by the same name. Kristofferson's lyrics helped jerk country music away from its soppy middle-of-the-road sound during the 1960s into a new, more dynamic realism that eventually spelled success for this type of music in a big way.

LaBelle Patti LaBelle, Nona Hendryx, Sarah Dash—These three women became a virtual phenomenon in the mid-1970s with their outrageous (and revealing) science fiction stage attire and suggestive lyrics (although the suggestion was in French) to their song "Lady Marmalade," which exploded onto the charts in 1976. The song, recounting the exploits of a New Orleans prostitute, was absolutely riveting, a virtuoso performance that made LaBelle an overnight household word. Actually the three had been working together since the early 1960s, when, as Patti LaBelle and the Blue Belles, they had a string of hits, beginning with "I Sold My Heart To The Junkman" (1962). The group became LaBelle in 1970 after consultation with former British television ace Vicki Wickham, who scrapped the sixties vocal group material for the science fiction fantasy material of the 1970s. While LaBelle became one of the most visible groups of the mid-1970s, the three lasted only until 1976, when the pressures of having been together for well over a decade sent Nona Hendryx, Patti LaBelle and Sarah Dash in search of successful solo careers, which have thus far eluded each of them.

Lane, Ronnie Best known as a member of Small Faces (later, simply the Faces), Lane, something of a bass-playing

Flying Dutchman, left that group in 1973. He has since worked with his own group, Slim Chance, and behind numerous others.

Larson, Nicolette Raised in Kansas City, Mo., Larson first came to attention in the mid-1970s as a polished studio singer on the West Coast (after briefly touring as vocalist with Commander Cody and working duets with Hoyt Axton). She worked with Emmylou Harris, Neil Young, Linda Ronstadt and many others in the West Coast scene before making *Nicolette,* her own critically acclaimed debut album in 1978, and its hit single "Lotta Love," written by friend Neil Young. She is also given credit for being the prime mover behind the nationwide craze for roller skating, since she badgered all her friends into trying it and her friends get their pictures taken a lot.

Leadbelly (Huddie Leadbetter) In a large part, Huddie Leadbetter is the man responsible for the continued interest in traditional black music today. Born in 1884 near Shreveport, La., Leadbetter's life—at least the early part of it—was violent in the extreme. He did time for murder, although he claimed he acted in self-defense; escaped from a chain gang, on which he was serving time for assault; and bore the scars of countless other fights. He was also a master of the 12-string guitar, and he absorbed music like a sponge. Wherever he went, he picked up the music of the area and added it to his huge repertoire. Blues, rhythm and blues, cowboy music,

dance tunes, jazz—all found their way into Leadbetter's seemingly limitless memory. In the late 1930s Leadbetter went to New York City, where he became the toast of Greenwich Village. He was in constant demand, and a good portion of his material was placed on record. Since his death in 1949 (shortly after a trip to Europe, where he spread the seeds of American black music in that fertile ground), his music has consistently led to the various rebirths of the blues and other black music, simply by being so accessible.

Led Zeppelin Robert Plant (vocals), Jimmy Page (guitar), John Paul Jones (bass, keyboards), John Bonham (drums)—The music of Led Zeppelin resembles a rock-and-roll thunderstorm, building to tremendous peaks of violence, then slipping quickly into calming lulls. The group was the undisputed king of heavy metal music and rated, with the Rolling Stones and the Who, as a contender for the title of the Greatest Rock-and-Roll Band in the World. Led Zeppelin grew out of the Yardbirds, or rather the New Yardbirds, which is what resulted when the rest of the band faded away and left guitarist Jimmy Page holding not only the name, but also an incomplete tour commitment. Page himself was practically a legend in English sessions circles. Born on Feb. 9, 1944 in Middlesex, England, Page had taught himself guitar by copying such thoroughly American licks as those of Scotty Moore on Elvis Presley records and James Burton on Ricky Nelson discs. He played on some of the most famous

English records, including the Who's "My Generation," Them's "Gloria" and even Tom Jones' debut hit, "It's Not Unusual," before joining the Yardbirds (on second invitation). When the group disbanded in 1968, Page scrambled around to find a band to fill in the tour dates. The first person he turned to was old friend and sessions star John Paul Jones (born Jan. 3, 1946 in Kent, England), and the two shopped around for the remainder of the band. The first choices, Procul Harum's Terry Reid and B.J. Wilson, were booked up, but they suggested the virtually unknown Robert Plant (born on Aug. 20, 1948 in Bromwich, England) and John Bonham (born on May 31, 1949 in Redditch, England) from the Band of Joy. The foursome recorded together for the first time on P.J. Proby's *Three Week Hero* album, and with that under their belt, they went on to complete the New Yardbirds' tour. The change of name supposedly came about when Who drummer Keith Moon remarked that the band would probably descend like a lead balloon." It stuck and Led—so spelled to avoid mispronunciation—Zeppelin hit the road. From the beginning the group concentrated on America, and the release of it's first album there in 1969 met with overnight success. By *Led Zeppelin II,* featuring the all-time heavy metal anthem "Whole Lotta Love" (a lift from bluesman Willie Dixon's "You Need Love"), the Zep was established as one of the biggest concert draws ever.

Perhaps the thing that set Led Zeppelin's music off from it's countless imitators, was the virtuosity of the band's individual members—some of the best rock musicians in the world. Furthermore, the band had the ability to mix ballad material with heavy metal in a format virtually unique to the Zep—witness perhaps the group's biggest hit ever, "Stairway To Heaven" (1971), a mystical ballad reflecting a general interest in mythology and Page's deep dabbling in the occult. By limiting its accessibility to the hungry public, the Zep managed to retain an aura of mystery, something that no other rock band had *ever* been able to sustain.

Drummer Bonham died on Sept. 25, 1980 of a reaction between liquor and a drug used in the treatment of alcoholism. In December 1980 the group announced that without Bonham, Led Zeppelin no longer existed.

Lee, Brenda   Spunky little Brenda Lee (born on Dec. 11, 1944 in Atlanta, Ga.) was all of 16 years old when "Rockin' Around The Christmas Tree" became an international hit song. Her other classics included "I'm Sorry" (1960), "I Want To Be Wanted" (1960), "Fool Number One" (1961) and "Break It To Me Gently" (1962), and she continued her career right through the 1970s. After about 1973 she drifted more toward country music. Her secret was her big, big voice, far too big for such a little person. She recently made a very successful comeback on the country charts, with her big voice still intact.

Lee, Dickey   Another veteran of Sun Records in Memphis, Lee (born on Sept. 21, 1940 in Memphis) first broke on the charts in 1962 with the tearjerker "Patches" and came back in 1965 with yet another weeper, "Laurie." Since then he's been a consistent country seller.

Le Fevre, Myron   One of the greatest "withs" in rock, Le Fevre has worked with practically everybody who is or was anybody—George Harrison, Eric Clapton, Dr. John, Stevie Wonder, Alvin Lee, Mick Fleetwood, the Atlanta Rhythm Section, Merry Clayton, Willie Nelson and Kansas, just to name a few. He is a great singer, trained in gospel music, but uneven in his recording. Somehow his guest appearances have always outweighed his solo work, although his album with guitar wiz Alvin Lee, *On The Road To Freedom,* shows him at his best.

Leiber and Stoller   Jerry Leiber and Mike Stoller were perhaps the most influential songwriting team in early rock—their songs had an immeasurable impact on the budding creature of rock and roll in the early 1950s, mainly through their expert shaping of the rhythm-and-blues idiom into younger-oriented rock music. Ironically, they were basically just a couple of white kids who really liked black music and decided to see if they were any good at writing it. The results were such classics as "Riot In Cell Block #9" (recorded by the Robins and later, in a revised version, by the Beach Boys), "Kansas

City" (originally "K.C. Lovin'," recorded by Wilbert Harrison and many others), "Hound Dog" (written for Willie Mae "Big Mama" Thornton and turned into household words by Elvis Presley, who tapped the duo to write the words and music for his movie *Jailhouse Rock*) and "Young Blood"/"Searchin' "(a two-sided hit for the Coasters, in addition to all the Coasters' other Leiber/Stoller hits— "Charlie Brown," "Yakety Yak," "Poison Ivy," "Along Came Jones" and "Little Egypt"). Later the two worked with the Drifters ("There Goes My Baby") and ex-Drifter Ben E. King ("Stand By Me") and many others. While they were not nearly so successful in the 1970s, they did produce the 1973 hit "Stuck In The Middle With You" for Stealers Wheel and have continued working as producers.

Lennon, John   Liverpool-born John Lennon was the first Beatle to record outside the fold, cutting his "Give Peace A Chance," an antiwar anthem, in 1969 with the Plastic Ono Band, basically whoever happened to be in his Toronto hotel room at the time. Born Oct. 9, 1940, he had formed the pre-Beatles group the Quarrymen while still in school. During the Beatles period Lennon combined with Paul McCartney to become the most famous and most successful songwriting team the entertainment world had (or has) ever seen, but his marriage to Yoko Ono in 1969 was one of the factors that contributed to the group's dissolution. After the Beatles, Lennon's recording career

John Lennon with Yoko Ono

ranged from mediocre to brilliant and all points in-between. He had several excellent hits, including "Instant Karma" (1970), "Imagine" (1971), "Mind Games" (1973) and "Whatever Gets You Thru The Night" (1974), as well as several numbingly dull albums. During the last half of the 1970s, Lennon went into semiretirement. In mid-1980 Lennon announced his return to recording, and his *Double Fantasy* album was released in late 1980, giving him a hit single, "Starting Over." On Dec. 8, 1980 Lennon was gunned down in front of his apartment house in New York City, the victim of an apparently deranged young man. Lennon's death touched off a worldwide mourning.

Lettermen, The   Bob Engemann (vocals), Tony Butalo (vocals), Jim Pike (vocals)—Beginning in 1960, while at Brigham Young University in Utah, the Lettermen became one of the most successful vocal groups of the 1960s with such songs as "When I Fall In Love" (1961), "Theme From *Summer Place*" (1965), "Secretly" (1965), "Traces" (1969) and "She Cried" (1970). They continue working, their soft harmonies still in demand.

Lewis, Furry   Bluesman, born in Mississippi around 1900 and best known as a fixture on the Memphis blues scene. Lewis was one of the most accessible of the bluesmen, being "rediscovered" time and time again (once by a writer from *Playboy* magazine while Lewis was cleaning streets for a living) and brought to the attention of white audiences. His blues had a particular effect on the Rolling Stones, who brought Lewis on stage for a couple of numbers during a mid-1970s tour, and Joni Mitchell, who was so impressed with the aging bluesman and his stories that she dedicated a song, "Old Furry Sings The Blues," to him several years ago.

Furry Lewis died on Sept. 14, 1981 in Memphis.

Lewis, Gary, and the Playboys   Gary Lewis (drums), Al Ramsey (guitar), John R. West (guitar), David Walker (keyboards), David Costell (bass)—The Playboys, headed by comedian Jerry Lewis' son Gary, began their career in California in 1964 as one of the house bands at Disneyland, moving from there to television's popular "Shindig" show. The band leaped onto the charts in 1965 with "This Diamond Ring" and continued the string until 1966, when Gary Lewis began a two-year stint in the service. Although the Playboys continued to release music recorded before Lewis' departure, the thrill was obviously gone. By the time Lewis was back in harness, it was impossible to rekindle the fire, and the Playboys faded away.

Lewis, Jerry Lee   Faced with Jerry Lee Lewis (born on Sept.

Jerry Lee Lewis

29, 1935 in Ferriday, La.), the other so-called wild men of rock and roll quail to pussycats. With his insane piano pounding, shouted lyrics and manic stage show, Lewis, who once studied the ministry and time and time again has threatened to go back, rivaled Elvis Presley as the greatest of the Sun Records rockabilly artists. In 1957 he cut "Whole Lotta Shakin' Goin' On" and "Great Balls Of Fire," securing his place in the rock pantheon. Not satisfied, he cut such classics as "High School Confidential," "Breathless," "You Win Again" and "High Heel Sneakers." Then, with his characteristic arrogance, he brought his career to a grinding halt when he married his 13-year-old cousin, Myra. America was scandalized, and Jerry Lee Lewis didn't care. He turned to country music, where, after several lean years, he became an established star.

In the mid-1970s he moved into the upper echelon of country artists, while working as a rock revivalist in the many nostalgia shows. In 1979, though, he decided to return to rock and roll, changing to Elecktra Records and releasing *Jerry Lee Lewis,* an incredibly hard rocking album that showed him completely in control and with none of the old fires diminished. Predictably it was a country and rock hit, particularly "Rockin' My Life Away," the four-word story of his life. Unfortunately his personal life remains in shambles—drugs, liquor, illness, back taxes and personal tragedy have combined to shackle the rock-and-roll wild man.

Lewis, Ramsey (Ramsey Lewis Trio)   Ramsey Lewis (piano), Eldee Young (bass), Isaac "Red" Holt (drums)—Formed in the mid-1950s as a jazz trio, the Ramsey Lewis Trio achieved a measure of pop success 10 years later with their version of Dobie Gray's "The In Crowd" (1965), "Hang On Sloopy" (1965) and "Wade In The Water" (1966). Holt and Young later left to form Young-Holt Unlimited ("Soulful Strut," 1968) and were replaced by Cleveland Eaton and Maurice White, who left in 1969 to organize Earth, Wind and Fire. Lewis continued as a solo artist.

Liar   Dave Taylor (vocals), Paul Travis (assorted instruments), Clive Brooks (drums), Dave Burton (vocals, guitar), Steve Mann (guitar)—Launched in 1977 in England by Dave Taylor, formerly with the very successful singles band Edison Lighthouse ("Love Grows" in 1970), the band has concentrated on straightforward rock and roll, beginning with *Set The World On Fire.* An up and coming ensemble.

Lightfoot, Gordon

Canadian folksinger Gordon Lightfoot (born around 1939 in Orillia, Canada) is best known as a prolific and expressive songwriter, with over 400 tunes to his credit, as well as a successful performer. He moved to Los Angeles in 1958 to study music, but soon dropped out to work in the business. An early association with the folk duo Ian and Sylvia, also Canadians, led to his first recorded song. His first album, *Lightfoot* in 1966, resulted in his being named Canada's top male vocalist. His songs, such as "Early Morning Rain" "For Lovin' Me," "Cotton Jenny," "The Last Time I Saw Her," "If You Could Read My Mind" and "Cold On The Shoulder," have been recorded by an impressive array of artists, including Bob Dylan, Johnny Cash, Jerry Lee Lewis, Elvis Presley, Barbra Streisand, Judy Collins, Waylon Jennings, the Carter Family, Peter, Paul and Mary, Anne Murray and Glen Campbell. Lightfoot's own biggest hits came in 1971 with "If You Could Read My Mind" and in 1976 with "The Wreck Of The Edmund Fitzgerald," an outstanding story song with an air of mythology.

Lighthouse   Robert McBride (vocals), Ralph Cole (guitar), Lawrence Smith (piano), Paul Hoffert (keyboards), John Naslen (trumpet), Rick Stepton (trombone), Dale Hillary (sax),

Donald Dinovo (violin), Richard Armin (cello), Al Wilmot (bass), Skip Prokop (drums)—Launched in the late 1960s in Canada, Lighthouse cut a number of albums before finding a top 20 American hit in 1971 with "One Fine Morning." The group folded in 1974.

Lightnin' Slim   Bluesman Otis Hicks, dubbed Lightnin' Slim, was born in 1915 in St. Louis, Mo. and is regarded as one of the better blues guitar players. He worked southern Louisiana, especially Baton Rouge, where he grew up and recorded for the Nashville-based Excello Records. He is remembered for such numbers as "Hoo-Doo Blues" and "Bad Luck And Trouble."

Limelighters, The   Leo Gottlieb (bass), Glenn Yarborough (guitar, vocals), Alex Hassilev (guitar, banjo)—Launched in Los Angeles in 1959, this harmony group is best known for "A Dollar Down," a hit in 1961, and for Glenn Yarborough, who went on to pursue a successful solo career ("Baby The Rain Must Fall" in 1965).

Lindisfarne   Alan Hull (guitar, vocals), Ray Jackson (harp, mandolin), Ray Laidlaw (drums), Rod Clements (bass, violin), Simon Cowe (guitar)—Originally started as a folk-rock act in England in the late 1960s, the band (working with Bob Johnson, famous as Dylan's producer) was a force on the U.K. charts, particularly in 1972 ("Meet Me On The Corner" and "Lady Eleanor") until its members went their separate ways in 1973. A re-

formation of the group several years later went nowhere.

Little Anthony and the Imperials   Dubbed Little Anthony by influential 1950s deejay Alan Freed, Anthony Gourdine (born Jan. 8, 1940 in New York, N.Y.) and his Imperials—Clarence Collins (vocals), Kenny Seymour (guitar), Ernest Wright (vocals) and Sam Strain (vocals)—burst out of Brooklyn in 1958 with "Tears On My Pillow" and went on to become one of the best-known and best-remembered groups of the 1950s and 1960s. Their hits included "Shimmy Shimmy Ko Ko Bop" (1959), "I'm On The Outside (Looking In)" (1964), "Goin' Out Of My Head" (1964), "Hurt So Bad" (1965) and "Take Me Back" (1965). The group continued to make the circuit of nightclubs and remained, even into the late 1970s, a strong draw. Little Anthony currently performs as a solo act.

Little Esther   Esther Phillips was born on Dec. 23, 1935 in Houston, Tex. and raised in Los Angeles, where she linked up with bandleader Johnny Otis in 1950, when she was 15. Singing in the tradition of Sarah Vaughan and Billie Holiday, Little Esther scored an R&B hit with the Otis-penned "Double Crossin' Blues" in 1950 and followed with other hits over the next two years. After a long layoff she cut a rhythm-and-blues version of "Release Me," which was a national hit in 1963. During the mid-1960s she toured England with the Beatles and recorded with Jeff Beck, and her records sold well, particularly in the early 1970s. She continues to perform her stylish rhythm and blues.

Little Eva   Eva Narcissus Boyd (born in 1944 in North Carolina) wanted to grow up to be either a nurse or a singer, but she ended up working as a baby-sitter for the songwriting team of Carole King and Gerry Goffin. What singing she did, she did around the house, prompting King and Goffin to write a song for her. That song was "The Loco-motion," a huge hit in 1962. Despite a few other releases, "The Loco-motion" remains her zenith.

Little Feat   Lowell George (guitar, vocals), Bill Payne (keyboards, vocals), Roy Estrada (bass), Paul Barrere (guitar, vocals), Kenn Gradney (bass), Sam Clayton (congas), Richard Hayward (drums, vocals)—Launched in the mid-1970s by former Mothers of Invention Lowell George and Roy Estrada (who soon left), Little Feat immediately built a reputation as a critics' favorite, although the group was never able to translate that good will into sales figures. One of its strongest points was the eclectic songwriting of George, who penned such classics as "Dixie Chicken" (for the 1973 *Dixie Chicken* album) and the truckers' anthem "Willin'" (for the earlier *Sailin' Shoes* album). Things picked up with the 1974 release of *Feats Don't Fail Me Now,* but the band headed into the end of the decade with cracks showing. In 1978 George left to go solo, producing a single successful album before his death from a heart attack the next year.

Little Richard   Richard Penniman was born on Dec. 5, 1932 in Macon, Ga. and pursued a recording career from 1951 on. That career was without particular success until 1955, when Penniman— working as a dishwasher at the Macon bus station—finally found a record company (Specialty) to listen to his bizarre brand of music. The result was "Tutti-Fruitti" (1955); with its mindless lyrics and machine gun piano playing, it became a giant hit. He followed that with "Long Tall Sally" (1956), "Slippin' And Slidin'" (1956), "Rip It Up" (1956), "Ready Teddy" (1956), "Lucille" (1957), "Jenny Jenny" (1957), "Good Golly Miss Molly" (1958) and "Kansas City" (1959). Since that time Little Richard has returned to the church, resurfacing briefly now and then for a bit of revival, then coming back to the fold.

What Little Richard brought to rock was a sense of the maniacal—the rock artist as lunatic—that far transcended anything which had come before. His shows were lunacy, but they were *inspired* lunacy. It was rock and roll pushed to the very limits of its new world,

Little Richard

125

and parents had some cause to be afraid for their children. Little Richard's exhortations to go all the way fell on receptive ears, and echoes of his music can still be heard throughout rock, from Beatle Paul McCartney's first tentative shouts on "She Loves You" to contemporary rock icon Bruce Springsteen's savage rendition of Little Richard's own "Jenny Jenny." More than any other early rock artist, Little Richard symbolized the free spirit of the new music. Ironically, one of the people who profited the most from Richard's work was crooner Pat Boone, who had a series of hits in the mid-1950s with extremely toned-down covers of Little Richard songs (most notably "Tutti Fruitti" and "Long Tall Sally," both in 1956).

Little River Band   Glenn Shorrock (vocals), David Briggs (guitar), Beeb Birtles (guitar, vocals), Graham Goble (guitar), George McArdle (bass), Derek Pellicci (drums)—Formed in 1975 in Australia, the Little River Band took America by storm with its 1978 hit "Help Is On The Way," from *Diamantina Cocktail* (1977). The secret? Catchy top 40 rock and roll.

Little Walter   Originally a harmonica player in Muddy Waters' band in the late 1940s, bluesman "Little Walter" Jacobs virtually defined the blues' harmonica. His style of blues harp introduced an element of jazzy bop to the blues, and that style has found its way into rock—most notably such English white bluesmen as John Mayall. Jacobs died in 1968. Among

his many R&B hits during the evolutionary years of rock, Jacobs cut two real classics, "Juke" in 1952 and "My Babe" in 1955.

Little Willie John   Born John Davenport in 1938 in Detroit, Mich., Little Willie John scored a hit on the R&B charts in 1956 with "Fever," which became a national pop hit for Peggy Lee two years later. He had another hit later in 1958 with "Talk To Me, Talk To Me" and in 1960 put "Sleep" on the R&B charts. He later died of pneumonia in prison, where he had been serving time for shooting a man. His style was emulated by the 1960s soul artists.

Lobo   Tallahassee, Fla.-born Kent Lavoie adopted the pseudonym in the early 1970s after a series of stints with local bands. His biggest success came in 1971 with the intensely hummable "Me and You and a Dog Named Boo." Although he had several other minor hits ("Rings" in 1974), he gradually shifted to producing, including Jim Stafford's quite successful "Spiders And Snakes" (1973).

Lofgren, Nils   Guitar wiz Nils Lofgren made a quick reputation for himself with a guest spot on the debut album by Neil Young and Crazy Horse in 1971. His own group, Grin, attracted a huge cult following. In 1975 he began a solo career with *Nils Lofgren.* While he continues making albums (mostly notably *Cry Tough* in 1976 and *I Came To Dance* in 1977) and enjoys substantial play on FM radio, he has yet to

step into the upper reaches of stardom.

Loggins, Dave   Born on Nov. 10, 1947 in Bristol, Tenn., Dave Loggins (a cousin of Kenny Loggins) had his first taste of success in 1972 when Three Dog Night, then riding high, cut his "Pieces Of April." Loggins' first solo success came in 1974 with his "Please Come To Boston." His music had since leaned more toward country.

Loggins and Messina   One of the most successful country-rock acts in the mid-1970s, Loggins and Messina was launched in 1971 when Jim Messina was tapped to produce Kenny Loggins' debut album. Messina was an accomplished engineer as well as a former member of the Buffalo Springfield (he sat in for the last album) and a founding member of the seminal country-rock group Poco. Loggins was a singer and songwriter, up until then best known as the author of the Nitty Gritty Dirt Band hit "House At Pooh Corner." Loggins and Messina struck it off immediately, and the album, *Sittin' In,* became a duet. It also became an FM hit, and the two cemented their place the next year with the rollicking hit single "Your Mama Don't Dance." By the mid-1970s, though, the pressures of superstardom began taking their toll, and Loggins' writing output dwindled to a trickle. In 1976 the pair parted with their *Best of Friends* album, and Loggins went on to launch a successful solo career.

Lomax, Jackie The first artist signed to the Beatles' Apple label in the late 1960s, Lomax has cut a series of vastly underrated albums, including *Livin' For Lovin'* and *Did You Ever Have That Feeling* in the early 1970s.

Los Bravos Michael Kogel (vocals), Antonio Martinez (guitar), Manuel Fernandez (keyboards), Miguel Vicens Danus (bass), Pablo Sanllehi (drums)—Originally formed in Spain (lead singer Kogel was from Germany; the remainder of the group were Spanish), the group moved to England early in the British Invasion years and changed its name from Mike and the Runaways to the more fitting Los Bravos. In 1966 the group had its biggest hit, "Black Is Black," featuring tour-de-force vocal work by Kogel. After a brief stint in the international limelight, Los Bravos returned to Spain.

Lost Gonzo Band Formerly the backup band for Jerry Jeff Walker, the Lost Gonzo Band began its own career in 1975 with the *The Lost Gonzo Band* album. Two more efforts failed to define the group, although the band's leader and lyricist, Gary Nunn, remains an excellent songwriter.

Loudermilk, John D. Born on March 31, 1934 in Durham, N.C., singer/songwriter John D. Loudermilk is best known as the author of a string of pop hits throughout the mid-1960s, including "Tobacco Road" (Nashville Teens, 1965), "Sad Movies" and "Norman" (Sue Thompson, 1961) and others. His own recording of "Language Of Love" became a

modest hit on both sides of the Atlantic in 1961.

Love, Darlene Born in Los Angeles, Darlene Love became one of producer Phil Spector's best finds. In 1962 she fronted for the Crystals on "He's A Rebel," shifting over to Bob B Soxx and the Blue Jeans for their 1962 hit "Zip-A-Dee-Doo-Dah." In 1963 she went solo, cutting "Today I Met The Boy I'm Gonna Marry" and "Wait 'Til My Bobby Gets Home," her best-known song. She presently works as a backup singer, with a brief excursion now and then into solo work.

Love Arthur Lee (guitar, vocals), Bryan MacLean (guitar, vocals), John Echols (guitar), Ken Forssi (bass), Alban Pfisterer (drums)—A band before its time, Love, formed in 1965 by ex-Memphian Arthur Lee, was one of the first Los Angeles rock

bands and a big underground hit through the mid-1960s. The band cut some great songs, including a cover version of Manfred Mann's "My Little Red Book" (1966) and its anthem "Seven And Seven Is" (1966), but never managed to crawl above the underground, despite numerous personnel changes (Lee was always looking for the right formula) and remarkably progressive music for the times. One interesting thing about the band was Lee himself, a black singer fronting a mostly white band, working hard to sound like Mick Jagger, a white singer who worked hard to sound black.

Lovin' Spoonful, The John Sebastian (vocals, guitar, harp), Zal Yanovsky (vocals, guitar), Joe Butler (drums), Steve Boone (bass)—One of the great good-time bands of the 1960s, the Lovin' Spoonful

The Lovin' Spoonful

was assembled by John Sebastian in 1965 after the breakup of the Mugwumps (which also featured soon-to-be Mamas and Papas Cass Elliott and Denny Doherty). Sebastian had spent some time down South and was impressed with the region's various types of music, which eventually found their way into the Lovin' Spoonful's music and set it apart from the run-of-the-mill New York City folk product. The group's 1965 album debut, *Do You Believe In Magic?*, was an overnight classic, featuring the title song (and the band's first big hit) plus "Younger Girl," "Did You Ever Have To Make Up Your Mind" and "Fishin' Blues." The Spoonful followed with an ebullient string of hits that included "Daydream" (1966), "Summer In The City," (1966), "Rain On The Roof," (1966), "Nashville Cats" (1966), "Darlin' Be Home Soon" (1967) and "You're A Big Boy Now" (1967). (Sometimes Sebastian's ebullience got the better of his knowledge, as when the Spoonful sung in "Nashville Cats" about those "Yellow Sun Records from Nashville." Yellow Sun Records were from Memphis.) In 1967 the group started coming apart, fueled by a drug bust that year. The next year, the Spoonful disbanded, with Sebastian weaving unsteadily toward a solo career.

Lowe, Nick Producer/bass player Nick Lowe began his career in the English pubs, eventually landing with the Brinsley Schwarz band in the ealry 1970s. In 1975 he signed with New Wave entrepreneurs Stiff Records and began

Nick Lowe & Rockpile

producing such hit acts as Elvis Costello, Graham Parker, the Damned and Clover. He also began working with Dave Edmunds in Edmunds' Rockpile band, which in 1979 enjoyed a very successful American tour.

Lulu Born Marie McDonald McLaughlin Lawrie on Nov. 3, 1948 in Scotland, Lulu began singing (as Lulu and the Lovers) in 1964. Three years later she was tapped to sing the title song for the Sidney Poitier movie *To Sir with Love*. The song went on to become an international hit, remaining on the top of the American charts for six weeks. She recently returned to recording with Elton John's Rocket Records.

Luman, Bob Country singer, born on April 15, 1938 in Nacogdoches, Tex. and best known for his 1960 country

and pop hit "Let's Think About Livin'." He died in 1979.

Lymon, Frankie, and the Teenagers Frankie Lymon (vocals), Herman Santiago (vocals), Jimmy Merchant (vocals), Joe Negroni (vocals), Sherman Garnes (vocals)— When the group was formed, Frankie Lymon wasn't even a teenager yet—he was 12 (all the other members were in their teens). In 1956, when Frankie was 13, the group recorded "Why Do Fools Fall In Love," which skyrocketed them into the national spotlight. They followed that up with a series of lightweight hits, including "I Want You to Be My Girl" (1956) and "ABC's Of Love" (1957) before Lymon left to go solo. In 1968 Lymon died of a heroin overdose.

Lynn, Loretta Perhaps the most famous female country

singer, Lynn was born on April 14, 1935 in Butcher Hollow, Ky., the daughter of a coal miner. Her life reads like one of her country songs—married by 14, six children, a grandmother by 32. But her songs have consistently struck out against the inequality of women—in fact, Lynn's song "The Pill" in the mid-1970s scandalized country music and made her something of a hero. Her autobiography, *Coal Miner's Daughter* (the title to one of her biggest hits), was on *The New York Times* best-sellers' list for nine weeks and was made into a movie.

Lynyrd Skynyrd   Ronnie Van Zant (vocals), Gary Rossington (guitar), Allen Collins (guitar), Steve Gaines (guitar), Billy Powell (keyboards), Leon Wilkeson (bass), Artimus Pyle (drums)—One of the best live bands in the history of rock and roll, Lynyrd Skynyrd (named after the group's high school gym coach, Leonard Skinner, who constantly rode the boys about their hair and manners) got together during the early 1970s in Jacksonville, Fla. and built a reputation as the South's best—and toughest—bar band. In 1973 the group was "discovered" in an Atlanta bar by Al Kooper. Kooper produced a first album, *Pronounced Leh-Nerd Skin-nerd,* which neither the band nor Kooper liked. But it did introduce what was to become Skynyrd's theme song—"Free Bird." The band opened for the Who on the English group's 1973 tour, which proved to be a major turning point. The second album, *Second Helping,* produced the hit single "Sweet Home Alabama," a chauvinistic answer to Neil Young's ridiculously anti-Southern "Southern Man." From then on there was no stopping Skynyrd. The group toured like maniacs, living on drugs and liquor and playing seven nights a week. By 1976 Skynyrd was one of the biggest concert draws in America; the band capped its touring with a live album called *One More From The Road.* On Oct. 20, 1977, en route to

Baton Rouge, La. to play another show, a private plane chartered by the band crashed, killing Van Zant, Steve Gaines, backup singer Cassie Gaines and roadie Dean Kilpatrick and ending one of the finest rock bands ever. Rossington and Collins re-formed into the well-received Rossington-Collins Band.

Mack, Lonnie   Born in 1941 in Harrisburg, Ind., Mack first broke on the music scene in 1963 with his instrumental version of Chuck Berry's "Memphis," which he followed with a second hit titled "Wham." The two songs revealed him to be an exceptional guitarist with a funky Duane Eddy-style twang to his playing. At that point Mack more or less disappeared, resurfacing seven years later to do two albums, then disappearing again. In 1977, seven years later, he released *Home At Last,* an

Lynyrd Skynyrd

excellent, though more country-flavored, album. He should be due again around 1984.

Maggard, Cledus   Also known as Jay Huguely, Maggard rode the crest of the craze for CB (citizens band radio) songs in the mid-1970s with his "White Knight" novelty hit. Oddly enough, Huguely was a former Shakespearean actor.

Mahal, Taj   Born on May 17, 1942 in New York City, Taj Mahal came into music through the back door — academia. While studying animal husbandry at the University of Massachusetts, Mahal developed an abiding interest in black music and culture, eventually becoming an expert musicologist. In the mid-1960s he decided on a full-time career in music and has been surprisingly successful — more than an academic, he evidences a deep love and understanding of the music, whether it be blues (*The Natch'l Blues*), West Indian folk music (*Music Keeps Me Together*) or his newer, funkier material (*Music Fuh Ya*).

Mahavishnu Orchestra, The   Launched as an informal gathering of sidemen for guitarist John McLaughlin in 1972, the Mahavishnu Orchestra became the most successful of the jazz-rock fusion groups, winning plaudits from both the jazz and rock ends of the spectrum. The first incarnation of the Orchestra consisted of Jan Hammer (piano), Jerry Goodman (violin), Billy Cobham (drums) and Rick Laird (bass), who

produced the outstanding *Inner Mountain Flame* in 1971. Incarnation Two included Jean-Luc Ponty (violin), Michael Walden (drums), Gayle Moran (keyboards, vocals), Bob Knapp (reeds), Steve Frankovitch (reeds), Ralph Armstrong (bass) and a string section; it lasted for two albums in the mid-1970s and then faded away. After a bit of solo work, McLaughlin turned to traditional Indian music, *sans* Orchestra.

Mahogany Rush   Hard rock Canadian cult band formed in 1970 and centered around guitarist Frank Marino, who emphasizes his Hendrix-like guitar style in every way possible. He is an extremely good guitarist, and the band has steadily picked up a following in the United States, especially among jaded rock critics.

Malo   Arcelio Garcia (vocals), Jorge Santana (guitar), Abel Zarate (guitar), Pablo Tellez (guitar), Richard Kermode (keyboards), Luis Gasca (trumpet), Forrest Buchtel (trumpet), Hadley Caliman (sax, trumpet), Leo Rosales (percussion), Raul Rekow (percussion), Richard Spremick (drums) — Soupy soft Latin rock from San Francisco, circa 1970; best known for the hit single "Suavecito," in 1972. Jorge Santana is Carlos Santana's brother.

Mamas and the Papas, The   John Phillips, Michelle Phillips, Cass Elliott, Denny Doherty — Billed by some as the first genuine "hippy" band,

the Mamas and the Papas were the brainchild of John Phillips in 1965. He saw the band as an extension of the New York City folk scene he'd been heavily involved with, and throughout the 1960s the group's superslick vocal harmonies (along with those of the Byrds) virtually defined folk rock. The Mamas and Papas began their career on the run with four huge hits in 1966 — "California Dreamin'," "Monday Monday," "I Saw Her Again" and "Words Of Love." Like Sonny and Cher, their hippy garb and outrageous looks were perfect for promotion, and they were soon seen regularly on television (which, incidentally, aided the budding counter-culture movement by providing acceptable models). The band came apart in 1968, precipitated greatly by the crumbling marriage of John and Michelle Phillips. Ironically, John Phillips heavily backed the Monterey Pop Festival in 1967, which launched the careers of Janis Joplin, Jimi Hendrix and the Who but showed the Mamas and the Papas as a band who hadn't grown in years. Cass Elliott went solo with some success, eventually dying of natural causes in London in 1974. John Phillips became a producer of both records and films, and Michelle Phillips became a surprisingly good actress, as did John's daughter from another marriage, MacKenzie Phillips.

Man   Mickey Jones (guitar, vocals), Deke Leonard (guitar, vocals), Terry Williams (drums, vocals), Phil Ryan (keyboards, vocals), John McKenzie (bass, vocals) —

Essentially a name in search of a band, Man was launched in the late 1960s in England and through the 1970s evolved into what one critic called England's answer to West Coast music. While the name remained the same, the band changed personnel on an apparently daily basis and finally broke up in 1976.

Manassas   Chris Hillman (guitar, vocals), Al Perkins (pedal steel), Dallas Taylor (drums), Calvin Samuels (bass), Paul Harris (keyboards), Joe Lala (percussion)—Best known as the backup band for Steve Stills after his departure from Crosby, Stills, Nash and Young, Manassas recorded two albums of its own (*Manassas* in 1972 and *Down The Road* in 1973) before being pulled apart from two different directions: ex-Byrd Hillman, Perkins and Harris left to join that short-lived "supergroup" the Souther-Hillman-Furay Band, while Lala was drawn into the brief CSN&Y reunion tour.

Manchester, Melissa   A superb vocalist who has yet to find her commercial niche, Manchester (born on Feb. 15, 1951 in the Bronx, New York City) was the daughter of a bassoonist in the Metropolitan Opera Orchestra. Her debut album, *Bright Eyes,* appeared in 1973, after an apprenticeship as a songwriter (with Paul Simon for a while), and her first hit came two years later with "Midnight Blue" from her *Melissa* album. She remains an excellent concert draw, and with the right song she should be able to take her place at the very top.

Mandel, Harvey   Best known as a member of Canned Heat, Mandel (born in Detroit) is one of the more renowned sessions men, playing guitar for such groups as the Rolling Stones (at one point it was rumored that he was the man slated to replace Mick Taylor, a job that Ronnie Wood finally got).

Mangione, Chuck   One of the more successful jazz-rock fusion musicians, trumpeter Chuck Mangione taught improvisation at the Eastman School of Music before having a fluke hit in 1969 with the album *Friends And Love,* which featured Mangione and the Rochester Philharmonic Orchestra. He became an underground legend several years later with the release of "Land Of Make Believe" (from the album of the same name), featuring a stunning vocal performance by Esther Satterfield, which was reissued in 1975 on his *Encore* album. Since then he has established himself as a consistent selling pop artist (closer to the rock end of the fusion) with such albums as *Chase The Clouds Away* and *Feels So Good.*

Manhattan Transfer   Tim Hauser, Janis Siegel, Alan Paul, Laurel Masse—At least once every couple of years a group appears on the horizon, becomes "the biggest thing since sliced bread," then is gone before anybody can memorize the names of its members. Around 1976 Manhattan Transfer burst out of the New York cult scene, complete with tails and tuxes and low-cut flashy dresses from the 1940s. The music was a melange of period

pieces, and for a while you couldn't turn on the television without seeing the group do "Tuxedo Junction" or "Chanson D'Amour." Manhattan Transfer quickly faded but hung on to its hard-core jazz following, even winning a Grammy in 1981 for "Birdland."

Manhattans, The   Blue Lovett (vocals), Sonny Bivens (vocals), Wally Kelly (vocals), Gerald Alston (vocals)—The Manhattans began their winning ways in 1965 with "I Wanna Be," and they've continued right on through the 1970s, sticking to the formula of soulful ballads, such as one of their biggest hits "Kiss And Say Goodbye" (1976).

Manilow, Barry   Born in 1947 in Brooklyn, New York City, Manilow seems an unlikely candidate for superstardom. He tends to be photographed with his beagle, Bagel, and he can't open his mouth without bringing down the wrath of critics everywhere. But beginning with "Mandy" in 1975, he became one of the biggest selling stars in music, and his songs routinely go to number one ("I Write The Songs" and "At The Copa"). Manilow began his career at the New York College of Music and, later, the prestigious Juilliard School of Music and then wrote commercial jingles and worked as an arranger for television shows. In 1972 he took a brief job as a pianist at New York City's trendy Continental Baths, where he met Bette Midler. He went to work for Midler as an arranger, director and pianist, coproducing her first two albums and guiding her musically. As her star seemed to decrease, Manilow's increased. His other hits include "Tryin' To Get The Feeling Again" (1976), "Looks Like We Made It" (1977) and "Can't Smile Without You" (1978).

Mann, Manfred Born Mike Lubowitz on Oct. 21, 1940 in Johannesburg, South Africa, Manfred Mann got to England just in time to join in the British Invasion. Mann (keyboards) and Mike Hug (drums, vibraphone) formed the group Manfred Mann and began turning out such hits as "Doo Wah Diddy Diddy" (1964) and "Pretty Flamingo" (1966). Although the original band—Hugg, Paul Jones (vocals, harmonica), Mike Vickers (sax, flute) and Tom McGuinness (bass)—sputtered out around 1968 (with a magnificent cover version of Bob Dylan's "The Mighty Quinn"), Mann quickly formed a new group with Hugg and kept on going until 1971, when it too collapsed. That year Mann put together Manfred Mann's Earth Band and in 1976 Mann and the band— Colin Pattenden (bass), Chris Slade (drums, percussion), Chris Thompson (vocals, guitar) and Dave Flett (guitar)—scored with another cover version, this time of Bruce Springsteen's "Blinded By The Light."

Marcels, The Cornelius Hart (vocals), Fred Johnson (vocals), Allen Johnson (vocals), Ronald Mundy (vocals), Walter Maddox (vocals)—Despite a brief appearance in the movie *Twist Around the Clock,* the Marcels

didn't outlive their superyear of 1961, when they made the top of the charts with their version of the Rodgers and Hart classic "Blue Moon," followed quickly by "Summertime" and "Heartaches."

Mark-Almond Band, The A jazz-rock ensemble centering around guitarist Jon Mark and reed man Johnny Almond, specializing in easy listening rock. The group reached its peak in the early 1970s.

Mar-Keys, The Steve Cropper (guitar), Jerry Johnson (drums), Donald "Duck" Dunn (bass), Charles Axton (sax), Don Nix (sax), Wayne Jackson (trumpet), Jerry Lee "Smoochie" Smith (piano, organ)—One of the original Memphis soul groups, the Mar-Keys began their instrumental career while still in high school. They had a national hit in 1961 with "Last Night," written by producer Chips Moman. The group went on to become the house band at Satellite Records, which became Stax, and two of its members, Cropper and Dunn, formed the basis of the much-vaunted "Memphis Sound" when they left the group to work with drummer Al Jackson and organist Booker T. Jones as Booker T. and the MGs (Memphis Group). Cropper and Dunn presently tour with the Blues Brothers.

Marley, Bob Reggae was going to be the Next Big Thing in American music—or so predicted most all the critics around the mid-1970s—and when reggae broke big, Bob Marley and his Wailers were

going to be superstars. Marley, born in 1947 in Jamaica, had been playing reggae since 1964. His name first became known in the United States in 1972, when rhythm-and-blues singer Johnny Nash had a hit with Marley's "I Can See Clearly Now." One year later Nash had another hit with Marley's "Stir It Up." In 1974 Eric Clapton recorded (and had a number one hit with) Marley's "I Shot The Sheriff," and the reggae revolution was supposedly full steam under way—at least as full steam as it ever got. Reggae, with its subtle—some say simplistic—rhythms and emphasis on Jamaican problems and the Rastafarian religion was not what American kids were looking for. Despite worldwide critical acclaim, Bob Marley's superstardom never arrived, although he moved a little closer to it in 1980 with a lively, infectiously rhythmic single titled "Could You Be Loved." Marley died of cancer on May 11, 1981.

Marriott, Steve Born on Jan. 30, 1947 in London, Marriott has launched two of the hardest rocking bands in the business, the Small Faces (in 1965 with Ronnie Lane) and Humble Pie (in 1969). In 1975 Humble Pie came apart, and despite fluttering attempts at a solo career, Marriott has found himself left by the wayside.

Marshall Tucker Band, The Toy Caldwell (guitar, vocals), George McCorkle (guitar), Paul Riddle (drums), Tommy Caldwell (bass, vocals), Jerry Eubanks (flute, sax, vocals), Doug Gray (vocals, percussion)—Formed

The Marshall Tucker Band

in Spartanburg, S.C. during the early 1960s, the Marshall Tucker Band is one of the better country-rock ensembles to surface, perhaps the very best. Most of the Tuckers (named for the owner of one of their rehearsal halls) went to high school together and by 1966 were working the grueling circuit of Southern bars. Their music, led by the outstanding songwriting of Toy Caldwell, was always a step ahead, and it wasn't until another Southern band, Wet Willie, caught their act and suggested they go to see Capricorn Records' Phil Walden in Macon, Ga. that their career really got under way. They signed with Capricorn in 1973, and Walden put them on

the road with the Allman Brothers. When that tour ran out, he decided to follow the proven method of breaking in an unknown band—keep them on the road, sometimes for 300 days out of the year. With such music as "Hillbilly Band," "Searchin' For A Rainbow," "This Ol' Cowboy," "24 Hours At A Time," "Fire On The Mountain," the single hit "Heard It In A Love Song" and "Can't You See," which has become a national anthem for Southern rock, the band soon had a tremendous following. It survived the collapse of Capricorn by an early move to Warner Brothers, and that label was rewarded with a hit single by the group in 1979, "Running Like The Wind."

In 1980 Tommy Caldwell was killed in an auto accident.

Martha and the Vandellas
Martha Reeves (vocals), Betty Kelly (vocals), Rosalind Ashford (vocals)—A genuine rags to riches story, Martha Reeves was a secretary-go-for at Motown Records, where part of her job was singing song lyrics onto tape for artists to learn. In a classic story, one day a singer got sick, and rather than cancel the session, the Motown heavies asked Reeves if she'd like to try her hand. They loved her, and soon she and two high school buddies were offered a contract as Martha and the Vandellas (changed in 1965 to Martha Reeves and the Vandellas).

Their first song in 1963, "Come And Get These Memories," was a hit, but later that year the girls turned to a much harder rocking style for "Heat Wave," which set the tone for their future releases. Their biggest hit came the next year with "Dancing In The Streets," a classic Marvin Gaye composition, which they followed with such catchy numbers as "Nowhere To Run" (1965), "I'm Ready For Love" (1966) and "Jimmy Mack" (1967). In 1971 Martha Reeves left the group for a solo career, which she's still trying to shake down.

Martindale, Wink   Born in 1934, in Bells, Tenn., Winston "Wink" Martindale, a disc jockey and television host, had a monster hit in 1959 with the T. Texas Tyler epic monologue "Deck Of Cards," which explains in great detail the religious significance a soldier attaches to a deck of cards.

Marvelettes, The   Gladys Horton (vocals), Katherine Anderson (vocals), Georgeanna Tillman (vocals), Juanita Cowart (vocals), Wanda Young (vocals)—The five women who made up the Marvelettes were all in their senior year at Inkster High School in Detroit when they met Berry Gordy, the head of Motown Records, who snapped them up very quickly. The result was "Please Mr. Postman," in 1961 (covered by Karen Carpenter in 1974). While they never again achieved the success of "Please Mr. Postman," they went on to record a string of songs justifiably considered rock classics: "Beechwood 4-

5789" (1962), "Too Many Fish In The Sea" (1964), "The Hunter Gets Captured By The Game" (1967) and "My Baby Must Be A Magician" (1968).

Mason, Dave   Dave Mason is something of a rock-and-roll institution. Born on May 10, 1946 in England, Mason first came to light as a roadie for the Spencer Davis Group, stepping up from the background to play guitar on the group's biggest hit, "I'm A Man." He went on to form Traffic in 1967, wrote some of its best music and left before a year was out. From there he went into production, working on Family's critically acclaimed first album, *Music In A Doll's House* in 1968, before taking a brief stab at solo work. After that, he worked for the likes of Jimi Hendrix, George Harrison and the Rolling Stones as a sessions guitarist; rejoined Traffic to record his "Feelin' Alright"—a rock-and-roll classic—and drifted to America to become one of Bonnie and Delaney's "friends." The year 1970 saw his first solo album, *Alone*

Dave Mason

Together, a hit in the United States, after which Mason drifted away again, this time for an unsuccessful stint with former Mama Cass Elliott. Beginning in 1972 Mason released a series of solo albums, including *Dave Mason, Split Coconut* and others, but he has yet to match his earlier success—although there is little doubt that he will eventually stumble on the winning combination again. His singles hits have included "We Just Disagree" (1977) and "Let It Go, Let It Flow" (1978).

Mathis, Johnny   Born on Sept. 30, 1935 in San Francisco, Calif., Mathis established a local high jump record in college before a chance encounter with a vacationing record company executive ended his plans to become a physical education teacher. Beginning in 1956 Mathis produced an incredibly successful string of ballads (under the tutelage of Mitch Miller), including "Wonderful Wonderful" (1956), "It's Not For Me To Say" (1957), "Chances Are" (1957) and "The Twelfth Of Never" (1957), all the way through 1979, revitalizing his career with a successful appeal to the disco market (beginning in 1976 with "When A Child Is Born" and his duets with Denise Williams). He is credited with one of the first *Best Of* albums (1957), which remained on the pop charts for 400 straight weeks. More importantly, he continued a career as a pop crooner through the very height of the rock-and-roll frenzy, making him one of the most durable artists in American history.

Matthews, Ian   Best known for his soft, country sounding group, Matthews Southern Comfort, Ian Matthews worked as lead vocalist for Fairport Convention before launching Matthews Southern Comfort in the early 1970s. The group had a hit with "Woodstock" in 1970, a reworking of the Joni Mitchell original, but Matthews left the group. Since then he has been steadily hammering away at a solo career, releasing an album a year without much more than a ripple on the FM radio.

Matthews Southern Comfort   Ian Matthews (vocals, guitar), Gordon Huntley (pedal steel), Mark Griffiths (guitar), Carl Barnwell (guitar), Ray Duffy (drums), Andy Leigh (bass)—Formed in 1970 by Ian Matthews, the group cut two albums and had one hit single, "Woodstock," before Matthews moved on. The group continued for several years as Southern Comfort, without particular success.

Mayall, John   The godfather of British blues was born on Nov. 29, 1933 in Manchester, England and first came across American blues when he was 13. Beginning in the early 1960s Mayall formed the first of a series of bands, the Bluesbreakers, which would include such future luminaries as Eric Clapton, Jack Bruce (Cream), John McVie (Fleetwood Mac), Peter Green (Fleetwood Mac), Mick Taylor (the Rolling Stones), Harvey Mandel (Canned Heat) and many others. Although he has produced countless albums, Mayall has never had the

commercial success of his many charges, perhaps because of his unswerving devotion to the blues, which, taken straight, has never been a particularly commercial proposition. In addition to the expert musicians nurtured in the various Bluesbreakers, Mayall also led a one-man crusade for the recognition (and payment) of the bluesmen he so admired. Some of that rubbed off on Clapton, who, when he recorded Skip James' "I'm So Glad," personally saw to it that the bluesman was paid his due.

Mayfield, Curtis   Born on June 3, 1942 in Chicago, Ill., Mayfield is one of the most important and most articulate black songwriters in America today. Starting in 1956 with the Impressions, Mayfield produced an impressive string of hits, from "Gypsy Woman" in 1961 until he broke from the group in 1970. His decision to go solo proved spectacularly successful with three hit albums *Curtis, Curtis-Live* and *Roots,* in rapid succession during 1970-71. But it was his agreement in 1972 to provide the soundtrack for the low-budget film *Superfly* that truly cemented Mayfield's place. The story of a Harlem cocaine dealer was hardly the inspirational, black pride material Mayfield usually dealt in, but in *Superfly* the singer-songwriter saw the perfect vehicle to express "the beauty, the anguish and the reality of the ghetto experience." The results were a masterpiece soundtrack album titled *Superfly* and two hit singles, "Superfly" and "Freddie's Dead." Since then Mayfield has

Curtis Mayfield

released the highly acclaimed *America Today* album, scripted the soundtrack for three more movies (he received an Academy Award nomination for *Claudine*) and continued to release albums of his own through his Curtom Company.

McCall, C.W.   Bill Fries, an advertising man masquerading as a country music singer, produced some of the best novelty hits of the 1970s. These included "The-Old-Home-Filler-Up-And-Keep-On-A-Truckin'-Cafe" in 1974 (originally designed as an advertising campaign for a bread company in Sioux City, Iowa, for which Fries created the character "C.W. McCall"), "Wolf Creek Pass" in 1975 and the huge country and pop hit "Convoy" in 1975, the story of a group of truckers in a cross-country dash that captured the imagination of the whole country. That song eventually became a perfectly horrible movie directed by Sam Peckinpah and starring Kris Kristofferson and Ali McGraw.

"Helen Wheels" (1973), "Jet" (1974) and "Junior's Farm" (1975), as well as some pretty strange items, such as "Give Ireland Back To The Irish" (1972) and "Mary Had A Little Lamb" (1972). His 1976 tour (and attendant three-record set), Wings over America, was an unqualified success, proving that the ex-Beatle could still pack 'em in. Although McCartney retains the name Wings for his touring group, the band actually has only one permanent member, ex-Moody Blue Denny Laine.

In 1980 McCartney was arrested for possession of marijuana upon his arrival in Japan for a concert series and, after spending several days in jail, was expelled from the country. *McCartney II* was released the same year, 10 years after *McCartney,* his initial solo effort.

McClinton, Delbert
Brought to public attention largely through the work of Blues Brother John Belushi on television's "Saturday Night Live" and through the virtually unanimous ecstatic praise of critics, McClinton (born in 1940 in Lubbock, Tex.) is indeed one of the finest white rhythm-and-blues singers. He was the man responsible for the superb harmonica intro on Bruce Channel's hit "Hey Baby" (1962), and while on tour in Europe with Channel, McClinton taught the then-unknown Beatles the fundamentals of the rock-and-roll harp (that later turned up on "Love Me Do"). Through a series of albums on the now-defunct Capricorn Records, McClinton showed himself to be a master, and his own "B

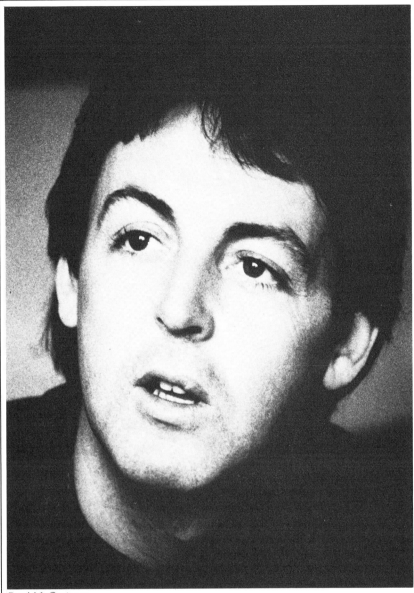

Paul McCartney

McCartney, Paul, and Wings Clearly the most successful of the solo Beatles, McCartney (born on June 18, 1942 in Liverpool) began work on his first solo album, *McCartney,* before the formal breakup of the group. *McCartney,* issued in 1970, was charming, its lightweight pop sound pointing the way for the ex-Beatle's future releases. The next album, *Ram,* was cut with New York City sessions men, and while it was critically derided, it produced the 1971 hit "Uncle Albert/Admiral Halsey." McCartney formed a touring ensemble called Wings in 1971, which consisted of Denny Laine, Denny Seiwell and McCartney's wife, Linda. Later, guitarist Henry McCullough was added to the band. Wings was both a success and a failure. McCartney generated some hard rocking hits, including

Delbert McClinton

Movie" became a hit for the Blues Brothers. He is one of the unsung geniuses of rock and roll, to be sure. Amazingly, he finally scored a top 10 hit in 1981, "Giving It Up For Your Love."

McCoy, Charlie Born on March 28, 1941 in Oak Hill, W. Va., McCoy is considered to be the finest sessions harmonica player in the world. Working out of Nashville, he was briefly a member of Area Code 615 and, earlier, played on Bob Dylan's *Highway 61 Revisited* and *Blonde On Blonde*.

McDonald, Country Joe Country Joe McDonald (born on Jan. 1, 1942 in El Monte, Calif.) and his band, the Fish (Barry Melton, guitar; David Cohen, keyboards; Chicken Hirsh, drums; and Bruce Barthol, bass), skyrocketed to attention at the 1969 Woodstock festival when they preceded their witty antiwar polemic "I-Feel-Like-I'm-Fixin'-To-Die-Rag" with the now-famous "Fish Cheer"— "Gimme an "F." "F!' Gimme a "U." "U!' "Gimme a "C." "C!'

"Gimme a "K." "K!' "Wassit spell?"—repeated over and over by the crowd of half-a-million. The band was a legend on the West Coast, where it had been formed in the mid-1960s, but after its big splash with a dirty word, it was hard-pressed for an encore. In addition, the changing mood of the times didn't lend itself to a career of protest, and the band passed with the coming of the new decade. Country Joe worked steadily but largely in the dark until his 1976 *Paradise With An Ocean View* album, which revealed a far more mellow balladeer.

Country Joe McDonald

McDowell, Fred Bluesman, born on Jan. 12, 1904 in Rossville, Tenn. and "discovered" during one of archivist Alan Lomax' many field trips in 1959. He became quite popular after the 1964 Newport Folk Festival, mainly because he had begun working in the mid-1920s and

therefore represented an outstanding repository of early blues works by such masters as Charlie Patton.

McGarrigle, Kate and Anna The darlings of the New York folk-rock scene, sisters Kate and Anna McGarrigle were raised in Canada and first came to attention when Linda Ronstadt recorded Anna's "Heart Like A Wheel." Additionally, Maria Muldaur recorded several McGarrigle compositions, including the excellent "Work Song" and "Cool River." The sisters' debut album, *Kate And Anna McGarrigle,* in 1976 was a critics' favorite, and many proclaimed a rebirth of the folk music scene. The next releases, though, found the sisters floundering, and the return of folk apparently will have to wait a while longer.

McGhee, Brownie Born in 1914 in Knoxville, Tenn., bluesman Brownie McGhee played dances in the Smoky Mountains and traveled with various minstrel shows before teaming up with Sonny Terry in 1939. McGhee, accomplished on the guitar and banjo, but with a soft, almost slurring singing style, matched well with Terry's gritty vocals and harp playing. The duo became quite popular in Europe.

McGuinn, Roger Born on July 13, 1942 in Chicago, Ill., McGuinn is best known as the founding father of the Byrds. Since that group's breakup in 1972, McGuinn has worked steadily as a solo artist, with limited success—hampered, in fact, by the remaining overwhelming aura of the

Byrds. Some of his best solo work can be heard on *Cardiff Rose* (1976). McGuinn toured with Bob Dylan's Rolling Thunder Revue in 1975-76.

McGuire, Barry Born on Oct. 15, 1935 in Oklahoma City, Okla. and originally the lead vocalist for the New Christy Minstrels, McGuire shocked an apparently naive world in 1965 with his "Eve Of Destruction," written by P.F. Sloan. The song was one of the first successful protest songs and was banned on numerous stations across the country and on the BBC for its bitter, forceful lyrics and its antiwar stance. In the late 1960s McGuire joined the cast of the rock musical *Hair*.

McKenzie, Scott Originally a New York City folkie, McKenzie (born on Oct. 1, 1944 in Virginia) made his mark in 1967 with the flower power anthem "San Francisco (Be Sure To Wear Some Flowers In Your Hair)." The song helped trigger an exodus of kids to the Bay City. The song was written by John Phillips of Mamas and Papas fame, an old friend of McKenzie from the folkie days. In fact, John Phillips daughter, television actress Mackenzie Phillips, is named for Scott.

McLaughlin, John Born in 1942 in Yorkshire, England, McLaughlin became one of the best jazz-rock guitarists (working with Graham Bond, Miles Davis and Buddy Miles) before adopting the Eastern teachings of mystic Sri Chinmoy. He then launched a string of Mahavishnu Orchestras and released a series of albums that ranged from brilliant (*The Inner Mounting Flame* in 1972 and *Birds Of Fire* in 1973) to downright dull (*Visions Of The Emerald Beyond* in 1975). After disbanding the last Orchestra, McLaughlin returned to his roots, releasing his critically acclaimed *John B. McLaughlin* album in 1979.

McLean, Don An overnight sensation with his hit single "American Pie," which boiled down the history of rock and roll to eight minutes and was the biggest hit of 1971, McLean (born on Oct. 2, 1945 in New Rochelle, N.Y.) worked steadily from 1963 to his break in 1971 as a singer and songwriter, including a stint with Pete Seeger. His career never recovered from the success of "American Pie," although he has recorded steadily since then, including such hits as "Vincent" in 1972. He is a facile and talented performer, but it is unlikely that he will ever again find the right amount of catchiness, cheek and soul searching so right for the times that marked "American Pie."

McPhatter, Clyde Born in 1931 in Durham, N.C., McPhatter was one of the biggest names in the early years of rock and roll. He began his singing career as a choirboy but soon left for the earthier rhythm-and-blues music of the Dominoes (biggest hit: "Sixty Minute Man" in 1951) and then the Drifters, a group he started with a bang in 1953 with "Money Honey." A year later he was drafted, but in 1955, while on leave from the Army, he cut his first solo effort, "Seven Days," which he followed the next year with "Treasure Of Love." He is probably best remembered for his 1958 hit, "A Lover's Question" and his "Lover Please" in 1962, but his actual influence goes far beyond individual hits. Through McPhatter (and a few others like Sam Cooke) the soul-wrenching frenzy of black gospel music was able to take root in secular white music. Since the 1920s black gospel music had been booming, but its rather strict conventions (gospel music was the music of the Lord; the blues was the work of the Devil) kept it segregated from the mainstream of music. In the early 1950s, though, a few singers—McPhatter foremost among them—began singing secular, blues-styled lyrics with a decided gospel flair and rhythm. In addition to vastly expanding the horizons of pop music, McPhatter and his kin laid the groundwork for the soul music of the 1960s—both the Southern branch at Stax Records in Memphis and the Northern contingent at Motown in Detroit. McPhatter benifited little from his innovations, however, and his later solo career was always overshadowed by his earlier work. He died of a heart attack in 1972 at his home in New Jersey.

McTell, Blind Willie Bluesman, born in 1898 in Statesboro, Ga., McTell, blind since birth, was one of the few Georgia bluesmen to survive the Depression with his popularity intact. He traveled widely, up and down the entire length of the East Coast. He was quite popular and in demand through the 1950s, supplying a bridge between the older rural blues and the newer, urban variety.

Meat Loaf   A true rock-and-roll spectacle, Meat Loaf (whose real name is allegedly Marvin Lee Aday, born on Sept. 27, 1947 in Dallas, Tex.) captured the late 1970s by storm. Possibly the world's largest rock singer (six foot two, 260 pounds), Meat Loaf (or Mr. Loaf, as *The New York Times* insists on calling him) worked in various bar bands and even sang lead for Ted Nugent's half-crazed Amboy Dukes before landing a roll in the classic 1970s cult movie *The Rocky Horror Picture Show.* He also linked up with shy, retiring songwriter Jim Steinman, who saw in Meat Loaf a vehicle for his wild science fiction/nostalgia fantasies. The result was an album produced by Todd Rundgren called *Bat Out Of Hell* (1977), which featured such 1978 hits as "Two Out Of Three Ain't Bad " and "Paradise By The Dashboard Light," the musical chronicle of a high school "date," complete with play-by-play commentary by New York Yankees TV and radio announcer Phil Rizzuto.

Melanie   Melanie Safka (born on Feb. 3, 1947 in New York City) rode the antiwar feelings of the late 1960s with her "Candles In The Rain" (1970), more or less the story of the 1969 Moratorium to end the Vietnam war. With the winding down of the antiwar movement, Melanie, the daughter of a jazz singer,

Meat Loaf

moved to cute, melodic tunes like "Look What They've Done To My Song" and covers of such standards as "Ruby Tuesday" (a hit for her in 1970) before finding the right combination in 1971 with the upbeat, excessively cheery "Brand New Key." Right about then the key stopped working, however, and her more serious work—at least six albums worth of it—has gone largely unnoticed.

Melvin, Harold, and the Blue Notes   Harold Melvin, Teddy Pendergrass, Lawrence Brown, Bernard Wilson, Lloyd Parks—Originally formed during the mid-1950s in Philadelphia, the Blue Notes first recorded in 1956. That year's "If You Love Me" was a modest hit, and the group eventually scored again in 1960 with the R&B-styled "My Hero." It wasn't until 12 years later, though, that Harold Melvin and the Blue Notes really hit the big time. After cruising through the 1960s as a lounge act, the group connected with Kenny Gamble and Leon Huff, who were in the process of refining their "soft soul" Philadelphia Sound. In the Blue Notes, Gamble and Huff found the perfect vehicle for their musical ideas—a rhythm-and-blues group refined through years on the club circuit. In 1972 the group scored big with the Gamble-Huff composition "If You Don't Know Me By Now," which helped define and popularize the Philly Sound. The Blue Notes followed the next year with "The Love I Lost" and continued their string of hits throught the 1970s, including "Bad Luck," one of the finest examples of soul-flavored disco to date. In 1976 Teddy Pendergrass left the group to become a solo act.

Memphis Minnie

Diminutive Minnie Douglas McCoy was born in 1900 in Algiers, La. and by the age of 15 was already singing the blues on Beale Street in Memphis. In the late 1920s she began an extensive recording career that carried her to Chicago, where she became one of the most-celebrated blues singers with her weekly "Blue Monday" parties. Her blues interpretations are considered some of the finest ever.

Memphis Slim Born Peter Chatman in 1915 in Memphis, Tenn., Memphis Slim got his start playing piano in that city's numerous bordellos. In the 1950s he moved to France and found himself in the middle of a tremendous appreciation of American black music. Today he remains a star in France, where he spends the vast bulk of his time, making only occasional forays to the United States.

Meters, The Art Neville (keyboards, vocals), Leo Nocentelli (guitar, vocals), Joseph Modeliste (drums), George Porter (bass, vocals), Cyril Neville (percussion, vocals)—Originally the backup group for Fats Domino, the Meters made their reputation as the house band for Seasaint Studios in New Orleans and as the backup for the Rolling Stones on their 1976 tour. The Meters have recorded several albums on their own, including *Cabbage Alley* (1972) and *Rejuvenation* (1974). They can also be heard on recordings by Dr. John, Paul McCartney and Robert Palmer.

Midler, Bette Born in 1945 in New Jersey and raised in Hawaii, Midler launched her career as the reigning chanteuse in New York City's Continental Baths, your basic gay bathhouse. The road to the bathhouse had been long and arduous, from a bit role in the film *Hawaii* that got her to New York to a three-year stretch in the Broadway production of *Fiddler on the Roof,* in which she worked her way up from the chorus. She was a brilliant performer, a cabaret artist with a zany range from blues to torchy songs from the 1940s to imitations of 1960s Phil Spector-type girl groups, and her debut album, *The Divine Miss M* (as the boys in the bathhouse tagged her), in 1973 was an overwhelming success. Her eclectic choice of material—from "Leader Of The Pack" to the country "Delta Dawn" to John Prine's introspective masterpiece "Hello In There"—and her brassy onstage persona boosted her

from star to phenomenon, a position she was not particularly fond of. Two albums later (after the furor had subsided a bit) she backed off until 1977, when she came slamming back with a television special, a Broadway revue and a new album, all of which were critically well received. She then immediately turned to the movies, taking the lead role in *The Rose,* a thinly disguised biography of Janis Joplin. The film, released in 1979, proved to be a triumph for Midler and a stepping stone to a much bigger career.

Midnighters, The Hank Ballard, Lawson Smith, Norman Thrasher, Billy Davis, Henry Booth—One of the most popular rhythm-and-blues groups of the 1950s, the Midnighters were originally formed as the Royals in 1952 in Cincinnati. They became the Midnighters the next year (after a modest hit with "Every Beat Of My Heart") and recorded "Get It," which was banned on many radio stations for being too sexually explicit. Taking their cue, the Midnighters went on to record a whole string of "dirty" songs, including "Work With Me Annie" (1954), "Sexy Ways" (1954), "Annie Had A Baby" (1954), "Annie's Aunt Fannie" (1954) and "Henry's Got Flat Feet" (1955), an answer to Etta James' answer song for all the "Annie" songs—"Roll With Me Henry." Hank Ballard left the group in 1958 and later wrote such rock classics as "The Twist" and "Let's Go Let's Go Let's Go."

Miles, Buddy Drummer Buddy Miles was born on Sept.

5, 1945 in Omaha, Neb. His first job was backing the Ink Spots, when he was 15, and his break came in 1967, when he joined Mike Bloomfield in the Electric Flag. Since the breakup of that group, he has alternated between solo work and sessions (actually supersessions, as with Carlos Santana in 1972), with a brief stint in Jimi Hendrix' Band of Gypsies.

Miller, Steve   Yet another one of rock's Flying Dutchmen, drifting from group to group, Miller was born on Oct. 5, 1943 in Milwaukee, Wis. and raised in Dallas, Tex., where he learned his first guitar licks from friends of the family Les Paul and Mary Ford. His first band was formed when he was 12, but it was at the University of Wisconsin where he got together with soulmate Boz Scaggs and formed the Knight Train, a prelude to the numerous Steve Miller Bands to come. He gigged steadily in Chicago with the blues greats and moved to San Francisco with the advent of flower power, cutting (with Scaggs) two of the classic "progressive rock" albums of the time, *Children Of The Future* and *Sailor.* From that point on he began recording a series of underground classics with a variety of Steve Miller Bands, including "Gangster Of Love," "Quicksilver Girl," "Going To Mexico" and "Enter Maurice." In 1973 he had a huge hit with "The Joker," from the album of the same name, a song that lampooned his earlier songs. He spent the next three years putting together *Fly Like An Eagle,* a less bluesy, more rock album that went on to become

his biggest hit ever, selling over a million copies, as did the follow-up *Book Of Dreams.* Miller is a talented guitarist, songwriter and bandleader, and whichever incarnation of the Steve Miller Band turns up next year, one can be sure the quality will remain.

Mills Brothers, The   John Mills (vocals), Herbert Mills (vocals), Harry Mills (vocals), Donald Mills (vocals)—The Mills Brothers began singing in the early 1940s, scoring their first hit in 1943 with "Paper Doll." Rather than fading away in the 1950s, they held their own with such hits as "Yellow Bird" (1959) and continued recording successfully until 1968. Along with the Ink Spots, the Mills Brothers set the stage for the waves of black harmony groups in the mid- and late-1950s, collectively known as doo-wop groups.

Milsap, Ronnie   Born in Robbinsville, N.C. and blind since birth, Milsap has emerged in the mid-1970s as one of the most successful country-pop artists ever. In the mid-1960s he quit his pre-law studies to join J.J. Cale's band and began making tough sounding rhythm-and-blues records, which soon had the white pianist playing alongside such black greats as Bobby Bland and Smokey Robinson and the Miracles. He moved to Memphis in 1969, honing his white rhythm and blues on the club circuit, until a lucrative deal drew him to Nashville in the early 1970s. He began a string of R&B-tinted ballads in 1973 (including "The Girl Who Waits On Tables") before shifting to a more heavily

orchestrated pop sound the next year. The result was a series of huge sellers, including the 1978 smash "It Was Almost Like A Song." He's won every award conceivable in country music, and his songs routinely cross over to the pop charts.

Miracles, The   William "Smokey" Robinson, Claudette Rodgers (later Robinson), Ronald White, Robert Rodgers, Pete Moore—One of the most successful and influential groups in modern music, the Miracles began in 1957 in Detroit, where they became acquainted with a struggling record producer and songwriter named Berry Gordy, Jr. Gordy, who was working with Jackie Wilson, was looking to get his own record label, which he called Tamla/Motown. The first two songs written by Gordy and Robinson were not particularly successful, but the third, "Way Over There," clicked in 1960, really getting Tamla/Motown off the ground. The next song, another Gordy/Robinson joint effort titled "Shop Around," put the group over the top as well as establishing Motown as a force to be watched. With Robinson writing most of the songs (Bob Dylan once called him one of America's leading poets), the Miracles followed with an impressive string of hits—"You've Really Got A Hold On Me" (1962), "Mickey's Monkey" (1963), "Ooo Baby Baby" (1965), "The Tracks Of My Tears" (1965), "Going To A Go-Go" (1966), "I Second That Emotion" (1967), "The Tears Of A Clown" (1970) and others. Robinson also wrote such soul classics as Mary

Wells' "My Guy," the Temptations' "My Girl" and "The Way You Do The Things You Do" and Marvin Gaye's "Ain't That Peculiar." Robinson left the group for more administrative-type duties at Motown in 1972, working sometimes as a solo artist, while the Miracles drifted effortlessly to slick, high-quality disco, such as "Love Machine" in 1975.

Mitchell, Joni   Joni Mitchell (born Nov. 7, 1943 in Alberta, Canada) first gained attention as a songwriter in the late 1960s, when Judy Collins ("Both Sides Now"), Tom Rush ("The Circle Game") and Fairport Convention ("Eastern Rain") recorded her songs. She'd begun her career as a conventional folkie, working the coffeehouse circuit in Canada, and her first two albums, *Joni Mitchell* (1968) and *Clouds* (1969), reflected those early days. With her 1970 release of *Ladies Of The Canyon,* Mitchell established herself as something special. That album included such classics as "Big Yellow Taxi" and "Woodstock" and established her as a major FM artist. Her album *Blue,* issued the next year, is considered both one of her finest statements and a turning point. From then on she began to dabble more and more in jazz (working with Tom Scott and his LA Express), which worked excellently on *Court And Spark* (1974). But beginning with *The Hissing Of Summer Lawns* (1976) and continuing through *Hejira* (1976) and *Don Juan's Reckless Daughter* (1977), her music became less and less

accessible, more and more deeply mired in jazz. Many critics considered the move a brilliant bit of growth on her part; others saw the change as overblown pretention. Her album *Mingus* (1979), a tribute to that jazz great, carried her new music to its extreme, and even her fans chafed. While Mitchell's work is definitely the work of a master, it remains to be seen whether it will ever again be the work of a popular master.

Mitchell, Willie   Most famous for his work with Al Green, Willie Mitchell is the president of Hi Records in Memphis and one of the great masters of soul music. He put his first band together in 1964 and recorded steadily through the 1970s, while taking over more and more administrative duties at Hi Records. He is also the head of Cream Records, which recently recorded veteran Memphis musician Don Nix, member of the original Mar-Keys.

Mitchum, Robert   Movie tough guy Robert Mitchum (born in 1917 in Connecticut) almost launched a recording career in 1958 with "The Ballad Of Thunder Road," from one of the great B movies of all time (with Mitchum in the starring role, of course). The movie is now immortalized in the title of the Bruce Springsteen song "Thunder Road," although Springsteen claims to have never seen the movie about moonshine runners, only the poster in the lobby.

Moby Grape   Skip Spence (guitar, vocals), Jerry Miller

(guitar, vocals), Bob Mosley (bass, vocals), Peter Lewis (guitar, vocals), Don Stevenson (drums, vocals)—Started by former Jefferson Airplane drummer Skip Spence in San Francisco in 1967, Moby Grape was a truly great band destroyed by a record company which didn't know what it had—the group's debut album, *Moby Grape* (1967), was *sooooo* great that the record company figured it would release five singles instead of just one, and they'd include every song on the 10 song album, and they'd all have the same cover . . . and on and on, until the Grape nearly self-destructed on the spot. A second album, *Wow/Grape Jam,* which featured studio work with Al Kooper, Mike Bloomfield and Stephen Stills (one of the first "supergroup" packages, i.e., built around artists who are already stars), still suffered from overhype, and by *Moby Grape '69,* the record company just didn't care. From then until 1974 the Grape concentrated on breaking up and then producing reunion albums, none of which amounted to anything.

Monkees, The   Davy Jones (vocals), Mike Nesmith (guitar, vocals), Peter Tork (bass, vocals), Mickey Dolenz (drums, vocals)—America's first totally prefabricated vocal group, the Monkees were put together by rock entrepreneur Don Kirshner (through an ad in *Variety* magazine), supplied with a seemingly inexhaustible array of hit songs (most through the good offices of Tommy Boyce and Bobby Hart) and trundled off to television, where they promptly became the biggest thing since marshmallows. Of the group, Nesmith was the only one who could call himself a musician with a straight face. Dolenz was a child actor who had played in television's "Circus Boy," Jones an English actor and Tork an aspiring musician. And no matter, really. For 1966, it was fun, and the songs, like "Daydream Believer," "Last Train To Clarksville," "I'm A Believer" and "Shades Of Grey," their "deep" song, weren't half-bad pop music. Sadly, it was all over within two years, although all but Tork struggled to keep things going for another year. Nesmith went on to prove himself a fine musician and songwriter, but the title of ex-Monkee was like a millstone around his neck. Jones and Dolenz tried to re-form the band in 1975 but failed. In retrospect, it really was great fun.

Montez, Chris   Born on Jan. 17, 1944 in Los Angeles, Calif., Montez grew up trying to imitate his hero Richie Valens. In 1962 he recorded "Let's Dance," which had an inescapably catchy organ track, and it went on to become a huge hit. He later recorded a string of other hits, including "Call Me" (1966) and "The More I See You" (1966).

Montrose   Ronnie Montrose (guitar), Bob James (vocals), Jim Alciver (keyboards), Alan Fitzgerald (bass), Denny Carmassi (drums)—A vehicle for heavy metal guitarist Ronnie Montrose, Montrose was formed in 1974 and began rocking that year with

Montrose. Ronnie Montrose had earlier worked with Van Morrison, Boz Scaggs and Edgar Winter. Their last work was the album *Open Fire* in 1978.

Moody Blues, The   Justin Hayward (guitar, vocals), Mike Pinder (keyboards, vocals), Ray Thomas (flute, vocals), John Lodge (bass, vocals), Graeme Edge (drums)—The Moody Blues were originally formed in 1964, at the height of the British Invasion, and they were quite successful with such basic rhythm and blues as "Go Now." In 1968, with their popularity ebbing, original members Denny Laine and Clint Warwick left the group, John Lodge and Justin Hayward took their places and the Moodies embarked on a new trip, this time with the London Symphony Orchestra. Their first album, *Days Of Future Passed,* was a tremendous success—a strongly orchestrated, "heavy" album that found immediate approval with the burgeoning rock underground in America. The Moody Blues stuck to that formula like glue, producing such lyrically and orchestrally ponderous albums as *In Search Of The Lost Chord* (1968), *On The Threshold Of A Dream* (1969), *To Our Children's Children* (1969) and *Seventh Sojourn* (1972). To be sure, the formula was wildly successful; there was much talk of "rock as poetry" and "poetry as rock," and the overt (and overplayed) symbolism of the group lent itself perfectly to group discussions in "hip" college classes. By 1974 the band members had moved on to

solo projects, getting together in the late 1970s for a much-ballyhooed and modestly successful reunion.

Moon, Keith   Manic drummer for the Who, Moon (born on Aug. 23, 1946 in England) was known for his kamikaze lifestyle as much as his drumming, which was excellent. He died on Sept. 7, 1978 from a reaction between prescription drugs and alcohol.

Moonglows, The   Harvey Fuqua, Bobby Lester, Pete Graves, Prentiss Barnes, Bobby Johnson—Formed in Kentucky in 1951, they are best known for their classic doo-wop "Sincerely," which stayed on the R&B charts from late 1954 to spring 1955, and "Ten Commandments Of Love," which, credited to Harvey and the Moonglows, was a big seller in 1958. The Moonglows were the pet group of disc jockey Alan Freed and his "Moondog Show"—in fact, the group's name reflects that relationship—and Freed was credited as coauthor of "Sincerely." They turned out a string of R&B hits before coming apart in the late 1950s. Harvey Fuqua went on to become a record producer. Bobby Lester, after getting a group together in the 1970s to play the oldies circuit, died of cancer in 1980.

Moore, Tim   Singer/songwriter Tim Moore won the American Song Festival in 1974 with "Charmer." He has since produced three albums, none of which have fared particularly well.

Jim Morrison

Morrison, Jim   Best known as the controversial, brilliant lead singer for the Doors, Jim Morrison, the son of a rear admiral, went on to become one of the most charismatic figures in rock. He died of a heart attack on July 3, 1971 in Paris, France. His grave in France has since become something of a shrine, with thousands of people making the pilgrimage each year. The closing months of 1980 saw a revival both in the music of the Doors and in the myth of Jim Morrison, fueled by a rerelease of Doors' music and a biography of Morrison by Jerry Hopkins, who also wrote a biography of Elvis Presley.

Morrison, Van   Impossible to categorize, unpredictable in his

recording, Van Morrison (born Aug. 31, 1945 in Belfast, Northern Ireland) has blazed an erratic, if at times brilliant, trail across popular music. From his initial work with the overhyped band Them ("Here Comes The Night" in 1965) and his composition of one of rock's all-time greatest classics, "Gloria" (a hit for the Shadows of Knight in 1966, a perennial standard for bar bands everywhere and a hit again for Patti Smith in late 1975—a superb rendition on her first album, *Horses),* to his own successes beginning with "Brown-Eyed Girl" in 1967, Morrison has set and stuck to high standards, disdaining what he saw as the manipulative music business and the less than top quality of

many of his fellow musicians. Starting with *Astral Weeks* in 1968, Morrison established himself as one of rock's top artists, blending acoustic folk, jazz and blues into what remains today as one of rock's finest moments. Although the album was a critical success, it didn't sell, but Morrison worked steadily, appearing at small concerts and honing his music. Each new album was different—*Moondance* in 1970 leaned heavily on a horn section; *Tupelo Honey* in 1971 put him back on the singles charts with its title song (the year before his "Domino" had also been a fluke hit). His 1974 *Veedon Fleece* marked a return to the acoustic simplicity of *Astral Weeks,* while the next album, *A Period Of Transition* in 1977, found him working with New Orleans heavy Dr. John. Morrison's tour in 1979 showed him to be a surprisingly strong concert draw—one of the best.

Morton, George "Shadow"
Best known for his work with songwiters Jerry Leiber and Mike Stoller and Wall of Sound producer Phil Spector, George "Shadow" Morton wrote and produced a string of hits that came to define the 1964-65 period, such as "Remember (Walking In The Sand)," "I Can Never Go Home Anymore" and "The Leader Of The Pack" for the Shangri-Las; "Chapel of Love" for the Dixie Cups; "The Boy From New York City" for the Ad Libs and "I Wanna Love Him So Bad" for the Jelly Beans. With Leiber and Stoller, he was one of the first producers to try for a biracial market.

Mothers of Invention, The Roy Estrada (bass), Jimmy Carl Black (drums), Ray Collins (vocals), Elliot Ingber (guitar) and numerous other musicians—Best known as the backup group for Frank Zappa, the Mothers of Invention changed constantly, both because of attrition and Zappa's constant disbanding and re-forming of the group. Some 120 musicians have worked on the various Zappa projects.

Motors, The British pub band formed around 1976, originally consisting of Bram Tchaikovsky, Ricky "Slaughter" Wernham, Andy McMaster and Nick Garvey. The Motors have the ability to tread the thin line between New Wave and chart/commercial music, although their initial successes have been limited to England. They are best known for their 1977 debut, *Motors*. A second album, *Approved By The Motors*, was released in 1978.

Motown See Tamla/Motown.

Mott the Hoople Ian Hunter (guitar, vocals), Pete Watts (bass), Dale "Buffin" Griffin (drums), Morgan Fisher (keyboards), Nigel Benjamin (vocals), Ray Major (guitar), Verden Allen (keyboards), Mick Ralphs (guitar), Ariel Bender (guitar)—Another critics' favorite, Mott the Hoople was formed in the late 1960s in England as sort of a low-budget Kinks. The group's eclectic, bitterly satirical rock reached its peak in 1972 (after the group broke up for the first time) with the David Bowie-produced *All The Young Dudes*, the title track of which became a modest hit single, and in 1973 with *Mott*, which featured the excellent "All The Way From Memphis" and "Honaloochie Boogie." After the departure of Hunter in 1974 for a critically acclaimed but commercially unsuccessful solo career, Nigel Benjamin took over lead vocals but within a couple of years he departed too.

Mountain Felix Pappalardi (bass), Leslie West (guitar, vocals), Corky Laing (drums), Steve Knight (keyboards)—Launched in the late 1960s by Felix Pappalardi, who'd gained public attention as the producer of Cream (becoming among the first of a long line of superstar producers), Mountain was essentially an American Cream, utilizing the slam-bang, Clapton-styled guitar playing of Leslie West (himself a virtual mountain). The band was a tremendous success, as Pappalardi figured it would be in the absence of Cream, with "Mississippi Queen" (1970) becoming its first hit. The peak for Mountain came in 1971 with the *Nantucket Sleighride* album, and the group's next two albums showed the fires were clearly banked. Pappalardi decided to return to the other side of the studio board in 1972, with West and Laing briefly joining ex-Cream bassist Jack Bruce for West Bruce & Laing. The band re-formed for no apparent reason in 1974, only to disband again the next year.

Van Morrison

Move, The Roy Wood (guitar, vocals); Carl Wayne (vocals); Bev Bevan (drums); Trevor Burton (guitar, vocals); Ace Kefford (bass); additional members: Rick Price (bass); Jeff Lynne (vocals)—Formed in 1965 in Birmingham, England, the Move was one of Britain's most successful singles bands, scoring hit after hit during its seven-year lifespan. Despite its popularity at home, the band was never very well known in the United States and is, in fact, best remembered as the incubator for the Electric Light Orchestra (ELO), formed by Wood, Lynne and Bevan. The Move jumped on the British charts in 1967 with the single "Night Of Fear" and were never far from the top thereafter. The Move's madcap antics made it famous. (One picture cover on another 1967 single, "Flowers In The Rain," so gravely offended Prime Minister Harold Wilson that he sued—successfully. As a result, all the royalties from that single were donated to charity, adding to the group's fame and endearing the members to the public.) But internal stresses eventually tore the Move apart in the early 1970s. All total, the group produced four albums, starting with *The Move* in 1967, and at least one of the Move's classics, "Do Ya," was later revived by ELO and a hit for them in 1977.

Muldaur, Geoff Originally a member of the Jim Kweskin Jug Band in the 1960s, Geoff Muldaur eschewed "commercial" music for years. He later joined the more commercial (although not much) Paul Butterfield Blues Band and in 1975 began a series of solo albums with *Geoff Muldaur Is Having A Wonderful Time,* a wry commentary on his ex-wife's (Maria Muldaur's) striking success at that time.

Muldaur, Maria Maria Muldaur became an "overnight sensation" in 1974 with the release of her first solo album, *Maria Muldaur,* featuring the sexy hit "Midnight At The Oasis." Previously she had been a folk singer in New York's Greenwich Village, where she met and married Geoff Muldaur, a member of the Jim Kweskin Jug Band, which she joined. She recorded two albums with Geoff before breaking up with him both professionally and personally to go solo. Her solo *Maria Muldaur* featured a wide blend of material, from Dolly Parton to Kate McGarrigle to Dan Hicks to Dr. John, and the blend was perfect for her sultry voice. Her follow-up, *Waitress In A Donut Shop,* leaned more toward jazz and was less well received. She recorded two more albums, both heavy on jazz, with *Sweet Harmonies* (1977) drifting back to rhythm and blues, but has yet to regain the momentum of *Maria Muldaur.* She was born Maria Grazia Rosa Domenica d'Amato on Sept. 12, 1943 in New York City.

Mull, Martin Comedian Martin Mull, a popular refugee from television's "Mary Hartman Mary Hartman" comedy and host of "America 2-Nite," continued his successful recording career in 1979 with his *Perfect/Near Perfect* album, featuring one great country cut titled "Pigs In A Blanket." Most of the record couldn't be played over the radio.

Murphey, Michael Self-confessed cosmic cowboy Michael Murphey was born in Texas but migrated to Los Angeles early on. After majoring in creative writing at UCLA, he began working as a singer/songwriter. His first album, the well-received *Geronimo's Cadillac,* was cut in Nashville in 1972, and the title cut became a hit that year. In 1975 he had a hit single with "Wildfire," from his *Blue Sky, Night Thunder* album. Murphey remains one of the most important country-rock musicians.

Murphy, Elliott Originally billed as "the new Dylan," Elliott Murphy tried his best in 1973 with *Aquashow.* Lyrically he is excellent, but he has yet to put the words and music together.

Murray, Anne Born on June 20, 1947 in Springhill, Nova Scotia, Canada, Murray has become one of the most popular pop singers in America. Her career got its start on Canadian television's "Sing Along Jubilee," and she scored her first American hit in 1970 with "Snowbird." That song established her as both a pop and country artist, a status she has consistently capitalized on with such hits as "Cotton Jenny" (1972), "Danny's Song" (1973), "You Won't See Me" (1974) and others. After a brief layoff to raise a family, she returned to the charts in 1979 with her *A New Kind Of Feeling* album.

Nash, Graham Born on Feb. 2, 1942 in Blackpool, England, Graham Nash has carved a successful niche for himself as a harmonious, laid-back California rocker, risen from the ashes of the 1960s supergroup Crosby, Stills, Nash and Young (CSN&Y). With David Crosby, Stephen Stills and mercurial Canadian Neil Young, Nash virtually defined the soft California Sound of the late 1960s in the *Deja Vu* album (1970). Since then he has made a good, if inauspicious, career working with the group's remnants, most notably David Crosby. Recently Nash has become involved in the antinuclear power movement and has

Graham Nash

been placing his talents at the movement's disposal. Before joining CSN&Y, Nash was the leader of the immensely successful group the Hollies (formed in 1963), one of the most consistent hitmakers of the British Invasion with such ditties as "Stop Stop Stop" (1966), "On A Carousel" (1967), "Carrie Anne" (1967) and "King Midas In Reverse" (1967).

Nash, Johnny Born on Aug. 19, 1940 in Houston, Tex., Johnny Nash was the first (and one of the few) pop singers to top the charts with a reggae song, "I Can See Clearly Now" (1972). He had had modest successes as a soul singer in the mid-1960s ("Hold Me Tight" in 1968), but it wasn't until he moved to London in 1971 and came across the music of Bob Marley that he found the reggae formula. Although he continues to work, "I Can See Clearly Now" remains his greatest contribution to rock music.

Nazareth Dan McCafferty (vocals), Darryl Sweet (drums), Pete Agnew (bass), Manny Charlton (guitar)—A Scottish band committed to the standard of loud, long and raucous, Nazareth had been playing together for six years before hitting big in America with the *Hair Of The Dog* album and the hit single "Love Hurts" in 1975. Lead vocalist McCafferty embarked on an unsuccessful solo career later that same year.

Nazz Todd Rundgren (guitar), Carson van Osten (bass), Robert Antoni (vocals, keyboards), Thom Mooney—

Launched in 1968 in Philadelphia, Nazz tried very hard to sound very British. It is best remembered as the incubator for performer/producer Todd Rundgren. The group disbanded in 1969 after three albums and one modest hit, "Hello It's Me."

Rick Nelson

Nelson, Rick In one of those strange cases of life imitating art—or perhaps art imitating art—Eric Hilliard Nelson, son of Ozzie and Harriet Nelson, America's favorite radio (and later television) couple, went from an actor to a singing star when a girlfriend revealed she preferred Elvis to Ricky. Born on May 8, 1940 in Teaneck, N.J., Ricky jumped from the little screen to the big stage, singing everything from Fats Domino ("I'm Walking" in 1957) to Hank Williams ("My Bucket's Got A Hole In It" in 1958) until his real break came later in 1958 with "Poor Little Fool." He assembled one of the finest bands in the business, including guitar flash James Burton, and spent the next few years in workmanlike pursuit of stardom. The closest he came was with "Travelin' Man" in 1961, after which Ricky became Rick. Ironically, he came back with a hit in 1972 after attending an oldies concert in Madison Square Garden, where he was so disgusted by the worshipful attitude of fans and performers alike toward the old days that he wrote a song about it— "Garden Party," a bitterly satiric and excellent look at the world of popular music, subsection nostalgia. He presently works as a country singer with his Stone Canyon Band, producing very good but little listened-to records.

Nelson, Willie Perhaps the most unlikely superstar ever, certainly the least likely person to become one of the biggest musical phenomenons of the 1970s. All Willie Nelson (born on April 30, 1933 in Abbott, Tex.) ever wanted to be was a country singer. Through a twisted, convoluted path that included selling Bibles door-to-door during the day and working the meanest honky-tonks at night, Nelson arrived in Nashville in the mid-1950s and immediately established himself as a major songwriting talent. Such songs as "Crazy," recorded by Patsy Cline (and, later, by Linda Ronstadt); "Hello Walls," by Faron Young; "Pretty Paper," by Roy Orbison; and "Night Life," by Ray Price and, eventually, 70 other artists, placed Nelson in the rarified ranks of Hank Williams.

Willie Nelson

But Nashville and Nelson never seemed to get along, and his own music, rooted in the simplicity of earlier country music and the blues, found little foothold in the heavily orchestrated Nashville Sound of the early 1960s.

In what has become one of the most-told stories in popular music, Nelson came back to his Nashville house one day in 1972 to find it on fire. Racing into the burning house, he returned seconds later slightly scorched and with a battered guitar case, which most people assumed contained a beloved guitar. Actually it contained high-quality marijuana, and on that note Willie Nelson went home to Texas. What he discovered in Texas was that young people, weaned on hard rock, were looking for something different, and Nelson was ready with a host of his own songs and numerous old standards. The results were nothing short of phenomenal. Nelson was already a hero in Texas when his *Red Headed Stranger* album boosted him to national stardom in 1975. That album and the compilation album *The*

Outlaws, with friends Waylon Jennings and Tompall Glaser, brought country music to national attention and established Willie Nelson as a pop as well as a country act, a move helped along by his Fourth of July "picnics" in Austin, Tex., his new home. The picnics became the 1970s incarnation of the 1960s pop festivals, and Nelson's skillful blending of country and pop acts won friends on both ends of that musical spectrum.

Since 1975 Nelson has blazed new trails, defying classification. One of his biggest hits since then has been his *Stardust* album (1977), which featured Nelson performing his favorite old standards, such as the title song, the hit single "Georgia On My Mind" and others. In addition, he has cut a gospel album, a tribute to Lefty Frizzell, a tribute to Kris Kristofferson and a series of wildly popular duets with Waylon Jennings and, for good measure, has gone into the movies in a big way with a critically acclaimed performance in the Robert Redford/Jane Fonda film *Electric Horseman* (1979).

In short, Nelson is one of the most iconoclastic—and influential—musical figures of the 1970s.

Nesmith, Michael The Monkee who made good, Nesmith was already established as a songwriter when he was tapped to become the token musical member of the television group the Monkees in 1965. (Linda Ronstadt later had her first hit with the Stone Poneys via a Nesmith composition,

"Different Drum," in 1967.) Born on Dec. 30, 1942 in Houston, Tex., Nesmith had discovered the guitar in the Air Force and become a competent musician. It was his constant badgering of the powers-that-be in television land that gave the Monkees the opportunity to be more than cartoon characters. He put together a backup group called the First National Band (John Ware, drums; John London, bass; and Red Rhodes, steel guitar) and cut an album, *Magnetic South,* in 1970, resulting in the hit single "Joanne." Since then Nesmith has worked the country-rock circuit with consistent critical success and almost total public apathy. He has had a few modest successes ("Rio" in 1977), to keep him from sinking completely out of sight.

New Christy Minstrels, The   Named for the famed Edwin P. Christy American minstrel group, which helped popularize the songs of such composers as Stephen Foster in the mid-1800s, the New Christy Minstrels rode the folk music revival of the mid-1960s with such hits as "Green Green" (1963) and "Today" (1964). The group was actually a shifting musical congregation formed around veteran performer Randy Sparks and his lead singer Barry McGuire, who went on to record "Eve Of Destruction," solo, in 1965.

New Riders of the Purple Sage   John Dawson (vocals, guitar), Spencer Dryden (drums), Buddy Cage (pedal steel), Stephen Love (vocals, bass)—New Riders of the

Purple Sage, NRPS for short, was originally cloned from the Grateful Dead in 1969 when Jerry Garcia, the Dead's godfather, bought his first steel guitar. Garcia began working with soulmate John Dawson as sort of a Dead country auxiliary, and NRPS was the outgrowth. Of course, Garcia couldn't continue working in two bands, and pretty soon the band was playing personnel roulette. Spencer Dryden was drafted from the Jefferson Airplane, Buddy Cage from Ian and Sylvia and Anne Murray and, eventually, Stephen Love from all over. The group's blend of country and rock has always managed to be out-of-sync with prevailing rock and country tastes, and to this day NRPS is welcome in neither camp.

New Vaudeville Band, The Consisting originally of Geoff Stephens (a teacher of English, French, games and religious instruction and, later, an advertising agency executive) and a group of sessions musicians, the New Vaudeville

Randy Newman

Band produced the most hummable hit of 1966, "Winchester Cathedral." Basically, Stephens was looking for the 1920s/1930s sound he so loved, and he got it—so much so that an appearance on Ed Sullivan's television show sparked a revival of Rudy Vallee and megaphones. Some 400 artists eventually covered Stephens' creation, making him one of the most-recorded pop composers ever.

New York Dolls, The Sylvain Sylvain (guitar), Johnny Thunder (guitar), David Johansen (vocals), Arthur Kane (bass), Jerry Nolan (drums)—Call it pre-punk punk or post-glitter rock, but given a couple of years in either direction and the New York Dolls could have been big stars. Formed in New York in 1973, the Dolls were soon the darlings of that city's sleazoid circuit with their Mick Jagger-in-drag antics and loud, raucous guitar rock. Two years and two albums later, the Dolls slid down the drain, but not before blazing a trail for such New Wave rockers as Patti Smith and the Ramones. Sylvain Sylvain, Johnny Thunder and David Johansen are all deeply involved in the New Wave scene they helped pioneer as artists and producers. Johansen presently works as a solo artist, out of the drag attire that made the Dolls famous.

Newbury, Mickey Born on May 19, 1940 in Houston, Tex., Newbury is a country singer and songwriter best known as the composer of "An

American Trilogy" in 1972, made famous by Elvis Presley, and "San Francisco Mabel Joy."

Newman, Randy   Although long known as a songwriter and arranger (Judy Collins recorded his "I Think It's Going To Rain Today" in 1966), it wasn't until his hit "Short People" in 1977 that the bizarre world of Randy Newman (born Nov. 28, 1943) became part of the public domain. In addition to lambasting little people, the Los Angeles-based Newman has recorded his own version of a siren song to lure Africans to the slave ships (the brilliant "Sail Away") and an ode to good ole boys everywhere (*Good Ole Boys,* a whole album featuring material from the biography of Louisiana demagogue Huey Long). After the success of "Short People," Newman declared he was only in it for the money, of which he has been getting a lot. Of course the royalties from the smash hit version of "Mama Told Me Not To Come" by Three Dog Night (1970) and cuts of Newman songs by Ringo Starr, Bonnie Raitt, Nilsson (who recorded an entire album of Newman numbers in 1970) and Ray Charles don't hurt.

Newton, Wayne   It's inordinately easy to write off Wayne Newton as a purveyor of middle-of-the-road *schlock* (witness his hits: "Danke Schoen" in 1963, "Red Roses For A Blue Lady" in1965 and "Daddy Don't You Walk So Fast" in 1972). Of course, that's probably true. It's also true that Wayne Newton is the highest paid performer in Las

Vegas, which happens to be the highest paying circuit in the world. His Vegas shows are invariably total sellouts, and visitors wait months for a ticket. Born on April 3, 1942 in Roanoke, Va., Newton got his start on the Jackie Gleason television show, where he practically became a fixture. In the late 1960s, after a modestly successful recording career, Newton began concentrating on club appearances, eventually settling into Vegas. He is an outstanding performer and, snide remarks aside, has managed to tap a major lode in music.

Newton-John, Olivia
Periodically a performer surfaces whose life reads like a storybook version of the same. For Olivia Newton-John (born Sept. 26, 1948 in England but soon transplanted to Australia) the legendary twisted path to stardom has been more of a greased rail. From her first all-girl group in Australia to her first talent show victory (the top prize was a trip to England) to her subsequent success on English television to a recording career, Newton-John has clung to her sweet, melodious voice with its tiny trace of accent. In 1971, after a brief unsuccessful stint with a group called Toomorrow, she inadvertently became a country music star in the United States, thanks largely to the careful handling of her hit "If Not For You" by her manager and record company. With her 1973 smash "Let Me Be There," she cemented her place at the top of both the country and pop charts,

capturing three Grammies and top Country Music Association awards. After a bundle of singing successes ("I Honestly Love You" in 1974, "If You Love Me" in 1974, "Please Mr. Please" in 1975, "Have You Never Been Mellow" in 1975, "Don't Stop Believing" in 1976 etc.), she captured the much sought-after female lead in the movie version of the Broadway nostalgia machine *Grease,* opposite John Travolta. Newton-John's managers negotiated an excellent deal—equal billing and equal money. By the time *Grease* came out in 1978, Travolta was one of the biggest movie stars in the country, courtesy of *Saturday Night Fever* (1977), and Newton-John eventually received some $8 *million* for her role. Unfortunately, she chose to invest all that money in the movie *Xanadu,* in which she had artistic control as well as a starring role. The movie, released in 1980, bombed, but Newton-John recovered with a smash single in 1981-82, "Physical," and a new image to go along with it.

Nice, The   Keith Emerson (keyboards), Brian "Blinky" Davison (drums), Lee Jackson (bass, vocals), David O'List (vocals, guitar)—Launched in 1967 as the backup group for British soul singer P.P. Arnold, the Nice soon developed into a stage for Keith Emerson's flamboyant keyboard antics. The group pioneered the use of musical classics and all manner of musical styles from Bach to Bernstein as grist for Emerson's mill. Eventually the other members of the Nice took issue with the complete emphasis on their superstar keyboardman. The group collapsed in 1970, with Emerson taking his flamboyance a step further to Emerson, Lake and Palmer.

Nico Born in the early 1940s in Berlin, Nico had been a largely unsuccessful singer in England before linking up with pop culture maven Andy Warhol in the mid-1960s. She appeared in Warhol's *Chelsea Girls* movie and joined in his formation of the Velvet Underground, one of the great cult groups of the period. She has since recorded a series of solo albums, mostly with producer John Cale, for a variety of record labels, but Nico is perhaps better known as a Warhol personality than as a performing artist.

Nighthawk, Robert
Bluesman Robert Lee McCoy, known as Robert Nighthawk, was born in 1909 in Helena, Ark. and ranged across the country, spending large chunks of time in Memphis, St. Louis and Chicago. He was an expert bottleneck slide guitar and harp player, and his bottleneck style has found its way into the rock repertoire.

Nilsson, Harry An odd case, Brooklyn-born Harry Nilsson (born June 15, 1941) has treated recording success as something of a revolving door, routinely spinning from public acceptance to equally public disdain. He first became popular as the singer of "Everybody's Talkin'," the theme song of the Dustin Hoffman/Jon Voight movie *Midnight Cowboy.* In 1970 he composed and sang the soundtrack to the animated fantasy *The Point,* which he followed with his two most successful albums, *Nilsson Schmilsson* (1971) and *Son Of Schmilsson* (1972). He thereafter set about alienating his audience and harpooning his career, slashing his way through a series of self-indulgent albums with Beatle-buddies John Lennon and Ringo Starr. His present taste tends toward snatches of verse and 1920s crooner material.

Nitty Gritty Dirt Band John McEuen (banjo, mandolin, guitar, accordian), Jeff Hanna (vocals, guitar, percussion), Jim Ibbotson (vocals, bass), Jimmie Fadden (vocals, bass, harp)—While the Dirt Band's output , if measured in hit records, is not particularly impressive ("Mr. Bojangles" in 1970; "The House At Pooh Corner" in 1971), its overall effect on popular music is both far reaching and impressive. Founded in the West Coast folkie scene of the mid-1960s, the band dabbled in folk, country and Western music until 1973, when it decided to undertake a seemingly impossible task, a triple-album set featuring the best of American country and bluegrass recorded in Nashville with as many of the original performers as possible. The result was the *Will The Circle Be Unbroken* album, featuring Roy Acuff, Merle Travis, Mother Maybelle Carter, Doc Watson and many others. Even today the album stands as a magnificent tribute to American music and the Dirt Band's excellent tastes.

Since then the band has gone its laconic way, producing periodic hits and touching all the bases of popular music, from bluegrass to hard rock. A 1976 triple album, *Dirt, Silver And Gold,* shows the band to its best advantage on its 10th birthday.

Nitzsche, Jack A superb arranger and producer, Nitzsche has worked as an arranger for producer Phil Spector (on the Crystals' "He's A Rebel"), as a pianist for the Rolling Stones, as a keyboard man and arranger for Crazy Horse (on the group's excellent debut album) and as an arranger for Neil Young. He is presently in heavy demand as an arranger for both records and movie soundtracks (he did the score for *One Flew Over The Cuckoo's Nest).*

Nix, Don Born on Sept. 27, 1941 in Memphis, Tenn., Don Nix was one of the original members of the Mar-Keys (with Steve Cropper and Donald "Duck" Dunn), the white group which provided the soul music for the much-vaunted Stax Sound. Since leaving the group Nix has drifted from Los Angeles to England and back to Memphis, working as a solo artist, a producer for Leon Russell and John Mayall and a member of various bands. He is presently working with Willie Mitchell (best known as the producer of Al Green) of Hi Records in Memphis to get his solo career into the high gear he never found before.

Nix, Larry Brother of Don Nix, Larry Nix is best known as the master engineer/producer of the Memphis Sound.

Nix, Willie   Bluesman, known as the Memphis Blues Boy, Willie Nix played guitar and drums with James Cotton in the early 1950s and became known for his distinctive T-Bone Walker-influenced style.

Nugent, Ted   One of the true wild men of rock and roll, Nugent has turned heavy metal thundering into some bizarre sort of art form. Born in 1949 in Detroit, Nugent and his Amboy Dukes hit the big time in 1968 with the mind-blowing psychedelic anthem "Journey To The Center Of The Mind." While the Amboy Dukes eventually faded away, Nugent slugged it out solo on the local club circuit, getting crazier with each passing year. Pretty soon the Midwest papers were full of Nugent exploits, wild guitar duels and savage stories of raw meat being ripped apart on stage. Such a talent couldn't be confined for long, and in 1975 Nugent burst out of Detroit to go nationwide with "Cat Scratch Fever," a hit in 1977, and "Wang Dang . . . Poontang." With the coming of the 1980s Nugent announced that he would follow the line of mainstream performers into

Ted Nugent

the wilds of the New Wave, although what this means for his mind-splitting music only time will tell.

Laura Nyro

Nyro, Laura   Born on Oct. 18, 1947 in the Bronx, New York City, Nyro established herself as a major songwriting talent ("And When I Die," recorded by Blood, Sweat and Tears; "Stoney End," by Barbra Streisand; "Stoned Soul Picnic," "Wedding Bell Blues" and "Sweet Blindness," by the Fifth Dimension; "Eli's Coming," by Three Dog Night), before failing spectacularly as a performer at the 1967 Monterey Pop Festival. Never a facile performer, she completely alienated the hippie culture of the times by trying to sing her soft, gospelish music backed by three black singers. Despite the failure she continued to pursue her concept of white soul until 1971, when she stopped recording and making public appearances. She returned in 1975 with the

album *Smile,* but she has never reached beyond a cult following. She remains reclusive, and a critic has referred to her as one of modern music's most faceless stars.

Oak Ridge Boys, The   Joe Bonsall (vocals), Duane Allen (vocals), Bill Golden (vocals), Richard Sterban (vocals) — Originally one of the best-known and most controversial white gospel groups, the Oak Ridge Boys (they are a continuation of the original Oak Ridge Boys, formed before World War II at the Oak Ridge, Tenn. nuclear research facilities) decided in 1975 to "cross over." Going from gospel to pop has been a fairly common phenomenon with

The Oak Ridge Boys

black gospel singers, but very rare for their white counterparts. After a slow start, the Oaks scored big on the country charts in 1978 with "Y' All Come Back Saloon" and with numerous other subsequent hits on both the country and pop charts. In addition, their dynamic stage show, a legacy of their gospel days, keeps the Oaks in constant demand for television guest spots and specials.

Ochs, Michael The younger brother of Phil Ochs and compiler of a double album of his brother's best work, *Chords Of Fame* (1976), Michael Ochs is best known for the Michael Ochs Archives, one of the most impressive collections of photographs about rock and roll and its various personalities in existence. He also works extensively on rock TV programs and film.

Ochs, Phil Born on Dec. 19, 1940 in El Paso, Tex., Phil Ochs flowered in the Greenwich Village folk scene of the early 1960s; he was a contemporary and friend of the greatest folkie graduate of them all—Bob Dylan. Ochs

moved his music vehemently from folk into the political arena and, unlike Dylan, kept it there at a time when "being political" meant not being commercially successful. The result was that Ochs, ever the activist, was permanently consigned to the cult cellars. His songs became widely known, especially "There But For Fortune," recorded by Joan Baez in 1965, and "I Ain't A Marchin' Anymore," written by Ochs in 1966 and perhaps the single best-known and most moving antiwar song of the Vietnam period. Ochs' own career remained stalled, however. In the late 1960s he became involved with the blossoming drug culture, and predictably, his work sagged. After struggling through the early 1970s, Ochs committed suicide on April 8, 1976, leaving behind at least a few ringing anthems for social change.

Odetta Born Odetta Holmes on Dec. 31, 1930 in Birmingham, Ala., Odetta turned from classical music to folk music when she was almost 20. It proved a perfect match, and she went on to

become one of the country's foremost folk interpreters. A two-record set of her work, *The Essential Odetta,* has been compiled by Vanguard Records and is a must for fans of American folk music.

Ohio Express, The Douglas Grassel (guitar), Dale Powers (guitar), Jim Pfahler (organ), Tim Corwin (drums), Dean Kastran (bass)—Launched in Ohio in 1965, the Ohio Express is best remembered for its two huge "bubblegum" hits in 1968—"Yummy Yummy Yummy (I've Got Love In My Tummy)" and "Chewy Chewy." "Yummy," by the way, sold one million records in two months.

Ohio Players, The Leroy "Sugar" Bonner (guitar, vocals), Marvin "Merv" Pierce (horns), William "Billy" Beck (keyboards, vocals), Ralph "Pee Wee" Middlebrooks (horns), "Diamond" Williams (drums), Clarence "Satch" Satchell (sax, flute)—For a while, it seemed that the Ohio Players were far better known for their album covers than for their music; the covers featured strikingly beautiful, almost totally nude women in rather odd positions, such as being covered with honey (*Honey* in 1975). Hailing from the Dayton, Ohio area, the Players have been working together since the early 1960s, but they have only struck it big since 1974 (*Skin Tight*), riding the crest of a funky disco wave. That wave appeared to have crested, at least for the Ohio Players, around 1977, although in the world of flashing lights and electric dance floors, anything is possible.

O'Jays, The Eddie Levert (vocals), Walter Williams (vocals), William Powell (vocals)—The high priests of the Philadelphia Sound, the O'Jays began working together in 1958, along with Bobby Massey and Bill Isles, in Canton, Ohio. They started as the Mascots, becoming the O'Jays a couple of years later in deference to their manager and mentor, Eddie O'Jay, a local disc jockey. Although they were modestly successful, it wasn't until producers Kenny Gamble and Leon Huff launched their Philadelphia International label in 1972 that the group really took off. Gamble and Huff (who'd worked with the O'Jays in the late 1960s) were looking to expand the Motown formula into lusher, more heavily orchestrated soul material, and the O'Jays' music fit the bill perfectly. The groups' second album on Philly International, *Backstabbers* (1972), is justly considered a classic, featuring the masterful title cut, "992 Arguments" and "Love Train," three of the very finest examples of the Philadelphia Sound. Since then the group has been consistent hitmakers, although the Gamble-Huff miracle work has worn a little thin around the edges. It should be noted that the O'Jays are one of the very few groups to work social commentary—"Backstabbers" (1972), "Love Train" (1973) "For The Love Of Money" (1974)—into the mass orchestration format of Philly dance music. Yet they can still do an outstanding job on a simple love melody, such as "Use Ta Be My Girl" (1978), a classic example of 1960s soul

harmonizing. In 1976 Sam Strain (a former member of Little Anthony and the Imperials) replaced William Powell.

Orbison, Roy One of the all-time greats, Orbison was born on April 23, 1936 in the little town of Wink, Tex. After doing some recording on his own (with Norman Petty, Buddy Holly's manager), he drifted to Memphis, where he became a part of Sam Phillips' Sun Records revolution. While Orbison found moderate success as a rockabilly singer, most notably "Ooby Dooby," a 300,000-selling single in 1956, it seemed more likely that he would make it as a songwriter. From Memphis he went to Nashville, where he eventually found his way to Monument Studios and its owner/producer, Fred Foster. Under Foster's tutelage, Orbison blossomed. By his third release, "Only The Lonely"

(1960), Orbison had found his niche as "the Voice," an incredible vocal talent. He then began a string of hits that remains awesome—"Crying" (1961), "Dream Baby" (1962), "In Dreams" (1962), "Blue Bayou" (1963), "Pretty Paper" (1963), "It's Over" (1964), "Oh Pretty Woman" (1964). At one point Elvis Presley commented that Orbison was the only vocalist he was really afraid of, and even the Beatles were forced to take second billing on an Orbison tour of England in 1963. But beginning in 1965, Orbison was haunted by professional problems, like switching record companies, and by a series of deeply personal tragedies, including the loss of his wife in a motorcycle accident and the death of two of his three children in a fire. Those tragedies affected his work, particularly his songwriting, and his career ground to a halt. Happily, that career is

Roy Orbison

beginning to move again, with a critically well-received album called *Laminar Flow* in 1979 and faithful remakes of his old hits by other artists.

Orioles, The   Sonny Til (vocals), George Nelson (vocals), Alexander Sharp (vocals), Johnny Reed (vocals), Tommy Gaither (vocals)— Formed in Baltimore during the late 1940s and named after Maryland's state bird, the Orioles were consistent rhythm-and-blues hitmakers in the late 1940s and early 1950s, pioneering doo-wop music. In 1953 the group achieved a landmark breakthrough—their R&B cover version of "Crying In The Chapel," a country song, was not only a hit on the R&B charts, but crossed over onto the pop charts as well, making it one of the very first such crossovers and heralding the beginning of the rock era (along with three other rock landmarks—Jackie Brenston's "Rocket 88" in 1951, considered by many to be the first rock-and-roll song; the Dominoes' "Sixty Minute Man" in 1951; and Bill Haley's "Crazy Man Crazy" in 1953). Tommy Gaither was killed in an auto accident in 1950; his place was taken by Ralph Williams.

Orlando, Tony, and Dawn
Tony Orlando, Telma Louise Hopkins, Joyce Wilson— Orlando began his recording career in the early 1960s working with rock impresario Don Kirshner, but it wasn't until 1970 when he was asked to overdub a vocal on a song titled "Candida" that his career really took off. The song was a hit, but ironically, Orlando was

unwilling to give up his secure job as a record promotion man. He was persuaded to cut another vocal track, titled "Knock Three Times." That song was a huge hit later in 1970, and Orlando was off on a new career. All he needed was a backup; so two veteran studio singers, Telma Hopkins and Joyce Wilson, were selected. The results were electrifying, including one of the largest hits of all time— "Tie A Yellow Ribbon (Round The Old Oak Tree)" (1973)— and soon the three had their own television series. The death of comedian Freddie Prinze, a close personal friend of Orlando, so shocked the singer that he temporarily quit show business in 1977. Two years later he returned, this time as a solo act.

Orleans   John Hall (vocals, guitar), Larry Hoppen (guitar, keyboards, vocals), Lance Hoppen (bass, vocals), Wells Kelly (drums, vocals)—One of the artsiest of the American "art rock" bands, Orleans was formed in 1972 out of the ashes of Boffalongo, which featured John Hall, Larry Hoppen and Wells Kelly and had the original of "Dancing In The Moonlight." Hall was a talented sessions musician, having worked with Taj Mahal, Al Kooper and Loudon Wainwright, and Orleans concentrated on virtuosity. That concentration paid off in 1975 with the hit "Dance With Me," followed the next year by "Still The One." The band has since built a strong, loyal following.

Otis, Johnny   White bandleader Johnny Otis (born

on Dec. 28, 1924) played the odd role of midwife to much of the early 1950s black rhythm and blues. During this period he boosted such artists as Etta James, Little Esther Phillips, Hank Ballard and Jackie Wilson. He also wrote such R&B classics as "So Fine" (recorded originally by the Sheiks and a hit for the Fiestas in 1959), "Double Crossin' Blues" (a hit for Little Esther in 1950) and "Every Beat Of My Heart" (later a hit for the Pips in 1961). With Etta James, Otis cowrote the notorious "Roll With Me Henry" (released as "The Wallflower" in 1955), the answer song to Hank Ballard's ribald 1954 hit "Work With Me Annie." Otis scored a hit of his own in 1958 with "Willie And The Hand Jive."

Ozark Mountain Daredevils, The   John Dillon (guitar, various instruments, vocals), Steve Cash (harp, vocals), Randle Chowning (guitar, harp, vocals), Michael Granda (bass), Larry Lee (drums), Buddy Brayfield (piano)—One of those good ideas that never seems to jell, the Ozark Mountain Daredevils grew out of a top-notch local group in Springfield, Mo. during the early 1970s. Since then they have made some outstanding country-rock music, including their hit "If You Want To Get To Heaven" in 1974 and the next year's "It'll Shine When It Shines." The problem seems to be the lack of a coherent vision as to how country and how rock the group is going to be (the Daredevils first albums were cut in England; later albums in Nashville) and a subsequent confusion on the part of the audience.

Pablo Cruise Cory Lerios (keyboards, vocals), David Jenkins (guitar, vocals), Steve Price (drums, vocals), Bud Cockrell (bass, vocals)— Formed from the remains of It's a Beautiful Day (Bud Cockrell) and Stoneground (Cory Lerios, David Jenkins and Steve Price), Pablo Cruise became an FM standard with its very heavily produced, lushly orchestrated music, and it eventually established an AM foothhold in the late 1970s, with a hit single titled "Love Will Find A Way" (1978). The best album is probably the group's debut, *Pablo Cruise,* released in 1975.

Page, Patti Born Clara Ann Fowler on Nov. 8, 1927 in Claremore, Okla., Patti Page became one of the most successful and most-copied vocalists of the 1950s with such monster hits as "The Tennessee Waltz" (1950), "Mister And Mississippi" (1951), "The Doggie In The Window" (1953), "Cross Of Gold" (1955), "Old Cape Cod" (1957) and dozens of others. In 1965 she had a hit with the theme song to a horror movie titled *Hush Hush Sweet Charlotte.* She began her career singing in a church choir in Tulsa, Okla. and changed her name after a successful stint on a Tulsa radio station.

Palmer, Robert Born in Yorkshire, England, Robert Palmer has become one of the

Robert Palmer

foremost practitioners of "blue-eyed soul," a white interpretation of black rhythm and blues. After working steadily for various British R&B ensembles for years, Palmer first came to attention in the United States through his *Sneakin' Sally Through The Alley* album in 1974, but it wasn't until 1979 that he broke out of the FM ghetto into widespread public acceptance with his "Bad Case Of Loving You" hit single.

Palmer, Robert Born in Little Rock, Ark., Robert Palmer is one of the country's foremost music critics. He is a regular contributor to *The New York Times, Rolling Stone* magazine and many other publications and is considered an expert on the blues and rockabilly. He played clarinet in a late 1960s band called the Insect Trust.

Pappalardi, Felix Best known as a member of the very heavy group Mountain and as a producer of the hit power trio Cream, Pappalardi was born in New York City in 1939 and did his time on the folkie circuit before turning to producing (Joan Baez, the Lovin' Spoonful and others). After his success with Cream in the late 1960s, Pappalardi was looking for a similar type group when he stumbled on the mountainous guitarist Leslie West, and by 1970 Mountain was a going concern, including the hit single "Mississippi Queen." After the group broke up in 1973, Pappalardi returned to his studio, where he has been content to age into something of a rock legend, with guest shots here and there.

Parker, Graham One of rock and roll's professional Next Big Things, Graham Parker leaped from service station attendant in Britain to rock star in 12 short months. After a homemade demo tape got the ball rolling, Parker put together the best members of the British pub bands— including Brinsley Schwarz, Martin Belmont, Bob Andrews, Andrew Bodnar and Stephen Goulding—into the Rumour, and in 1976 the group's first album, *Howlin' Wind,* was released to worshipful reviews. Parker's formula was simple— rock and roll just like the stuff he grew up with, from Van Morrison to the Four Tops— music you could dance to. Since *Howlin' Wind* and the follow-up, *Heat Treatment,* the road has been straight up, but there's some question as to whether Parker is willing to

Graham Parker and the Rumour

follow it. He's recently been working with buddies Nick Lowe and Dave Edmunds, and his Next Big Thing image is beginning to tarnish slightly. Part of the problem seems to be that Parker's no-frills approach to rock, founded in pub rock, is at odds with New Wave rock, which plays off the more flamboyant of rock's performers.

Parker, Junior Bluesman Junior Parker was born in 1932 in West Memphis, Ark. and learned the blues harp from Sonny Boy Williamson. After a stint in Howlin' Wolf's band, Parker formed his own Blue Flames, one of the most popular rhythm-and-blues groups in the Memphis area. He made the first recording of "Mystery Train," a song he had written with Sun Records head Sam Phillips. That song later became one of Elvis Presley's first and one of his best-remembered hits.

Parks, Michael Stone-faced actor Michael Parks had one hit

single, "Long Lonesome Highway" in 1970, in conjunction with his sole television series, "Then Came Bronson."

Parks, Van Dyke Rock has produced more than its share of mystery men, and Van Dyke Parks ranks right up there with the best of them. Best known for his songwriting and production work, especially with Beach Boy Brian Wilson's "Surf's Up" and "Heroes and Villains," Parks began his career as a child actor and eventually became a songwriter for Walt Disney Productions. He drifted from his own work into production, including such artsy mid-1960s groups as Harper's Bizarre ("Anything Goes") and the Mojo Men ("Sit Down I Think I Love You") and then more ambitious tasks, such as the *Smile* album with Beach Boy Brian Wilson in the late 1960s. Throughout the 1970s he has worked on a variety of projects in a variety of positions, from producer (Arlo

Guthrie's moderately successful *Running Down The Road* album) to sessions piano work (with Little Feat and Judy Collins, among others).

Parsons, Gram Born on Nov. 5, 1946 in Winterhaven, Fla., Parsons was the most important pioneer in country rock, the fusion of rock and roll and country music that was to dominate much of the mid-1970s through such groups as the Eagles. While he is famous for his work with the Byrds (specifically the 1968 *Sweetheart of the Rodeo* album), he actually began his musical career with the International Submarine Band, formed while he was an 18-year-old student at Harvard. The band's single album, *Safe At Home,* is considered one of the starting points for country-rock music. By the time the album was released, Parsons had moved on to the Byrds, with whom he lasted three months—he quit after refusing to go on a tour of South Africa in 1968. *Sweetheart Of The Rodeo* was a landmark album, the first successful attempt to blend country and rock, but Parsons benefited little from it. In late 1968 he formed the Flying Burrito Brothers and participated in their first two albums, *The Gilded Palace of Sin* (1969) and *Burrito Deluxe* (1970), before moving on again. In late 1972 he began work on a solo album, *G.P.,* which featured Emmylou Harris as vocalist. *G.P.* and his second solo album, *Grievous Angel,* (also with Harris) served to define the country-rock genre he created and still stand as masterful statements.

Parsons died on Sept. 19,

1973 while rehearsing a new project. Shortly after, his body was snatched by longtime friend Phil Kaufman, who, apparently according to Parsons' wishes, cremated the body at the Joshua Tree National Monument. No cause of death was ever established.

Parton, Dolly   Born on Jan. 19, 1946 in Sevier County, Tenn., Parton became one of country music's premier singers and songwriters, only to turn her back on Nashville in the successful pursuit of pop stardom. One of a family of 12, Parton's early life read like a country song and indeed served as the inspiration for some of her best-known compositions. The family was big, country and poor, and when she turned 18, she headed for Nashville to make her career. Eventually she linked up with veteran country singer Porter Wagoner, and the pair became something of an institution. Beginning in 1974 she concentrated more on a solo career, spurred by her hit single "Jolene." About then she became close friends with Linda Ronstadt and Emmylou Harris, both of whom had been instrumental in popularizing Parton songs (Ronstadt cut "I Will Always Love You," Harris "Coat Of Many Colors"). Parton began drifting more and more toward her successful rock friends, until by 1977 RCA was financing a multimillion dollar "image change" for her, which included more rock-oriented albums, appearances at rock clubs and seemingly endless television exposure. The success of Parton's much-ballyhooed switch is still being tallied up. While she is without a doubt far more successful in terms of money and audience, she has, in turn, moved from a brilliant singer/songwriter to a conventional stylist of popular material.

Passions, The   Jimmy Gallagher (vocals), Tony Armato (vocals), Albee Galione (vocals), Vinnie Aciero (vocals)—Formed in 1959 in Brooklyn, New York City, the Passions are best remembered for their first hit, "Just To Be With You" (1959). That particular song was originally cut as a demo by the Cousins, Paul Simon and Carole King.

Paul, Les   Born Lester Polfus on June 9, 1916 in Waukesha, Wis., Les Paul is famous as the creator of tape overdubbing—superimposing tape tracks to put together the final version of a song—and for his constant improvement of the electric guitar. He pioneered the now-familiar solid body electric guitar fitted with several pick-ups, originally using a crudely cut log as the basis for his guitar. In addition, he worked for years with singing partner Mary Ford, their most notable hits being "Goofus" (1950) and "How High The Moon" (1951). In recent years Paul has been involved in two albums and a tour with Nashville guitar virtuoso Chet Atkins. Their latest album was appropriately titled *Guitar Monsters* (1979).

Dolly Parton

Les Paul

Paul and Paula Best remembered for their two 1963 hits, "Hey Paula" and "Young Lovers," Paul and Paula were actually Ray Hildebrand (born on Dec. 21, 1940 in Joshua, Tex.) and Jill Jackson (born on May 20, 1942 in McCaney, Tex.). Paul and Paula were the creation of flashy entrepreneur Major Bill Smith, a Texas legend.

Paxton, Tom Born on Oct. 31, 1937 in Chicago, Ill., Paxton began his folksinging career in the early 1960s with such soft ballads as "The Last Thing On My Mind" (1963). His lyrics became increasingly strident, and he rode the protest wave of the 1960s until it crested in the waning years of

that decade. He then shifted to England, where he quickly built a large cult following with such albums as *Heroes* (1978).

Paycheck, Johnny Born Don Lytle on May 31, 1941 in Ohio, Johnny Paycheck might have remained a journeyman country singer had it not been for the wildly successful 1978 hit "Take This Job And Shove It," written by country music bad boy David Allan Coe. The song became a national mania and was soon adopted by labor unions, political candidates and workers' groups everywhere. At one show in Texas, Paycheck had to sing the song 10 times in a row before the crowd would let him off stage. After a spell in the national limelight, he reverted to journeyman status once again, proving once again that it is impossible to follow up a hit of that magnitude.

Pearls Before Swine Tom Rapp (guitar, vocals), Jim Bohannon (keyboards), Roger Crissinger (keyboards), Wayne Harley (guitars), Lane Lederer (bass)—Described by one critic as "acid folk music," Pearls Before Swine managed to build and sustain a substantial cult following (especially on college campuses) in the late 1960s. When the band decided to get serious about its music and move to a bigger, more commercial label, it failed. According to legend, Pearls Before Swine founder Tom Rapp once beat out Bob Dylan in a talent contest.

Pendergrass, Teddy Originally a member of Harold Melvin and the Bluenotes,

Teddy Pendergrass went solo in 1976. His first album, *Teddy Pendergrass,* came the next year, and Pendergrass quickly established himself as something unique in Gamble and Huff's Philly International stables. He became maybe the last soul singer in the tradition of, say, Otis Redding. With such hits as "Close The Door" (1978), Pendergrass quickly claimed the soul turf as his own, adding a depth to the slick Philly Sound that was heretofore absent.

Penguins, The Cleveland Duncan (vocals); Dexter Tisby (vocals); Curtis Williams (vocals); Bruce Tate; and others, including Teddy Harper, Randy Jones— Formed in 1954 by Cleveland (Cleve) Duncan in Los Angeles, the group took its name from the penguin on the Kool Cigarettes package. In 1954 they recorded one of Williams' songwriting efforts, "Earth Angel," written for his girl friend. The song began as a monster hit on the rhythm-and-blues charts and quickly crossed over to the pop charts—one of the first records to do so on a national scale. "Earth Angel" also helped trigger a wave of doo-wop, ushering in one of the most famous eras of rock.

Pentangle, The Bert Jansch (guitar, vocals), Terry Cox (percussion), Danny Thompson (bass), John Renbourn (guitar, vocals), Jacqui McShee (vocals)— British folk-rock group formed in 1967 by a congregation of top-notch British folkies. The group developed a fairly large cult following in the United

States with its folky blend of blues, jazz and traditional folk music. That formula held until 1973, when the group disbanded.

Perkins, Carl One of popular music's saddest "also rans," Carl Perkins (born on April 9, 1932 in Lake City, Tenn.) once rivaled Elvis Presley for the title of King of Rock and Roll, only to be knocked out of the running by a personal tragedy. Perkins was already a local rockabilly star in Jackson, Tenn. when he decided to make the big move to Memphis to try his hand at Sun Records. One of his first cuts there was a number he had penned after observing a young man on a dance floor who was obviously afraid that the dancers were going to scuff his new shoes. The song, of course, was "Blue Suede Shoes," and the recording by Carl Perkins and his two brothers immediately topped the country, pop and rhythm-and-blues charts—a trick once considered impossible, since each chart was aimed at a totally different audience. An invitation to a treasured guest spot on "The Ed Sullivan Show" was forthcoming, but on the way to that show in March 1956, Perkins was critically injured in a car wreck, and his brother Jay was killed. Perkins spent almost a year in the hospital, and when he was released, his song had been covered by Elvis Presley, and the rockabilly fires were already dying.

He continued recording and eventually toured with Johnny Cash, finally putting together a critically well-received comeback album, *Ol' Blue*

Suede's Back, in 1978 for Jet Records. Perkins now regularly plays the clubs, where he credits Presley with opening the door for acts like himself.

Perry, Richard Although record producer Richard Perry cut his teeth on such acts as Tiny Tim and Ella Fitzgerald, it wasn't until he worked with Barbra Streisand's *Stoney End* album in 1970 that he found his niche as perhaps one of the most influential producers of the 1970s. His brand of soft rock and sophistication became the trademark of the times, boosting such acts as Carly Simon, Art Garfunkel, Ringo Starr, Harry Nilsson, Diana Ross, Leo Sayer and the Pointer Sisters. In the late 1970s he established his own record company, Planet, distributed by Warner Brothers.

Persuasions, The Jerry Lawson (vocals), Jimmy Hayes (vocals), Joe Russell (vocals), Jayotis Washington (vocals), Herbert Rhoad (vocals)—The Kings of A Capella from Brooklyn, New York City, the Persuasions have elevated doo-wop to an art form. Theirs is perhaps the ultimate fusion of rhythm and blues and gospel roots expressed in superbly crafted street-corner harmonies. When the Persuasions sing Sam Cooke's "She Was Only Sixteen" or Elvis Presley's "Return To Sender" or Joe South's "Don't It Make You Wanta Go Home," the songs come to life with an energy, spirit and emotionalism that is the essence of rock and roll and what really makes it worth listening to. The group plays to a devoted following in clubs

around the country; their albums include *We Came To Play* and *Chirpin'*.

Peter and Gordon Peter Asher and Gordon Waller exploded on the American musical scene in 1964, riding the peak of the British Invasion with such hits as "World Without Love" (1964), "I Don't Want To See You Again" (1964) and such novelty tunes as "Lady Godiva" (1966). Asher and Waller first met in boarding school, where they began working together. On the strength of "World Without Love," written for the duo by Beatles John Lennon and Paul McCartney, the group became major figures in the British Invasion. Asher went on to become an even more important figure in popular music as a manager, handling such superstar acts as Linda Ronstadt and James Taylor.

Peter, Paul and Mary Peter Yarrow, Paul Stookey and Mary Travers practically defined the folk period of the early 1960s with such classic hits as "If I Had A Hammer" (1962), "Blowin' In The Wind" (1963), "Puff The Magic Dragon" (1963), "Don't Think Twice It's All Right" (1963) and others. They also introduced numerous songwriters to a widespread public, including Bob Dylan ("Blowin' In The Wind," "Don't Think Twice"), Pete Seeger ("If I Had A Hammer") and Woody Guthrie ("Puff"). The group held on until the turn of the decade, recording the sardonic "I Dig Rock And Roll Music" (1967) and introducing yet another songwriter, John Denver, with his "Leaving On A Jet Plane"

Peter, Paul & Mary

(1970) before disbanding in 1971. After checkered solo careers (Yarrow wrote and coproduced "Torn Between Two Lovers," a huge hit for Mary MacGregor in 1976), the group re-formed in late 1978, with critical success.

Petty, Tom, and the Heartbreakers   Tom Petty and the Heartbreakers (Mike Campbell, guitar; Stan Lynch, drums, vocals; Benmont Tench, piano, organ, vocals; and Ron Blair, bass) were one of the first New Wave acts to really break big, although many critics consider them more traditional rock than New Wave. The group was formed in Los Angeles during the mid-1970s and began drawing attention to its hard rocking music with its second album, *You're Gonna Get It!* The group's music ranged from driving guitar-based rock to, oddly enough, a Byrd-flavored number titled "Listen To Her Heart," an FM radio favorite. With the third album, *Damn The Torpedoes!* in 1979, Tom Petty and the Heartbreakers were established as one of the hottest new rock acts around— as well as one of the biggest sellers.

P.F.M.   Franz Di Ciccio (drums, vocals), Flavio Premoli (keyboards, vocals), Franco Mussida (guitar, vocals), Mauro Pagani (flutes, violin, vocals) Patrick Djivas (bass), Bernardo Lanzetti (guitar, vocals)— Actually Premiata Forneria Marconi, P.F.M. was formed in Italy in 1971 and became one of the few Italian rock groups to achieve international success (largely thanks to Keith Emerson of Emerson, Lake and Palmer, who signed the group to ELP's special label). The group's albums have included *P.F.M. Cook* (1975) and *Chocolate Kings* (1976).

Phillips, Esther.   See Little Esther.

Phillips, Sam   The near-legendary creator of Sun Records was born in 1925 in Florence, Ala. and studied engineering, podiatry and embalming before settling for a career in radio. After moving to Memphis in the mid-1940s, Phillips was struck by the wealth of musical talent— mostly black—that the city had to offer. Phillips had always been fascinated by the blues, and he set about to put it on record. The result was Sun, originally conceived to record such greats as Howlin' Wolf, B.B. King, Rufus Thomas and other lesser known blues artists. But Phillips was always on the lookout for a white man who could tap the feelings of the blues. That person appeared in 1954, when Elvis Presley walked into the studio to cut a record for his mother. Phillips and Presley went on to produce some of the most powerful rock-and-roll music to date, music that over a quarter of a century later remains fresh and vital. (The best anthology is the RCA package *The Sun*

Tom Petty & the Heartbreakers

Sessions, released in 1976.) Phillips went on to discover or attract such talents as Jerry Lee Lewis, Carl Perkins, Roy Orbison, Johnny Cash, Charlie Rich and a host of others, from Ike Turner, who first recorded for Phillips and later acted as his talent scout, to Billy Sherrill, who went on to become one of Nashville's most successful producers. Phillips has recently come out of his self-imposed retirement from the music business to produce several cuts by John Prine and other local acts. There is little that happens in popular music today that hasn't been touched on some level by the magic of Sam Phillips.

Phillips, Shawn Born in 1943 in Texas, Shawn Phillips began recording in 1963 with a version of "Frankie And Johnny." Some 15 albums later Phillips is an international star, although not so much in the United States. His music has moved from folk to an increasingly more orchestrated style. His album *Transcendence* in 1978 featured an orchestral arrangement and Herbie Hancock's jazz group. Nevertheless, he remains best known for his West Coast-sounding soft rock.

Pickett, Bobby "Boris" Born on Feb. 11, 1942 in Massachusetts, stand-up comedian Bobby Pickett, during a stint with a lounge singing group, wrote his masterpiece—"Monster Mash" in 1962. The song, recorded with the Crypt Kickers, has been released three times and will probably be released many more.

Pickett, Wilson Born on March 18, 1941 in Prattville, Ala., "The Wicked" Wilson Pickett started singing rhythm and blues in 1959 with a group called the Falcons in Detroit, where Pickett was raised. In 1963 he got his first taste of stardom when his "If You Need Me" grew from a hit to a rhythm-and-blues standard. But it wasn't until the next year, when he signed with Atlantic Records, that his career as one of the top soul singers of the 1960s really took off. First working with the legendary rhythm section at Stax Records in Memphis and later with the equally talented section in Muscle Shoals, Pickett produced a string of classic soul songs—"In The Midnight Hour" (1965), "634-5789" (1966), "Mustang Sally" (1966),"Funky Broadway" (1967), "Hey Jude" (1969).

Pinetoppers, The A Macon, Ga. group formed around local singer Johnny Jenkins. Otis Redding was hired to drive the Pinetoppers' bus to Memphis in 1963 for an audition at Stax Records. Redding, of course, also sang at that audition and went on to become a star. The Pinetoppers went back to Macon.

Pink Floyd Rick Wright (keyboards); Nick Mason (drums); Roger Waters (piano, bass); Dave Gilmour (guitar); additional member: Syd Barrett—The quintessential psychedelic group, Pink Floyd has survived long enough to be dubbed incredible, at the very least. Launched in England during the mid-1960s, the group began playing Chuck Berry covers at local pubs before being caught up in the psychedelic vibrations coming from San Francisco. Growing weirder by the minute, Pink Floyd became the darling of

London's underground, along with the Crazy World of Arthur Brown and the Soft Machine. In 1966 Pink Floyd took a giant step forward (at least for performing rock bands) when they developed a slide presentation to be shown on a screen over their heads while they performed. The novelty was quickly dubbed a "lightshow," and within a couple of years *everybody* had to have one. While the group was quite successful in Britain, it wasn't until 1973—well after the psychedelic wave had petered out—that the Floyd stormed the American market with *Dark Side Of The Moon,* a wildly successful album that carried the group's mysterious conception of the psychedelic era into the decidedly good-natured 1970s. Pink Floyd founder Syd Barrett, who took his psychedelia too seriously, was replaced by Dave Gilmour in 1968. Nevertheless, the group has proved surprisingly durable; their ● *The Wall* album was one of the most popular of 1980—*the* most popular, according to *Rolling Stone.*

Pink Lady   Would you believe Japan's most popular disco duo as an American variety show? No one else did either, which is why the much-hyped American Invasion by the incredibly long-legged Mie and Kei, collectively Pink Lady, died abirthing. The girls were a national mania in Japan, where you could get everything from Pink Lady dolls to Pink Lady hot dogs, and their sharp manager, Paul Drew, tried for a country transplant. The result was a couple of leggy album covers and a television series in

1979, neither of which worked particularly well. The duo broke up in 1980.

Pirates   Johnny Spence (guitar), Mick Green (vocals, guitar), Frank Farley (drums, vocals)—British New Wave group formed in the mid-1970s and heavily influenced by Chuck Berry and various rockabilly acts. As with many of the other British New Wavers, the Pirates can be summed up simply by saying "no-frills rock." They are best known for their 1978 single "Shakin' All Over."

Pitney, Gene   Born on Feb. 17, 1941 in Rockville, Conn. Pitney first came to attention as a songwriter, penning "Hello Mary Lou" (1961) for Rick Nelson, the Crystals' classic "He's A Rebel" (1962) and other hits. In 1962 he began a string of hits on his own, starting with "Town Without Pity." His strong, distinctive voice was best suited to urgent ballads, such as "The Man Who Shot Liberty Valance" (1962), "24 Hours From Tulsa" (1963) and "It Hurts To Be In Love" (1964).

Plastic Bertrand   A brief respite from the stupifying seriousness of rock in the late 1970s, the Belgian known as Plastic Bertrand (actually his name is Plastoc) released his infectious "Ca Plane Pour Moi" in 1978, which went on to become a worldwide hit on the radio and in discos. He was once fired from his position as mail boy at a major record company because the brass there thought he dressed strangely.

Plastic Bertrand

Platters, The   Tony Williams (vocals); Zola Taylor (vocals); David Lynch (vocals); Paul Robi (vocals); Herb Reed (vocals); additional member: Alex Hodge—Originally formed in Los Angeles in 1953, the Platters worked steadily through the 1950s and well into the 1960s (their last hit, "With This Ring," was in 1967), cutting such classics as "Only You" (1955), "The Great Pretender" (1955), "My Prayer" (1956), "Twilight Time" (1958) and "Smoke Gets In Your Eyes" (1958). In the closing minutes of the 1970s, the Platters enjoyed something of a revival, thanks to late night television advertisements, and their repackaged albums once again became big sellers.

Poco   Tim Schmit (bass, vocals); George Grantham (drums); Rusty Young (pedal steel, banjo, guitar); Paul Cotton (guitar, vocals); and others, including Richie Furay, Jim Messina, Randy Meisner—

Originally one of the better country-rock ensembles, Poco (the group wanted to be called Pogo, but the creator of the comic strip of the same name wouldn't allow it) was formed from the ashes of the Buffalo Springfield by Richie Furay and Jim Messina. The band produced excellent music, and nobody—least of all Furay and Messina—could figure out why it didn't sell. Randy Meisner drifted away after the first album, *Pickin' Up The Pieces,* with its classic title cut, and eventually ended up with the Eagles. Messina lasted two more albums before leaving to join Kenny Loggins and get famous and successful. Furay hung on for three more albums, including Poco's two best known, *A Good Feelin' To Know* and *Crazy Eyes,* before quitting in disgust with the musical direction of the group to form Souther-Hillman-Furay, which didn't work either. Today Poco plods on and on, scoring just enough minor hits to keep it working.

The Pointer Sisters

Pointer Sisters, The   The Pointer Sisters—Ruth, June, Anita and Bonnie—were responsible for some of the most eclectic and dynamic music of the mid-1970s. The daughters of a preacher, they were raised in a strictly religious household in Oakland, Calif., hearing no secular music until high school. They developed a unique style, rooted, understandably, in gospel music but touching every other form from psychedelic rock to hard country. In 1973 the four sisters, decked out in thrift store chic and singing an incredible range of songs, fell into the wave of nostalgia for the 1940s and found themselves on television almost constantly. Their music ranged from the New Orleans sound of Allen Toussaint's "Yes, We Can-Can" (1973) to country, with their "Fairy Tale" (1974), which the sisters premiered to a wild reception on the stage of Nashville's hallowed Grand Ole Opry. They went on to the scat-singing "How Long (Betcha Gotta Chick On The Side)" (1975) and older material, such as "Salted Peanuts." In 1977 the sisters broke up, but eventually Anita, June and Ruth re-formed (Bonnie maintained a solo career) and had a hit in 1978-79 with a stunning rendition of Bruce Springsteen's "Fire."

Police, The   Andy Summers (guitar), Gordon Sumner (bass), Stewart Copeland (drums)—English New Wave group originally formed around sessions man Andy Summers. The group was one of the first English New Wave bands to score big in the American market with it's 1979 hit, "Roxanne," a hypnotic single. In 1980 the Police released *Zenyatta Mondatta,* which made the top 10.

164

Ponty, Jean-Luc Born in France, jazz violinist Jean-Luc Ponty developed a large following among rock fans for his work with Frank Zappa (*Hot Rats* in 1969) and John McLaughlin and the Mahavishnu Orchestra in 1974. He also played violin on Elton John's *Honky Chateau* album in 1972 and has recorded several solo albums.

Pop, Iggy James Jewel Osterburg (born in 1947 in Ann Arbor, Mich.) adopted the name Iggy when he became vocalist for a local Detroit group called the Prime Movers. However, it was as the moving force behind the Stooges (Ron Asheton, guitar; Scott Asheton, drums; and Dave Alexander, bass), that Iggy came into his own. The Stooges represented the grossest, most depraved example of pre-punk punk. The music was raw and wild, as were the audiences—on *Metallic K.O.*, released in 1976 and originally recorded on a cassette, one can actually hear the band being pelted with beer bottles. Ah, art. Some say Iggy's music is quintessential rock and roll, and to be sure, it is one of the spiritual fathers of today's New Wave music (which Iggy continues, more or less, to perform). Others claim the beer bottles on *Metallic K.O.* represent the most eloquent statement ever made about the Stooges' music. In either case Iggy Pop remains rock's wildest and most-demented performer.

Pratt, Andy Born in Cambridge, Mass., Andy Pratt is best known as a soft rock singer (*Resolution* in 1976) and as a songwriter ("Avenging Annie," recorded by Roger Daltrey of the Who on his solo album *One Of The Boys*).

Presley, Elvis The King of Rock and Roll, Elvis Aron Presley was as much a creature of myth as of reality. He was the pivot point on which the whole popular music world turned. To be sure, there were other rock-and-roll artists and songs before Elvis Presley and Sam Phillips walked into the Sun Records recording studio in Memphis in 1954. Phillips himself was responsible for Jackie Brenston's "Rocket 88" (produced by Ike Turner) in 1951, considered by many to be the "first" rock record, and Bill Haley and the Comets were already stars. But Presley was different—he would become the center of the storm, the vehicle by which rock and roll would be spread throughout the country. After Elvis nothing would remain the same.

He was born on Jan. 8, 1935 in Tupelo, Miss. and began singing early on. In fact, in 1943 he won a local talent contest with the soppy ballad "Old Shep," which he would later record. In the late 1940s the family moved to Memphis, where Elvis eventually got a job as a truck driver for a local electric company.

The Police

Elvis Presley

He had driven past the Memphis Recording Service, owned by Sam Phillips as part of Sun Records, before he built up enough nerve to go in. The occasion was not an audition, but rather to make a gift record for his mother, Gladys, whom he adored. Within a few minutes he had cut "My Happiness" and "That's When Your Heartaches Begin," accompanying himself on guitar. A snatch of the session was recorded by Sun secretary Marion Keisker, who was impressed with Elvis' voice. So was Sam Phillips when he heard the tape, and he remembered the singer. When Elvis dropped by the studio almost a year later, Phillips cut a demo by him, and when a tape came in that Phillips had no singer for, he called Elvis.

Phillips also called up a guitar player, Scotty Moore, and a slap-bass man, Bill Black, and the two musicians began working with Elvis. Nothing much happened until July 6, 1954, when the three and Phillips, after a particularly discouraging session, began working with Arthur "Big Boy" Crudup's "That's All Right." Phillips was electrified—here was a white man singing in a black idiom—and he ordered a quick second take. That take was put on record, and the world spun.

Elvis Presley went on to cut a series of brilliant songs on Sun (collected on the 1976 RCA album *The Sun Sessions*) before linking up with country promoter Col. Tom Parker, who knew a gold mine when he saw it. Under Parker's canny management, Elvis was sold to RCA Records for what was, at that time, a staggering amount of money—$35,000. Elvis' first RCA release, "Heartbreak Hotel" (1955), turned him into a national mania. Girls fainted; parents fretted and Elvis rocked like no one had ever rocked before. "Blue Suede Shoes," "Hound Dog" "Don't Be Cruel" (all in 1956) and "All Shook Up" (1957) galvanized America, and a Presley appearance on Ed Sullivan's TV show—from the waist up to save the country from Elvis' thrusting hips—only fed the fires. Under the tutelage of Col. Tom, Elvis turned to Hollywood, making *Love Me Tender* in 1956, the first of a long string of Elvis movies. In 1958 the King was drafted and sent to Germany. Meanwhile Parker began releasing his already-recorded material, which resulted in making Elvis an even bigger star when he got out of the Army in 1960 than when he went in.

But the fires had abated (or Col. Tom had decreed that the fires abate), and the new Elvis was more interested in ballads than in rockabilly fury. He continued making movies— one bubble-headed film after another—and piling up an unprecedented number of hit records, one on top of the other. While his audience remained stable, the younger kids were being lured away during the mid-1960s by the British Invasion, much of which was, ironically, rockabilly repackaged and shipped back home. 1967 marked the first year in Presley's career that he did not have a top 20 single.

Elvis seemed oblivious to it all until Christmas 1968, when

he made his much-vaunted TV special comeback, rocking as hard as ever and showing that he'd lost none of the old edge during the previous 10 years of fluff. He then returned to touring with a vengeance, smashing Vegas attendance records like pins in a bowling alley, and started making outstanding recordings again—"In The Ghetto" (1969), "Suspicious Minds (1969), "Kentucky Rain" (1970) and "Burning Love" (1972).

In 1973, Presley was divorced by his wife of six years, Priscilla, who took custody of their daughter, Lisa Marie. Although Elvis kept touring, the spirit was clearly gone. He developed major health problems, which he kept at bay with an increasingly large barrage of drugs. On Aug. 16, 1977 he died at the age of 42, the victim of a normally minor heart ailment.

His death caused an almost unprecedented outpouring of national grief, and it was painfully clear that an era had passed. Every one of his albums began selling like wild, and even now it's impossible to compute how many records he has sold during his life and since his death. He is the single most important figure in the history of rock and roll, the very bedrock on which the music is founded.

Preston, Billy   The perennial sideman, Preston was born on Sept. 9, 1946 in Houston, Tex. Growing up in Los Angeles, he was involved with the entertainment business practically as soon as he could walk, from playing with Mahalia Jackson to touring with Little Richard. He cut his first record in 1962, under the tutelage of Sam Cooke, and ended up on "Shindig," television's answer to the rock revolution. His work caught the ear of Beatle George Harrison, and Preston was invited to play on the Beatles' "Get Back," which for the first time carried a non-Beatle credit—"The Beatles with Billy Preston." That led to a series of guest appearances and tours with the Beatles and the Rolling Stones and eventually to two hits on his own, "Will It Go Round In Circles" (1973) and "Nothing From Nothing" (1974). He still turns up regularly as a guest and sideman, although the solo hits have stopped coming.

Pretenders   Chrissie Hynde (vocals), Martin Chambers (drums), James Honeyman Scott (guitar), Peter Farndon (bass)—Centered around flamboyant, hard-edged vocalist Hynde, a native of Akron, Ohio (the other members of the group are English), the Pretenders have become one of the best-received bands to emerge in the New Wave movement. Their first album, *Pretenders,* produced by Nick Lowe in 1980, showed Hynde as a particularly effective and evocative vocalist, with a sense of both 1960s rock and earlier rhythm and blues. The album became a top 10 seller that year.

Pretty Things, The   Phil May (vocals), Jack Green (bass, vocals), Gordon Edwards (keyboards, guitar, vocals), Peter Tolson (guitar, vocals), John Povey (keyboards, vocals), Skip Alan (drums)—Once rivals to the Rolling Stones, the Pretty Things (the name is from a Bo Diddley song) were meaner, tougher and nastier than the Stones, and for a while it looked like they might give them a run for the money. That's not the way things worked out, though, and despite critical approval for many years, the Pretty Things kept sinking. Before they sank completely in 1976, they had "invented" the rock opera— *S.F. Sorrow* in 1968, which inspired Peter Townshend of the Who to write the landmark *Tommy.* In one of life's little ironies, the release of the Pretty Things' opera was held up for over a year and when it came out in the United States, it was lambasted for ripping off *Tommy.* They also produced some great albums, including *Parachute* (1971) and *Freeway Madness*(1973).

Previn, Dory   Cult artist Dory Previn began her career writing movie scores (for such films as *The Valley of the Dolls* and *Last Tango in Paris*), moved on to making albums, such as *Mythical Kings And Iguanas* and *We're Children Of Coincidence And Harpo Marx,* and has written an autobiography.

Price, Lloyd   Born on March 9, 1933 in New Orleans, La., Price began a distinguished career in the early 1950s when he wrote the now-legendary "Lawdy Miss Clawdy." He recorded that song himself in 1952, but it wasn't until his 1958 retelling of the "Stagger Lee" myth that he had a big national hit. The next year he recorded another hit that has become a standard on the rock revival circuit—"Personality."

Pride, Charley Country singer Charley Pride (born on March 18, 1938 in Sledge, Miss.) was the first successful black entertainer to emerge in country music. He is best known for such hits as "Kiss An Angel Good Morning" (1971), "Amazing Love" (1973) and "Mississippi Cotton-Pickin' Delta Town" (1974). Pride is also one of the few—perhaps the only—modern country singers to have ever actually picked cotton.

John Prine

Prine, John The latest convert to Memphis rockabilly madness, John Prine (born on Oct. 10, 1946 in Maywood, Ill.) was well known as a folk singer extraordinaire before falling in with Sam Phillips and his son, Knox. Prine had been discovered by the unlikely combination of Paul Anka and Kris Kristofferson and was best known for his "Sam Stone," a painful song about a Vietnam veteran on drugs, and "Hello In There," a poignant song about old people, recorded by Bette Midler. In 1978 Prine, at the suggestion of "Cowboy" Jack Clement, went to Memphis to record his *Pink Cadillac* album with Knox Phillips. Knox was joined by his father, who came out of retirement to work on the Prine album. The results were particularly satisfying— rockabilly of the 1950s successfully translated into the music of 1979. Predictably, the album failed to sell.

Prisonaires, The Johnny Bragg (vocals), William Stewart (guitar, vocals), Ed Thurman (vocals), Marcell Sanders (vocals), John Drue (vocals)— Formed at the Tennessee State Prison in Nashville in 1944, the Prisonaires were a group of black inmates organized by Johnny Bragg, who, by special dispensation of the warden, recorded "Just Walkin' In The Rain." The song became a big hit for Johnnie Ray in 1956, and the royalties were held in trust for Johnny Bragg. The governor of Tennessee heard of the Prisonaires and was so impressed that he allowed them to travel to Memphis, under heavy guard, to record for Sun Records. In addition, the group once backed Elvis Presley. He later repaid the favor by a visit to the prison.

Proby, P.J. Born James Marcus Smith on Nov. 6, 1938 in Houston, Tex., P.J. Proby's career really took off when he established residency on television's "Shindig" in the mid-1960s. Eventually he moved to England, where he became a huge star. His biggest American song came in 1967 with "Nicki Hoeky," a top 20 hit.

Procol Harum Gary Brooker (piano, vocals); Chris Copping (organ); Mick Grabham (guitar); Alan Cartwright (bass); B.J. Wilson (drums); Keith Reid (lyrics); and others, including Robin Trower (guitar), Bob Harrison (drums), Ray Rowyer (guitar), Dave Knights (bass), David Ball (guitar)—Originally formed as your basic mid-1960s rhythm-and-blues group, Procol Harum shot to the top of the charts in May 1967 with the haunting "A Whiter Shade Of Pale," based, oddly enough, on a Bach cantata. The stunning success so rattled the group that they almost collapsed, with various personnel changes and a general thrashing about in search of direction. They found that direction in 1973 with *Grand Hotel,* and briefly soared to the top for a second go-round. Although the second time did last longer than the first, Procol Harum again failed to consolidate its victory and went down once more by the mid-1970s.

Professor Longhair Henry Roy Byrd, better known as Professor Longhair, was a fixture in New Orleans dancehalls from the end of World War II until his death in 1980. Although never nationally successful himself, Byrd's barrelhouse piano style was a major influence on such New Orleans greats as Fats Domino, Huey "Piano" Smith, Dr. John and Allen Toussaint and helped lay the ground work for rock and roll. Byrd died of a heart attack on Jan. 30, 1980.

Puckett, Gary, and the Union Gap Gary Puckett (vocals, guitar), Dwight Bement (sax), Gary Withem (keyboards), Kerry Chater (bass), Paul Wheatbread (drums)—Formed during the mid-1960s in San Diego by Puckett, the group originally gained a reputation of sorts by appearing in Civil War uniforms. In 1967, though, the group managed to achieve a different sort of reputation through their reworking of the old Tompall Glaser and the Glaser Brothers' hit "Girl, Girl" into "Woman, Woman." The group then began a string of licentious hits, beginning with "Young Girl," (1968), "Lady Willpower" (1968), "Don't Give In To Him" (1969), "This Girl Is A Woman Now" (1969) and finally (and perhaps appropriately) "Let's Give Adam And Eve Another Chance" (1970). Puckett then left the group and quickly sank.

Quatro, Suzi Born on June 3, 1950 in Detroit, Mich., Suzie Quatro, decked out in leather, had a brief fling in the mid-1970s as the "raunchiest female rock-and-roll star" in England, compliments of her flashy manager, Mickie Most. Her songs about cars and teenage angst were very successful in England, but the formula failed to generate the proper excitement in the jaded American market. She eventually ended up parodying herself as an occasional

Queen

character in the television nostalgia series "Happy Days."

Queen Freddy Mercury (vocals), Brian May (guitar), John Deacon (bass), Roger Taylor (drums)—Wildly pretentious, outrageously derivative, stylish to a flaw, the British group Queen formed around Freddy Mercury in 1972, filling a void left by the absence of such masters as Led Zeppelin and David Bowie. But while the Zep sledgehammered, Queen was content to use a very stylish jackhammer to achieve the same results. Such strange songs as "Killer Queen" (1974) and "We Are The Champions (Of The World)" (1977) established the band as not only consistent sellers, but

critics' favorites as well. Queen managed to reach a plateau of outrageousness in 1979, when, in an attempt to promote its new single, "Bicycle Races/Fat Bottom Girls," the group invited women to London, especially those with the aforementioned posteriors, to turn out for a nude bicycle race. A staggering number did so, and the result was a classic poster (actually a posterior poster) and a hit song.

Question Mark and the Mysterians "Question Mark" (vocals), Bobby Balderramma (guitar), Frank Lugo (bass), Eddie Serrato (drums), Frank Rodriquez (organ)—One of the greatest one-shot groups of all time, Question Mark and the

Mysterians (usually written ? and the Mysterians) became legends in 1966 with their hit "96 Tears," which remains a standard for bar bands everywhere. Although "discovered" in Detroit, the group was actually formed in Acapulco, Mexico, where it undoubtedly picked up its bluesy Latin rhythms. Question Mark, by the way, was something of a mystery man, never revealing his real name and never taking off his dark glasses.

Quicksilver Messenger Service

Gary Duncan (guitar, vocals), John Cipollina (guitar), David Freiberg (bass, vocals), Greg Elmore (drums), Dino Valenti (guitar, vocals)—One of the first San Francisco psychedelic bands and perhaps the best example of the San Francisco Sound of the mid-1960s, Quicksilver Messenger Service was formed in 1965 and produced two outstanding albums, *Quicksilver Messenger Service* (1968) and *Happy Trails* (1969), and some hit singles, particularly "Fresh Air" (1970), before coming unhinged creatively. Although hampered by drug arrests, the band worked steadily through 1972, when it tossed in the towel, only to re-form in 1975, cutting *Solid Silver* that year.

Quotations, The

Larry Kaye (vocals), Richard Schwartz (vocals), Lew Arno (vocals), Harvey Hershkowitz (vocals)— Formed in Brooklyn, New York City in 1959, the Quotations are best known for their 1961 hit, "Imagination," which is, incidentally, their only hit.

Rabbitt, Eddie

Country singer Eddie Rabbitt (born on Nov. 27, 1941 in Brooklyn, New York City) first came to public attention as the author of Elvis Presley's hit "Kentucky Rain" (such was the power and prestige of Presley that even his songwriters basked in the reflected glory, often becoming wealthy or stars on their own thanks to a boost from the King). Beginning in 1975 Rabbitt launched a very successful country career with such hits as "Rocky Mountain Music" (1976) and "Two Dollars In The Jukebox" (1977), all the while keeping an eye on the lucrative pop charts. He made those charts in 1979 with "Suspicion," a straight soul rendition that found favor on all the charts. And in 1981 he cracked the top 10 with "I Love A Rainy Night."

Eddie Rabbitt

Rafferty, Gerry

Originally a member of the group Stealers Wheel ("Stuck In The Middle With You" in 1973), Rafferty achieved startling solo success in 1978 with "Baker Street," an excellent, unpretentious ballad from his *City To City* album. Born in Scotland, Rafferty was already a well-known local musician there when some of his tapes found their way to Mike Leiber and Jerry Stoller, who produced the first Stealers Wheel album. Rafferty returned in 1979 with yet another ballad, "Right Down The Line."

Bonnie Raitt

Raitt, Bonnie

One of the most durable of the so-called cult artists, Raitt has never been able to parlay her bluesy, powerful voice into a means of

170

capturing a national audience. Born in 1950 in Los Angeles, Calif., the daughter of Broadway actor John Raitt, she grew up immersed in the blues and after a brief fling at folksinging soon began working with such bluesmen as Mississippi John Hurt and Fred McDowell. Her recording career began in 1971 with *Bonnie Raitt*, a critically well-received album—as most of her material has been. Her voice was compared favorably to both Janis Joplin's and Linda Ronstadt's, and many critics feel Raitt is superior to both of them in terms of range and material. But although she has made several mini-masterpieces—*Takin' My Time* (1974), *Streetlights* (1975) and *Home Plate* (1976)—stardom has remained one step away. She's had one major hit, "Runaway" (1977), a remake of Del Shannon's classic.

Ramones, The   Joey Ramone (vocals), Johnny Ramone (guitar), Dee Dee Ramone (bass), Marky Ramone (drums)—Actually, they're not brothers, but rather prototypical punks who brought back the two-minute three-chord rock-and-roll song. Formed in the outer reaches of New York City in 1974, the Ramones exploded onto the "progressive"—read, long, pretentious and boring—rock music scene of 1976 with their debut album, *Ramones,* a collection of quick, loud and at times atonal rock that set the staid progressive world on its ear. Like their spiritual forefathers, the Monkees, the Ramones were cartoon character rock and roll, the main difference being that the Ramones were filtered through the New York "punk" scene. The group became the most successful of that scene, whipping through five albums

in three years. At present the Ramones are trying to deal with that demon success, particularly tough for a group that began as a parody. The group's album *Rock And Roll Radio* even includes a *ballad.*

Ramrods, The   Best known for their 1961 hit of the classic cowboy song "Ghost Riders (In The Sky)." The Ramrods' version, one of the early instrumental successes, featured cattle calls and cowboy side effects.

Randolph, Boots   Premier Nashville sessions player Boots Randolph is best known for his "yakety" saxaphone, which led to a string of country and pop hits in the mid-1960s, beginning with "Yakety Sax" (1963). His horn style has become one of the most copied in rock-and-roll music.

Rare Earth   Gil Bridges (horn, vocals), John Persh (bass, trombone, vocals), Rod Richards (guitar, vocals), Kenny James (organ, piano), Pete Rivera (drums, vocals)—Originally launched as the Sunliners in 1961, Rare Earth became a major force for Motown Records in 1970 with its hit "Get Ready," a straight rocker originally recorded by the Temptations and written by Motown ace Smokey Robinson four years earlier. The group went on to produce a string of very non-Motown sounding hits throughout the early 1970s, including "(I Know) I'm Losing You" (1970), "I Just Want To Celebrate" (1971) and "What'd I Say" (1972).

Rascals, The   Felix Cavaliere (keyboards, vocals), Eddie

The Ramones

Brigati (vocals), Dino Danelli (drums), Gene Cornish (guitar)—Once labeled by *Rolling Stone* magazine as the blackest sounding white group ever, the Rascals (originally the Young Rascals) were launched in 1965 in New York City out of the wreckage of Joey Dee's Starlighters. Working the chic clubs on Long Island, the Rascals soon gained a reputation as a slick white soul group, with music you could dance to. In 1966 they solidified that reputation with the classic "Good Lovin'," one of the finest examples of "blue-eyed soul" you're likely to find. They followed that with "You Better Run," and, changing directions slightly, the more jazz-oriented *Groovin'* album, containing the hit title cut, in 1967. However, musical tastes were changing—the San Francisco revolution was already in full swing, and white soul music was on the way out. Although the group scored additional hits (most notably "A Girl Like You" and "How Can I Be Sure" in 1967 and "A Beautiful Morning" and "People Got To Be Free" in 1968), the original members disbanded in 1971 and Cavaliere and Danelli became the nucleus of a new group, adding Ann Sutton, Buzzy Feiten and Robert Popwell. The re-formed group dissolved a year later.

Raspberries, The Eric Carmen (vocals, piano, bass), Wally Bryson (guitar), David Smalley (guitar), Jim Bonfanti (drums)—Originally from Cleveland, Ohio, the group surfaced in 1972 with "Don't Want To Say Goodbye" and the wildly popular bubblegum

hit "Go All The Way," written and arranged by Eric Carmen. The Raspberries had some other minor hits ("I Wanna Be With You" in 1973) before Carmen split to go solo in 1974.

Raspberry, Larry The leader of a little-known cult band from Memphis, Tenn. called the High-Steppers. They are famous for a rollicking late 1960s instrumental, "Dixie Diner," and their one album, *High Steppin', Fancy Dancin'* (1974), now commands a high price among aficionados.

Ravan, Genya Ravan was a vocalist for the jazzy Ten Wheel Drive in the late 1960s, after having toured with the Rolling Stones in the old days as the lead singer of Goldie and the Gingerbreads. She has since discovered New Wave rock, produced the Dead Boys and, in 1979, cut her own New Wave album, with the help of Lou Reed, titled *Urban Desire.* Her photo on the record jacket, transparent shirt and all, helps contribute to that desire, one supposes.

Ravens, The Maithe Marshall (vocals), Len Puzey (vocals), Warren Scuttles (vocals), Jimmy Ricks (vocals)—Formed in 1946 in New York City, the Ravens (so named because everybody was "ravin'" about their sound) were similar to the Mills Brothers/Ink Spots style of black harmony, although they featured more vocal gymnastics in the background. With such songs as "Bye Bye Baby Blues" (1946) and "Deep Purple" (1949), the Ravens helped set the style that would

become known as doo-wop. They also sparked a wave of groups named for birds—the Orioles, the Penguins, the Larks—in the 1950s.

Rawls, Lou Born on Dec. 1, 1936 in Chicago, Ill., Rawls is best known for his stunning vocal performance on "Love Is A Hurtin' Thing" in 1966, although it wasn't until 1969 that he had his biggest hit, "Your Good Thing (Is About To End)," written by the top songwriting team of David Porter and Isaac Hayes. In 1971 he scored a top 10 single with "A Natural Man" and has continued making hits since then. Rawls began singing in the church when he was seven years old and eventually joined a gospel group, the Pilgrim Travelers, before turning to secular songs in the late 1950s. His distinctive style of soul songs and nonstop patter was developed as a device to be heard over the noise in small clubs.

Redbone, Leon Eclectic singer Leon Redbone (his real name and age are a mystery) has made a career by unearthing and performing his favorite hits of the last several decades, from Emmit Miller to Jelly Roll Morton to Blind Lemon Jefferson to Jimmie Rodgers. On stage Redbone has been known to growl, hum, cackle, whistle, imitate a trombone or trumpet, shoot off a blank pistol at the audience, consult a compass to ascertain where he is, measure the microphone stand and, once in a while, sing and play the guitar quite well. He's become quite popular through extensive exposure on "Saturday Night

Leon Redbone

Live," the late night TV comedy show.

Redding, Otis One of the greatest—if not *the* greatest—soul singers of all time, Otis Redding (born on Sept. 9, 1941 in Macon, Ga.) hailed from the same part of Georgia as Little Richard and James Brown. It was the association of the black Redding and the white Phil Walden (late of Capricorn Records) in the early 1960s that was to lead to Redding's all-too-brief success. When another Walden-sponsored group, Johnny Jenkins and the Pinetoppers, went to Memphis to audition for Stax Records, Walden arranged to have Redding drive their bus and when the Jenkins session (a bust) was finished, Redding cut two songs, one of which was "These Arms Of Mine." Signed to Volt, a newly formed Stax subsidiary, Redding grew

steadily, capturing the American rhythm-and-blues market and the entire European pop market, as well as making Stax a major power in the recording industry. At the 1967 Monterey Pop Festival, Redding virtually stole the show, establishing soul as a "legitimate" part of the rock market, something white kids could listen to as well as blacks. His triumph was short-lived. On Dec. 10, 1967 Redding was killed in a plane crash in Wisconsin, along with four members of his backup band, the Bar-Kays. Redding's masterpiece, "(Sittin' On The) Dock Of The Bay," had been released three days prior to the crash, and it went on to become one of the biggest hits of the new year—a tribute to one of the most important men in American popular music—winning two Grammies.

Otis Redding

Reddy, Helen Born on Oct. 25, 1942 in Melbourne, Australia, Reddy began her career like a political lioness but quickly settled down into a more moderate lamb. With the prompting of husband/manager Jeff Wald, she pursued a singing career, eventually hitting with a song from the rock musical *Jesus Christ Superstar,* "I Don't Know How To Love Him" (1971). What really put her over the top, however, was her stirring anthem to the womens' movement, "I Am Woman" (1972), after which she was a star. Since then she has routinely had hit records ("Peaceful" in 1973, "Leave Me Alone" in 1973, "Delta Dawn" in 1973 "Angie Baby" in 1975), her own television series, various television specials and what have you, although the ringing sincerity of "I Am Woman" has been noticeably lacking. She remains, however, one of pop music's foremost stars.

Reed, Jimmy Bluesman Jimmy Reed (born in 1926 in Leland, Miss.) had such rhythm-and-blues hits as "Baby What You Want Me To Do" (1960), "Big Boss Man" (1961) and "Bright Lights, Big City" (1961). He died in San Francisco on Aug. 29, 1976. He is best known for his influence on such artists as Gregg Allman.

Reed, Lou Born on March 2, 1944 in Freeport, New York, Lou Reed is the best-known survivor of the Velvet Underground, New York City's landmark underground group of the late 1960s. Since the Velvet Underground broke up

Lou Reed

in 1970, Reed has been trying, with varying degrees of success, to put his bizarre visions on record. The high point came in 1973 with his huge hit "Walk On The Wild Side," which despite sexually explicit (and fairly offbeat) lyrics got substantial airplay and ended up on jukeboxes everywhere. The low point was unquestionably his *Metal Machine Music* album in 1975, which is best described by its title. It sounded like tape hum, actually, and RCA Records was so embarrassed by the whole thing that they recalled it and apologized. Somewhere between those two poles lies the bulk of Reed's music. He continues recording complex and, at times, moving music.

Reeves, Martha   Originally a secretary at Motown Records in her home town of Detroit,
Martha Reeves became famous as the lead singer for Martha and the Vandellas with their monster hit "Heat Wave" in 1963. (The song was released at the height of a Los Angeles heat wave, and many newscasters used the song as a background for their weather reports—which didn't hurt sales any.) The group had a string of classic hits throughout the 1960s (including "Quicksand" in 1963, "Dancing In The Street" in 1964, "Nowhere To Run To" in 1965, "Jimmy Mack" in 1967), changing their name to Martha Reeves and the Vandellas around 1965. In 1971 Reeves left the group for a solo career after a bitter court fight with Motown Records. That solo career has yet to really take root.

Renaissance   Michael Dunford (guitar, vocals), Jon Camp (bass, vocals), John Tout (keyboards), Terence Sullivan (percussion), Annie Haslam (vocals)—Assembled in the late 1960s in England from bits and pieces of other groups, including the Yardbirds and the Nashville Teens, Renaissance became best known for its slightly pretentious rock-classical fusions (*Scheherazade And Other Stories* in 1975) and for the powerful singing voice of Annie Haslam, who eventually turned to a solo career in the late 1970s.

REO Speedwagon   Gary Richrath (guitar), Kevin Cronin (guitar, vocals), Bruce Hall (bass), Alan Gratzer (drums), Neal Doughty (keyboards)— Formed in Illinois during the mid-1970s, REO Speedwagon has forged ahead with a steady formula of hard rock with a melody. One of the group's albums was titled *You Can Tune A Piano But You Can't Tuna Fish* (1978). In 1981, thanks to a revival of hard rock, they had a number one album, *Hi Infidelity.*

Return To Forever   Chick Corea (keyboards, electronics), Stanley Clarke (bass), Lenny White (drums), Al DiMeola (guitar)—Chick Corea's landmark jazz-rock fusion group, Return To Forever, was formed in 1973, the name taken from the previous year's Chick Corea album, which featured, among others, Stanley Clarke. The band became one of the most popular fusion groups.

Revere, Paul, and the Raiders   Mark Lindsay (vocals); Paul Revere (keyboards); Freddie Weller (guitar); Michael Smith (guitar); Drake Levin (drums); Phil Volk (bass); and others, including Jim Valley, Joe Correro, Charlie Coe—Originally launched in 1962 in Portland, Ore., the Raiders became one of the best-known rock bands in America, thanks to Dick Clark's "Where the Action Is" television show, where the group performed every day. With their Revolutionary War costumes and their carefully choreographed act, it was a miracle the Raiders survived as long as they did in an era of long hair, beads and jeans. They also produced some excellent hit singles, including "Kicks" (1966), "Hungry" (1966), "Good Thing" (1966), "Him Or Me" (1967) and "Too

Much Talk" (1969). With the coming of the 1970s, the group disbanded.

Rhinocerus   John Finley (vocals), Michael Fonfara (keyboards), Danny Weis (guitar), Alan Gerber (piano, vocals), Doug Hastings (guitar), Jerry Penrod (bass), Billy Mundi (drums)—Formed in 1968 out of a group of successful sessions men and Billy Mundi from the Mothers of Invention, Rhinocerus is less well known for its music (uninspired) than for the fact that it was one of the first rock bands to be treated seriously by the "straight" press, in this case *Harper's Magazine,* who tagged the band as the Next Big Thing. Needless to say, it wasn't.

Rice, Tim (and Andrew Lloyd Webber)   The inventors of *Jesus Christ Superstar* met in England in 1965 and produced a less successful rock Biblical epic, *Joseph and the Technicolor Dream Coat,* before striking it big with *Superstar* in 1970. The album, stage productions and movie kept the *Jesus Christ Superstar* phenomenon going for years, and in 1974 they began working on a new rock opera based, incredibly enough, on the life of Eva Peron, titled *Evita.* While that opera, released in 1976, did quite well in England (especially the recurring theme, "Don't Cry For Me Argentina," which reached number one there), it was generally greeted with chuckles in the United States. However, once again proving that he or she who laughs lasts, laughs best, Rice and Webber

saw their newest creation go on to become the biggest Broadway stage hit of 1979.

Rich, Charlie   Born on Dec. 14, 1934 in Colt, Ark., Rich is yet another member of the Sun Records stable in Memphis—although one of the last. He first hit in 1959 with "Lonely Weekends," a fine showcase for his bluesy voice. Unfortunately, Sun Records was in its twilight, and very soon Rich was without a label. He rallied in the mid-1960s with such hits as "Big Boss Man" (1965) and "Mohair Sam" (1965), but he seemed quite willing to let stardom pass, thank you. But stardom caught up with him in 1973 with "Behind Closed Doors," a masterpiece of the heavily orchestrated Nashville Sound, as handled by producer Billy Sherrill. After a few more hits in the same vein, though, Charlie Rich once more stepped down, producing a small amount of sometimes great, sometimes awful material each year.

Richard, Cliff   Originally thought of as Britain's answer to Elvis Presley (at least in Britain), Cliff Richard (born Harry Webb on Oct. 14, 1940 in India) began his career in one of the many English skiffle bands during the early 1950s. He formed his own group, the Drifters (later renamed the Shadows to avoid confusion with the American Drifters), and in 1958 the group's first demo recording resulted in a record called "Move It." Britain was hungry for rockers, and Cliff Richard and the Shadows rose quickly. In the early 1960s he shifted to the movies, with such teen epics as *The Young*

Cliff Richard

Ones (1962) and *Wonderful Life* (1964), while continuing a successful recording career. As the movies wound down, he switched to television and in 1976 launched a revival of his career (which had obviously never faded) with his *I'm Nearly Famous* album. A single from that album, "Devil Woman," gave him his first substantial American hit, a position he consolidated in 1979 with the smash "We Don't Talk Anymore."

Richman, Jonathan   Art rock at its finest, Richman (born in 1952 in Boston, Mass.) formed his group, the

Modern Lovers, because, as he says, "I was lonely." The group began recording in 1971, producing such classics as "Pablo Picasso" and "Roadrunner," less songs, perhaps, than recitations in Richman's odd, deadpan voice. Despite a wildly enthusiastic cult audience, the group faded, only to return triumphantly in 1977 with such *new* classics as "I'm In Love With The New Bank Teller." In short, suburban rock with a wild sense of humor.

Righteous Brothers, The   Bill Medley (born on Sept. 19, 1940 in Los Angeles, Calif.) and Bobby Hatfield (born on Aug. 10, 1940 in Beaver Dam, Wis.) became perhaps the premier blue-eyed singing act of the mid-1960s, with such consumate Phil Spector Wall of Sound productions as "You've Lost That Lovin' Feelin'" (1965) and "Unchained Melody" (1965) and the Medley-

Jonathan Richman

produced "Soul And Inspiration" (1966), until 1968, when the "brothers" split up. They re-formed in 1974 to cut "Rock And Roll Heaven," a grisly chronicle of rock casualties that became quite a hit, but the reunion stalled soon after. Their early work, though, remains a testament to Medley and Hatfield's fine voices and Spector's absolute mastery of the rhythm-and-blues idiom.

Riley, Billy Lee   Born on Oct. 5, 1933 in Pocahontas, Ark. Billy Lee Riley is one of the least-known Sun Records rockabilly stars, although he did extensive sessions work for Sun. His principal recognition is for his often-copied "(My Gal Is) Red Hot" and he is once again recording.

Riley, Jeannie C.   Born on Oct. 19, 1945 in Anson, Tex., country singer Jeannie C. Riley is best known as the mini-skirted singer of "Harper Valley P.T.A." (1968), written by country storyteller Tom T. Hall. The song refuses to die and ended up as a very successful movie in 1978 and a television series in 1980.

Rip Chords, The   Phil Stewart (vocals), Arnie Marcus (vocals), Rich Rotkin (vocals), Bernie Bringas (vocals)—At the peak of the cars-and-beach craze of the mid-1960s, the Rip Chords, veterans of the southern California car scene since 1961, cut their one and only hit, "Hey Little Cobra" (1964), an uncanny imitation of Jan and Dean.

Riperton, Minnie   Originally trained to be an opera singer,

Riperton (born in 1948 in Chicago) first came to attention as the lead singer for the Rotary Connection, a vastly underrated group formed by Chess Records, but by 1971 she was disillusioned enough to leave music entirely. After much coaxing, she returned to recording and cut *Perfect Angel,* which yielded "Lovin' You," a simple ballad designed to show off her remarkable vocal range. That song became a number one hit in 1975, and her career was in high gear when she was forced off the road in 1976 for major cancer surgery. Although she returned to recording and performing the next year, she died from the disease in 1978.

Ritter, Tex Although one of the best-known and most-beloved country stars, Ritter (born in Panola, Tex. on Jan. 12, 1906; died on Jan. 3, 1974) is best remembered for his two major excursions onto the pop charts—the theme to one of the first great "adult" Westerns, *High Noon,* in 1952; and his rendition of "Wayward Wind" in 1956. About the same time he recorded "High Noon," he also cut the gory, totally off-the-wall Western epic "Blood On The Saddle," which was adopted years later as something of a theme song for the mechanical android animals at Walt Disney World in Orlando, Fla., where a stuffed bear and a stuffed buffalo now echo Tex's voice.

Rivers, Johnny Born John Ramistella on Nov. 7, 1942 in New York City but raised in the bayou country of Baton Rouge, La., Rivers became, in the mid-1960s, the logical successor to the frenzied rock-and-roll stars of the 1950s. Although his work was heavily derivative, his powerful voice and black-influenced stylings provided some of the strongest hits of that era, beginning with a remake of Chuck Berry's "Memphis" in 1964 and continuing with "Maybellene" (1964), "Mountain Of Love" (1964), "Midnight Special" (1965), "Seventh Son" (1965), "Secret Agent Man" (1966), "I Washed My Hands In Muddy Water" (1966), "Poor Side Of Town" (1966) and others, including a fluke hit in 1972 with Huey "Piano" Smith's "Rockin' Pneumonia And The Boogie Woogie Flu." He really took off in 1962 when, as a favor to a friend, he stood in at the Whiskey A Go Go disco on Sunset Strip. He is also noted as one of the first performers to assemble a regular group of studio musicians and actually give them credit on an album cover. He has tried at least one modestly successful comeback in the mid-1970s and remains in steady demand.

Rivingtons, The Carl White (vocals), Sonny Harris (vocals), Al Frazier (vocals), Rocky Wilson (vocals)—Named for a street on the Lower East Side of New York City (where their producers, not the group members, grew up), the Rivingtons were formed in Los Angeles around 1960 and produced three of the more bizarre and imitated rock-and-roll hits: "Papa-Oom-Mow-Mow" (1962), "Mama-Oom-Mow-Mow" (1962) and "The Bird's The Word" (1963), all three of which sound almost identical.

Robbins, Hargus "Pig"
Nashville sessions piano player best known in the rock world for having contributed the piano parts on Bob Dylan's *Blonde On Blonde* album. His solo work doesn't do the blind piano man credit, but he's heard on probably every record coming out of Music City USA.

Robbins, Marty Like so many other Nashville icons, country superstar Marty Robbins (born on Sept. 25, 1925 in Glendale, Ariz.) first received national attention as a rock-and-roll singer in the mid-1950s with such hits as "Singing The Blues" (1956), "A White Sport Coat" (1957) and "Teenage Dream" (1957). Unlike the other rockers, though, Robbins had already established a solid reputation as a country singer, joining the Grand Ole Opry and scoring a top 10 country hit, "I'll Go On Alone," in 1953. Robbins continued his rock-and-roll ways quite convincingly until 1959, when he recorded what was destined to be one of the greatest country classics of all time—"El Paso," a Western soap opera boiled down to a few minutes. That song put him on the top of the pop and country charts, and he followed up with such hits as "Big Iron" (1960), another Western ballad, and "Devil Woman" (1962). Since then Robbins has remained at the very top of the country hit lists, while pursuing such diverse interests as automobile racing and a career in the movies (*Buffalo Gun* in 1962, *Ballad of a Gunfighter* in 1963). In 1976 he released one of the most clever follow-up songs ever— "El Paso City," a song that chronicled a modern man's strange attraction to El Paso and that city's famous "legend," which, of course, Robbins himself had started in 1959.

Robins, The Carl Gardner (vocals), Ty Terrell (vocals), Grady Chapman (vocals), Billy Richards (vocals), Roy Richards (vocals), Bobby Nunn (vocals)—Best known as the forerunner of the Coasters, the vehicle for Mike Leiber and Jerry Stoller's classic 1950s compositions, the Robins had a hit with the Leiber and Stoller composition "Smokey Joe's Cafe" in 1955. Shortly thereafter Carl Gardner and Bobby Nunn broke off to form the Coasters.

Robinson, Smokey Born on Feb. 19, 1940 in Detroit, Mich., William "Smokey" Robinson, in addition to having his own successful career as a member of Smokey Robinson and the Miracles (and, later, as a solo act), is one of Motown's prime movers as well as the creative kingpin of Motown Records. With Robinson singing lead, the Miracles helped to get the Motown juggernaut off the ground in 1960 with "Shop Around." In addition to writing that song and other material for the Miracles, Smokey penned "Ain't That Peculiar," a hit for Marvin Gaye in 1964; "My Guy," a hit for Mary Wells in 1964; and "The Way You Do The Things You Do" and "My Girl" for the Temptations in 1964 and 1965 respectively. His later songs for the Miracles (renamed Smokey Robinson and the Miracles in 1967) are worth noting as well—"The

Smokey Robinson

Tracks Of My Tears" (1965), "I Second That Emotion" (1967) and "The Tears Of A Clown" (1970), to name just a few. Motown administration began taking up more and more of his time, and in 1972 he left the Miracles. His debut album, *Smokey,* arrived soon after, and he continued making albums throughout the 1970s, although without great distinction. Then in 1979 he came back to the top of the charts with a distinctly Robinsonesque song titled "Cruisin' Together," just slick enough to be played in the discos, but just Motown enough to set it apart from the run of the mill.

Robinson, Tom Tom Robinson and his band burst onto the New Wave scene from England in 1978. Although they appeared to be yet another hard driving rock

band, the difference was Robinson's politics—slightly left wing and defiantly gay. While some of his songs bogged down in rhetoric (the bane of political rockers everywhere), such English hits as "2-4-6-8 Motorway" in 1978 found a surprisingly large following on American radio and marked the band as one to really watch.

Robinson, Vicki Sue Basically a Gloria Gaynor clone from the disco explosion of the late 1970s, Vicki Sue Robinson started out in New York City as an aspiring Broadway singer before "Turn The Beat Around" (1976) and "Hold Tight" (1977) introduced her to a larger, more active audience. She was born in 1955 in Philadelphia, Pa.

Roches, The When New York City is not swooning under the influence of New Wave, it's heralding the rebirth of folk music. The latest rebirth has been in the form of the sisters Maggie, Terre and Suzze Roche (their first album, *Seductive Reasoning* in 1975, featured only Maggie and Terre), whose *The Roches* was named one of the top albums (according to critics, not sales) of 1979. Their music is vintage Loudon Wainwright.

Rodgers, Jimmie Known as the Father of Country Music, Jimmie Rodgers (born on Sept. 8, 1897 in Meridian, Miss.) was responsible for popularizing the music of the Appalachian Mountains in the mid-1920s. The country music of Jimmie Rodgers, though, had as much to do with the black blues as with the white fiddle music of the mountains. He grew up in the fields of rural Mississippi, where the music of black and white readily flowed together. Although his first love was working on the railroads, tuberculosis soon forced him to give up that tough life. He then became a performer, sometimes working in blackface. He eventually found himself in Bristol, a town straddling the Tennessee-Virginia state line, where the Victor Talking Machine recording company was holding an audition. On Aug. 4, 1927 Rodgers recorded two songs, "The Soldier's Sweetheart" and "Sleep, Baby, Sleep." The songs were released two monthe later, and Rodgers became a superstar. From then until his death from tuberculosis on May 26, 1933, Rodgers recorded a classic body of work, including "Mule Skinner Blues," "T For Texas," "Brakeman's Blues" and dozens of others. Along the way, he gave America back its folk music and, through the blending of black blues and white country music, helped lay down a path that eventually led to rock and roll.

Rodgers, Jimmie   Born on Sept. 18, 1933 in Washington State, Jimmie Rodgers is best known for his string of lightweight, upbeat hits—the antithesis of the "bad" rock and roller of that time—in the late 1950s, including his biggest, "Honeycomb" (1957), "Kisses Sweeter Than Wine" (1957) and "Oh-Oh I'm Falling In Love Again" (1958). Rodgers was one of the artists instrumental in making rock and roll safe for mommy and daddy.

Roe, Tommy   Born on May 9, 1942 in Atlanta, Ga., Roe proved to be a suprisingly durable, if slightly lightweight, artist throughout the 1960s with such hits as "Sheila" (1962), "Everybody" (1963), "Sweet Pea" (1966), "Hooray For Hazel" (1966), "Dizzy" (1969) and "Jam Up Jelly Tight" (1969). He based his singing style on that of the late Buddy Holly, and he proved it still worked.

Rogers, Kenny   In 1979 Kenny Rogers emerged as a pop star for the 1980s, carefully straddling rock, country and middle-of-the-road pop to become the most sought-after and most successful star in the waning minutes of the decade. Rogers was born on Aug. 21, 1941 in Houston, Tex. and his story really gets under way in the mid-1960s, when he (and several other members of the New Christy Minstrels) organized the First Edition. The First Edition had a series of hits throughout the late 1960s and early 1970s, drawing on such well-known country writers as Mickey Newbury ("Just Dropped In To See What Condition My Condition Was In"), Alex Harvey ("Reuben James") and Mel Tillis ("Ruby, Don't Take Your Love To Town"). By 1971

Kenny Rogers

the First Edition had run down, and Rogers sought a solo career, which never seemed to ignite until 1977, when he recorded a straight country song, "Lucille," a hit that won a Grammy and numerous country awards. With the country music world in hand, Rogers took his gravelly vocals to the pop world in 1978 with "The Gambler," a huge pop and country hit that, in addition to winning many awards, spun off an above average television movie, featuring Rogers in the lead role. The result has been that going into the 1980s, everything Rogers touches turns to gold, and he is a major force in the music world.

Rolling Stones, The Mick Jagger (vocals, harp); Keith Richards (guitar); Bill Wyman (bass); Charlie Watts (drums); Ron Wood (guitar); and others, including Brian Jones (died, 1969), Mick Taylor—One of the most successful and certainly the most durable of the British Invasion rock groups of the mid-1960s, the Rolling Stones, with flamboyant superstar-singer Mick Jagger at the helm, have easily made the transition from rock to disco. Their 1978 album, *Some Girls,* with its hit disco single "Miss You," confirmed the band's place at the top, becoming one of the year's biggest-selling albums and establishing the Stones' popularity with a younger, second generation of rock listeners. The Rolling Stones were formed in late 1962 in Surrey, England, after members of the group had met at London's notorious Marquee Club. Initially their style was one quite common in England at that time—the blues. The Stones, along with such groups as John Mayall's Bluesbreakers, had adopted the music of America's rural blacks and repackaged it for the British pubs. They were quick to break away from the strict blues idiom, though, recognizing that success hinged on being commercial, and the blues had never been commercial. The group then found ample material in the Chicago electric blues scene, with Mick Jagger and Keith Richards borrowing from the likes of Muddy Waters and Chuck Berry for both style and inspiration. The group quickly became a success, signing with Decca after a frenetic

The Rolling Stones

bidding war among various record companies. Their first releases included "Come On" (1963), Lennon and McCartney's "I Wanna Be Your Man" (1964) and Buddy Holly's "Not Fade Away" (1964). Their first million seller worldwide was "The Last Time," penned by Jagger and Richards, but it wasn't until later in 1965 that another Jagger/Richards number, "(I Can't Get No) Satisfaction," hit the United States charts like a storm. Since then the group has had some 27 million-selling records, including 11 albums, which ranks them behind only Elvis Presley and the Beatles in terms of worldwide sales. They have had nine number one songs in the U.S. and continue to turn out hit singles and albums. In 1980 their *Emotional Rescue* album made the top five.

The Stones were largely responsible for awakening American teens to the blues in their midsts, as well as triggering a wave of white blues bands that persist to this day. It is one of the ironies of popular music that the blues were not appreciated in their homeland until they were sung by young English gentlemen.

Ronettes, The   Veronica "Ronnie" Bennett (vocals), Estelle Bennett (vocals), Nedra Talley (vocals)—The group first began as part of the Joey Dee Revue at the Peppermint Lounge in New York City at the height of the twist craze. There they were discovered by Phil Spector, who produced a string of hits for them (and helped trigger a craze for girl groups), beginning with "Be My Baby" (1963) and probably

The Ronettes

climaxing with "Walkin' In The Rain" (1964), which earned Spector a Grammy for his inclusion of rain noises and thunder on the record. In 1968 he married Ronnie Bennett. They were divorced in 1974, and she resumed her career in 1977.

Ronson, Mick   English guitarist Mick Ronson originally came to public notice with David Bowie's Spiders from Mars band in the early 1970s. While his solo career has never gotten off the ground (despite two albums), he's continued making a name for himself, first as a member of Mott the Hoople, then as a part of Bob Dylan's Rolling Thunder Revue in 1975-76.

Ronstadt, Linda   Born on July 15, 1946 in Tucson, Ariz., Ronstadt has emerged from the 1970s as that decade's premier woman vocalist and

chief rock-and-roll pinup girl, despite her efforts to downplay the latter. Her family was musically inclined, and there never seemed to be any doubt of her career in music. In 1964 she split from her family trio and headed for Los Angeles to make it on her own. There she linked up with Bobby Kimmel and Kenny Edwards, and collectively they became the Stone Poneys. Ronstadt's voice was always the biggest selling point of the trio. They recorded three albums and managed one hit, Monkee Mike Nesmith's "Different Drum" in 1967, before Ronstadt left to pursue a solo career. That solo career was slow getting off the ground, as she thrashed around looking for a single coherent direction. She cut an album in Nashville, *Silk Purse* (1970)—which she reportedly hates—and finally formed her own backup group with Glenn Frey, Don Henley and Randy

Linda Ronstadt

Meisner, who left six months later to form their own group, the Eagles. That sense of direction finally came in 1973, when she connected with Peter Asher (of Peter and Gordon). Under Asher's astute guidance, she began a series of albums that turned her career around and in two short years put her on the very top of the music business. Beginning with *Don't Cry Now* in 1973 and *Heart Like A Wheel* (*Heart* was owed to Capitol Records, while the other was on her new label, Asylum), Ronstadt consistently topped the charts with such memorable hits as "You're No Good" (1974), "When Will I Be Loved" (1975), "Heat Wave" (1975), "Tracks Of My Tears" (1975), "That'll Be The Day" (1976), "Blue Bayou" (1977) and "Tumbling Dice" (1978). Apparently unhappy with her interpretations of 1950s and 1960s songs and the material of such West Coast standards as Warren Zevon, Ronstadt made a much-publicized attempt at New Wave with her 1979 *Mad Love* album. Although the album was not as well received across the board as her other work, it made the charts in early 1980 and showed the powerful vocalist still in control. In 1981 she tried her hand at acting with the Broadway production of *The Pirates of Penzance* in New York City.

Rose, Tim   Folksinger Tim Rose (born in September 1940 and raised in Washington state) worked with Mama Cass Elliott and produced the arrangement of the traditional "Hey Joe" that was picked up by Jimi Hendrix. His career, however, has never really managed to get out of the starting gate. He is best known for his beautiful folk ballad "Morning Dew," which he wrote in the early 1960s.

Rose Royce   Gwen "Rose" Dickey (vocals), Kenji Brown (guitar, vocals), Kenny Copeland (horns, vocals), Duke Jobe (bass, vocals), Henry Garner (drums), Michael Nash (keyboards), Terry Santiel (percussion), Freddie Dunn (horns), Michael Moore (horns, vocals)—Originally launched as a backup group, Rose Royce (with the addition of singer Gwen Dickey) stepped out on its own in the late 1970s with the soundtrack to the hit movie *Car Wash,* which captured numerous awards (including a Grammy) and spun off two substantial hits, "Car Wash" and "I Wanna Get Next To You." The group's sound might be described as super-Motown, funk you can dance to.

Ross, Diana   Born on March 26, 1944 in Detroit, Mich., Ross won a high school singing contest in 1960 with two of her close friends, Mary Wilson and Florence Ballard, singing as the Primettes. The Primettes were quickly spotted by Berry Gordy, Jr., the godfather of Motown Records, and as soon as the girls finished high school, they were rechristened the Supremes and launched in their spectacular career in 1962 with "Your Heart Belongs To Me." Beginning two years later with "Where Did Our Love Go," the Supremes became one of the most successful and most durable of the Motown

artists. But in 1967 Florence Ballard left the group (replaced by Cindy Birdsong), and the emphasis shifted from the group to the lead singer, Diana Ross. In Ross, Gordy saw a potential star of tremendous proportions, the ultimate canvas for his production and managerial genius. Under Gordy's direction Diana Ross left the Supremes in 1969 and started her solo career (with such hits as "Ain't No Mountain High Enough" in 1970 and "Touch Me In The Morning" in 1973) without ever missing a beat. When Motown turned to movies, Gordy selected Ross for the Billie Holiday role in *Lady Sings the Blues* (1972), an outstanding acting debut that netted Ross an Oscar nomination for her performance. She continued her movie career through the modestly successful *Mahogany* (1975) and the stupendous flop *The Wiz* (1978), in which she was inexplicably cast as the young Dorothy character. Her singing hits have continued into the 1980s ("Upside Down" in 1980), although she is closer to the high-paying club circuit now than the charts, and lately she has put some distance between herself and Gordy.

Roxy Music   Bryan Ferry (vocals, keyboards), Phil Manzanera (guitars), Paul Thompson (drums), Andy Mackay (sax, oboe), Eddie Jobson (keyboards)—Originally launched in 1971 by art student Bryan Ferry and guitarist Graham Simpson, Roxy Music, with its artsy-jazzy approach to rock, was quickly a critics' favorite, although a commercial stiff. The band's

eclectic repertoire led to friction between Ferry, the creator and perpetual art student, and original member Brian Eno, who sought a more rock-oriented direction. Eno eventually left the band in 1972, leaving Ferry free to pursue his wry visions. That pursuit yielded one hit single, "Love Is The Drug" in 1975, and for a while it looked as if Roxy Music had captured the American market. Perhaps predictably, the band broke up the next year, again over artistic directions. Although the various and sundry members pursue solo careers, the parts have not proved as successful as the whole; Ferry has come the closest to success.

Royal Teens, The   Joe Villa (vocals); Bob Gaudio (piano); Tom Austin (drums), Bill Crandall (sax); Billy Dalton (bass); and others, including Larry Qualaino, Al Kooper—Formed in 1957 as the Royal Tones in New York, they are best known for their 1958 hit "Short Shorts." In addition, Bob Gaudio went on to the Four Seasons, while Al Kooper became one of the best-known white blues advocates.

Rubinoos, The   Jon Rubin (guitar, vocals), Tommy Dunbar (guitar, keyboards, vocals), Royse Ader (bass, vocals), Donn Spindt (drums, percussion, vocals)—One of the late 1970s groups dedicated to recycling early 1960s rock and loosely tagging along under the banner of New Wave, the Rubinoos specialize in four-part harmony. The group had a hit with a remake of the Tommy James and the Shondells 1967 hit "I Think We're Alone Now." The Rubinoos rely heavily on recycled girl group material.

Ruby and the Romantics
Ruby Nash (vocals), Edward Roberts (vocals), Robert Moseley (vocals), Leroy Fann (vocals), George Lee (vocals)—Originally launched by the four male members of the group in the late 1950s. In 1962 Ruby Nash joined what was then called the Supremes. After a quick name change, the group enjoyed its biggest hit, "Our Day Will Come," in 1963.

Ruffin, David   Born on Jan. 18, 1941 in Meridian, Miss., Ruffin is best known as the lead singer of the great Motown group the Temptations. The Temps were one of Motown's most solid groups, with hits beginning in 1964 ("The Way You Do The Things You Do") and continuing through the mid-1970s, although without Ruffin. Ruffin left the group in 1969 and had an immediate hit with "My Whole World Ended (The Moment You Left Me)." Subsequently his career ground to a halt, and it wasn't until 1975 that he put together another hit, "Walk Away From Love," from his successful *Who I Am* album. He is one of the most distinctive and most-copied soul stylists.

Rufus   Chaka Khan (vocals), Tony Maiden (guitar), Bobby Watson (bass), Kevin Murphy (keyboards), Andre Fischer (drums)—Not for nothing is this band usually referred to as Rufus, Featuring Chaka Khan, which was the name of the group's 1975 album. Sexy, flamboyant Chaka Khan is the pivot for this Chicago-based band formed in 1972. The group's first hit came in 1974 with "Tell Me Something Good," a Stevie Wonder number. Rufus later joined Wonder on tour the following year, on the heels of its wildly successful *Rags To Rufus* album and its follow-up, *Rufusised.*

Runaways, The   Sandy West (drums, vocals), Lita Ford (guitar), Joan Jett (guitar, vocals), Cherie Currie (vocals, piano), Jackie Fox (bass, vocals)—Originally launched in the mid-1970s by master hype artist Kim Fowley (perpetrator of the Hollywood Argyles of "Alley Oop" fame), the Runaways were going to become the biggest all-woman rock-and-roll group ever, along the way fulfilling all their fans sleaziest dreams. The idea was to get a bunch of 16- and 17-year-old girls together, dress them in sort of late leather or early hooker and put them on the road to see what came up. What came up was vast amounts of media coverage and underwhelming sales. Various permutations of the group are still around, as are expatriate members, trying to carve out a piece of the New Wave scene, with Joan Jett ("I Love Rock And Roll" [1982]) the most successful.

Rundgren, Todd   Rundgren keeps resurfacing throughout pop music, sometimes as a performer, sometimes as a producer. Born on June 22, 1948 in Upper Darby, Pa., he picked up his moves as the frontman for the Nazz, a local Philly imitation-English group in the late 1960s. Following the collapse of the band, he turned

Todd Rundgren

to a solo career that more or less culminated in 1972 with *Something/Anything*, his masterwork album. He promptly began sinking deeper and deeper into electronics, and his albums, including those with his band, Utopia (Roger Powell, synthesizer; Kasim Sulton, bass; and John Wilcox, drums), have reflected his leanings. His music tends to sway wildly from simple rock ballads like "Hello It's Me," (once a hit for the Nazz and once for Rundgren solo) to Emerson, Lake and Palmer-style epics to early rock tunes. As a producer, he knocked out some of the best (some say the strangest) work of the 1970s, including Meat Loaf's debut album, *Bat Out Of Hell*, and Grand Funk Railroad's parting shot, *American Band.*

Rush, Merilee   Best known for her 1968 ballad "Angel Of The Morning," Merilee Rush—

managed by Paul Revere and the Raiders—was a fixture on late 1960s rock television. A 1978 comeback attempt failed.

Rush, Otis   Contemporary bluesman Otis Rush was born in 1935 in Philadelphia, Miss. When he was 25 years-old, he went to Chicago, where he became a fixture in the South Side blues clubs, usually working with his friend Buddy Guy. With such songs as "So Many Roads So Many Trains," Rush eventually came to the attention of the Chicago folklorists and their unique spinoffs, the white blues musicians—middle-class kids, most notably Paul Butterfield, Mike Bloomfield and Nick Gravenites, committed to mastering the blues on its own turf. Gravenites produced a brilliant album by Rush in 1971, one of the finest examples of contemporary blues. But the album was never released, and after years of negotiating, Rush finally purchased the master tapes himself, and *Right Place, Wrong Time* was released on the Bullfrog label in 1976.

Rush, Tom   Folksinger Tom Rush (born Feb. 8, 1941 in Portsmouth, N. H.) began his career with the other folk heavies of the early 1960s but distinguished himself on two counts—he recorded material other than his own, including songs by such then-unknown writers as Joni Mitchell, Jackson Browne and James Taylor, and he was unafraid to venture into electric rock, *a la* Bo Diddley and Buddy Holly. Although he continues performing, he remains best known for the *The Circle*

Game album (containing "No Regrets"), released in the late 1960s.

Rush   Neil Peart (drums), Alex Lifeson (guitars), Geddy Lee (vocals)—Hailing from Toronto, Canada, Rush

Rush

(formed in 1974) is a strange mix of Ayn Rand and Led Zeppelin, concentrating on very long, very loud science fiction epics ("Cygnus X-1" in 1977, for example, chronicled the journey of a spaceship pilot plunging through a black hole in outer space. That musical trip was nothing, however, compared to the group's *2112* album in 1978, which concerned the tale of a battle between the gods Apollo and Dionysus in which the deity Cygnus intervened). Nevertheless, Rush is enormously popular.

Russell, Ken   Eccentric filmmaker Ken Russell (*Women In Love* in 1970, *The Devils* in 1971) brought the Who's epic *Tommy* album to

the screen in 1974, complete with Ann-Margret and Roger Daltrey and enough special effects to awe Cecil B. DeMille. His next movie *Lisztomania,* begun the following year, also starred Daltrey, this time as Franz Liszt.

Russell, Leon   One of rock's more commanding figures, Leon Russell has been everything from a sessions man (for Jerry Lee Lewis, the Byrds, the Rolling Stones, Delaney and Bonnie—you name it) to a Svengali (he orchestrated Joe Cocker's Mad Dogs and Englishmen tour, movie, album and what-have-you), along the way producing a series of outstanding solo albums and writing some of rock's more memorable songs ("Delta Lady," recorded by Joe Cocker in 1969; "Superstar," by the Carpenters in 1971; and his own hits, such as "Song For You" in 1970 and "This Masquerade" in 1972). He has been, virtually at the same time, one of the foremost technologists in rock, quickly

Leon Russell

seeing the importance of and utilizing 40-track tape machines and enough support electronics to launch an Apollo moonshot, then turning around to record a duet album with country music superstar Willie Nelson, cutting most of the songs on the first take with only his piano for accompaniment. And that's not to mention his own country album (*Hank Wilson's Back* in 1973) or his own record label (Paradise, formed after his marriage to Mary McCreary in 1976). Whew! He was born on April 2, 1941 in Lawton, Okla. and studied classical piano for 10 years, starting at the age of three. He formed his first band at age 14 and a couple of years later was on the road with Jerry Lee Lewis. He reached his peak of popularity in the early 1970s and since then has slipped to a lower, although stable, plateau. He works steadily with country musicians while pursuing his own muse on such Paradise albums as *Life and Love* in 1979.

Russell, Mary   Originally Mary McCreary, a vocalist with Little Sister, a part of Sly Stone's "family," Mary Russell's career took an upswing in 1976 with the release of *The Wedding Album*, with new husband Leon Russell, featuring the hit single "Rainbow In Your Eyes." She continues recording for their Paradise label and remains perhaps one of the most beautiful women to grace popular music.

Mary Russell

Rydell, Bobby   Born Robert Lewis Ridarelli on April 26, 1942 in Philadelphia, Pa., Rydell was a star by the ripe old age of seven, playing the drums like his idol Gene Krupa. In his teens he turned to recording, beginning in 1959 with "Kissin' Time." In 1961 he headlined at the posh Copacabana Club in New York City, riding such hits as "Wild One" (1960), "Little Bitty Girl" (1960) and his trademark "Volare" (1960). He appeared in the film version of *Bye Bye Birdie* in 1963 and his last big

hit, "Forget Him," entered the charts at the end of that year.

Ryder, Mitch, and the Detroit Wheels   Mitch Ryder (vocals), John Badenjek (drums), Jimmy McCartney (guitar), Earl Eliot (bass), Joe Cubert (guitar)—Just when everybody thought you had to be English to be cool, Mitch Ryder came thundering out of Detroit with a bad case of rhythm and blues, to set the English boys temporarily on their guitars. The scene was Detroit, 1965, and the Detroit Wheels (a popular local band formerly known as Billy Lee and the Rivieras) were scheduled to open the show for the superpopular, supercool, super-English Dave Clark Five. The Wheels were slated to play two songs, and when they finished up an hour and a half later, the Dave Clark Five could barely slink on stage. Their first national hit came that year with the combination of Little Richard's "Jenny Jenny" and Chuck Willis' "C.C. Rider" called "Jenny Take A Ride," and they followed that up with some of the hardest driving rhythm and blues ever cut by any band, much less any white band— "Little Latin Lupe Lu" (1966), "Devil With A Blue Dress/Good Golly Miss Molly" (1966) and "Sock It To Me Baby" (1966). The problem with the Detroit Wheels was that the English Invasion fed directly into the flower power era of psychedelic rock, where white rhythm-and-blues groups were considered only slightly less quaint than brontosaurs. Their music, though, has been resurrected in the late 1970s by Bruce Springsteen—

himself strongly influenced by Ryder—who closes his shows with a Detroit Wheels medley. It's still great.

Sadler, Sergeant Barry
Army Staff Sergeant Barry Sadler (born in 1941 in New Mexico) became a member of the much-vaunted Green Berets combat unit as a medic in the early 1960s. While serving in Vietnam he was injured in a trap and retired from combat duty. Along the way he'd become an accomplished country singer, writing songs during the lulls. One of those songs was "The Ballad Of The Green Berets" in 1966, which, although intended for internal Army consumption, was brought to the attention of RCA Records by author Robin Moore, who had written a book called *The Green Berets* and was looking for someone to pose for the cover. "The Ballad Of The Green Berets" became one of the fastest selling songs in RCA's history, and Barry Sadler's face ended up on the cover of Robin Moore's book.

Sager, Carole Bayer
Lyricist Carole Bayer Sager, along with usual collaborator Marvin Hamlisch, has written an impressive string of 1970s hits. She began with Wayne Fontana and the Mindbenders' "A Groovy Kind Of Love" and Melissa Manchester's "Midnight Blue," then ran through Carly Simon's "Nobody Does It Better," the James Bond movie theme, in 1977 and numerous other songs recorded in 1978-79, from Dolly Parton's "Heartbreaker" to Paul Anka's "Starmaker." She is also working steadily on a solo career that began in 1978 with her *Carole Bayer Sager... Too* album.

Sahm, Doug
Born on Nov. 6, 1941 in Texas, Sahm is best known as the founder of the Sir Douglas Quintet, one of the oddest congregations to surface in flower power San Francisco. In 1965 he brought a wild-eyed collection of crazies to the Psychedelic City, and although attempting to pass as English rockers, the Quintet played music that reflected their blues, Western swing, country, fifties rock-and-roll, Cajun, Mexican and rhythm-and-blues backgrounds. The results included two masterpieces: "She's About A Mover" (1965) and "Mendocino" (1969). Since then Sahm has produced a number of generally excellent, though completely obscure, albums. (An exception was *Doug Sahm And Band,* recorded with the help of Bob Dylan and produced by Jerry Wexler for Atlantic Records in 1973. But that record did not accurately represent Sahm's music.) He continues to pursue his fusion of the many and varied musical elements of south Texas into a single soul stew.

Sainte-Marie, Buffy
Buffy Sainte-Marie, a Cree Indian, was born on Feb. 20, 1941 in Saskatchewan, Canada and is best known for her two huge folk hits "Universal Soldier"—an all-purpose protest song—and the haunting "Until It's Time For You To Go." She began her career in the folk music boom of the mid-1960s and has retained her tough left-wing slant—especially concerning the problems of American Indians—although she has at times sought a more commercial vein with such albums as *Moonshot.*

Saints, The
Chris Bailey (vocals), Ed Kuepper (guitar), Ivor Hay (drums), Alastair Ward (bass)—Australian New Wave group founded in 1973 in Brisbane, the Saints began their career in 1976 by pressing 500 copies of their own record, "I'm Stranded." It went on to be named one of the top English singles of 1977. Since, the band has produced two albums for Sire Records with limited success.

Sam and Dave
Sam Moore (born on Oct. 12, 1935 in Miami, Fla.) and Dave Prater (born on May 9, 1937 in Ocilla, Ga.) made some of the finest soul music to come out of the Memphis soul explosion, including "Hold On I'm Coming" (1966), "Soul Man" (1967), "Thank You" (1968) and others. Dave, who had originally intended to be a gospel singer, was working as a baker in Miami when he ran into Sam at a local club and joined him on stage—still in his white baker's clothes—for a little singing. By 1967, thanks in a large part to the writing of David Porter and Isaac Hayes and the superb Stax musicians, Sam and Dave were the hottest soul act in the country. As soul music waned, so did their

fortunes, and a personal split between the two kept them apart for years. Happily, they got back together in 1978 and have been touring again with a suprisingly vibrant, suprisingly powerful stage show.

Sam the Sham and the Pharaohs   Sam the Sham (Domingo Samudio) was the leader of a popular Memphis bar band during the mid-1960s, famous for arriving at their gigs in a hearse, wearing outrageous outfits and going through semicrazed stage antics. Well-known Memphis producer Stan Kessler was able to do an admirable job of translating that craziness onto wax with "Wooly Bully" (1965) and "Lil' Red Riding Hood" (1966). Despite the obvious lighweight nature of his lyrics, Sam the Sham's music remains a surprisingly powerful example of rhythm and blues, sort of a missing Memphis link between Sun Records rock and Stax Records soul. The Pharaohs were Ray Stinnet (guitar), David Martin (bass), Jerry Patterson (drums) and Butch Gibson (sax).

Sandpipers, The   James Brady (vocals), Richard Shoff (vocals), Michael Piano (vocals)—Folk group famous for its popularization of the Cuban revolutionary ballad "Guantanamera" (1966) and for "Come Saturday Morning" (1970), the theme to *The Sterile Cuckoo* (1969), starring Liza Minnelli.

Sang, Samantha   A protege of Bee Gee Barry Gibb, Samantha Sang (born on Aug. 5, 1953 in Melbourne,

Australia) became the toast of the discos in 1978 with "Emotion," a top 10 hit that was produced by Gibb, and rode the crest of the Bee Gees frenzy of that period.

Santana   Carlos Santana (guitar, vocals); Greg Walker (vocals); Ndugu Leon Chancler (drums); Armando Peraza (percussion); Francisco Aquabella (percussion); David Brown (bass); Tom Coster (keyboards); and others, including Jose Chepito Areas, Michael Carabello, Gregg Rolie, Michael Shrieve, Neal Schon—Native Mexican Carlos Santana launched the group that bore his name during the late 1960 s in a very successful attempt to blend Latin and rock music. The group's back-to-back hits, "Evil Ways" (1970) and "Black Magic Woman" (1970), both from *Abraxas*, coupled with an appearance at Woodstock and in the successful *Woodstock* movie got Santana off in a spectacular manner. Band members came and went while the music alternately became more Latin, with a reworking of Tito Puente's "Oye Coma Va" in 1971, and more jazzy, with the *Caravanserai* album in 1972. By 1972, though, Carlos Santana had become a disciple of Sri Chinmoy, and that guru's Eastern disciplines led him down a completely different path (*Love, Devotion, Surrender* in 1973, with fellow Chinmoy disciple John McLaughlin). In recent years Carlos Santana has been striving to regain his commercial appeal; he was moderately successful in 1977 with *Amigos,* a return to his Latin roots.

Savoy Brown   Kim Simmonds (guitar), Tom Farnell (drums), Ian Ellis (bass, vocals), Paul Raymond (guitar, keyboards, vocals) and numerous others—Originally formed in 1966 as the Savoy Brown Blues Band by Kim Simmonds, Savoy Brown has at times resembled a revolving door for musicians, with 20-some-odd members coming and going throughout the years. While the members have changed, the music has not— hard driving blues-based rock, loud enough to cause internal injuries among the uninitiated. The group is best known for *Hellbound Train* (1972) and the earlier *Blue Matter* (1968).

Sayer, Leo   Originally best known as a songwriter, the author of the more memorable cuts on Roger Daltrey's (of the Who) first solo album, *Daltrey, Sayer* (born on May 21, 1948 in England) went on to become, oddly enough, the king of the discos. Although his first hit, "Long Tall Glasses" (1974), had almost a novelty flavor, his subsequent "You Make Me Feel Like Dancing" (1976) and "When I Need You" (1977) established him as a solid star on the disco circuit. Late 1978, though, found him leaving the dance floor and returning to acoustic music, even recording an old Buddy Holly number on his *Leo Sayer* album that year.

Scaggs, Boz   At the tender age of 15, Boz Scaggs (born William Royce Scaggs on June 8, 1944 in Ohio) joined a band with white soulmate Steve Miller, eventually following Miller to the University of Wisconsin to work in Miller's band the Ardells, aka the Fabulous Night Train. Under Miller he developed a fierce love and understanding of rhythm and blues, which was to serve him well in later years. Scaggs drifted to Europe in the mid-1960s, where he worked as a folksinger, and stayed until 1967, when Miller called him back to join the psychedelic Steve Miller Band. In 1969 he began a solo career, returning to his R&B roots, but it wasn't until his *Silk Degrees* album in 1976 that he found the groove with such hits as "Lowdown" and "Lido Shuffle." Today he remains an outstanding singer and stylist.

Scott, Tom, and the LA Express   Tom Scott (sax), Max Bennett (bass), John Guerin (drums), Robben Ford (guitar), Larry Nash (piano)—One of the most successful jazz-rock fusion groups of the mid-1970s, best known for their backup work behind such artists as Steely Dan and Joni Mitchell (particularly her live *Miles Of Aisles* album in 1974). Their numerous solo albums have not fared so well commercially, although such albums as *New York Connection* (1975) and *Intimate Strangers* (1979) earned critical accolades.

Scott-Heron, Gil   Black poet Gil Scot-Heron was born in Chicago, Ill. and raised in Jackson, Tenn., where as a teenager he wrote detective stories. He wrote his first novel at the age of 19, his first book of poetry the next year, but it wasn't until the waning hours of the 1960s that he came to the attention of the rock audience with his rap poem

"The Revolution Will Not Be Televised," also recorded by LaBelle. He had an international hit (in 1975) with "Johannasburg" and has recently been active in the antinuclear power movement.

Scruggs, Earl   Born on June 19, 1914 in Overton County, Tenn., Scruggs is best known for his development of the modern five-string banjo technique as well as for his work with Lester Flatt. He gained the attention of rock audiences for "Foggy Mountain Breakdown," first recorded in 1960 and used as background in the violent film *Bonnie and Clyde.* Scruggs presently works in a more rock-oriented group with his sons.

Sea Level   Formed by Allman Brothers Band keyboard man Chuck Leavell (the band is a pun on his name: C. Leavell) and bassist Lamar Williams after the first breakup of the band in the mid-1970s, Sea Level sought a more jazzier ground than the blues-boogie of the Brothers. After three albums—the first, *Sea Level,* is probably the best—the band is still going strong, so much so that Leavell and Williams declined an invitation to join the re-formed Brothers in 1978.

Seals and Crofts   Texans Jim Seals (born on Oct. 17, 1941) and Dash Crofts (born on Aug. 14, 1940) first got together in the mid-1950s with a group called the Champs, famous for "Tequila" (1958). Won over to the Baha'i faith, they resurfaced in 1970 with a patented MOR duo sound that immediately shot up the charts

with such hits as "Summer Breeze" (1972), "Hummingbird" (1973) and "Diamond Girl" (1973). Some of their glitter faded in 1973, when they sang "Unborn Child," a bitter tirade against abortion that won them few friends. Their success since then has been tempered, although they have continued to make the charts.

Searchers, The   Anthony Jackson (vocals, bass), Michael Pendergast (guitar), John McNally (guitar), Chris Curtis (drums); additional member: Frank Allen—An English group formed in 1960, the Searchers rode in on the British Invasion wave of 1963 and 1964, hitting the charts with "Needles And Pins," "Don't Throw Your Love Away" and "When You Walk In The Room" in 1964 and staying there pretty steadily through the halcyon days of British Rule. They also produced a minor hit with a remake of a classic—"Love Potion Number Nine" (1964).

Seatrain   Richard Greene (violin), Andy Kulberg (bass, flute), Don Kretmar (sax, bass), John Gregory (guitar, vocals), Roy Blumenfeld (drums)—A spinoff of the Blues Project formed in Marin County, Calif. during the late 1960s, Seatrain leaned heavily on Richard Greene's violin, which lasted through three albums—the best probably being the first, *Seatrain* (1969).

Sebastian, John   Born on March 17, 1944 in New York, N.Y., Sebastian is yet another of that city's famous folkies. He was the cofounder (with Zal

Yanovsky) of the most famous folkie group of them all, the Lovin' Spoonful, and when the Spoonful packed it in, he seemed destined for solo stardom. That stardom never really worked out, although he produced some excellent singles (the whole albums were more uneven). An appearance at Woodstock and in the *Woodstock* movie, which he claims to have forgotten thanks to drugs, revitalized his career, but not for very long. His most recent boost came when he recorded the theme for "Welcome Back Kotter," the Gabe Kaplan/John Travolta television comedy. The song was a big hit in 1976.

Neil Sedaka

Sedaka, Neil   Neil Sedaka (born on March 13, 1939 in Brooklyn, New York City) has had two successful careers in pop music: one in the 1960s and one in the 1970s. After being trained in classical piano at the prestigious Juilliard School of Music and chosen as

the top young classical pianist in New York, Sedaka went on to become a very successful pop songwriter ("Stupid Cupid," recorded by Connie Francis in 1958, for example). He moved on to become a teen idol with such hits as "Oh Carol" (1959), for girl friend Carole King, "Calendar Girl" (1960) and "Little Devil" (1961). He staged a spectacular comeback in 1974 with "Laughter In The Rain" and returned to writing solid gold hits ("Love Will Keep Us Together" for the Captain and Tennille and "Solitaire" for the Carpenters).

Seeds, The   Sky Saxon (vocals), Daryl Hopper (keyboards), Rick Andridge (drums), Jan Savage (guitar)— Formed in Los Angeles in the flower power 1960s, the Seeds are best remembered for their tough psychedelic rock, such as "Pushin' Too Hard" (1966) and "Can't Seem To Make You Mine" (1967).

Seeger, Pete   Born on May 3, 1919 in New York, N.Y., Seeger is perhaps the most influential of the professional folk singers. His work as a guitarist and banjo player led many of a new generation of rock musicians into the fold, and his work as a lyricist and supporter of unpopular causes presaged the whole protest movement in popular music. (When he was blacklisted from the popular television program "Hootenanny" in the mid-1960s for alleged "communist" sympathies, a host of other big-name talent, including Joan Baez and the Kingston Trio, refused to perform on the show at all.)

Seeger formed the Weavers, one of the most popular folk groups ever, in 1949. His songwriting (and arranging of folk ballads) speaks for itself: "We Shall Overcome," "Where Have All The Flowers Gone" and "Kisses Sweeter Than Wine," among many others.

Seger, Bob   Originally one of rock's greatest regional acts, Bob Seger came thundering out of the wilderness around Detroit in 1976 with "Night Moves," perhaps the only time rock and roll has ever effectively dealt with the subject of growing older in a pop culture geared for 14-year-olds. Seger (born on May 6, 1945 in Ann Arbor, Mich.) got his first taste of stardom in 1966, when his song "Heavy Music" made the national charts and became a huge hit in the Midwest. That more or less set the pattern. While Seger would make a minor dent nationally, he became a legend in Detroit. His "Ramblin' Gamblin' Man" was enough of a hit to get him some national attention in early 1969, but it was not enough to boost him out of the Midwest ghetto. That boost came in 1976 with his *Live Bullet* album, recorded live in (where else?) Detroit, and the subsequent release of the *Night Moves* album (with its hit title track), which remains one of the finest examples of American rock ever. One critic described Seger's music as rock and roll for grown-ups, and his album *Against The Wind* (with another hit title song) in 1980 aptly fit the description.

Sensations, The   Yvonne

Baker (vocals), Richard Curtain (vocals), Sam Armstrong (vocals), Alphonso Howell (vocals)—Launched in Philadelphia in 1956, the Sensations enjoyed several minor hits before their classic "Let Me In" in 1962. The song was written by Yvonne Baker, who had been coaxed into coming out of retirement the year before.

Seville, David   Born on Jan. 27, 1919 in Fresno, Calif., Seville established himself as a songwriter (the Rosemary Clooney standard "Come On-a My House" in the mid-1950s) and a master of the novelty number ("Witch Doctor" in 1958), before the creation that made him famous. That creation was the Chipmunks—Theodore, Simon and the precocious Alvin—actually speeded up tapes of his voice. "The Chipmunk Song" (1958) is still heard with regularity each year at Christmas time. Seville died in 1972.

Sex Pistols, The   Johnny Rotten (vocals), Steve Jones (guitar, vocals), Sid Vicious (bass), Paul Cook (drums)—All hype aside (which is no mean feat in this case), the Sex Pistols stand as perhaps the most important band of the 1970s. They almost single-handedly launched the punk movement in Britain (although its beginnings are clearly American), which opened the door for the explosion of New Wave rock that ended the 1970s. And they did so in the accepted manner of rockers since the beginning —by being outrageously rude, crude, uncouth, unmannered, spoiled, gross and incredibly

vibrant and alive. Formed in 1975 by former New York Dolls manager Malcom McLaren, the Sex Pistols soon grabbed the all-time title for raunchiness with a series of concert/brawls. Their music, as snarled by vocalist Rotten (so named, legend goes, because of his rotten teeth) was raw, powerful rock. Their dealings with record companies were about

The former Johnny Rotten of the Sex Pistols, now John Lydon of Public Image Ltd. (Pil)

equally as raw—they were signed by three companies, paid $200,000 to get lost and produced three singles in 1976-77, "Anarchy In The U.K.," "Pretty Vacant" and "God Save The Queen," which managed to bring the might of the English government down on their heads. Despite the publicity the group failed to crack the American market.

They signed with Warner Records, which had no trouble with them, figuring that if the Pistols made money, nothing they could do would be sufficiently offensive to let them go. After one American album, *Never Mind The Bollocks Here's The Sex Pistols,* and a busted U.S. tour, the group blew up. Vicious died of a drug overdose in 1979 after being arrested for the murder of his girl friend.

Shadows of Knight, The Jim Sohns (vocals, percussion), Joseph Kelley (guitar, bass, harp), Warren Rogers (guitar, bass), Jerry McGeorge (guitar), Thomas Schiffour (drums)—Your basic Chicago club band, the Shadows of Knight flared briefly in 1966 with "Gloria," a remake of the Van Morrison song, which became a standard for high school bands everywhere. Along with "Louie-Louie," "Gloria" remains one of the most durable dance hits.

Sha Na Na   Screamin' Scott Simon (piano), Frederick Dennis Greene (vocals), John "Bowzer" Bauman (piano), John "Jocko" Marcellino (drums), Donald York (vocals), Tony Santini (vocals), Lenny Baker (sax), Johnny Contardo (vocals), Dave "Chico" Ryan (bass), Dan McBride (guitar)— The group that institutionalized nostalgia, Sha Na Na (the name taken from the chorus of the Silhouettes' 1958 hit song, "Get A Job") began at Columbia University in New York City in 1969 playing for a "1950s" dance. The group really took off after Woodstock and the subsequent movie, the members' wild stage antics and greaser looks monumentally clashing with the jeans-and-long-hair rockers of the time. Musically the band is little more than an oldies jukebox, never venturing far from the fifties material that made it. At present the group is best known for its weekly television show, which has turned Sha Na Na into more of an institution than a band. Former member Henry Gross has done well in his solo career, with the hit "Shannon" (1976).

Shangri-Las, The Mary Weiss (vocals), Betty Weiss (vocals), Mary Anne Ganser (vocals), Marge Ganser (vocals)—Formed in the early 1960s at Andrew Jackson High School in Queens, New York City, the Shangri-Las were the "bad girls" of the girl group craze. Under the tutelage of George "Shadow" Morton, the Shangri-Las really took off with "Remember (Walking In The Sand)" (1964), a Morton-penned number, but it wasn't until Morton found a Jeff Berry/Ellie Greenwich number titled "Leader Of The Pack" (1964) that the group became superstars in the black leather mold. They went on to make several other mini-classics, including "Give Him A Great Big Kiss" in 1964 and "I Can Never Go Home Any More" the next year. Marge Ganser later died of a drug overdose, but the group still performs as a trio.

Shannon, Del Shannon's distinctive voice (with its falsetto sweeps) punctuated the early 1960s, just before the British Invasion. Born on Dec. 30, 1939 in Grand Rapids,

Mich., Shannon began working around clubs in his home state after his discharge from the Army in 1959. His hits began in 1961 with "Runaway" and continued throughout the early 1960s with such songs as "Hats Off To Larry" (1961), "Hey Little Girl" (1961), "Little Town Flirt" (1963), "Handy Man" (1964) and "Do You Want To Dance" (1964). He also composed such songs as "I Go To Pieces" for the English duo Peter and Gordon, a hit in 1965.

Sharp, Dee Dee Born on Sept. 9, 1945 in Philadelphia, Pa., Sharp began her recording career by answering an ad from Cameo Records for a girl who could read music, play the piano and sing. Her first and biggest hit came in 1962 with "Mashed Potato Time," riding the current dance craze. She later married producer Kenny Gamble, who produced a series of Philadelphia Sound albums by Sharp in the late 1970s.

Sherman, Allan Born on Nov. 30, 1924 in Chicago, Ill., Sherman created the television staple "I've Got A Secret" before taking his Jewish humor one step further with a series of *My Son The...* albums, including folk singer, celebrity etc. In 1963 he had a hilarious hit single with "Hello Muddah, Hello Faddah," about life in a summer camp. Sherman died on Nov. 21, 1973.

Sherrill, Billy Nashville producer Billy Sherrill began his career producing rhythm and blues in Muscle Shoals, Ala., but he soon turned to

country music. He is best known for his work with Charlie Rich ("Behind Closed Doors," "The Most Beautiful Girl"— both in 1973) and for the creation of the supersmooth, superheavily orchestrated "cosmopolitan" country sound.

Shines, Johnny Bluesman Johnny Shines (born in 1915 in Memphis, Tenn.) continues as one of the most prolific modern bluesmen still performing. He came to Chicago in 1941, but a promising recording career took a long time to materialize. That career for the fine singer and songwriter finally began in the 1970s, when he was "discovered" by white musicians. His most recent album, in fact, was produced by noted blues authority Peter Guralnick. Shines claims legendary bluesman Robert Johnson as his stepfather, and whether the claim is valid or not, Johnny Shines is one of the very few bluesmen who are comfortable with both the rural blues of the Mississippi Delta and the hard-edged urban blues of the Chicago bars.

Shirelles, The Shirley Alston (vocals), Beverley Lee (vocals), Micki Harris (vocals), Doris Kenner (vocals)—After going to high school together in Passaic, N.J., the four formed the Shirelles (the name taken from leader Shirley Alston's first name) in 1957. The Shirelles began recording the next year with "I Met Him On A Sunday," written by the members themselves, and then went on to record a string of classic girl group hits— "Tonight's The Night" (1960), the Carole King/Gerry Goffin composition "Will You Still Love Me Tomorrow" (1960), "Dedicated To The One I Love" (1961), "Mama Said" (1961), "Soldier Boy" (1962) and many others. The group continues to perform (sans Doris Kenner), and most of their hits have been rerecorded by other groups at least once.

Silverstein, Shel   Well known to readers of *Playboy* magazine as the iconoclastic cartoonist and offbeat poet, Silverstein has almost single-handedly introduced insanity into country music through such songs as Johnny Cash's "A Boy Named Sue," Dr. Hook's "The Cover Of The Rolling Stone" and Bobby Bare's "The Winner." He's also produced a series of solo albums, although his voice is perhaps closer to a grunt than a melodious instrument, and done some outstanding work on children's books, including his classic *The Giving Tree*.

Simmons, Gene   Not to be confused with the Kiss member of the same name, "Jumpin'" Gene Simmons became popular in the late 1950s with his hit "Haunted House." He was born in 1933 in Tupelo, Miss.

Simon, Carly   Carly Simon's music sounds exactly like what it is—the laments of a very wealthy Sara Lawrence graduate whose life reads like your basic fairy tale. Born on June 25, 1945 in New York, N.Y., the daughter of Richard Simon of the Simon and Schuster publishing empire, she began singing with her sister Lucy in college. When

Carly Simon

Lucy got married, Carly Simon headed for Europe, where she ran into Albert Grossman, then Bob Dylan's manager. Grossman hatched a plan to make Simon the female Bob Dylan, which failed spectacularly. It did ultimately result in her first album, *Carly Simon* (1971), which established her as a master of the slick vocal. The album produced two hits, "That's The Way I've Always Heard It Should Be" and the more

powerful "Anticipation," which, in one of life's little ironies, ended up as a successful television commercial for ketchup. From there on, the rails were greased as she honed her slick and slickly produced vocals with each subsequent album. Her 1972 *No Secrets* featured the hit "You're So Vain," a wry look at celebrityhood, with accompanying vocals by Mick Jagger. *Playing Possum* in 1975 featured a stunningly

193

sexy (but tasteful) album cover. In 1973 she married singer James Taylor, and they have had two children and one hit duet, "Mockingbird" (1974).

Simon, Joe Soul singer Joe Simon was born on Sept. 2, 1943 in Simmesport, La. and began recording in 1960. Although he recorded steadily throughout the early and mid-1960s, it wasn't until "The Chokin' Kind" in 1969 that he had a million seller. In the early 1970s he began working with Philadelphia Sound producers Kenny Gamble and Leon Huff, a collaboration that resulted in the huge hit "Drowning In The Sea Of Love" (1971) and the follow-up hit "Power Of Love" (1972). Simon has had numerous other hits during his career.

Simon, Paul Without a doubt one of the most important pop artists in the history of rock and roll, Paul Simon began his solo career in 1970 after the breakup of the phenomenally successful duo Simon and Garfunkel. Born on Oct. 13, 1941 in Newark, N.J. but raised in Queens, New York City, he'd been friends with Art Garfunkel since grade school. They recorded together briefly as Tom and Jerry, even scoring a modest hit, "Hey Schoolgirl," in 1957 before returning to school. At Queens College, Simon worked briefly with songwriter Carole King, went to law school for a while and ultimately left to bum around Europe. Upon returning to the United States in the mid-1960s, he once again linked up with Garfunkel and thereafter they practically redefined folk music, giving it a much-needed

boost out of its strictly traditional confines into more topical areas. By 1970, however, Simon and Garfunkel, although very successful, had become stale, and Simon left to go it on his own. His first album, *Paul Simon,* laid out the basics of his style with such hits as "Mother And Child Reunion" (named for an egg and chicken dish in a Chinese restaurant) in 1972 and "Me And Julio Down By The School Yard" the same year. Simon's style was spare, in direct contrast to the last Simon and Garfunkel opuses, and he was willing to experiment with such rhythms as reggae and gospel. His songwriting continued to improve, becoming more sophisticated and more able to comment on life without sacrificing simplicity. Songs like "Kodachrome" in 1973, "Loves Me Like A Rock" (backed by the great gospel group the Dixie Hummingbirds) in 1973, "American Tune" (named by *Rolling Stone* magazine as the best song of 1975), "My Little Town" (his reunion song with Art Garfunkel) in 1975 and "Still Crazy After All These Years" in 1976 did for the 1970s what the music of Simon and Garfunkel did for the 1960s.

Simon and Garfunkel Paul Simon and Art Garfunkel had been friends in school in New York City and even recorded a sort-of hit in 1957, "Hey Schoolgirl" (as Tom and Jerry), but it wasn't until 1964 that the magic of Simon and Garfunkel began to work. At a time when the world was afire

with the sound of folk music, the two drifted back together and cut a folkie album of their own, *Wednesday Morning 3 A.M.,* which went exactly nowhere when it was released in 1965. Dispirited, Simon headed for Europe with Garfunkel in tow in the hopes of making a little money on the coffee club circuit. While they were gone, producer Tom Wilson decided to release a cut from the album as a single. He chose "The Sounds Of Silence" and since neither Simon nor Garfunkel was around either to consult or complain, Wilson added electric guitars, drums and all sorts of rock paraphernalia to the record. It was an overnight hit, reaching the top of the charts in late 1965, and by the time the duo got back to America, they were big stars. The two then began laying the groundwork for what would be known as soft rock, with such hits as "Homeward Bound" (1966), "I Am A Rock" (1966), "A Hazy Shade Of Winter" (1966), "At The Zoo" (1967) and the landmark "Mrs. Robinson" (1968), from the movie *The Graduate.* Simon's songwriting was becoming increasingly sophisticated, and in addition, the duo was having to contend with a shifting musical terrain. The soft protest of the folkies era sounded more outdated in the post-Woodstock years of the late 1960s. In 1970 Simon and Garfunkel did their piece de resistance—"Bridge Over Troubled Water"—then, within a year, announced that they were parting ways. Simon went on to new heights as a songwriter and singer, moving into areas outside the realm of the duo, while Garfunkel began a modestly successful acting career. The two got back together briefly in 1975 for "My Little Town," which sounded as good as they had ever sounded.

Simone, Nina   Born Eunice Waymon on Feb. 21, 1933 in Tryon, N.C., and trained at the Juilliard School of Music in New York City, Nina Simone has drifted from her stunning interpretation of "I Loves You Porgy" in 1959 to the Bee Gees "To Love Somebody" in 1969. She has also recorded some outstanding versions of such rhythm-and-blues hits as "Please Don't Let Me Be Misunderstood" and "I Put A Spell On You." Her increasing involvement with black causes led to her stepping down from the music business in 1974. Recently, however, she has done some concert work.

Sinatra, Frank   For most of the rock generation, Francis Albert Sinatra is best known as the guy who recorded "My Way" before Elvis Presley got around to it. Over the years he's had scores of hits (beginning with "All Or Nothing" in 1943, when he was a vocalist with the Harry James orchestra), record sales of over 40 million units and millions of loyal fans. But what Frank Sinatra gave to rock was a sense of vocal style, that of the ultimate crooner. Sinatra's sensual style has been copied by dozens and dozens of rock singers, including Elvis Presley, who was able to blend Sinatra's crooning with his own rockabilly fury.

Sinatra was born on Dec. 12, 1915 in Hoboken, N.J. and

began singing in the late 1930s. He had a number one pop hit, "Strangers In The Night," in 1966 and another chart topper, "Somethin' Stupid," the following year in a duet with his daughter, Nancy. Nancy Sinatra also had solo hits ("These Boots Are Made For Walkin'" in 1966) and duet hits with Lee Hazlewood ("Jackson" in 1967).

Sir Douglas Quintet, The Doug Sahm (vocals, guitar), Augie Meyer (keyboards), Jack Barber (bass), Leon Beatty (percussion), John Perez (drums)—The Sir Douglas Quintet was the brainstorm of Tex-Mex rocker Doug Sahm and canny promoter Huey Meaux. Meaux correctly perceived that the world in 1965 was not ready for a group of semi-crazed Texans and Mexicans playing flamboyant rock and roll. What the world wanted was Englishmen, so Meaux and Sahm created the Sir Douglas Quintet, a group of crazed Texans and Mexicans masquerading as an English rock band (the cover of the group's first album showed unclear pictures of the members, lest the sham be discovered). The Sir Douglas Quintet produced two absolutely classic rock songs, "She's About A Mover" (1965) and "Mendocino" (1969), before falling apart. Sahm and various pieces of the Quintet still perform together occasionally, and they are still one of the most dynamic and powerful acts in rock.

Slade   Noddy Holder (vocals, guitar), Dave Hill (guitar), Jimmy Lea (bass, piano), Don Powell (drums)—Launched in

the late 1960s in England, Slade was scheduled to "take America by storm" in the early 1970s with its perpetually recycled heavy rock. While the band had a tremendous power base in England, it failed miserably in the American market, fading quickly after a mid-1970s assault.

Sledge, Percy   Born in 1941 in Muscle Shoals, Ala., soul crooner Percy Sledge began singing when he was 15 years old, but it wasn't until the mid-1960s that his career really got started. He recorded "When A Man Loves A Woman" in 1966 at a small Alabama studio, and when Phil Walden, then manager of Otis Redding, and Atlantic Records executives heard the cut, they knew it was a hit. Sledge continued recording throughout the 1960s and early 1970s, producing some of the best soul music of that period, including "Warm And Tender Love" (1966), "Take Time To Know Her" (1968) and "Any Day Now" (1969).

Slick, Grace   Born on Oct. 30, 1943 in Chicago, Ill., Slick had worked as a fashion model and as a singer for the band Great Society in San Francisco before joining forces with the Jefferson Airplane for the group's *Surrealistic Pillow* album in 1967. Her work with that San Francisco group made her reputation, although during one of the band's several collapses she tried a solo career with an album titled *Manhole*. The band re-formed as the Jefferson Starship for a series of mid- and late-1970s hits, but in 1978 Slick, troubled by recurring bouts with the

195

bottle, left the band for good. At the time her move was considered by some to be more of a bad omen for the Jefferson Starship than for Grace Slick. Ironically, the Starship came back strong in 1979, while little was heard from Slick until 1981, when she returned with a solo album, *The Wrecking Ball.*

Sly and the Family Stone
Sly Stone (organ, vocals), Rose Stone (piano, vocals), Freddie Stone (guitar, vocals), Larry Graham, Jr. (bass, vocals), Greg Errico (drums), Jerry Martini (sax, flute, accordion, piano), Cynthia Robinson (trumpet, vocals)—Sly and the Family Stone was formed in San Francisco around 1967 by jive disc jockey Sylvester Stewart (born on March 15, 1944 in Dallas, Tex.) after meeting Cynthia Robinson. Band members included brother Freddie and sister Rose, cousin Larry Graham and, shocking at the time, two whites—Greg Errico and Jerry Martini. Beginning with "Dance To The Music" in 1968, the band produced a series of jazzy, infectiously cheery soul hits, including "Everyday People" (1968), "Stand" (1969), "I Want To Take You Higher" (1969), "Hot Fun In The Summer Time" (1969), "Thank You (Falettinme Be Mice Elf Agin)" (1970), "Everybody Is A Star" (1970) and "Family Affair" (1971). The importance of Sly Stone's music is that it represented a bridge between the soul music and Motown Sound of the 1960s and the jazzier, can-you-dance-to-it music of the 1970s. The band fell apart in the early 1970s, largely due to Sly

Stone's disinterest, but has since re-formed several times, most recently in 1979.

Small Faces, The Steve Marriott (vocals, guitar), Ronnie Lane (bass), Ian McLagan (organ), Kenny Jones (drums)—One of the die-hard English rock-and-roll bands of the mid-1960s, the Small Faces refused to grow up and become progressive. They are best known for their nasty hit "Itchycoo Park" in 1967 and for the fact that two years later they broke up to spawn Humble Pie, with Steve Marriott and Peter Frampton, and the Faces, with Rod Stewart and Ron Wood joining Lane, Jones and McLagan. They returned as the Small Faces in 1977, to no avail.

Smith, Huey "Piano" Born on Oct. 10, 1924 in New Orleans, La., Huey "Piano" Smith, like Fats Domino, Allen Toussaint and other well-known New Orleans R&B piano players, was another disciple of Professor Longhair. His first hit came in 1957 with the infectiously rhythmic "Rocking Pneumonia And The Boogie Woogie Flu," followed the next year by "Don't You Just Know It."

Smith, O.C. Born on June 21, 1932 in Mansfield, La., O.C. Smith honed his performing career in the Air Force during the early 1950s before breaking into the big time with his two huge hits in 1968, "The Son Of Hickory Holler's Tramp" and "Little Green Apples."

Smith, Patti Chicago-born (in 1946), Jersey-raised Patti

Patti Smith

Smith began her career as a poet, deeply influenced by the works of Arthur Rimbaud and such rock "poets" as Jim Morrison, Bob Dylan and the Rolling Stones. Her work found outlets in *Creem* and *Rolling Stone,* as well as in readings in New York City's numerous rock clubs and coffeehouses. In 1975 she took the next logical step and recorded an album, *Horses,* which featured a stunning version of Van Morrison's "Gloria" and in general marked her as one of the most important rock personalities to surface in those bare times. Her success focused attention on the budding "punk" scene in New York City and, in turn, helped to fuel the scene. A second album, *Radio Ethiopia* (1976), did little, but her third, *Easter* (1978), yielded a major surprise, a hit version of Bruce Springsteen's "Because The Night," one of the finest rock moments of the waning 1970s.

Smith, Ray Best known for his infectious "Rockin' Little

Angel" in 1960, Ray Smith was born on Oct. 31, 1938 in Paducah, Ky.

Smith, Warren Born on Feb. 7, 1933 in Louise, Miss., Warren Smith was one of the earliest successful Sun Records artists in Memphis, with such hits as "Rock And Roll Ruby" and "So Long I'm Gone" in the rockabilly years of the mid-1950s.

Phoebe Snow

Snow, Phoebe Born Phoebe Laub on July 17, 1952 in New York, N.Y., Phoebe Snow began performing in the early 1970s in Greenwich Village, using her remarkable vocal range to pursue a fusion of blues, jazz and folk. Not suprisingly, that voice soon came to the attention of music business professionals, and her first album was released in 1973. That album, *Phoebe Snow,* encompassed her many styles and yielded a hit single, "Poetry Man." It also caught the attention of Paul Simon, who recorded a duet with Snow, "Gone At Last," on

his *Still Crazy After All These Years* album in 1975. Contractual hassles with her record company held up Snow's work for a time, and it really wasn't until 1977 that she got back on track with the single "Shaky Ground." One of the most promising female vocalists to emerge in the 1970s.

Soft Machine Karl Jenkins (keyboards, reeds), Alan Wakeman (sax), John Marshall (drums), Roy Babbington (bass), John Etheridge (guitar)—Originally formed as the group Wilde Flowers in England in 1961, the Soft Machine was one of the preeminent English underground bands of that period. Early on, they worked jazz-rock fusions, experimented with multimedia happenings and used long improvisational techniques (one of the group's best albums, *Third,* in 1970 was a two-record set with four songs). The last original member, Mike Ratledge, left the band in 1978.

Sonny and Cher Sonny Bono was working as an assistant and singer for producer Phil Spector in 1964 when a half-Indian girl named Cherilyn Sakisian walked into his life. Sonny, a former artist and repertoire (A&R) man for Specialty Records and a moderately successful songwriter ("Needles And Pins," by Jackie DeShannon and, later, the Searchers), knew there was something special about Cher, as she called herself, but Phil Spector wasn't buying it. She sang backup on a Spector opus, "Da Doo Ron Ron," before she and Sonny

struck out on their own, first as Caesar and Cleo, then as Sonny and Cher. After a few initial misses, the duo recorded "I Got You Babe" in 1965. The record was an immediate hit, and Sonny and Cher, with their weird clothes and cuddly personas, became immediate heroes of the counterculture, making, as one critic pointed out, love fashionable again. They produced a string of hits throughout the 1960s, including the classic "The Beat Goes On" in 1967. That beat continued for another year, when Cher, with Sonny as her mentor, went on her own with a string of fairly memorable hits and a couple of so-so movies. In the early 1970s, the duo made the shift from pop stardom to Vegas, where they were able to revive their flagging act. Vegas led to television, where Sonny was ultimately reduced to a bumbling straight man for Cher's increasingly sophisticated bits. In 1974, with Cher's solo career soaring and Sonny's still at the starting gate, the pair broke up, the TV show was canceled and Sonny and Cher went their separate ways, at least for a couple of years, until 1975, when a television reunion failed.

Sons of Champlin Bill Champlin (vocals, keyboards), Geoff Palmer (keyboards, vocals, reeds), Mike Andreas (woodwinds), Phil Wood (brass, keyboards), Terry Haggerty (guitar), Dave Schallock (bass, vocals), Jim Preston (drums), Mark Isham (brass, keyboards)—Formed in San Francisco in 1966, the Sons of Champlin (aka the Sons) shuffled names, personnel and record companies until around 1976, when they disbanded. Although they never achieved better than cult status, they were one of the better San Francisco bands in an era that included the Jefferson Airplane and the Grateful Dead.

Sopwith Camel Peter Kraemer (vocals, sax), Terry MacNeil (guitar), William Sievers (guitar), Martin Beard (bass), Norman Mayell (drums)—Formed in the middle 1960s and named for a World War I airplane, Sopwith Camel was the ringer in the San Francisco music community. While everybody else was being psychedelicized, the Camel threatened to nod out with bliss. The group had a superlaid-back hit, "Hello Hello," in 1966 and a modest follow-up, "A Postcard From Jamaica," in 1967 before disbanding. In 1973 Sopwith Camel regrouped without Sievers and without success.

Soul, David Hutch in the popular late-1970s television show "Starsky and Hutch," your standard-issue cop shoot-and-chase. Soul launched a surprisingly successful recording career in 1977 with "Don't Give Up On Us Baby." Since the demise of "S&H" though, his twin careers of records and stage have been noticeably low key.

South, Joe A sessions man who made good, South (born on Feb. 28, 1942 in Atlanta, Ga.) established himself as a sessions guitar player in Muscle Shoals, Ala. and as a songwriter ("Down In The

Boondocks" for Billy Joe Royal in 1965 and "Hush" for Deep Purple in 1968) before going on his own. In 1968 he went solo, with the resulting 1969 hit "Games People Play." His career seemed preordained, especially after subsequent hits like "Don't It Make You Want To Go Home" (1969) and "Walk A Mile In My Shoes" (1970), but the death of his brother, Tommy, in 1971 caused him to retire abruptly. He returned on a much lower key in 1975.

Souther, John David Born in Detroit, Mich. and raised in Amarillo, Tex., Souther has written successful songs for Linda Ronstadt and Bonnie Raitt and worked with the abortive "supergroup," the Souther-Hillman-Furay Band, before striking out on his own in 1976 with his *Black Rose* album. Nothing much happened until 1979, when his Roy Orbison-styled single, "You're Only Lonely," gave his career a much-needed boost.

J.D. Souther

Souther-Hillman-Furay Band, The John David Souther (guitar, vocals), Chris Hillman (bass, vocals), Richie Furay (guitar, vocals), Al Perkins (pedal steel), Paul Harris (keyboards), Jim Gordon (drums)—Basically a group that never got off the ground, the Souther-Hillman-Furay Band was formed in 1973 by ex-Byrd Chris Hillman, Richie Furay from the Buffalo Springfield and Poco and J.D. Souther, songwriter for Linda Ronstadt and Bonnie Raitt. Despite two albums and all the right moves, the band quickly folded—the only thing missing, it seems, was inspiration.

"Southside" Johnny and the Asbury Jukes "Southside" Johnny (vocals, harp), Kevin Kavanaugh (keyboards, vocals), Kenny Pentifallo (drums, vocals), Billy Rush (guitars), Alan Berger (bass), Carlo Novi (tenor saxophone), Eddie Manion (baritone sax), Tony Palligrosi (trumpet), Ricky Gazda (trumpet), Richie Rosenberg (trombone)—Out of the Asbury Park, N.J. wastelands have come two of the 1970s greatest live acts—Bruce Springsteen and his E Street Band and Springsteen's old knockaround buddy "Southside" Johnny Lyon and the Asbury Jukes. Both bands (in various permutations) worked steadily throughout the late 1960s and early 1970s, but it took the astonishing success of Springsteen to focus attention on "Southside" Johnny. In 1976 E Street bandmember Miami Steve Van Zandt produced the first "Southside" Johnny album, *I Don't Want To Go Home,* with guest vocalist Ronnie Spector and Lee Dorsey; it was a masterpiece of soul not seen since the fading of Stax Records in Memphis. Johnny and the Jukes remain one of the great bar bands of all time.

Soxx, Bob B, and the Blue Jeans See Bob B Soxx and the Blue Jeans.

Spanky and Our Gang
Elaine "Spanky" McFarlane (vocals), Lefty Baker (guitar), Malcolm Hale (guitar), Geoffrey Myers (bass), John George Seiter (drums), Oz Bach (kazoo), Nigel Pickering— Working both as a jazz singer and a folk singer, Spanky McFarlane formed Spanky and Our Gang with Oz Bach and Nigel Pickering in 1966 in Chicago. They produced a short string of exceedingly pop hits, including "Sunday Will Never Be The Same" (1967), "Lazy Day" (1967), "Sunday Morning" (1968), "Like To Get To Know You" (1968) and their stab at social commentary (which actually wasn't bad) "Give A Damn" (1968). The group broke up the next year when McFarlane returned to her family. A re-formation in the mid-1970s amounted to zip.

Spann, Otis Bluesman Otis Spann made his career in the 1950s as the piano player in Muddy Waters' outstanding blues band. Spann learned the piano in the Mississippi Delta country from veteran bluesman Friday Ford, and he was easily able to translate the Mississippi blues into the high-energy Chicago electric style. Much of his piano style found its way into rock through the

adoration of the British blues players, and Spann later worked with the white blues aficionados—mostly Paul Butterfield and Mike Bloomfield—in the 1960s on such classics as Muddy Waters' *Fathers And Sons* album. Spann died in 1971, at the age of 40.

Sparks Ron Mael (keyboards), Russell Mael (vocals), Dinky Diamond (drums), Ian Hampton (bass), Trevor White (guitar)— Originally formed in England in 1971 around the brothers Ron and Russell Mael, Sparks became an extremely successful singles group in England during the mid-1970s, catering to your basic glitter rock crowd. They were unable to repeat their English success in the United States, however. Recently a re-formed American version of the band has turned to rock-disco material.

Spector, Phil Perhaps the greatest rock-and-roll producer of all times, Spector revolutionized rock in the 1960s by recording layers and layers of sound until it blended together into his much-vaunted "Wall of Sound." Born on Dec. 25, 1940 in the Bronx, New York City but transplanted to Los Angeles at age 12, he began his career by hanging around the studios of Mike Leiber and Jerry Stoller, the two white songwriters who were able to translate black rhythm and blues for the white rock audience. Spector's own recording work started with the Teddy Bears' "To Know Him Is To Love Him" in 1958, the first of many Spector hits. He followed that up with Ray

Peterson's "Corinna Corinna" and Curtis Lee's "Pretty Little Angel Eyes." But it wasn't until he formed his own label on the West Coast, Philles, and signed his first act, the Crystals, that he found the appropriate canvas for his work. After a near miss in 1961, Spector and the Crystals came back in 1962 with one of the great rock classics of all time, "He's A Rebel" (which featured such musicians as Leon Russell and Sonny Bono). The Crystals continued with such hits as "Da Doo Ron Ron" (1963) and "Then He Kissed Me" (1963) while Spector added other girl groups, such as the Ronettes ("Be My Baby," "Baby I Love You"—both in 1963), Bob B Soxx and the Blue Jeans— including Darlene Love—("Zip-A-Dee-Doo-Dah" in 1962) and Darlene Love solo ("Today I Met The Boy I'm Gonna Marry" in 1963). Branching out from girl groups in 1964, he turned to producing the Righteous Brothers on their greatest hit, "You've Lost That Loving Feeling" (1965), and— continuing his early love of rhythm and blues—the next year began work with the volatile Ike and Tina Turner. But with the British Invasion in full swing, Spector couldn't buck the trend, not even with such unequivocally brilliant work as their "River Deep Mountain High" (1966). From that point on, Spector, always eccentric, drifted into retirement. He resurfaced in the 1970s, working with individual Beatles (George Harrison's *Concert For Bangladesh,* for example), and has since gone into the studio with the likes of Cher and Nilsson. In the early 1970s he bankrolled *Enter The Dragon,* perhaps the greatest Kung-Fu movie of all time, and the last movie by master Bruce Lee.

Spencer Davis Group, The   Spencer Davis (guitar, vocals, harp); Stevie Winwood (keyboards, vocals, guitar); Muff Winwood (bass, vocals); Peter York (drums); and others, including Ray Fenwick, Dee Murray, Dave Hynes, Eddie Hardin, Phil Sawyer, Charlie McCracken, Nigel Olsson—Although formed by Spencer Davis in 1963, the real fire in the British band bearing his name was 16-year-old Stevie Winwood. The group produced such high-power rock as "Gimme Some Lovin'" (1966) and "I'm A Man" (1967) before Winwood left to form the renowned group Traffic. Without Winwood the Spencer Davis Group wasted away, despite continual shuffling of personnel and styles.

Spinners, The   Pervis Jackson (vocals); Henry Fambrough (vocals); Billy Henderson (vocals); Bobby Smith (vocals); Jonathan Edwards (vocals); and others, including Crathman Spencer, Edgar Edwards, G.C. Cameron, Phillipe Wynne—The nucleus of the Spinners—Pervis Jackson, Henry Fambrough, Billy Henderson and Bobby Smith—began singing together in 1955 at Ferndale High School in Ferndale, Mich. Predictably, they found their way to nearby Detroit, where they went to work for Motown Records in the early 1960s, scoring some R&B hits. They

eventually scored with "It's A Shame" (1970), produced by Stevie Wonder. Yet it wasn't until 1971, when the group left Motown for the Philadelphia Sound of Thom Bell and Atlantic Records, that things really began to happen. That year yielded two hits, "I'll Be Around" and "Could It Be I'm Falling In Love," the next year "One Of A Kind (Love Affair)." The Spinners continued with their excellent music throughout the 1970s, expanding and defining the "super-Motown" Philadelphia Sound with such hits as "Mighty Love" and "Then Came You" (with a guest appearance by Dionne Warwick) in the mid-1970s.

Spirit   Randy California (vocals, guitar), Ed Cassidy (drums), Mark Andes (bass, vocals), Jay Andes (bass, vocals), John Locke (keyboards), Jay Ferguson (vocals)—Surprisingly articulate California band from the late 1960s. Spirit was formed around Randy California, a 13-year-old guitar flash who had worked with Jimi Hendrix, and Ed Cassidy, a jazz journeyman who had played with the likes of Cannonball Adderley and Thelonious Monk and who happened to be dating Randy's mother. Eventually, Cassidy married Randy's mother, and the original Spirit (first named Red Rooster) got under way in 1965. The group's music was a slick blend of jazz and psychedelia, marked by a fluid grace that is seldom heard on rock records. Such hits as "I Got A Line On You" (1968), from *The Family That Plays Together* album, captured the

critics but not sufficient crowds to boost the group out of cult status. Jay Andes and Jay Ferguson moved on to form Jo Jo Gunne, and Spirit eventually re-formed in the mid-1970s, although the group never succeeded in recapturing its old spark.

Spooky Tooth   Gary Wright (keyboards, vocals), Mike Harrison (keyboards, vocals), Luther Grosvenor (guitar), Greg Ridley (bass), Mike Kellie (drums)—A great name for a band, to be sure, Spooky Tooth was a British progressive rock band of the late 1960s who found reasonable fame and fortune with an American singer named Gary Wright. The group's best material came in 1969 ("Evil Woman," for example), but by 1970 the band had bit the dust, with that year's album, *Last Puff,* becoming Spooky Tooth's biggest hit. (Ironically, the only true member of Spooky Tooth on *Last Puff* was Mike Harrison.) A reunion in 1973 went nowhere, although the re-formed group cut more albums, most notably *You Broke My Heart So I Busted Your Jaw* (1973). Wright has gone on to a successful solo career.

Springfield, Dusty
Originally a member of the British folk trio the Springfields ("Silver Threads And Golden Needles"), Dusty Springfield (born on April 16, 1939 in London, England) went solo after the group's collapse in 1963 and immediately chalked up a string of hits, including "I Only Want To Be With You" (1963), "Wishin' And Hopin'" (1964) and "All I See Is You"

The Boss—Bruce Springsteen

(1966). In 1968 she cut a classic album of soul music interpretations, *Dusty In Memphis,* under the production of Jerry Wexler, which yielded the 1969 hit single "Son Of A Preacher Man."

Springsteen, Bruce   It's hard to make heads or tails of Bruce Springsteen after the hurricanes of hype that have surrounded both him and his music since the very beginning. To be sure, he is the most electrifying stage act to surface in the 1970s. His legendary three-hour shows can (and do) bring audiences to their knees, and his cult of followers is among the most rabidly loyal in rock. Springsteen's music is, at times, brilliant, a synthesis of the many styles that have come before it. Clearly, Bruce Springsteen knows the streets better than any other rock composer, and his music reflects a gut-level understanding that numerous New Wave composers try so hard to communicate. Springsteen (born on Sept. 23, 1949 in Freehold, N.J.) began

as yet another "new Bob Dylan," signed to Columbia Records after his manager had successfully badgered Columbia head John Hammond, Sr. into listening to Springsteen do his own "It's So Hard To Be A Saint In The City" in 1972. The first two albums, *Greetings From Asbury Park, New Jersey* and *The Wild, The Innocent, And The E Street Shuffle,* saw Springsteen trying to work around the "new Dylan" label and were critically successful, but it wasn't until *Born To Run,* one of the greatest rock albums ever, came out in 1975 that Springsteen's career was made. Ironically, Columbia almost scuttled that career by launching the most wretchedly excessive hype campaign in the history of pop music, keying on an observation by *Rolling Stone* critic Jon Landau (who eventually helped produce *Born To Run*), who said, "I have seen the future of rock and roll, and his name is Bruce Springsteen." Although the campaign netted *Time* and *Newsweek* covers, it also generated vast amounts of ill will. For five years legal

problems limited Springsteen to two other albums, *Darkness On The Edge Of Town,* issued in 1978, and *The River,* in 1980, which seem to confirm his genius. As one critic has pointed out, Springsteen has faced the future of rock and roll and come out rocking. For his legions of fans, that's enough.

Stampeders, The   Rick Dodson (guitar), Ronnie King (guitar, bass), Kim Berly (guitar, drums)—The Stampeders were a Canadian trio formed in Calgary, Canada (the home of the world famous rodeo) in 1963. Their big intrusion into the American market came in 1971 with "Sweet City Woman," a finely produced and arranged number, following which they returned to being consistent hitmakers in Canada.

Staple Singers, The Roebuck "Pop" Staples (vocals), Cleo Staples (vocals), Mavis Staples (vocals), Yvonne Staples (vocals), Pervis Staples (vocals)—Born in 1915 in Drew, Miss., Pop Staples took the traditional route from the Delta to Chicago in the 1930s. In the late 1940s and early 1950s, he and the Staple Singers became one of the foremost gospel groups. In 1967 the group made the tough decision to "go pop," initially recording Stephen Stills "For What It's Worth." In 1968, though, the group linked up with Stax Records in Memphis, producing perhaps the ultimate fusion between soul and gospel (with Mavis' unique lead vocals and Pop's distinctive guitar work) on such compelling hits as "Respect

Yourself" in 1971 and "I'll Take You There" in 1972. In 1975 the Staple Singers worked with Curtis Mayfield on the soundtrack to the comedy film *Let's Do It Again*. Pervis left the group in the early 1970s, and Mavis has periodically recorded solo.

Starbuck   Bruce Blackman (vocals, keyboards), Jimmy Cobb (vocals, bass), Sloan Hayes (vocals, keyboards), Darryl Kutz (vocals, guitar), David Shaver (vocals, keyboards), Bo Wagner (percussion, vibes), Ken Crysler (drums)—Just a bunch of Atlanta, Ga. boys who got together in 1973 and made the club circuit until 1976, when a song written by Bruce Blackman titled "Moonlight Feels Right," produced at the Atlanta Rhythm Section's Studio One in Doraville, Ga. became a runaway national hit. The song was slickly produced and reminiscent of many mid-1960s pop hits.

Starland Vocal Band   Bill Danoff (vocals), Kathy Danoff (vocals), Jon Carroll (guitar, keyboards, vocals), Margot Chapman (keyboards, vocals)—Bill Danoff was working the coffeehouse circuit in the early 1970s when he met up with John Denver, who was getting ready to launch his phenomenally successful career. Danoff's contribution to Denver was coauthoring a song with him called "Take Me Home Country Roads," and when Denver formed his own record label, Windsong, in the mid-1970s, he went looking for old friend Danoff, who had formed a group, the Starland Vocal

Band, the year before. The group's first outing on Windsong produced "Afternoon Delight" in 1976, a song that rivaled the first Danoff/Denver hit for sheer media saturation. Besides a hit song the group got its own television show (briefly) and enough exposure to turn its members into instant superstars. For some reason success didn't quite take, though, and "Afternoon Delight" remains the group's zenith.

Starr, Ringo   Born Richard Starkey on July 7, 1940 in Liverpool, England (as any true Beatles' fan should know right off), Ringo Starr appeared to be the least promising of the post-breakup Beatles. That analysis has held pretty true. Despite some interesting (and some excellent) records, including the country-styled "Beaucoups Of Blues" (1970), "It Don't Come Easy" (1971), "Back Off Boogaloo" (1972), "Photograph" (1973) and "You're Sixteen" (1973), Starr's recording work has been decidedly low key. At the same time, however, he's also pursued a career in films, such as *The Magic Christian* (1970) and *That'll Be The Day* (1973), in which his offbeat mannerisms won critical acclaim.

Starz   Michael Lee Smith (vocals), Brenden Harkin (guitar), Richie Ranno (guitar),

Ringo Starr

Peter Sweval (bass), Joe X. Dube (drums)—Despite the flashy name, Starz remains a journeyman rock ensemble, formed in the mid-1970s in New York City and pretty much swamped in the New Wave juggernaut of the late 1970s. Their hits include "Cherry Baby" (1977) and "Hold On To The Night" (1978).

Statler Brothers, The Lew DeWitt (vocals), Don Reid (vocals), Harold Reid (vocals), Phil Balsley (vocals)—A country quartet, the Statler Brothers (named for a box of tissues, by the way) collect country music awards the way some people collect stamps. They were formed during the mid-1950s in rural Virginia and are best known to rock audiences for their offbeat hit "Flowers On The Wall" in 1965. They routinely top the country charts several times a year.

Status Quo Francis Rossi (guitar, vocals), Alan Lancaster (bass), Rick Parfitt (guitar, vocals), John Coughlan (drums)—First formed as Britain's answer to flower power in 1965, Status Quo has the dubious distinction of being hated by every critic in the world for its bland interpretations of the present trend. Nonetheless, the band has done quite well (it had a U.S./U.K. hit in 1968 with "Pictures Of Matchstick Men," plus several other British hits since then), moving from psychedelia to boogie to progressive rock to wherever the river flowed without once losing its sense of fun, which—critics aside—is what rock and roll is all about anyway.

Stax Records Formed in the early 1960s in Memphis, Stax Records was the next step in that city's musical progression from blues to rockabilly to soul music. The label was created by Jim Stewart and his sister, Estelle Axton. Although they were white, they were quick to notice—as had Sam Phillips before them—that the city was rich in unexploited black talent. They also assembled a stunning rhythm section, including Steve Cropper, Donald "Duck" Dunn, Booker T. Jones and Al Jackson, which also recorded on its own as Booker T. and the MGs. Stax began cutting a series of soul singers—that is, black singers using a strongly gospel style in front of the tough rhythm section. The array of talent and the results were startling—Wilson Pickett, Otis Redding, Sam and Dave, Eddie Floyd, the durable Rufus Thomas, Carla Thomas and many others. The music was classic soul: Sam and Dave's "Soul Man," Wilson Pickett's "In The Midnight Hour," Otis Redding's "The Dock Of The Bay." In fact, throughout the 1960s Stax and its Detroit competition, Motown, came to represent the two opposing poles of black music: Stax was the rhythm-and-blues, gospel sound, although it was produced by whites; Motown, a predominantly black organization, produced a strongly white-influenced form of pop/rhythm and blues/gospel. Stax went under during the early 1970s in a wave of court cases and accusations, leaving one of the most durable and exciting catalogues in pop music.

Stealers Wheel Gerry Rafferty (vocals, guitar), Joe Egan (vocals, keyboards)—Formed in the late 1960s and seemingly more concerned with shifting personnel than making records, Stealers Wheel scored its first hit with the Leiber and Stoller-produced album *Stealers Wheel* in 1973. Ironically, when "Stuck In The Middle With You" from that album became a hit, Rafferty had already left the group. The band was quickly re-formed with Rafferty to capitalize on the success of that song, and a second Leiber and Stoller-produced album, *Ferguslie Park,* was completed. Although the critics liked it, the public didn't. Rafferty and Egan completed another album, *Right Or Wrong* in 1975, before Rafferty went on his way again, this time to a successful solo career.

Steeleye Span Maddy Prior (vocals), Tim Hart (vocals, guitar, dulcimer), Peter Knight (fiddle, mandolin, vocals), Bob Johnson (guitar, vocals), Rick Kemp (bass, vocals), Nigel Pegrum (drums, flute)—Formed in 1969 when former Fairport Convention member Ashley Hutchings met up with a pair of folk singers, Tim Hart and Maddy Prior, Steeleye Span was one of the most literate of the folk-rock bands of the period. The group fused rock rhythms with the traditional songs of Britain and did occasional sojourns into everything from remakes of Four Seasons hits to recording New Wave music (dirty, even) under an assumed name. The band broke up in 1978, with lead vocalist Maddy Prior working on a solo career.

Steely Dan Walter Becker (bass, vocals), Dan Fagen (keyboards, vocals)—Named for a dildo in William Burrough's *Naked Lunch,* Steely Dan was one of those bands whose lyrics required an Acme Decoder Ring to understand and whose music ranged from hummingly infectious to irritatingly artsy. Formed around songwriters Walter Becker and Dan Fagen, the group took off in 1972 with *Can't Buy A Thrill,* featuring the hit "Reeling In The Years." Steely Dan reached a peak the next year with *Countdown To Ecstasy* and managed to sustain it through 1974's *Pretzel Logic.* The band's insistence on being lyrically obtuse and musically artsy eventually took its toll. However, Steely Dan recovered with its album *Gaucho* (1980); both the album and the single "Hey Nineteen" from it made the top 10 in 1981. After that success Becker and Fagen parted. Seventy-some-odd musicians and vocalists participated in Becker/Fagen projects.

Steppenwolf John Kay (vocals, guitar), George Biondo (bass, vocals), Jerry Edmonton (drums, vocals), Bobby Cochran (guitar), Wayne Cook (keyboards)—The inspiration of German vocalist John Kay, Steppenwolf refused to bow to the psychedelic trappings of the late 1960s, sticking to straight-ahead, bad-ass rock and roll. In 1968 the group achieved virtually legendary status with "Born To Be Wild," the bikers' national anthem, "Magic Carpet Ride" and a bitterly antidrug rendition of

Hoyt Axton's "The Pusher," banned on many radio stations for its language. Two Steppenwolf numbers made it to the ultimate cult movie *Easy Rider,* boosting the band's already superimage—eight gold albums in very few years—but in 1972 that old demon "artistic differences" brought it all to an end. Solo careers didn't pan out, nor did a reunion effort in 1974. Steppenwolf's best music, though, can still make your hackles rise.

Stevens, April, and Tempo, Nino See Tempo, Nino, and Stevens, April.

Stevens, Cat Steven Demetri Georgiou (born on July 21, 1948 in London, England) began working as a musician almost as soon as he could walk and in 1966 had his first folkish hit—"I Love My Dog," followed by the somewhat tougher "Matthew & Son" the next year. A bout with tuberculosis temporarily halted his promising career, but in 1970 he began working again. His *Tea For The Tillerman* album, released that year, catapulted him to virtually superstar status, and he cemented his position with the next year's album, *Teaser And The Firecat.* Such singles as "Wild World" (1971), "Moon Shadow" (1971), "Peace Train" (1971), "Morning Has Broken" (1972) and others quickly established him as a major artist. Paradoxically, he grew more and more reclusive, and his work drifted more and more toward middle-of-the-road pop.

Stevens, Connie Concetta Ann Ingolia was born on April

8, 1938 in Brooklyn, New York City. She changed her name to Connie Stevens when she became an actress at the tender age of 16. She had an offbeat hit "Kookie, Kookie (Lend Me Your Comb)" with Ed "Kookie" Byrnes—the star of television's "77 Sunset Strip"—in 1959 while she was featured in "Hawaiian Eye."

Stevens, Ray Funnyman Ray Stevens (born in 1939 in Clarksdale, Ga.) is an accomplished instrumentalist, arranger and producer in Nashville, but what he is best known for is his off-the-wall excursions into song—"Ahab The Arab" (1962), "Gitarzan" (1969), "The Streak" (1974) and "Shriners' Convention" (1979).

Stevenson, B.W. One of the tremendous number of talented musicians and singers who make their home in the Austin, Tex. area, Stevenson (born in 1949 in Austin) broke through on a national level briefly in 1973 with "Shambala" before the song was wiped off the charts by a Three Dog Night cover version. Later that year Stevenson enjoyed modest success with "My Maria." His biggest influence in recent years has been on the evolving Austin "country" Sound (a Texas blend of rock and country) of which he is considered one of the foremost proponents.

Stewart, Al Born in Scotland in 1945, Al Stewart is best known for his 1976 hit, "Year Of The Cat." He has shifted from rhythm and blues to folk to electric, his music changing with each album.

Stewart, Gary Born in Kentucky but raised in Florida, Gary Stewart is one of the finest singers to emerge from the country-rock boom of the mid-1970s, although he is far and away best known by the country branch of that family. Such honky-tonk anthems as "Drinkin' Thing" (1974), "Out Of Hand" (1975) and "She's Acting Single (I'm Drinking Doubles)" (1975) practically define the country-rock idiom and deserve far more exposure than they originally received.

Stewart, Jim Former bluegrass fiddle player best known as the founding father of Stax Records in Memphis. (See also Stax Records.)

Stewart, John Originally a member of the Kingston Trio, John Stewart (born on Sept. 5, 1939 in San Diego, Calif.) wrote songs for the Monkees and the Lovin' Spoonful and, throughout the 1960s and 1970s, produced solo albums of his own. It wasn't until 1979, though, that Stewart linked up with Fleetwood Mac's incomparable Stevie Nicks and recorded two of the best sounding and best selling singles of the year, "Gold" and "Midnight Wind," which showcased Stewart's powerful, graphic voice.

Rod Stewart

Stewart, Rod With all the strutting, posing and gossip that surrounds Rod Stewart these days, it's almost hard to believe that he is one of the finest blues interpreters to ever come out of England. Born on Jan. 10, 1945 in London, England and originally obsessed with becoming a soccer player (a desire that

died a quick death when he discovered how little they got paid), Stewart drifted into music almost by accident, bumming around Spain with British folksinger Wizz Jones. Upon returning to England (compliments of the British government, who bailed him out when he went totally broke in Spain), he began singing for

a series of R&B-based bands, including Jimmy Powell and the Dimensions, Long John Baldry's Hoochie Coochie Men and the semilegendary London blues outfit Steampacket, formed by Baldry, Brian Auger and Julie Driscoll. In 1968 he joined the Jeff Beck Group and worked as a vocalist on two albums before the Group disintegrated. At that point Stewart decided to hedge his bets, on the one hand launching a solo career with *An Old Raincoat Will Never Let You Down* (1969) and the highly acclaimed *Gasoline Alley* (1970), while simultaneously joining the Small Faces, now officially called the Faces. It was obvious to everyone except Stewart that such an arrangement would eventually backfire—the amazing thing is that it lasted as long as it did (until 1975). His *Every Picture Tells A Story* album in 1971 was the turning point. "Maggie May," the single from that album, was brilliant and immediately topped the charts, establishing Stewart as a superstar. He followed that with *Never A Dull Moment* in 1972, and its hit "You Wear It Well" continued his successful singles trend. On *Smiler* in 1974 Stewart reached for such material as "Bring It On Home To Me" and "You Send Me" from Sam Cooke. Beginning in 1975 with the successful *Atlantic Crossing* album, Stewart began drifting more and more to slick material and arrangements, perhaps at the behest of steady pal Britt Ekland, and by 1977 he was a full-blown sex symbol, a more accessible Mick Jagger. And that move, of course, has done nothing except make him bigger and bigger. His 1979 album, *Blondes Have More Fun,* produced the disco single "Da Ya Think I'm Sexy," which became the fastest selling single in the history of Warner Brothers Records. Obviously, somebody thought he was.

Stigwood, Robert   Head of RSO Records (Eric Clapton) and superpromoter (*Hair* and *Jesus Christ Superstar*), Stigwood (born in 1934 in Australia) is famous as the man behind the Bee Gees' stunning success in 1977 with the soundtrack from *Saturday Night Fever,* one of the biggest selling records in the history of the business and the music that practically defined the late 1970s.

Stills, Stephen   Born on Jan. 3, 1948 in Dallas, Tex., Stills knocked around the country working as a singer— even auditioning for a part as a

Stephen Stills

Monkee—before linking up with the band that would mean the most to his career, the Buffalo Springfield, in 1966. Stills wrote some of the group's most memorable material, including its first hit, "For What It's Worth." After the Buffalo Springfield's demise in 1968, Stills worked on the *Super Session* album with Al Kooper and Mike Bloomfield before forming his own supergroup, Crosby, Stills and Nash, with David Crosby and Graham Nash in late 1968. Stills wrote the definitive CS&N song—"Suite: Judy Blue Eyes"—for girl friend Judy Collins. In 1970 he began a solo career when it became obvious that CSN&Y (the "Y" being Neil Young, with whom Stills reputedly could not get along) was on the skids. *Stephen Stills* in 1970 yielded the hit "Love The One You're With"; *Stephen Stills II* in 1971 produced "Change Partners." Since then his career has been rocky. He has gone from solo work to heading his own band, Manassas, which lasted for two albums and featured ex-Byrd Chris Hillman; cutting an album with former non-friend Neil Young in 1976; and doing a reunion tour with CSN& (sometimes) Y. Recently he has been involved (with C&N) in the antinuke movement.

Stone Poneys, The   Linda Ronstadt (vocals), Robert Kimmel (guitar), Kenny Edwards (keyboards)— Formed in the mid-1960s, the Stone Poneys became popular with their rendition of the Michael Nesmith (of Monkee fame) composition "Different Drum" in 1967, although the band is clearly best remembered as a starting ground for Linda Ronstadt.

Stone the Crows   Maggie Bell (vocals), Les Harvey (guitar), Jim Dewar (bass), John McGinnis (keyboards), Collin Allen (drums)—

Launched in the late 1960s in Scotland, Stone the Crows is primarily known for the tough, soulful vocals of Maggie Bell, who went solo when the band broke up in 1973.

Stooges, The Iggy Pop (vocals), Ron Asheton (guitar), Scott Asheton (drums), Dave Alexander (bass)—Bizarre backup group for all-around contortionist and demented rock personality Iggy Pop, the Stooges, formed in Detroit in the late 1960s, managed to fare even worse than Iggy, whose career was no prize. By 1977, when Iggy had achieved some modest sort of success, the Stooges were long gone, leaving behind a handful of albums (most notably *Raw Power* from 1973) beloved by their fans and misunderstood by everybody else.

Storm, Gale TV and film actress Gale Storm (born on April 5, 1922 in Bloomington, Tex.) became a very successful "cover" artist—a singer specializing in remakes of original material, in Storm's case rhythm-and-blues "race" records—during the 1950s, beginning with Fats Domino's "I Hear You Knocking" in 1955.

Stranglers, The Hugh Cornwell (guitar, vocals), Jean Jacques Burnel (bass, vocals), Dave Greenfield (keyboards), Jet Black (drums)—Formed in 1975 and given their initial boost by opening for Patti Smith on her 1975 English tour, the Stranglers are considered the New Wave band most likely to become "the new Doors," largely due to the hypnotic vocals of Hugh Cornwell and the Doors-styled

organ playing of Dave Greenfield. They are older than most of the English punks (their ages, God forbid, are over 30, although they'll never tell). Their 1977 *IV Rattus Norvegicus* album won favorable reviews in the United States.

Strawbs, The Dave Cousins (vocals, guitar, banjo, dulcimer), Rod Coombes (drums), Chas Cronk (bass), Dave Lambert (guitar, vocals)—Dave Cousins started the Strawbs as a bluegrass group in England in 1967, and they grew to be one of the best-known cult bands of the late 1960s and early 1970s. Their most noted work was with singer/songwriter Sandy Denny early on in their career, although alumni include Rick Wakeman as well.

Streisand, Barbra The larger-than-life little girl from Brooklyn, New York City (born there on April 24, 1942) began her performing career in amateur theatricals, eventually working her way up to Broadway in 1962 in *I Can Get It For You Wholesale.* That performance won her a role in a major movie, *Funny Girl,* and a recording contract. *Funny Girl* and her first song, "People" (1964), established her as a major, if conservative, vocalist, a pose she maintained throughout the 1960s and 1970s. Her songs read like a greatest hits package for a couple of decades—"Funny Girl" (1964), "Free Again" (1966), "Stoney End" (1970), "The Way We Were" (1973), "Evergreen" (1976) and "A Woman In Love" (1980), to name just a few. (She also had

a duet hit with Neil Diamond, "You Don't Bring Me Flowers," in 1979.) There are two albums worth noting: *Stoney End* (1970), a lean, superb album produced by rock master Richard Perry; and the more heavily orchestrated soundtrack album to *A Star Is Born* (1976), which showcased Streisand as the most popular female vocalist in America.

Strunk, Jud Born on June 11, 1938 in Jamestown, N.Y., Strunk traveled the world as a one-man show before striking it big in 1973 with "A Daisy A Day." He is perhaps better remembered for his tremendous underground hit of 1975 "(She's Got) The Biggest Parakeets In Town," which also happened to be Motown Records' single attempt to break into country music.

Stylistics, The Russell Thompkins, Jr. (vocals), Herb Murrell (vocals), James Dunn (vocals), James Smith (vocals), Airrion Love (vocals)—Formed from two local groups in Philadelphia—the Monarchs and the Percussions—in the late 1960s, the Stylistics came to attention in the mid-1970s as the leading proponents of the soft branch of the Philadelphia Sound—rhythm and blues, derided one critic, without the rhythm or the blues. Just the emotion backed with a lot of orchestration. Nevertheless the Stylistics anchored the Philly Sound for years with such hits as "You Are Everything" (1971), "Betcha By Golly Wow" (1972), "Break Up To Make Up" (1973) and "You Make Me Feel Brand New" (1974).

Styx James Young (guitar, vocals); Tommy Shaw (guitar, keyboards); Dennis DeYoung (keyboards); Charles Panozzo (bass); John Panozzo (drums); additional members: John Curulewski—Formed in Chicago in 1970 from an earlier bar band called the Tradewinds, Styx built its reputation throughout the early 1970s with incessant touring and a repertoire that borrowed heavily from the pyrotechnics of the flashy British rock outfits. In 1974, Styx hit the top of the charts with the melodic ballad "Lady," which didn't sound a bit like the bulk of the band's harder rock material.

Sugarloaf Jerry Corbetta (vocals, keyboards), Robert Webber (guitar), Robert Raymond (bass), Robert MacVitte (drums), Robert Yezal (guitar), Robert Pickett (guitar, bass)—Formed by Corbetta in Colorado during the late 1960s, Sugarloaf is best known for its 1970 hit, "Green Eyed Lady." After a quick fade, the group returned in 1974 with "Don't Call Us, We'll Call You," a humorous and more than a little bitter look at how the record business operates. That song is as true today as it was in 1974.

Summer, Donna Disco chanteuse Donna Summer was already one of the best-known stars in the dancing world when, in 1978 and 1979, she really blossomed, taking the rock music world by storm. Born on Dec. 31, 1948 in Boston, Mass., Summer got her break in the late 1960s while performing in the German cast of the pop musical *Hair.* From there she

Donna Summer

went on to capture the budding disco market with such heavy breathing specials as "Love To Love You Baby" (1975). All her protestations about being more than just another disco queen fell on deaf ears until 1978, when she recorded the Academy Award-winning theme to the movie *T.G.I.F.* titled "Last Dance," a stunning ballad performance. She followed that up with a tough R&B-styled disco performance on "Hot Stuff" (1979), which won her a Grammy, and another ballad, "On The Radio" (1979), and all of a sudden the very rock audience that had ignored her for so long sat up and took notice. She followed her back-to-back recording success with a television special in 1979 that completely captivated both

critics and audience alike, a series of low-key performances that removed the disco queen stigma from Summer's career. Which is only fair, since she is one of the finest vocal stylists to emerge in the 1970s.

Sun Records Founded in the early 1950s by ex-radio announcer Sam Phillips in Memphis, Sun Records became the touchstone for the rock- and roll-revolution of the 1950s. Sun launched the careers of Elvis Presley, Johnny Cash, Carl Perkins, Jerry Lee Lewis, Roy Orbison, Charlie Rich and a host of lesser-known artists. The key to Sun Records was rockabilly, a fusion of blues and country and honky-tonk music, all common to the area around Memphis. With Elvis Presley,

Phillips found his "white boy who sounds black," and his release of "That's All Right" b/w "Blue Moon Of Kentucky" in 1954 is generally considered one of the birthpoints of rock. In 1969 Phillips sold Sun Records to Nashville entrepreneur Shelby Singleton, who is still releasing material from the Sun vaults almost 30 years later.

Supertramp   Roger Hodgson (vocals, keyboards, guitar), Richard Davies (vocals, keyboards), Dougie Thompson (bass), John Anthony Helliwell (sax, clarinet, vocals), Bob Benberg (drums, percussion)—Supertramp got together in England around 1970, perhaps the only rock band to be bankrolled by an anonymous millionaire. The band worked the grind, shuffling personnel, until 1974, when its *Crime Of The Century* album yielded a modest hit, "Dreamer," in 1975. All the investment and the work paid off in 1979, when Supertramp became the hottest group in America with its melodious, superbly produced hit "Long Way Home."

Supremes, The   Diana Ross (vocals); Florence Ballard (vocals); Mary Wilson (vocals); and others, including Jean Terrell, Shari Payne—The epitome of the Motown Sound, the original Supremes began singing together in 1960 as the Primettes, capturing a high school talent contest and the attention of Motown president Berry Gordy, Jr.. They signed with Motown two years later and, after a couple of false starts, hit it big in 1964 with

"Where Did Our Love Go," "Baby Love" and "Come See About Me," becoming the only American group to challenge the Beatles' domination of the charts. They were Gordy's masterwork, the girls' voices working in perfect harmony with Motown's outstanding sessions players and the crack songwriting team of Eddie and Brian Holland and Lamont Dozier (see Holland-Dozier-Holland). In 1967 Florence Ballard left the group (she died on Feb. 22, 1976 in total poverty, the victim of drugs) and was replaced by Cindy Birdsong from Patty LaBelle and the Bluebells. The name of the group was also changed to Diana Ross and the Supremes, reflecting Gordy's decision to groom Diana Ross for stardom. In 1969, Ross left the group to pursue (and eventually catch) that stardom, at a time when "Someday We'll Be Together" was the top song in the country. After that, the Supremes had several modest hits, including "Nathan Jones" in 1971, but were shadows of their former selves. The Supremes logged a staggering 12 number one hits, including such classics as "Stop! In The Name Of Love" (1965), "Back In My Arms Again" (1965), "I Hear A Symphony" (1965), "You Can't Hurry Love" (1966), "You Keep Me Hanging On" (1966), "Love Is Here (And Now You're Gone)" (1967), "The Happening" (1967) and others.

Surfaris, The   Jim Pash (vocals), Jim Fuller (vocals), Bob Berryhill (vocals), Pat Connolly (vocals), Ron Wilson (vocals)—Formed in Glendale, Calif. in 1963, the Surfaris

gained national attention that year with the classic instrumental "Wipe Out." The high-pitched laugh at the beginning of the song belonged to the group's manager, Dale Smallins.

Swan, Billy   Born on May 12, 1944 in Cape Girardeau, Mo., Swan has done everything from living in a hearse in Nashville to working as a gatekeeper at Elvis Presley's Graceland Mansion to touring the country as one of Kinky Friedman's Texas Jewboys. He has also produced a string of outstanding—if largely unknown—albums. His biggest hit, written with buddy Kris Kristofferson, was knocked together one evening on a small electric organ that had been a gift to Swan from Kristofferson. The result was "I Can Help," a runaway hit song around the world in 1974. Swan also wrote "Lover Please" for Clyde McPhatter in 1962, while Swan was still in high school.

Sweet   Brian Connolly (vocals), Frank Torpy (guitar), Steven Priest (bass), Mick Tucker (drums)—Launched during the late 1960s in England by Mick Tucker and Brian Connolly, the remnants of the British "soul" group Wainwright's Gentlemen, Sweet became famous during the mid-1970s for its bubblegum rock songs (one of which, "Little Willie," made the American charts). Since 1975 the group has been trying to get back to the funky soul music of its roots. Among its hits are "Ballroom Blitz" (1975) and "Love Is Like Oxygen."

Sweet Inspirations Cissy Houston (vocals), Myrna Smith (vocals), Sylvia Shamwell (vocals), Estelle Brown (vocals)—Originally a backup group for the extensive Atlantic Records soul stable, the Sweet Inspirations went on their own in the late 1960s. Their biggest hit was "Sweet Inspiration" in 1968. Cissy Houston left the group in the early 1970s to become a solo artist.

The Talking Heads

Talking Heads, The David Byrne (guitar, vocals), Jerry Harrison (keyboards, guitar, vocals), Chris Frantz (drums), Tina Weymouth (bass)—Created in 1975, the Talking Heads (the name is television terminology for what most television shows degenerate into) quickly became the top band on the punk-New Wave circuit. And justly, since their accomplished musicianship and their off-the-wall lyrics (beginning in 1977 with "Psycho Killer," "Don't Worry About The Government" and "The Girls Want To Be With The Girls," to name a few) set them above most of the other New York underground denizens. Moreover, their two albums—*Talking Heads '77* and the Brian Eno-produced *More Songs About Buildings And Food*—are entertaining without being irritating.

Talley, James James Talley's career seemed made in 1976 when First Lady Rosalynn Carter revealed that

Talley was her favorite singer. His 1975 debut album, *Got No Bread,* had already established him as a substantial country poet, perhaps closer to Pete Seeger and Woody Guthrie than Waylon Jennings and Conway Twitty. Born in Tulsa, Okla., Talley, who holds a degree in fine arts, is an unlikely country singer. Yet his work is simple and surprisingly effective, a subtle blending of blues, folk and country. Lamentably, his career has never jelled, despite the presidential publicity, and he is presently floating without a record label.

Tamla/Motown One of the most successful record companies in the history of popular music, the Tamla/Motown organization was founded in the late 1950s by former fighter and successful songwriter Berry Gordy, Jr. with the specific intent of only making hit records. At that, he has been

spectacularly successful. Motown performers such as the Supremes, the Four Tops, Smokey Robinson and the Miracles and the Temptations were the only American groups to stand against the British Invasion. Almost single-handedly Gordy hammered out the Motown Sound, a drastic redefinition of black music. While he had grown up in Detroit listening to the blues and rhythm and blues, Gordy realized that the sound was too raw to appeal to mainstream America. When he launched Motown in Detroit in 1958, he began searching for local groups to mold into his new idea, sort of cleaned-up rhythm and blues with sanitized gospel vocals. His first big hit came in 1960 with the Miracles' "Shop Around," followed in 1961 by the Marvelettes' classic "Please Mr. Postman," but it wasn't until he began steady work with the Supremes and the Four Tops that his fortune really soared. The Motown formula began to wane in the early 1970s after the company moved to the West Coast, although Gordy was successful in turning ex-Supreme Diana Ross into a superstar via Motown's first movie, *Lady Sings The Blues.* Since the late 1970s, though, the Motown Sound has been staging a comeback with new groups, and many Motown artists, including Smokey Robinson, have found a new life in the discos. Some of the artists, particularly Stevie Wonder, have proven to be totally consistent hitmakers, despite the prevailing musical styles.

Tampa Red Bluesman Hudson Woodbridge Whittaker was born on Christmas Day, 1900 in Atlanta, Ga., but he spent his early years in Tampa, Fla. Making his way to Chicago in the mid-1920s, he linked up with a piano player called Georgia Tom—Thomas Dorsey—and the two began playing a wild amalgam of what they'd picked up on the road—blues, rhythm and blues, kazoo music, imitation country string bands—but all with a slick sense of the city. Tampa Red is credited by some with single-handedly inventing the slide guitar technique so well known today and with adapting the Hawaiian guitar to the blues. He is also famous for some of the bawdiest blues around, such as his own "Let's Get Drunk And Truck" and a number of Georgia Tom's he recorded in 1928, "It's Tight Like That." Ironically, Georgia Tom turned away from the blues, practically launching the black gospel movement and going on to

write two of the greatest gospel songs of all time, "Precious Lord" (1932) and "Peace In The Valley" (1939).

Tangerine Dream Edgar Froese (synthesizers, keyboards, guitar), Christoph Franke (synthesizers), Peter Baumann (synthesizers, keyboards, flute)—The Germans have, naturally, taken a shine to machinery, as this synthesizer-oriented trio clearly shows. Tangerine Dream, formed in Germany in 1967, makes metal music, sort of a mechanical Lou Reed sound. The group's avant-garde sound found little takers in America during the late 1960s, but Tangerine Dream has become something of a cult band—especially with its 1970 German release, *Electronic Meditation,* and, later, with its English releases, *Phaedra* in 1974 and *Rubycon* in 1975.

Tavares Chubby Tavares (vocals), Butch Tavares (vocals), Tina Tavares (vocals), Ralph Vierra Tavares (vocals), Arthur Tavares (vocals), Vic Tavares (vocals)—Born in New Bedford, Mass., the Tavares made a substantial reputation for themselves playing the club circuit in New England. The brothers really began to click in the mid-1970s, when their soft soul sound began to find a home with the disco crowd. The group's inclusion on the *Saturday Night Fever* album in 1977 didn't hurt, and "More Than A Woman" from that album became a runaway hit not once but twice.

Taylor, Chip Originally known as a songwriter (most notably the underground

classic "Wild Thing" for the Troggs in 1966 and "Angel Of The Morning" for Merilee Rush in 1968, but also "Take Me For A Little While" for the Vanilla Fudge in 1968 and "Bend Me, Shape Me" for the American Breed in 1967), Chip Taylor stumbled in his career as a singer, although he did produce the mildly interesting album *Somebody Shoot Out The Jukebox* in the mid-1970s. He was born in Yonkers, N.Y. and is the brother of actor John Voight.

Taylor, James Born on March 12, 1948 in Boston, Mass., but raised in North Carolina, James Taylor has overcome personal adversity to become one of the finest singers/songwriters in the history of rock music. Indeed, he is credited with popularizing the whole concept of singer/songwriter, which, during the 1960s, languished under the influence of the British bands. Brought up in a well-to-do family (the son of a medical school dean and a conservatory-trained singer), Taylor had a brief stay in a mental hospital for depression before trying his first coffeehouse group, the Flying Machine, which lasted until 1967. From there he went to London, where he fell in with Peter Asher, who was then with the Beatles' Apple Records. Asher liked Taylor and wangled a contract with Apple, resulting in his *James Taylor* album (1968), which went nowhere. Taylor turned to drugs and returned to the United States, where it was back to the mental hospital again. Upon Taylor's release for the second time, Asher spun yet another deal

211

James Taylor with Carly Simon

Taylor, Johnny Born on May 5, 1937 in West Memphis, Ark., Johnny Taylor began his career in the mid-1950s as the replacement for Sam Cooke in the gospel group the Soul Stirrers. Secular music also called to Taylor, who found his way to Stax Records in the early 1960s. There he recorded a string of tough sounding soul hits, including the classic "Who's Making Love" (1968). In 1976 he surfaced again with the leering "Disco Lady," a fairly frank dissertation about what said lady enjoyed doing, setting the tone for his later career—a long way from the Soul Stirrers.

Taylor, Kate Younger sister of James Taylor, born on Aug. 15, 1949 in Boston, Mass. An early album, *Sister Kate* (1971), established her as an artist to watch. Subsequently she did nothing until 1978, when she produced her *Kate Taylor* album, which was little better than her earlier work.

Taylor, Livingston Younger brother of James Taylor, Livingston Taylor has been recording since the early 1970s, following in the style of his brother. His first two albums were produced by rock critic Jon Landau, who went on to produce Bruce Springsteen's epic *Born To Run*. The two albums were basically undistinguished. In 1979 he released *Three Way Mirror*.

Taylor, R. Dean Country singer R. Dean Taylor was born in Toronto, Canada. He enjoyed a number one pop hit in 1970 with "Indiana Wants Me"—the first number one hit

out of the ashes of Apple, this time with Warner, and together Taylor and Asher produced *Sweet Baby James,* perhaps the definitive singer/songwriter statement. That album, with the powerful single "Fire And Rain," which chronicled his life in the mental institution, the breakup of the Flying Machine and the suicide of a close friend, established Taylor as a superstar and gave him an extraordinary act to follow. In fact, he wasn't able to follow that act until the release of his *Gorilla* album in 1975, which showed him coming to grips with his own stardom. He also

delved a little deeper into his bag of rock, folk and rhythm and blues to come up with his mellow reworking of the R&B hit "How Sweet It Is." Since *Gorilla,* the road has been pretty smooth. He has had continued recording success, including a *Greatest Hits* album in 1976 that featured some excellent recordings of his early work. He has also benefited again from his blue-eyed soul material with the hit "Handy Man" in 1977, from the album *JT*. His marriage to Carly Simon in 1973 yielded a duet hit, "Mockingbird," in 1974. They have two children.

on Motown Records by a white artist. He is also the writer for one of Motown's best-known songs, "Love Child," a hit for the Supremes in 1968.

Teddy Bears, The Phil Spector (vocals), Marshall Leib (vocals), Annette Bard (vocals)—The Teddy Bears got together while all three were in high school in Los Angeles in 1958. Later that year they decided to cut a record Phil Spector had written, inspired by the inscription on his father's tombstone: To Know Him Was To Love Him. The song, "To Know Him Is To Love Him," became a major hit and launched Spector on a career that would help shape American popular music for years to come.

New Wave movement. Eventually the group released two albums, *Marquee Moon* (1977) and *Adventure* (1978), before breaking up. The albums were very much showcases for Verlaine—Hell having been dumped in 1975—and he quickly went on to a solo career.

Tempo, Nino, and Stevens, April April Stevens (born on April 29, 1936 in Niagara Falls, N.Y.) and brother Nino Tempo (born on Jan. 6, 1937 also in Niagara Falls) began singing together in the early 1960s, recording the hit "Deep Purple" in 1963 and a follow-up titled "Whispering" later that same year. "Whispering" made the charts the first week of 1964.

Television

Television Tom Verlaine (guitar, vocals), Richard Lloyd (guitar, vocals), Fred Smith (bass, vocals), Billy Ficca (drums)—Formed around Verlaine in New York during the early 1970s, Television—with hypnotic vocalist Richard Hell—was one of the original standardbearers of that city's

Temptations, The Otis Williams (vocals); Eddie Kendricks (vocals); David Ruffin (vocals); Melvin Franklin (vocals); Paul Williams (vocals); additional members: Damon Harris, Glenn Leonard, Richard Street, Dennis Edwards, Louis Price— The original Temptations got

together in 1960, with Otis Williams, Eddie Kendricks, Melvin Franklin and Paul Williams singing together in Detroit as the Elgins. They were discovered at a local talent show by Berry Gordy, Jr., head of Motown Records, and with the addition of David Ruffin, the group became the Temptations. They were off and running in 1964 with "The Way You Do The Things You Do," and the next year's "My Girl" established them as one of Motown's top sellers, a position they held for the better part of a decade. Lyrically, the Temps were the most innovative and daring of any of the Motown groups, shifting from the "safe" Motown Sound (hits like "Ain't Too Proud To Beg" in 1966 and "I Wish It Would Rain" in 1968) to "psychedelic soul," a surprisingly effective attempt to fuse the Motown formula with the psychedelic rock of the late 1960s ("Cloud 9" in 1968, "Psychedelic Shack" in 1970). The Temps also cut some powerful social commentaries, something that Gordy's groups had never chanced, although Gordy himself was deeply committed to social change. Such songs as "Ball Of Confusion" (1970) and the spectacular "Papa Was A Rolling Stone" (1972) took the Motown formula one step further. Ruffin and Kendricks eventually left the group for solo careers, but the Temps keep right on rolling along. Recently they have recorded disco material.

10 cc Eric Stewart (guitar); Graham Gouldman (bass); Paul Burgess (drums); and others, including Lol Creme,

The Temptations

Kevin Godley—10 cc was formed in 1973 in England around former Mindbenders Eric Stewart and Graham Gouldman. The group eventually hit the American market in 1975 with "I'm Not In Love" and again the next year with "The Things We Do For Love." The band's ability to knock out hit singles, particularly in Britain, should have taken no one by surprise since Gouldman has been a prolific and successful songwriter, a sampling of whose hits includes "For Your Love" (1965) and "Heart Full Of Soul" (1965) for the Yardbirds, "Look Through Any Window" (1965) and "Bus Stop" (1966) for the Hollies and "No Milk Today" (1966) for Herman's Hermits. The music of 10 cc (which is the amount of sperm in an average ejaculation) has been both praised for its slickness and criticized for being "too calculatedly pop."

Ten Years After   Alvin Lee (guitar, vocals), Chick Churchill (keyboards), Ric Lee (drums), Leo Lyons (bass)—Originally started in England during the mid-1960s, Ten Years After (TYA) played a slick blues-based rock (and was considered one of the best blues bands of the times) until 1969, when the band began to dabble in more straightforward guitar rock. The 1969 Woodstock festival marked the band's high and low watermark—high, because Ten Years After emerged from Woodstock as a superstar band; low, because to achieve that status it scrapped its meticulous blues playing and concentrated on *fast* and *loud.* The group's boogie version of "Going Home" became a festival rallying cry, and Ten Years After kept its reputation as the fastest band in the West until 1974, when the pressures of stardom did the band in. Alvin Lee, the self-styled fastest guitarist in the world, began a largely uneventful solo career. In 1975 there was a TYA reunion tour, which didn't work either.

Terrell, Tammi   Born in Philadelphia, Terrell hooked up with the Motown organization in the mid-1960s and cut a series of successful duets with soul master Marvin Gaye, including "Ain't No Mountain High Enough" (1967), "Your Precious Love" (1967) and "Ain't Nothing Like The Real Thing" (1968). In 1967 she collapsed onstage into Gaye's arms, and after being rushed to the hospital, she was found to be suffering from a brain tumor. Three years later, on March 16, 1970, she died from the disease.

Terry, Sonny   Blind bluesman Sonny Terry is renowned for his blues harp work with Brownie McGhee. Terry (born Teddell Saunders Terry on Oct. 24, 1911 near Durham, N.C.) is considered one of the most important popularizers of the blues in the 1940s and 1950s and even into the 1960s, steadily working the budding folk coffeehouse circuit.

Tex, Joe   Soul singer Joe Tex (born on Aug. 8, 1933 in Rogers, Tex.) worked steadily as a rhythm-and-blues singer at such venues as the Apollo Theater in Harlem before cashing in on the soul music boom of the mid-1960s. Working with country producer Buddy Killen, Tex produced such soul classics as "Hold On To What You Got" (1964), "Skinny Legs And All" (1967), "Men Are Getting Scarce" (1968) and "I Gotcha" (1972). After an extended retirement for religious reasons, he returned to recording in 1977, producing some powerful soul backed by the great Nashville sessions men.

Thin Lizzy

Them   Van Morrison (vocals); Jim Armstrong (guitar, drums, sitar); Alan Henderson (bass); Ray Elliot (organ); and others, including Ken McDowell— Founded in Ireland in 1963, the original Them was ahead of their time, although by their first album, *Them,* in 1965, the times had caught up with the group. That album yielded "Here Comes The Night," "Mystic Eyes" and the classic bar band song of all time—the

Morrison composition "Gloria." When the band failed to capitalize on its initial success, Morrison struck out on his own, and Ken McDowell took over the vocals for Them. The band folded in 1968.

Thin Lizzy   Brian Downey (drums), Brian Robertson (guitar), Phil Lynott (vocals, bass), Scott Gorham (guitar)— Formed in the early 1970s in Ireland, the group grabbed a chunk of "overnight" stardom in 1976, when the single "The Boys Are Back In Town" from its *Jailbreak* album became one of the biggest rock songs of the year. Prior to *Jailbreak,* Thin Lizzy had steadily been the top rock band in Ireland and a major seller in Britain. The group is known for its free-swinging, frequently violent concert appearances. Brian Robertson left Thin Lizzy in 1977 because of illness— which took some of the glitter off the band's touring—but returned to the fold the next year.

.38 Special   Donnie Van Zandt (vocals, guitar), Steve

10 cc

Brookins (drums), Ken Lyons (bass)—Essentially a bar band copy of Lynyrd Skynyrd formed by Donnie Van Zandt, younger brother of Ronnie Van Zandt, Skynyrd's moving force. Two albums, *.38 Special* (1977) and *Special Delivery* (1978), have failed to put things in any better perspective.

Thomas, B.J.   Born on Aug. 7, 1942 in Houston, Tex., B.J. Thomas began his recording career in 1965 with a version of Hank Williams' "I'm So Lonesome I Could Cry." That song was enough to get his career off the ground early in 1966, and thereafter he produced a series of minor hits ("The Eyes Of A New York Woman" and "Hooked On A Feeling," both 1968) throughout the late 1960s. His biggest break came in 1969, when he recorded the themesong to the movie *Butch Cassidy and the Sundance Kid.* "Raindrops Keep Falling On My Head" was a number one smash and spent 15 weeks on the charts. Since then Thomas has continued with a strong, predictable series of hits, including "I Just Can't Help Believing" (1970), "Rock And Roll Lullaby" (1972), "Another Somebody Done Somebody Wrong Song" (1975) and "Everybody Loves A Rain Song" (1978).

Thomas, Carla   The daughter of soul singer Rufus Thomas was born in 1947 in Memphis, Tenn., and although she eventually assumed the title of Queen of Soul (largely for her brief work with Otis Redding), her music has always been closer to 1960s girl group pop than soul. She broke big in 1961 with a song she'd written herself, "Gee Whiz." Her biggest hit came in 1966 with "B-A-B-Y."

Thomas, Rufus   Soul man Rufus Thomas worked with the legendary Rabbit Foot Minstrels and along the sleazy haunts of Beale Street in Memphis before beginning a recording career with Sam Phillips at Sun Records. Thomas' classic performance on "Bearcat (An Answer To Hound Dog)" in the early 1950s not only gave Sun one of its first hits, but also landed the company in legal hot water because it lacked the necessary copyright permission. Undaunted, Thomas went on to become one of Memphis' most popular disc jockeys, vying for that honor with Riley "Blues Boy" (B.B.) King. In 1962 he returned to recording with the fledgling Stax label, delivering that company's first hit, "The Dog," and its follow-up, "Walking The Dog," also a hit. He continued to milk the dance craze (from "Can Your Monkey Do The Dog" all the way to "Do The Funky Chicken" in 1970), but he faded in the light of Stax' bigger name artists (including daughter Carla Thomas). Thomas began an involvement with the church and gospel music, but he returned to the limelight in the late 1970s, when the craze for disco gave a whole new life to his wild dances. Thomas was born on March 28, 1917 in Collierville, Tenn.

Three Dog Night   Cory Wells (vocals), Danny Hutton (vocals), Chuck Negron (vocals), Mike Allsup (guitar), Jim Greenspoon (keyboards), Floyd Sneed (drums), Joe Schermie (bass)—One of the biggest selling groups ever (14 gold albums—their entire output—10 gold singles and some 50 million records sold), Three Dog Night spent its four-year career as a superstar band being castigated by the critics and laughed at by the "hipper" hard rock audiences. The band got together in the late 1960s at the behest of Danny Hutton, who felt that three lead vocals were better than one. The group's first album proved Hutton right; *Three Dog Night* in 1969 yielded three hits: "Nobody," "Try A Little Tenderness" and the top 10 song "One," written by Harry Nilsson. From then on the rails were greased, and the hits just kept coming: "Easy To Be Hard" (1969), from the rock musical *Hair;* "Celebrate" (1970); "Mama Told Me Not To Come" (1970); "Joy To The World" (1971); "Never Been To Spain" (1972) and "Shambala" (1973). In retrospect, Three Dog Night was always a better band than the critics gave it credit for—much of the criticism leveled at the band was because of its concentration on singles rather than albums and its success with them. Three Dog Night also made a habit of engaging the best new songwriters, including Laura Nyro, Hoyt Axton, Harry Nilsson, Elton John/Bernie Taupin and Randy Newman, giving those writers important exposure and money to live on. The band wound down in 1974, although various permutations still make the rounds.

Thunderclap Newman

Andy Newman (keyboards), Jimmy McCulloch (guitar), John "Speedy" Keen (vocals, drums)—Best known for "Something In The Air," the climactic song for the climactic scene in Peter Sellers' bizarre film *The Magic Christian* (1969), which featured Ringo Starr in his first acting role. Thunderclap Newman was actually the brainchild of the Who's guiding spirit, Peter Townshend, producer of Thunderclap and its bass player under the pseudonym "Bijou Drains." "Something In The Air" was so successful that the group collapsed trying to capitalize on it, with guitarist McCulloch joining Paul McCartney in Wings.

Tillotson, Johnny   Born on April 20, 1939 in Jacksonville, Fla., Tillotson began his career in central Florida as a country singer, but he soon graduated to the pop charts with his "Poetry In Motion" in 1960. He produced a string of country sounding ballads throughout the early 1960s, including "It Keeps Right On A-Hurtin'" (1962) and "Talk Back Trembling Lips" (1963).

Tiny Tim   Probably more words have been written about the rise and fall of Herbert Khaury, aka Tiny Tim (born on April 12, 1933 in New York, N.Y.), than about half the groups in rock music put together. In the summer of 1968 Tiny Tim (whose earlier *noms de guerre* included the Human Canary and Judas K. Foxglove) took his high whiney voice and his ukulele on television's popular "Laugh-In," where he sang "Tip-Toe

Through The Tulips." Wham! Bam! He's a national sensation, doing Vegas at $50,000 a week, appearing on television nightly, even getting married to the lovely Miss Vicki on Johnny Carson's late night TV show, where he drew some of the highest ratings in the history of the biz. Press agents were quick to point out that Tiny had paid his dues, working the clubs in Greenwich Village and even recording for rock producer Richard Perry before becoming an overnight sensation. But "overnight" pretty well described it. Trusting Tiny managed to lose most of his money; the marriage to Miss Vicki was terminated; and the light of his life ended up in the altogether in a well-known men's magazine, describing in detail just what Tiny wouldn't do. Many pounds heavier, alas, he is again on the comeback trail.

Tokens, The   Jay Siegal (vocals, guitar), Phil Margo (vocals, piano, drums, guitar), Mitchell Margo (vocals, piano, drums), Henry Medress (vocals, piano, bass)—The Tokens got together in New York City during the mid-1950s with vocalist Neil Sedaka, but the group became famous on its own after Sedaka left, scoring in 1961 with "Tonight I Fell In Love" and "The Lion Sleeps Tonight," a reworking of the South African Zulu folk song "Mbube."

Tom and Jerry   Recorded one minor hit, "Hey Schoolgirl," in 1957. They are perhaps better known by their given names: "Tom" is Art Garfunkel and "Jerry" is Paul Simon.

Toots and the Maytals

Frederick "Toots" Hibbert (vocals), Raleigh Gordon (vocals), Jerry Matthias (vocals)—One of the most popular groups in Jamaica, Toots and the Maytals have been working together since the early 1960s, with a brief break for Toots to do time on a

Toots and the Maytals

drug charge in 1965. Toots worked with Baptist choirs as a child and absorbed vast amounts of American soul music over the radio. Not surprisingly, Toots' reggae (a term he helped to define in the early 1960s) is heavily tinted with the upbeat soul of, say, Otis Redding. While Toots and the Maytals have been reasonably well received in the United States (his *Funky Kingston* album in the mid-1970s was popular with the FM programers), like Bob Marley and the Wailers his primary effect on American rock has been his influence on others, most notably the New Wave groups such as the Clash.

Tosh, Peter   Born on Oct. 19, 1944 in Jamaica and originally a member of Bob Marley's Wailers—the foremost proponents of reggae,

Jamaican pop-soul music—Tosh moved on to a solo career in the mid-1970s, riding his hymn to marijuana, "Legalize It." In 1978 Tosh linked up with Rolling Stones Mick Jagger and Keith Richards, who signed him to the new Rolling Stones label and began using him as an opening act. Despite the exposure, reggae remains a largely Jamaican phenomenon.

Toto   David Paich (keyboards), Jeff Porcaro (drums), David Hungate (bass), Steve Porcaro (keyboards), Steve Lukather (guitar), Bobby Kimball (vocals)—Largely a sessions group formed in the late 1970s and best known for its work behind Boz Scaggs (David Paich wrote and arranged Scaggs' celebrated *Silk Degrees* album). The group had a hit in 1978 with "Hold The Line."

Toussaint, Allen   Born in 1938 in New Orleans, La., Toussaint has been one of the moving forces behind New Orleans music for over three decades. Beginning as a performer in the 1950s, he soon moved to producing and playing piano with the likes of Fats Domino. He was instrumental in the second wave of New Orleans rock during the early 1960s, producing such acts as Ernie K. Doe ("Mother-In-Law" in 1961); Aaron Neville ("Tell It Like It Is" in 1966) and Lee Dorsey ("Working In A Coal Mine" in 1966, which Toussaint wrote as well). His songwriting has found its way to the top with many other artists as well, including

"Southern Nights" (1977) for Glen Campbell, "Yes We Can-Can" (1973) for the Pointer Sisters, "Sneakin' Sally Through The Alley" (1974) for Robert Palmer and many others. Although he has cut solo albums (*Southern Nights* in 1975), it is through his work with other groups that his influence has really been felt. Dr. John, Little Feat, the Band, Wings, the Pointer Sisters, LaBelle (he cowrote, arranged and produced "Lady Marmalade") and Claudia Lennear, to name just a few, have all used the master's touch, and rock music is the better for it.

Tower of Power   Hubert Tubbs (vocals), Lenny Pickett (sax, flute), Emilio Castillo (sax, vocals), Steve Kupka (sax, vocals), Greg Adams (trumpet, flugelhorn, vocals), Mic Gillette (trumpet, trombone, vocals), Bruce Conte (guitar, vocals), Chester Thompson (keyboards, vocals), Frank Prestia (bass), David Garibaldi (drums)—Formed in the early 1970s in California, Tower of Power was one of the first horn-oriented bands to find widespread acceptance with the rock audience, playing what has come to be called funk. The group's horn section has also been fielded out to do studio work for the likes of Elton John and Carlos Santana. In addition to making big selling albums (*Bump City* in 1972), Tower of Power has put several singles on the charts ("So Very Hard To Go" in 1973 and "What Is Hip" in 1974).

Townshend, Peter   Born on May 19, 1945 in England,

Townshend is famous as the lead vocalist for the Who and the composer of the bulk of the group's material, including the epic rock opera *Tommy*. He briefly tried a solo career in 1972, while the Who was going through one of its periodic upheavals. The result was a ho-hum album titled *Who Came First* (1972). On his *Rough Mix* album in 1977, he collaborated with Ronnie Lane, a onetime Face. Townshend released another solo album, *Empty Glass,* in 1980.

Traffic   Stevie Winwood (guitar, keyboards), Chris Wood (sax, flute), Dave Mason (guitar), Jim Capaldi (drums)—Organized in England in 1967 by Stevie Winwood after his exit from the Spencer Davis Group, Traffic became one of the finest soft rock/flower power groups of the late 1960s. The secret was Winwood's commitment to high quality musicianship, reflected right off the bat in the band's first singles, "Paper Sun" (1967) and "Hole In My Shoe" (1968). The balance of four excellent musicians didn't last long, though, and Dave Mason found himself on the outs. The group continued as a trio until Winwood left to join Blind Faith. But that band's career didn't take up much time at all, and pretty soon Winwood was back in the fold (along with fellow Blind Faith refugee Rick Grech). In 1971 Traffic produced *John Barleycorn Must Die,* a superb album that was well received in the United States and remains something of an FM favorite. The next year *The Low Spark Of High Heeled Boys* went gold, and the band enjoyed a two-year heyday. Things began coming apart around 1973, and no amount of personnel shuffling seemed to stem the problem. Although Traffic periodically shows signs of life out of the grave, the spirit flew off around 1974.

Stevie Winwood and Jim Capaldi of Traffic

Trammps, The   James Ellis (vocals), Dennis Harris (guitar), Doc Wade (guitar), Ron Kersey (keyboards), John Hart (keyboards), John Davis (sax), Fred Jointer (trombone), Roger Stevens (trumpet), Stan Wade (bass), Michael Thompson (drums), Earl Young (drums)—The Trammps have been knocking around together since the start of the 1960s (an early incarnation called the Volcanoes had a hit in 1965 with "Storm Warning") in Philadelphia, where they soaked up the slick Philadelphia Sound. The early 1970s found them committed to disco but maintaining a sense of humor ("Zing Went The Strings Of My Heart" and a disco version of "Sixty Minute

Man"). In 1977 they were included in the legendary soundtrack of *Saturday Night Fever,* the single most important album of the 1970s, and their staggeringly powerful version of "Disco Inferno" became a huge pop hit and gave disco music the best publicity it ever got. The Trammps' disco represents just another step in the long evolution of black music, and their roots in rhythm-and-blues, black vocal groups and soul music are there for all the world to see.

Travers, Mary   Famous as a member of the hugely successful folk group, Peter, Paul and Mary, Travers was

born on Nov. 7, 1937 in Louisville, Ky. After the breakup of the group in 1971, she pursued a solo career, but it never seemed to get off the ground. Much more successful was her syndicated radio talk show, which got off the ground rather well thanks to an exclusive interview with the reclusive Bob Dylan. In 1978 Peter, Paul and Mary re-formed.

Travolta, John   Hey! You mean he sings, *too!* Right, only not very well. John Travolta (born on Feb. 18, 1954 in Englewood, N.J.) touched on a recording career in 1976 with a series of syrupy albums before he captured the entire rock world with the movies

John Travolta

Saturday Night Fever (in which he danced) in 1977 and *Grease* (in which he posed) in 1978. Of course, *Grease* yielded a couple of hit singles, including his duet with Olivia Newton-John, "You're The One That I Want" (which came out sounding something like "Yuhddawhan datta waunt").

T. Rex Marc Bolan (vocals, guitar), Steven Peregrine Took (vocals), Jack Green (guitar), Steven Currie (bass), Bill Legend (drums); additional member: Mickey Finn—In 1967 former male model Marc Bolan founded T. Rex (originally Tyrannosaurus Rex) in England as a sort of science fiction theater in acoustic rock; the group's first album was titled *My People Were Fair And Had Sky In Their Hair.* That phase lasted until 1970, when Bolan started slipping in a little electric guitar on the *Beard Of Stars* album. It was downhill for a while, but in 1972 Bolan found himself a full-fledged teen star, complete with an electric rock-and-roll band. The same year he had his biggest success in the United States, "Bang A Gong (Get It On)," a long way from people with sky in their hair. In September 1977 Bolan was killed in a traffic accident.

Troggs, The Reg Presley (vocals), Chris Britton (guitar), Peter Staples (bass), Ronnie Bond (drums)—Weird stuff indeed, the Troggs came roaring out of England in 1966 with the nastiest sounding rock-and-roll song since Elvis

did "Heartbreak Hotel"—"Wild Thing." Subsequent songs either stiffed or never got played because they were *too* nasty ("I Can't Control Myself," for one), and the Troggs called it quits in 1968 after their totally uncharacteristic hit "Love Is All Around." They re-formed in 1975.

Trower, Robin Born on March 9, 1945 in England, Trower first gained recognition playing guitar with Procol Harum. At best Procol Harum was never very satisfying, and after one of that group's many breakups in the early 1970s, Trower went on his own. Following the lead of his idol Jimi Hendrix, Trower eventually settled on a straight-ahead rock group centered around his multilayered guitar playing. He has since drifted a bit back toward his rhythm-and-blues roots (Procol Harum was, after all, originally an R&B-oriented group), maintaining his high standards.

True, Andrea When porn star Andrea True told her friends in her hometown of Nashville that she was going to become a famous singing star, they sniggered. When she had a huge hit in 1976 with "More More More," concerning a subject she's had *more* than a passing interest in, they stopped sniggering. Disco.

Tubes, The Bill Spooner (guitar, vocals), Roger Steen (guitar, vocals), Fee Waybill (vocals), Re Styles (vocals),

Praire Prince (drums), Vince Welnick (keyboards), Rick Anderson (bass), Michael Cotton (synthesizers), Mingo Lewis (percussion)—The Tubes got started during the mid-1970s in (where else?) San Francisco. They are not so much a band as a whacko revue, featuring characters like rock star Quay Lude and neo-Nazi Dr. Strangekiss, lots of strange posturing and T&A, when available. Their song titles tell all—"White Punks On Dope," "Don't Touch Me There," "Young And Rich" and "Cathy's Clone."

Tucker, Tanya Born on Oct. 10, 1958 in Seminole, Tex., Tucker broke into the music business in a big way in 1972 with her rendition of "Delta Dawn." Her powerful voice seemed to be coming from a woman of the world, not a 14-year-old kid. In 1974 she cut David Allan Coe's "Would You Lay With Me (In A Field Of Stone)," described by one critic as about as close to metaphysical as country music is likely to get, and after that her career was made. In recent years she's been trying to establish herself as a rock act, shifting producers, arrangers, fashion designers and publicists with each album, to no avail. Her 1978 effort, *T.N.T.,* did show her maturity as a rock-oriented singer, but nobody was listening.

Tuff Darts New Wave band best known as the early home for rockabilly revivalist Robert Gordon and, at present, nothing else.

Tina Turner

Turner, "Big" Joe
Bluesman "Big" Joe Turner (born on May 18, 1911 in Kansas City, Mo.) had already had a successful career as a blues stylist when he began cutting R&B songs in 1950 for what would become the rock market, including "Chains Of Love" (1951), "Sweet Sixteen" (1952), "Shake, Rattle And Roll" (1954), later a big pop hit for Bill Haley, and "Flip, Flop And Fly" (1955). Two of his biggest hits came in 1956, with the blues standard "Corinna Corinna" and the absolute classic "Lipstick, Powder And Paint."

Turner, Ike and Tina Ike Turner was originally a talent scout and bandleader for Sun Records in Memphis — as a talent scout, he discovered Howlin' Wolf; as a bandleader (with his Kings of Rhythm, featuring Jackie Brenston as vocalist) he cut "Rocket 88," widely considered to be the very first rock-and-roll record. Not bad for starters. Turner (born on Nov. 5, 1931 in Clarksdale, Miss.) followed rock and roll north, developing his show into a revue. Part of that revue was a pistol-hot singer named Tina Braddock (born on Nov. 26, 1938 in Brownsville, Tenn.). She became Tina Turner in 1958, and the pair began recording in 1960. They worked steadily throughout the 1960s, eventually adding the Ikettes, three girl singers whose function was as much to wiggle as to harmonize, and Tina's act got wilder and more sultry. In 1966 they linked up with producer Phil Spector, who put together the brilliant "River Deep Mountain High," but the song couldn't buck the British Invasion, driving the volatile Spector out of the business and putting Ike and Tina back on the road. The Ike and Tina Turner Revue shot through the 1970s like a bullet, Tina and the Ikettes causing heart failure wherever they appeared. They opened for the Rolling Stones on the group's 1969 tour, and in 1971 they cracked the charts in a big way with a cover of Creedence Clearwater Revival's "Proud Mary." Tina played the Acid Queen in Ken Russell's movie version of *Tommy* in 1975, and her performance was considered to be one of the high points of the movie. In the late 1970s Ike and Tina separated — a disaster for rock.

Turtles, The Howard Kaylan (vocals); Marc Volman (vocals);

John Barbata (drums); Jim Tucker (guitar); Jim Pons (bass, vocals); Al Nichol (guitar); and others, including Don Murray, John Seiter, Chuck Portz—The odd thing about the Turtles, formed in 1965 in Los Angeles during the heyday of folk rock, was that they never much liked the idea of being teen idols. It was hard to tell that from their first superhit, a cut of Bob Dylan's "It Ain't Me Babe" (1965), which they followed with two more quick hits, "Let Me Be" (1965) and "You Baby" (1966). Beginning in 1967 they turned out one hit right after the other, including "Happy Together" (1967), "She'd Rather Be With Me" (1967), "You Know What I Mean" (1967), "She's My Girl" (1967) and "Elenore" (1967). Their "B" sides, however, showed the Howard Kaylan/Marc Volman insanity at its peak—"Chicken Little Was Right," "Umbassa And The Dragon," "Can't You Hear The Cows," "Surfer Dan," "I Think I'll Run Away" and "Grim Reaper Of Love." In 1970 insanity won over hits, and the band parted ways with a remake of "Eve Of Destruction" and a perfectly crazy album titled *Battle Of The Bands,* on which the Turtles all pretended to be some other groups playing different kinds of music. Kaylan and Volman formed the Phlorescent Leech and Eddie, now known as Flo and Eddie, working briefly with the Mothers of Invention. Barbata ended up with the Jefferson Starship.

Twitty, Conway Born Harold Lloyd Jenkins on Sept. 1, 1933 in Friars Point, Miss.,

country singer Conway Twitty (so named for two towns, Conway, Ark. and Twitty, Tex.) began his career in the mid-1950s singing rockabilly. He worked briefly at Sun Records, touring with such Sun stars as Elvis Presley and Carl Perkins before hitting it big on his own in 1958 with "It's Only Make Believe." But Twitty saw the handwriting on the wall, and by 1960, when the rockabilly fever was already a dimming memory, he was writing country songs. Six years later he was a bonafide country singer. He and Loretta Lynn were named country duet of the year by the Country Music Association for four years in a row (1972-75). Twitty has produced some of the most striking songs in country music ("You've Never Been This Far Before," "Play Guitar Play") and—when he chooses—can still rock with the best of them.

Tyler, Bonnie Gravel-voiced Bonnie Tyler grew up in a Welsh village called Mumbles. After establishing herself as a pub singer, Tyler required an operation on her vocal chords. The result was an even more gravelly voice, which paid off in 1977, when her "It's A Heartache" became an across-the-charts hit in America, Britain, Australia, Sweden, Norway, Austria, South Africa, Germany, Holland, Belgium, Switzerland, Finland, Denmark and Israel. It also did well in France, New Zealand and Brazil. The tune was (it almost goes without saying) extremely catchy, and her vocals unique. Two albums later no one can remember her name. Such things, though, can change very fast.

UFO Phil Mogg (vocals), Pete Way (bass), Andy Parker, (drums), Paul Raymond (keyboards), Michael Schenker (guitar)—British hard rockers formed around 1970, UFO produced six albums, including *UFO* (1971), *Lights Out* (1977) and *Strangers In The Night* (1978), without ever finding the key to the American market. The group had its biggest success in Japan during the early 1970s with a version of Eddie Cochran's "C'mon Everybody," which turned UFO into an overnight sensation in that country.

Undisputed Truth, The Billie Calvin, Brenda Evans, Joe Harris—Motown group best known for its stunning hit single "Smiling Faces Sometimes" (1971), one of the most powerful evocations ever to come out of Motown. The group is still around, featuring Chaka Khan's sister, Taka Boom, but it hasn't come up with anything like the first big hit.

Uriah Heep David Byron (vocals), Mick Box (guitar), Ken Hensley (keyboards), John Wetton (bass), Lee Kerslake (drums)—The bastard offspring (at least stylewise) of Deep Purple and Led Zeppelin, Uriah Heep is probably one of the most critically dumped-on groups ever. In a moment of wretched rock excess, a critic wrote of its first album, *Very* 'eavy... Very 'umble (1970), "If this group makes it, I'll have to commit suicide." Not only did Uriah Heep make it, the group became a mainstay of the 1970s with such singles hits as "Easy Livin'" (1972) and such albums as *Demons And Wizards* (1972).

Valens, Ritchie   Born Ritchie Valenzuela on May 13, 1941 in Los Angeles, Valens began his brief career with "Come On, Let's Go" in 1958, followed by the slow-dance classic "Donna" later that year. On Feb. 30, 1959 he was killed in a plane crash with Buddy Holly and the Big Bopper.

Van Halen   David Lee Roth (vocals), Edward Van Halen (guitar), Alex Van Halen (drums), Michael Anthony (bass)—The Van Halen brothers, both from Holland, formed their group (known by many names) in southern California during the mid-1970s, touring the area for years as a top-notch bar band. After being discovered in a Hollywood rock club in 1977, the group's first album, *Van Halen,* went on to sell some two million copies, proving that loud, powerful rock, *a la* the bar circuit, was still overwhelmingly popular. The band followed that album with *Van Halen II* in 1979.

Van Zandt, Townes   Texas songwriter Townes Van Zandt

Van Halen

is best known for such songs as "For The Sake Of The Song" (1968) and "Pancho And Lefty" (1972). His singing voice is weak but surprisingly effective, and over the years he has built a steady cult following.

Vanilla Fudge   Carmine Appice (drums), Mark Stein (organ), Tim Bogert (bass), Vinnie Martell (guitar)— Formed during the late 1970s on Long Island, N.Y., the Vanilla Fudge's forte was ominous, creaking versions of pop hits, such as the group's biggest hit, an undertaker's version of the Supremes' upbeat "You Keep Me Hanging On" (1967). The band's main contribution was the idea that something good could come from reworkings of rock standards.

Vaughan, Sarah   Born on March 27, 1924 in Newark, N.J., Vaughan first came to public attention as a vocalist for Earl "Fatha" Hines' band. Beginning in the late 1940s with "It's Magic" (1948), she cut a series of pop hits that defined her smooth style—a bridge between the tougher blues singers of the 1930s and the more rock-oriented women vocalists of the 1960s. In 1955 she had three hits: "Make Yourself Comfortable," "How Important Can It Be" and "Whatever Lola Wants." Her biggest hit came in 1959 with "Broken-Hearted Melody."

Vee, Bobby   Born on April 30, 1943 in Fargo, N.D., Bobby Vee (actually Robert Velline) was a member of the band that replaced Buddy Holly after his plane crashed on the way to a show in Fargo. Vee was tapped to be vocalist, the story goes, because he knew more Buddy Holly songs than anyone else in the band. Despite this rather macabre beginning, Vee went on to record a series of memorable hits throughout the early 1960s, including "Devil Or Angel" (1960), "Take Good Care Of My Baby" (1961) and "The Night Has A Thousand Eyes" (1962), which made the charts in early 1963.

Velvet Underground, The Nico (vocals), Lou Reed (guitar, vocals), John Cale (bass, viola), Maureen Tucker (drums), Sterling Morrison (guitar)—Originally formed in New York City in 1966, the Velvet Underground went on to become one of the most influential groups in rock, although it was neither long-lived or successful. The group's main influence came from its jarring, menacing instrumental style—in drastic contrast to the peace and love vibes of the late 1960s—and its return to the streets of New York City for inspiration. Instead of finding love all around them, the Velvet Underground found heroin and crazies and decadence, all of which were reflected in its music, and which now echo through the punk groups that idolize the Velvets' music. The group actually seemed destined to go under in 1966, when pop artist Andy Warhol took them under his wing as part of his multimedia experiments. He added German vocalist Nico and a good bit of money to get them going, even providing the cover art for the first album, *The Velvet Underground And*

Nico in 1967. That album features perhaps the band's best-known (and most-criticized) song, "Heroin," an eerie incantation. A second album, *White Light/White Heat,* came in 1968, but by then Nico had already moved on. At the start of the next year, the Velvet Underground began to come apart, producing two more albums before self-destructing, with Cale and Reed going on to reasonably successful solo careers.

Ventures, The Don Wilson (guitar); Bob Bogle (guitar); Howie Johnston (drums); Nokie Edwards (guitar); additional member: Mel Taylor (drums)—The Ventures were an instrumental group formed in Tacoma, Wash. during the late 1950s. Don Wilson and Bob Bogle were in construction work when they decided to take up the guitar, eventually teaming up with Nokie Edwards and Howie Johnston. Their first hit, "Walk—Don't Run" (1960), was turned down by numerous people before the group decided to circulate it themselves. They followed that up with "Perfidia," a Latin American oldie, in 1961, "Walk—Don't Run '64" in 1964 and the hit theme from the television show "Hawaii Five-O" in 1969.

Verlaine, Tom Originally the lead vocalist for Television (Richard Lloyd, Fred Smith and Billy Ficca), one of the most literate of the New Wave bands. Verlaine went on his own in 1978 after the breakup of the band. His lyric work shows an eclectic sense of humor and a good eye for

Tom Verlaine

street weirdness, and his guitar playing reflects his early attempts to imitate Jimi Hendrix, then not realizing that the master recorded several guitar tracks one at a time, building up the sound a layer at a time.

Vibrations, The James Johnson (vocals), Richard Owens (vocals), Carl Fisher (vocals), Dave Govan (vocals), Don Bradley (vocals)—First formed as the Jayhawks in Los Angeles during the mid-1950s, the group changed names in the early 1960s and had its biggest hit in 1961, "The Watusi," riding the dance craze of the times. The group also had a classic hit as the Marathons—"Peanut Butter" in 1961.

Village People, The David Hodo (vocals), Felipe Rose (vocals), Alex Briley (vocals), Victor Willis (vocals), Randy Jones (vocals), Glenn Hughes (vocals)—Originally conceived by French producer Jacques Morali, the Village People are a disco group composed of the stereotypical gay men seen at various times in New York City's Greenwich Village—a hard hat, a sailor, a cop, a cowboy, an Indian and a biker. Morali was right on target—the group was campy enough to grab television coverage and titillating enough to bring in the hipper crowd. The results were several 1978-79 hits, including "Macho Man," "In The Navy" and the outrageously successful bit of double entendre "YMCA." A movie starring the Village People, *Can't Stop the Music,* was released in 1980.

Village Stompers, The An eight-man Dixieland ensemble that got its name gigging in Greenwich Village in the early 1960s. The group had one major hit, the catchy "Washington Square" (the large park smack in the center of Greenwich Village) in 1963.

Vincent, Gene Rockabilly rebel Gene Vincent was born on Feb. 11, 1935 in Norfolk, Va. and developed into the toughest of the rockabilly singers of the 1950s. His classic "Be-Bop-A-Lula" (written in 1956 with Sheriff Tex Davis) was considered the "blackest sounding" record to come out of rockabilly, and the song, with its attendant heavy promotion of the leather-jacketed Vincent, led to Vincent's inclusion in two movies, *The Girl Can't Help It* and *Hot Rod Gang* (1958). But rock and roll in America was getting cleaner by the hour, and Vincent found himself in the position of a greaser

dinosaur. He went to England, where he became nothing short of a national craze until an automobile accident severely injured him and killed his friend and fellow rocker Eddie Cochran (April 17, 1960). Vincent never really recovered, and after a bout with the bottle, he died on Oct. 12, 1971. The Vincent mania continues nonetheless with the French Gene Vincent Society working steadily to see to it that every single scrap of tape on Vincent is released on record.

Vinton, Bobby Born on April 16, 1935 in Canonsburg, Pa., Vinton organized his first band in high school. After two unsuccessful records he had to persuade the record company to let him finish out his contract for two more songs. Those songs were "Roses Are Red" and "Mr. Lonely," two number one hits (the first in 1962, the second in 1964). Following that, he produced a string of crooner hits throughout the 1960s and into the 1970s, including "Blue Velvet" (1963), "There! I've Said It Again" (1963) and "Please Love Me Forever" (1967).

Vogues, The Bill Burkette (vocals), Don Miller (vocals), Hugh Geyer (vocals), Chuck Blasko (vocals)—The Vogues translated 1950s group harmonies into a 1960s setting and had a hit in 1968 with "Turn Around Look At Me." The group was formed in Turtle Creek, Pa. in 1960 and had several modest hits in the same vein (including "Five O'Clock World" in 1965 and "Magic Town" in 1966) before striking it big.

Wagoner, Porter Flashy country singer Porter Wagoner (born on Aug. 12, 1927 in West Plains, Mo.) is best known for his early duets with Dolly Parton. His own recording career began in 1955 and includes such country standards as "Satisfied Mind" (1955) and "Green Green Grass Of Home" (1965). He is presently one of Nashville's busiest producers, concentrating lately on disco groups.

Wainwright, Loudon, III Son of *Look* magazine writer Loudon Wainwright, II, Loudon Wainwright, III (born on Sept. 5, 1946 in Bedford, N.Y.) became prominent in the early 1970s with his sarcastic, sardonic songs, delivered in a voice that can be most kindly described as whining. He covered such topics as politics and suicide, and his songs rarely found their way to the radio. That changed in 1973 during his much-vaunted "mellowing," when his "Dead Skunk" song—which described various and sundry animals smashed flat on the highway—became a hit. He was formerly married to Kate McGarrigle of the McGarrigle sisters.

Waits, Tom Born on Dec. 7, 1949 in Pomona, Calif., Waits is the master barroom troubadour, a self-proclaimed night creature who intersperses his songs about sleazy nightlife with a beatnik rap about the same. He is an accomplished sessions man (backing the likes of Charlie Rich and Frank Zappa) and a surprisingly powerful composer, with such songs as "Closing Time" and "Ol' 55" almost being swamped under his beery persona. Waits is also one of the finest rock interpreters, dipping into country for a left-field version of Red Sovine's "Phantom 309," about a ghost truck, and pop for a twist of *West Side Story*'s "Somewhere" to his own ends. Among his albums are *Nighthawks At The Diner* in 1975, *Blue Valentine* in 1978 and *Heartattack And Vine* in 1980, containing the evocative, 1960s-styled "Jersey Girl." He is basically one of the last links to the Beat Generation and is available for consultation at the rundown Los Angeles hotel where he lives. Waits is also credited with orginating the phrase, "She looks like she could suck the chrome off a trailer hitch," made famous by Willie Nelson in the Robert Redford/Jane Fonda film *The Electric Horseman* (1979).

Wakeman, Rick Perhaps the premier keyboard man in rock, Wakeman was born on May 18, 1949 in London. He first acquired recognition as a sessions man (Cat Stevens, T. Rex, David Bowie), worked with the Strawbs in 1970 and joined the group Yes in 1971. He made his reputation as that group's flamboyant keyboard man but, chafing at the bit, went on his own in 1973. Since then he has staged a number of ambitious (some say overly so) projects—including his *Myths And Legends Of King Arthur* (1975), featuring a full

orchestra and choir—most of which failed. He wrote the score for Ken Russell's *Lisztomania* film in 1976 and the next year rejoined the flagging Yes.

Walden, Phil The founder and president of the late, lamented Capricorn Records was born on Jan. 11, 1940 in Greenville, S.C., but his family soon moved to Macon, Ga. An early interest in rhythm and blues and an unsuccessful attempt at forming a band led the young Walden to start managing his own black acts. Eventually he linked up with soul singer Otis Redding, whom he successfully managed until the singer's death in 1967. In 1969 Walden heard tapes of a sessions guitarist at Muscle Shoals who so impressed him that he flew there to meet him. The guitarist was Duane Allman, and with Walden's encouragement Allman formed a band with his younger brother Gregg, called the Allman Brothers Band. That group was to be the flagship for Walden's new record label, Capricorn, formed at the behest of Atlantic Records' vice president Jerry Wexler (both he and Walden were Capricorns). The label—and the band— became spectacularly successful, with Capricorn eventually managing some of the biggest and most lucrative acts in the country, including the Allman Brothers Band, the Marshall Tucker Band, Wet Willie and Grinderswitch.

Walden was also instrumental in the 1976 election of President Jimmy Carter, the former governor of

Georgia and a close friend of Walden. When Carter's campaign faltered in the early days because of a lack of money, Walden engineered a series of concerts by Capricorn acts that netted, in a very short span of time, almost a million dollars for the cause.

The late 1970s saw Walden's empire crumbling, however, as shifting musical tastes (he refused to record or even acknowledge disco music) and a series of bitter lawsuits and group defections gnawed away at Capricorn. The label went under in 1979, with Walden firmly proclaiming that Capricorn would return.

Waldman, Wendy Although known as a singer and songwriter ("Mad Mad Me" and "Vaudeville Man" for Maria Muldaur; "Pirate Ships" for Judy Collins), Waldman's singing career has never really jelled—perhaps, as one critic has suggested, because her style is too close to the Ronstadt/Emmylou Harris female singer axis. Beginning in 1973 with *Love Has Got Me,* she has made several albums. Waldman was born in 1951 in Los Angeles.

Walker, Jerry Jeff Born a Yankee on March 16, 1942 in upstate New York, Jerry Jeff Walker left home at 16 to make his way as a musician. He quickly discovered that regardless of where he was born, Texas was his spiritual home, and he made it official when he moved to Austin in the late 1960s to escape the New York music biz. He'd been successful in his early career as a folk-rock singer, producing one classic song—"Mr. Bojangles," which he recorded in 1968 and which became a hit for the Nitty Gritty Dirt Band in 1970. Once permanently ensconced in Austin, he began a series of "redneck" albums, using his gruff voice to its greatest effect on such story songs as Guy Clark's "LA Freeway" and "Desperadoes Waiting For A Train." In 1973 he cut *Viva Terlingua* in the Texas ghost town of Luckenbach, later made famous in a song by Willie Nelson and Waylon Jennings. Walker remains a central focus of the Austin movement in country music, although his recent material has suffered from endless repetition and his frequent surrender to the bottle. His former backup group, the Lost Gonzo Band, has gone on to a modestly unsuccessful solo career.

Walker, Junior, and the All-Stars Junior Walker (sax, piano, vocals), Willie Woods (guitar), Vic Thomas (keyboards), James Graves (drums)—Motown's rhythm-and-bluesiest sounding group, formed by Junior Walker in the early 1960s in Battle Creek, Mich. Although Walker's raunchy saxophone honky-tonk piano and gruff voice ran against Motown's polished grain, he was successful with such infectiously rollicking songs as "Shotgun" (1965) and "Road Runner" (1966). Later he became mellower with hits like "What Does It Take To Win Your Love" (1969). In recent years he's come back a couple of times, his largely unchanged party music finding a new home in the discos as well as the rock clubs.

Walker, T-Bone Bluesman Aaron "T-Bone" Walker was born in 1913 in Linden, Tex. and was already recording by the age of 16. He was the master of the acoustic blues guitar, flamboyant and flashy, but when he met up with the electric guitar, he knew he'd found his instrument. Walker became one of the first bluesmen to adopt the electric guitar wholeheartedly, and his guitar style became more and more attuned to that instrument—faster, jazzier, upgrading the Texas blues into its modern offspring. That influence can be heard today in the works of B.B. King and Eric Clapton and dozens of other rock guitarists, especially the late Duane Allman. Walker also wrote "Stormy Monday," one of the great blues songs of all time.

Walker Brothers, The Gary Leeds (vocals, drums), John Maus (vocals, guitar), Scott Engel (vocals, bass)—A British Invasion group that wasn't British, the Walker Brothers (they weren't brothers either) left California, where they'd gotten together in college, for swinging London in the early 1960s. Their vocal styles and long hair fit in perfectly with the movement under way there, and pretty soon the group found itself exported back to the U.S. with "Make It Easy On Yourself" (1965) and "The Sun Ain't Gonna Shine Anymore" (1966).

Walsh, Joe Eagles guitarist Joe Walsh (born in Cleveland, Ohio) first came to attention in the early 1970s as the moving spirit behind the James Gang. Leaving that group in 1971, he formed a new group, Barnstorm, and had a gold album in 1973, *The Smoker You Drink, The Player You Get,* and a hit single, "Rocky Mountain Way," from the album. He left the group that year and flirted with a solo career. In 1976 Walsh joined the Eagles, providing an excellent leavening of hard

War

Dionne Warwick

synthesizer), Charles Miller (sax, clarinet, vocals), Lee Oskar (harp, vocals), Howard Scott (guitar, percussion, vocals)—Originally formed in 1959 as the Night Shift, a popular bar band on the West Coast, War joined ex-Animal Eric Burdon during the late 1960s. Their first hit was the bizarre "Spill The Wine" (1970), featuring long recitations by Burdon. Burdon and War split in 1971, and War began carving out a name for itself as a funk-soul group. In 1972 the band had a hit of its own with "Slippin' Into Darkness" from the album of the same name, followed by the excellent *The World Is A Ghetto* album later that year, which featured yet another title track hit plus a song that reached number two on the charts, "Cisco Kid." In 1975 War hit again with the upbeat "Why Can't We Be Friends." The group's work has grown increasingly erratic.

Warwick, Dionne   Born on Dec. 12, 1941 in East Orange, N.J., the professionally trained Dionne Warwick was the perfect vocalist for the Burt Bacharach/Hal David hit machine, which she first encountered in 1962. The results were a quick string of memorable hits—"Don't Make Me Over" (1962), "Anyone Who Had A Heart" (1963), "Walk On By" (1964), "You'll Never Get To Heaven" (1964), "Message To Michael" (1966) and "I Say A Little Prayer" (1967). Since she left the songwriting team, her output has ranged from her excellent teaming up with the Spinners for "Then Came You" (1976) to her Grammy-winning single

rock guitar for that mellow West Coast group. Two years later he wrote "In The City," the theme song for the teenage gang movie *The Warriors*; the song was included on the Eagles' *Long Run* album. Also in 1978 he cut "Life's Been Good To Me," a wry view of a rock star's life, included on the *But Seriously Folks...* album.

Wammack, Travis   Muscle Shoals sessions guitarist best known for his 1963 hit "Scratchy." Although only a modest hit, the song influenced a generation of Southern guitarists. A brief solo career failed to get off the ground.

War   Harold Brown (drums, percussion, vocals), Papa Dee Allen (percussion), B.B. Dickerson (bass, percussion, vocals), Lonnie Jordan (keyboards, vocals,

"I'll Never Love This Way Again" (1979), produced by Barry Manilow.

Washboard Sam Bluesman Robert Brown was probably born around 1910 in Arkansas and made his reputation playing the corrugated metal washboard. He surfaced in Chicago in 1932, washboard in tow, to take part in that city's blues heyday.

Washington, Dinah Born Ruth Jones on Aug. 29, 1924 in Tuscaloosa, Ala. and raised in Chicago, Ill., Dinah Washington grew up singing gospel music. Drawn to black secular music, she joined Lionel Hampton's big band in 1943 and began to record shortly thereafter. During the 1950s she was one of the top female R&B vocalists, blending blues and gospel phrasing with her own unique vocal intensity. She successfully made the transition to pop in the late 1950s. Her biggest hit came in 1959 with "What A Difference A Day Makes," followed by "Unforgettable" later that year and "September In The Rain" in 1961. During this period she had two top 10 duet hits with Brook Benton: "Baby (You Got What It Takes)" and "Rockin' Good Way"—both in 1960. Her career was cut short in 1963, when she died from an accidental overdose of sleeping pills.

Washington, Grover, Jr. Born on Dec. 12, 1943 in Buffalo, N.Y., Grover Washington, Jr. is best known for his excellent jazz-rock fusion work with a saxophone. His biggest selling album to date came in the mid-1970s with *Mr. Magic,* a low-key

instrumental recording that sold nearly a million copies.

Waters, Muddy Without a doubt the single most influential blues player in the history and development of rock and roll. Born McKinley Morganfield on April 4, 1915 in Rolling Fork, Miss., Muddy Waters was playing the blues by the time he was 15 years old. In the early 1940s Waters was recorded by folk researchers Alan Lomax and John Work, singing unamplified hard-core Delta blues. Soon after, Waters gave up working in the fields and followed the conduit north to the Chicago ghettos. In 1944 he bought his first electric guitar and was introduced to the Chess brothers, who had their own record label. What Waters brought to the blues was the idea of an electrified band, playing loud and hard with all the energy that could be summoned. It was this very tradition that rock and roll would soon tap so successfully, borrowing such Waters' classics as "Hoochie Coochie Man," "Mannish Boy" and "Got My Mojo Working" along the way. In 1954 he wrote and recorded a song called "Rollin' Stone," which would later inspire Bob Dylan to write and record "Like A Rolling Stone," an English group to name themselves after the Waters classic and a rock magazine to follow suit. His direct influence is staggering, touching most of the first- and second-generation rock players in America and England. Indirectly he happened to introduce Phil Chess to Chuck Berry, thereby planting the very

seeds of rock. Although his own career has had its ups and downs (like his psychedelic blues albums in the 1960s, a definite down), it's currently going strong again with the help of guitarist Johnny Winter, who produced the highly acclaimed *Hard Again* album in 1977. Waters is a true king of rock and roll.

Watson, Arthel "Doc" Blind guitar picker Doc Watson was born on March 2, 1923 in Deep Gap, N.C. Working as a traveling musician throughout the 1950s, his initial exposure to the folk ballads of the mountains was broadened to include bluegrass, swing, the blues, rhythm and blues and string band music. With his phenomenal memory Watson became a storehouse of American music, which he played with an incredible picking style on the guitar. In the 1960s he became the darling of the folk crowd and in the 1970s an excellent recording artist (with his son Merle) in his own right.

We Five Beverly Bivens (vocals), Peter Fullerton (vocals), Jerry Burgan (vocals), Robert Jones (vocals), Michael Stewart (vocals)—Formed in 1965 in California, the group had a hit that year with the Ian and Sylvia composition "You Were On My Mind," a great summer song. It was their only major hit, however.

Weather Report Josef Zawinul (keyboards, synthesizer), Wayne Shorter (saxophone), Jaco Pastorius (bass), Manolo Badrena (percussion, vocals), Alejandro Neciosup Acuna (percussion)—Jazz-rock fusion

229

group (closer to jazz than rock) formed by Vienna-born Josef Zawinul and Jersey-bred Wayne Shorter in 1970. At this point Weather Report is something of an institution in jazz circles, although it does not have the same overall acceptance in the rock market. Nevertheless, the group's *Heavy Weather* album in 1977 provided a hit single, "Birdland."

Webb, Jimmy   Born on Aug. 15, 1946 in Elk City, Okla., Webb became prominent in the mid-1960s as one of that decade's most commercial— if not most outstanding— songwriters. He provided "Up, Up And Away" (1967) for the Fifth Dimension, "By The Time I Get To Phoenix" (1967), "Wichita Lineman" (1968) and "Galveston" (1969) for Glen Campbell and Richard Harris' epic "MacArthur Park" (1968), which has since won awards both in a country rendition by Waylon Jennings and a disco version by Donna Summer. The 1970s saw Webb in eclipse, with a solo singing career that has never caught on. He remains a fine songwriter, however, and it's not surprising for a Jim Webb number to pop to the top of the charts every now and then.

Weir, Bob   Born on Oct. 16, 1947 in San Francisco, Calif., Bob Weir is best known as a lead singer and guitarist for the Grateful Dead. In 1976 he formed his own moderately successful group, Kingfish.

Welch, Bob   Formerly a member of Fleetwood Mac, Welch (born on July 31, 1946 in Los Angeles, Calif.) left that group just in time to see Mac make it big. Undaunted, he cut

a solo album, *French Kiss,* which yielded a big hit single, "Sentimental Lady" (1977) and proved that Lady Luck does have her softer moments. The following year he had another hit with "Ebony Eyes."

Wells, Junior   Bluesman Junior Wells (born on Dec. 9, 1934 in West Memphis, Ark.) was the blues harp player who replaced "Little Walter" Jacobs in the Muddy Waters' band during the mid-1950s. His solo career began in the 1960s, and he often tours with guitarist Buddy Guy, playing rock and jazz clubs.

Wells, Kitty   Born on Aug. 30, 1918 in Nashville, Tenn., Kitty Wells was the first woman country music superstar, based largely on her huge hit in the early 1950s "It Wasn't God Who Made Honky-Tonk Angels," which she followed with such successes as "Making Believe," "One By One," "I Can't Stop Loving You" and others in the 1950s and 1960s.

Wells, Mary   Motown star Mary Wells was born on May 13, 1943 in Detroit, Mich. and became one of Motown's hit acts in the early 1960s. Her career started in 1961 with a song she'd written called "Bye Bye Baby." The following year she had three top 10 hits— "The One Who Really Loves You," "You Beat Me To The Punch" and "Two Lovers"— but it wasn't until 1964, when she recorded the Smokey Robinson classic "My Guy," that she reached the top of the charts and the height of her success. Wells eventually left Motown because of the heavy

emphasis that label was putting on its other acts.

Werewolves   Another attempt to cash in on the mercurial rock market of the 1970s, this one by former Rolling Stones guiding light Andrew Loog Oldham. The Werewolves were formed by guitarist Seab Meador and vocalist Brian Papageorge in Dallas, in 1970. They are best known for their single "Waking Up Is Hard To Do," circa late 1970s.

West, Bruce and Laing   Leslie West (guitar), Jack Bruce (bass, vocals, keyboards), Corky Laing (drums)—Sort of son of Mountain meets Cream, West, Bruce and Laing was tinkered together in 1972 as a supergroup by Felix Pappalardi, who produced both Mountain and Cream. Although the trio stuck to the same basic formula as the other two groups, the grafting didn't take, and by 1974 West, Bruce and Laing had disappeared.

Weston, Kim   Another Motown singer, Kim Weston's greatest success came from her duets with Marvin Gaye, most notably "It Takes Two" in 1967.

Wet Willie   Jimmy Hall (vocals, sax, harp), Rick Hirsch (guitar), Jack Hall (bass), John Anthony (keyboards), Lewis Ross (drums), Donna Hall (vocals), Ella Avery (vocals)— Part of the Capricorn Records boogie axis, Wet Willie took its first breath in Mobile during the late 1960s. In 1971 the group signed with Capricorn and began releasing a series of tough R&B-based boogie records, which won Wet Willie fans if not record sales. A 1974 hit, "Keep On Smiling," kept things alive, and the late 1970s found Wet Willie regrouped after the collapse of Capricorn and very much alive and sticking to the boogie formula—"Street Corner Serenade" (1977) and "Make You Feel Love Again" (1978).

Wexler, Jerry   Recording executive Jerry Wexler was responsible for Atlantic Records' landmark move into black and Southern music in the late 1950s and 1960s. His trips down South had put him in touch with Jim Stewart of Stax Records and Phil Walden, then manager of Otis Redding and other soul groups, as well as the whole New Orleans circuit of performers. Wexler was able to give Atlantic Records the jump on soul music during virtually the whole decade of the 1960s, recording such soul acts as Wilson Pickett (Wexler produced many of his greatest hits and is credited with helping fuse Pickett's soul sound), Aretha Franklin (whose work with Wexler in Muscle Shoals remains some of the most powerful soul work ever to emerge) and others. He persuaded Phil Walden to form Capricorn Records and had earlier arranged for Atlantic Records to distribute Stax. He helped steer Atlantic Records into rock and ultimately deserves the credit for fusing that label into one of the most powerful in music. He is presently an executive at Warner Brothers.

Whitcomb, Ian   Born in 1941 in England, Ian Whitcomb is known for his two novelty hits, "You Turn Me On" and "N-E-R-V-O-U-S," in 1965. He is perhaps more famous for his book on popular music titled *After the Ball: A History of Pop,* published in 1972.

White, Barry   The undisputed king of the moan, Barry White was born on Sept. 12, 1944 in Galveston, Tex. and first made his reputation in the 1960s as a producer. In the early 1970s White put together Love Unlimited, a three-girl vocal group that included his wife, and scored with "Walkin' In The Rain (With The One I Love)" in 1972. He also put together the Love Unlimited Orchestra, which made the charts in 1973 with the instrumental "Love's Theme." Bolstered by his successes, White launched himself as a solo artist in 1973 with "I'm Gonna Love You Just A Little Bit More Baby," which introduced White as the breathless lover—a persona that's worked amazingly well since. Such hits as "Never, Never Gonna Give You Up" (1973) and "You're The First, The Last, My Everything" (1974) revealed White as the master of the bedroom moan, backed by an incredible number of strings and sweeping orchestral arrangements.

White, Bukka   Bluesman Booker T. "Bukka" White (born in 1909 in Houston, Miss.) served time for murder in the notorious Parchman Prison Farm in Mississippi, where his blues playing helped him to avoid the worst of that prison's horrors. Until his death in 1977, he was a fixture in the Memphis blues community, where he was renowned for his work with the steel-bodied guitar.

White, Tony Joe   White soulman Tony Joe White was born on July 23, 1943 in the bayou country of Oak Grove, La. and originally formed a group called Tony Joe and the Mojos. After working as a producer and songwriter in Nashville, White produced a string of solo hits, including "Polk Salad Annie" in 1969 (a top 10 song for him), "Roosevelt And Ira Lee Jones" in 1969 and "Rainy Night In Georgia" in 1970 (a top 10 song for Brook Benton), all accented by White's deep, powerful voice. In recent years his career has been low key, with no repetition of the earlier successes in sight, although he remains a popular live act around the world.

Whitlock, Bobby   Originally a member of Derek and the Dominos (with Eric Clapton and Duane Allman), Bobby Whitlock later toured with Delaney and Bonnie and tried briefly for a solo career on Capricorn Records before settling into sessions work.

Who, The   Pete Townshend (guitar); Roger Daltrey (vocals); John Entwistle (bass); Kenny Jones (drums), replacement for Keith Moon (drums), died 1978—Formed in London in 1963 as a Mod rock group, the Who have managed to survive both the 1960s and the 1970s to become one of the rock world's all-time great bands. The Who were always different. Playing typical R&B music, the group soon allied with the

The Who

nattily dressed Mods, a ready-made audience. The band members began closing their shows by smashing most of their equipment—dramatic, expensive and perhaps symbolic of the budding music. The Who's break came in 1965, when Townshend penned one of the all-time rock classics, "My Generation," which gave the generation without a cause at least a voice, While "My Generation" took off in England, it wasn't until the more liberal FM radio was firmly established in the United States that the Who's eclectic music found success here. Meanwhile the group's reputation as a touring ensemble was growing, and in the late 1960s Townshend chanced on the vehicle that would make the Who virtually a household word. In 1969 the Who released the rock opera Tommy, which wasn't an overnight success. Instead, it grew and grew and grew—and by all standards is still growing. Tommy, the story of a deaf, dumb and blind rock everyman, has so far gone from a record to a stage performance to a movie to a soundtrack album. The reason for its unprecedented success is simple: Tommy remains an awesome achievement, one of the high watermarks in rock music. Post-Tommy releases found Townshend trying to top his masterpiece and suffering for the effort, and during the mid-1970s the Who seemed on the verge of breaking up to pursue individual projects (the flashy Daltrey seemed the most insistent, producing a series of well-received albums). In the late 1970s, though, the Who regrouped and set about to bring "My Generation" to a whole new generation of rock fans, at which it succeeded amazingly well. Even the tragic drug-related death of manic drummer Keith Moon in 1978 did not stop the group.

The Who have produced some of the most memorable music in rock, bouncing from the powerful overture to Tommy to the 1975 offbeat country music success "Squeeze Box" (most country disc jockeys who played the song had no idea who the group was). The Who's songs have ranged from light ("Happy Jack" in 1967 and "The Magic Bus" in 1968) to brooding ("Behind Blue Eyes" in 1971) to bitter ("Won't Get Fooled Again" in 1971). Who Are You (1978), released just before the death of Moon, showed the group still the master of the rock format.

Williams, Andy Although hardly anyone's idea of a rocker, Andy Williams has chalked up an impressive string of pop hits throughout the years, beginning with "Canadian Sunset" in 1956 and "Butterfly" in 1957 right on up through the "Love Theme From The Godfather" in 1972. He first gained notoriety during the 1950s as a singer on Steve Allen's "Tonight Show," and in 1959 he began his own enormously successful television show. He is probably best known for his 1963 recording of "Moon River" from the movie *Breakfast at Tiffany's* (1961) and his 1971 "Love Story," the theme from the movie of the same name. He was born on Dec. 3, 1928 in Wall Lake, Iowa.

Williams, Hank, Jr.   Son of country music superstar Hank Williams, Hank Williams, Jr. (born on May 26, 1949 in Shreveport, La.) developed into a country star in his own right, touring from the age of eight. By 15 he was considered one of the biggest stars in country music, but the same forces that acted on his father—drugs and drink—also took their toll on him. With a career in decline, he turned himself around in the mid-1970s with his *Hank Williams, Jr. And Friends* album, which featured such Southern rock stars as Toy Caldwell of the Marshall Tucker Band and fiddler Charlie Daniels. The album was a masterpiece of country-rock fusion, but before Williams could take advantage of it, he was injured in Montana—falling some 500 feet onto a rock face—while scouting for a hunting trip. Two years of surgery and recovery were required, but in 1979 he came back stronger than ever with a series of superb country songs, including one of the biggest country hits of that year, "Family Tradition."

Williams, Hank, Sr.
Perhaps the most important figure ever in country music and one of the most powerful songwriters to emerge on the pop scene, Hank Williams was born on Sept. 17, 1923 in Georgiana, Ala. He began singing in the church choir, but it was from a black street musician, a bluesman named Rufe Payne, that Williams got his all-important early training. He took his black-styled country vocals to Nashville and in 1949 scored big with a Tin Pan Alley tune called "Lovesick Blues" (his debut performance at the Grand Ole Opry featured seven encores of "Lovesick Blues," and Williams left the stage as the biggest star country music had yet produced). Working with Nashville producer Fred Rose, Williams began writing (sometimes alone, sometimes with Rose) some of the most striking and powerful music ever created for pop—a fact attested to by the number of Williams' songs that make the charts for other artists each year and the fact that his song catalogue is perhaps the most lucrative in the world, rivaling Lennon and McCartney's. A sampling of Williams classics written from 1949 to 1952 includes "I'm So Lonesome I Could Cry," "Long Gone Lonesome Blues," "Mansion On The Hill," "Cold Cold Heart," "Your Cheatin' Heart," "Jambalaya," "Hey Good Lookin'" and "I Can't Help It If I'm Still In Love With You." Despite his successes, he was haunted by the demons of drugs and drink. On New Years Day, 1953 he died from a drug- and alcohol-induced heart attack in the back of a car on

the way to a show in Canton, Ohio.

Williams, Mason   Born on Aug. 24, 1938 in Abilene, Tex., Mason Williams briefly became a household word working on the Smothers Brothers' television show in the late 1960s. In 1968 he had an infectious instrumental hit with "Classical Gas," effectively combining chamber music and rock.

Williams, Paul   Born in 1940 in Omaha, Neb., the diminutive Paul Williams began his career as a comedy writer and "child" star. When he was 25, he began writing songs on a movie set, and a few years later he was penning such hits as "We've Only Just Begun" (1970) and "Rainy Days And Mondays" (1971) for the Carpenters and "Out In The Country" (1970) and "Just An Old Fashioned Love Song" (1971) for Three Dog Night. He wrote a bizarre soundtrack for a bizarre rock film called *Phantom of the Paradise* (1974) and continued performing, singing and songwriting. During the late 1970s he rewrote the lyrics for the immortal Tex Ritter theme to the Gary Cooper/Grace Kelly movie *High Noon* (1952) for use in a television sequel, starring Lee "The Six Million Dollar Man" Majors, aired in 1980. The show's producers had deemed the original lyrics unsuitable for the 1980s.

Williams, Roger   Born Louis Weertz in 1925, Roger Williams began his enormously successful recording career in 1955 with "Autumn Leaves." In 1966 he came to the attention of a whole new generation with "Born Free."

Williamson, Sonny Boy
Two bluesmen shared the name Sonny Boy Williamson. The first Sonny Boy, John Lee Williamson, was a blues harp player during the early 1930s in Chicago. The second, harp player Rice Miller (born in Mississippi), styled himself after the first Sonny Boy when the latter was killed. The second Sonny Boy is best known in the rock world for his extremely influential work with the English blues-styled musicians of the early 1960s, especially the Yardbirds and a young Eric Clapton.

Wills, Bob   Western swing bandleader Bob Wills was born on March 6, 1905 in Limestone County, Tex. He formed his first band, a duo, in the summer of 1929, and four years later he got together Bob Wills and His Texas Playboys, one of the most influential bands in popular music. They played swing music with country overtones, mixing country ballads, blues and swinging jazz into a conglomeration people could dance to. Wills signature song, his composition "San Antonio Rose" (1940), has become a standard of pop music. Although Western swing faded with the coming of World War II, it has since enjoyed a tremendous revival that began, luckily, before Wills' death in 1975.

Wilson, Al   Soul singer Al Wilson (born on June 19, 1939 in Mississippi) worked with a number of successful vocal groups before scoring as a

solo artist in 1968 with "The Snake," a soul recitation of sorts. In 1973 he had a number one hit with "Show And Tell."

Wilson, Brian, Carl and Dennis   The brothers Wilson (Brian, born on June 20, 1942; Dennis, born on Dec. 4, 1944; and Carl, born on Dec. 21, 1946—all in Hawthorne, Calif.) were the nucleus of the Beach Boys. The mercurial Brian was (and is) considered the soul of the group, providing some of its greatest singles and almost single-handedly hammering out the sun-and-fun style of the band.

Wilson, Jackie   Born on June 9, 1934 in Detroit, Mich., singer Jackie Wilson was a Golden Gloves champion at the age of 16. In 1953, while still a teenager, Wilson became the lead singer for the Dominoes (then known as Billy Ward and His Dominoes), replacing Clyde McPhatter. He left the group in 1956 and shortly afterward met future Motown king Berry Gordy, Jr. The combination produced a string of quick hits, starting with "Reet Petite" (1957), that established Wilson as a slick vocalist and Gordy as a songwriter. The third hit was "Lonely Teardrops" (1958), a rock-and-roll classic. From then on Wilson pursued an uneven career, mixing schmaltzy ballads and gospel-inspired shouters in an electric stage show. In the mid-1960s he had two million sellers, "Whispers" (1966) and "(Your Love Keeps Lifting Me) Higher And Higher" (1967). In 1975 he suffered a heart attack while performing in Cherry Hill, N.J. He remains in a coma.

Winchester, Jesse   Born in 1945 in Shreveport, La. and raised in the musically fertile city of Memphis, Winchester moved to Canada in the late 1960s to avoid the draft. Working with the Band's Robbie Robertson, Winchester produced some outstanding, lyrically powerful music, including such minor classics as "Yankee Lady" (1971), "The Brand New Tennessee Waltz" (1971) and "Mississippi You're On My Mind" (1974). His songs were quite sucessful for other artists (including Jimmy Buffett, Joan Baez and Jonathan Edwards). Following President Jimmy Carter's amnesty for draft dodgers, Winchester returned to the United States for the first time in 1977. Since then his career has continued in a modestly successful vein. He still lives with his family in Canada.

Wings   Basically, Paul McCartney's backup band, whose only steady member has been Denny Laine, previously of the Moody Blues. The "band" was formed in 1973.

Winter, Edgar   Born on Dec. 28, 1946 in Beaumont, Tex., Edgar Winter originally worked with brother Johnny, and when Johnny's career took off, Edgar joined his brother's band. Forming several bands of his own, he eventually hit on the right combination with Rick Derringer, and in 1974 the Edgar Winter Group Featuring Rick Derringer took the concert circuit by storm. Despite this earlier success Edgar's career has apparently been in somewhat of a self-imposed eclipse, although he has appeared on subsequent Rick Derringer albums and Bette Midler's *Songs For The New Depression* (1975). His own albums have included *White Thrash* (1973) and *They Only Come Out At Night* (1973)—both produced by Rick Derringer—and *Recycled White Thrash* (1979). Edgar also had a singles hit in 1973 with "Frankenstein."

Winter, Johnny Albino bluesman (as is brother Edgar) Johnny Winter (born on Feb. 23, 1944 in Beaumont, Tex.) served as a backup musician in the blues clubs of Chicago before returning to Texas to make his mark. In 1968 Johnny was working locally in Texas when an article in the fledgling *Rolling Stone* magazine cast him as the Next Big Thing. Thereafter his career took off—although never fulfilling the excessive predictions of rock journalists—and he cut *Johnny Winter* in 1969 and *Second Winter* a year later. Over the years his work has shown him to be one of the finest blues interpreters to emerge in rock. In 1977 Johnny Winter produced the "comeback" album for Muddy Waters, *Hard Again,* a minor masterpiece and by far and away the best example of a blending of old and new. Winter joined Waters on tour and produced a second excellent album, *Still Hard.* Winter's own *White Hot And Blue* appeared in 1978.

Winwood, Steve Best known for his work with the influential English group Traffic, Winwood (born on May 12, 1948 in England) made his debut as vocalist for the Spencer Davis Group at the tender age of 16. In 1977, several years after the passing of Traffic, Winwood relaunched a solo career with the modestly successful *Winwood* album. In early 1981 his *Arc Of A Diver* album was released in the United States.

Wiseman, Mac Born on May 23, 1925 near Waynesboro, Va., Malcolm "Mac" Wiseman is one of the best-known and most-revered figures in bluegrass music, leaning toward the older folk traditions and serving as a vehicle for carrying those traditions to a newer, younger audience.

Wishbone Ash Andy Powell (guitar), Laurie Wisefield (guitar), Martin Turner (bass, vocals), Steve Upton (drums)—Formed in England in 1969, Wishbone Ash gathered a strong cult following with what amounted to straightforward rock and roll. The group continued going well throughout the 1970s. Wishbone released several albums during this period, perhaps most notably *Argus* in 1972.

Withers, Bill Born on July 4, 1938 in Slab Fork, W. Va., Withers shot to the forefront of popular music in 1971 with the powerful "Ain't No Sunshine," produced by Booker T. Jones of Booker T. and the MGs fame. Two subsequent hits, "Lean On Me" (1972) and "Use Me" (1972), exploited his soulful voice, but since then he has been sliding.

Womack, Bobby Soul singer Bobby Womack (born on March 4, 1944 in Cleveland, Ohio) was involved with some classic rock songs early on in his career, including his composition of "It's All Over Now," covered quite successfully by the Rolling Stones in 1964. Womack later worked with Wilson Pickett and in 1968 began a solo career utilizing slicker production techniques and a more laid-back vocal style. His "Lookin' For A Love" was a hit for the J. Geils Band in 1971.

Wonder, Stevie One of the most prolific voices in rock and roll, Stevie Wonder began his incredible career at the age of 12, when he met Motown genius Berry Gordy, Jr. Wonder was born on May 13, 1950 in Saginaw, Mich. and has been blind since birth. Gordy signed him on the spot, dubbed him Little Stevie Wonder and immediately cut "Fingertips-Pt.2," a number one hit in 1963, with the young harmonica player. Rather than remain a child prodigy, Wonder worked constantly to refine his playing, learn new instruments and improve his delivery. By the mid-1960s he was writing his hits as well as singing them—"Uptight" (1966), "I Was Made To Love Her" (1967), "For Once In My Life" (1968), "My Cherie Amour" (1969)—as well as providing some startling cover versions of such songs as Bob Dylan's "Blowin' In The Wind" (1966). At the age of 21, a millionaire several times over, Wonder embarked on an amazing musical journey, leaving behind the pop Motown stylings of the 1960s and experimenting in jazzier, more heavily orchestrated arrangements. At first Motown couldn't figure out what to do, since the label was strictly oriented toward hit singles. But by *Music Of My Mind* in 1972, Wonder had reestablished himself as pop's foremost composer. That year's *Talking Book* album returned him to the top of the singles charts with "Superstition" and "You Are The Sunshine Of My Life." Since then his career has been a juggernaut, with classic hits (such as "Living In The City" in 1973) and accolades (his 1977 *Songs In The Key Of Life* album won five Grammy awards). He overcame a severe automobile accident in 1973.

His 1979 album, *The Secret Life Of Plants,* showed him moving in yet another direction—more personal, more low key. Recently, Wonder has also been working as a producer (of Rufus, B.B. King). A major figure in rock music.

Wood, Ron   Rock guitarist Ron Wood (born on June 1, 1947 in England) is perhaps the best-known rock sideman, having played with Jeff Beck, the Faces and the Rolling Stones before formally becoming a Stone in 1976. He has followed an on-again, off-again solo career without too much seriousness, and in the late 1970s he toured with a band laughingly referred to as the New Barbarians, featuring himself, Keith Richards, Stanley Clarke, Bobby Keyes, Ian McLagan and Meter Zig Modeliste.

Woodstock   The Woodstock Music and Arts Fair, held on Aug. 21, 1969, and the subsequent *Woodstock* movie represented the culmination of the waves of San Francisco flower power that had been sweeping the country for years. Around half a million people gathered at Max Yasgur's farm in upstate New York to get stoned, groove and listen to the music, which included Joan Baez; Crosby, Stills, Nash and Young; the Band; the Grateful Dead; Blood, Sweat and Tears; Mountain; Ten Years After; Santana; Sha Na Na; Arlo Guthrie; the Who; Sly and the Family Stone; Janis Joplin; Paul Butterfield; Joe Cocker; Canned Heat; Country Joe and the Fish; Jimi Hendrix; John Sebastian and God alone knows who else. The movie—by far more important than the concert itself—was released in 1970 and spawned a wave of imitation concerts; it defined the music of the 1960s, as *Saturday Night Fever* later did for the music of the 1970s.

Wooley, Sheb   Wooley (born on April 10, 1921 in Erick, Okla.) is best known to rock fans (and UFO fanatics) for his 1958 smash, "Purple People Eater." He has also worked as an actor (he had a bit part as one of the killers in *High Noon*) and as a country music humorist, parodying famous country hits in his alter ego of Ben Colder.

Wray, Link   Absolute proof that if you cut one good song, your place in rock's pantheon is assured. In Link Wray's case the song was "Rumble." Apparently first recorded in 1954, it became a national hit in 1958 and remains to this day perhaps the most ominous rock instrumental ever recorded. The song was Wray's re-creation of a gang fight he saw in Virginia. He had a second million-selling hit in 1959, "Rawhide," and then virtually retired from public life, working steadily in a home studio to record what he considered the "perfect" sound. In 1971 his first album, *Link Wray,* emerged from those years of experimentation and became something of an instant classic. His early guitar style influenced numerous musicians, particularly Peter Townshend of the Who, Jeff Beck and Bob Dylan. In the late 1970s Wray began a comeback with punk-rockabilly revivalist Robert Gordon and released a solo album *Bullshot* (1979). He was born on May 2, 1935 near Fort Bragg, N.C.

Wright, Gary   Born in 1943 in Cresskill, N.J., Wright began his career as a child actor and became a vocalist and keyboardist for Spooky Tooth before scoring big with his solo *Dream Weaver* album in 1975. Wright's vocals have drifted from the frenetic screams of the Tooth days to ethereal and densely atmospheric—a formula that has worked extremely well.

Wynette, Tammy   The queen of middle-of-the-road country music, Tammy Wynette (born Wynette Pugh on May 5, 1942 near Tupelo, Miss.) was a beautician before breaking as the biggest female star in country music. Her tear-soaked ballads ("D-I-V-O-R-C-E," "Stand By Your Man"—both in 1968) are perfectly matched with her voice, which seems to have a permanent catch on the verge of tears. She was married to country star George Jones, a marriage broken up by Jones' bouts with the bottle and chronicled in numerous songs, most notably "(I Still Believe In) Fairy Tales" (1975). Recently she has turned to more pop-styled material, *a la* the Vegas-bound Dolly Parton.

Yarbrough, Glenn   Born on Jan. 12, 1930 in Milwaukee, Wis., Yarbrough first came to the attention of rock audiences in 1965 with the theme to the movie *Baby the Rain Must Fall*. Originally a member of the Limelighters, he re-formed that group in 1973.

Yardbirds, The   Jimmy Page (guitar), Jeff Beck (guitar), Eric Clapton (guitar), John Paul Jones (bass, organ), Paul Samwell-Smith (bass, organ), Robert Plant (vocals), John Bonham (drums), Keith Relf (vocals), Jimmy McCarty (drums), Chris Dreja (guitar)— This landmark British blues group ranks as one of the most influential, largely because of the incredible successes of various Yardbird members in later years. Originally formed in London in 1963, the Yardbirds became the house band at the Crawdaddy Club, succeeding the Rolling Stones. Unlike the Stones, though, the Yardbirds lacked a charismatic Mick Jagger, and all the elements for superstar success never seemed to line up just right. In

1965 the group began a short string of hit singles—"For Your Love," "Heart Full Of Soul" and "I'm A Man" in 1965 and "Shapes Of Things" and "Over Under Sideways Down" in 1966—which established the Yardbirds but caused Eric Clapton, unhappy at the group's obvious turn away from straight blues, to leave. Personnel shuffles and management problems eventually sank the Yardbirds. Clapton went on to Cream, Blind Faith, Derek and the Dominos and his soaring solo career; Jeff Beck formed the Jeff Beck Group; Jimmy Page, John Paul Jones, Robert Plant and John Bonham (who died in 1980) created Led Zeppelin. And dozens of other rock performers adopted the Yardbirds' style.

Yes   Jon Anderson (vocals), Steve Howe (guitar), Rick Wakeman (keyboards), Chris Squire (bass), Alan White (drums)—Formed in 1968, the band's career really took off when Jon Anderson suggested that his band Yes sub for Sly and the Family Stone at a London concert where that group had pulled another one of its legendary no-shows. One of the key factors in the band's unique sound was the brilliant keyboard work of Rick Wakeman, who left Yes for a solo attempt in 1973 but eventually returned to the fold. The music of Yes is heavily arty, often drifting into various and sundry imaginary worlds (demons and dragons apparently have an irresistible appeal to rock and rollers). It can range from punchy rock hits, such as "Roundabout" and "Long Distance

Runaround" (both in 1972), to ponderous excursions into fantasy, such as the songs on *Tales From Topographic Oceans* (1974). With Wakeman back in line, Yes is a powerful, if slightly overblown, ensemble.

Yost, Dennis, and the Classics IV   Dennis Yost (vocals), James Cobb (guitar), Wally Eaton (guitar), Joseph Wilson (bass), Kim Venable (drums)—Originally organized by Dennis Yost and Wally Eaton as a bar band in Florida, the Classics IV scored in 1967 with "Spooky" and again in 1968 with the similarly titled, similar sounding "Stormy." After several more hits in the same vein, the group disbanded, only to be re-formed by Yost with new members in 1972.

Young, Jesse Colin   Originally the leader of the Youngbloods, Jesse Colin Young (whose original name was the more mundane Perry Miller) went solo in 1972 and has produced an album a year since then. His music, like the music of the Youngbloods, is rooted in the folk-flower child traditions of the 1960s, primarily love ballads and endless rehashing of the Youngbloods' biggest hit, "Get Together," which became a top 10 song in 1969. Young was born in New York City on Nov. 11, 1944.

Young, Neil   It wasn't until the 1977 release of *Decade*, the 10-year compilation of Neil Young's work, that the moody Canadian singer/songwriter's full contribution to rock was realized. Born on Nov. 12,

Neil Young

Through the 1970s he flatly refused to play the rock star. The mood of his music has gone from bitter (as in the 1971 CSN&Y hit "Ohio") to despairing ("The Needle And The Damage Done" in 1972 and "Tonight's The Night" in 1975) to light and airy ("Love Is A Rose"). In the late 1970s Young reluctantly stepped to the forefront with a movie titled *Rust Never Sleeps,* an album of the same name and an extensive tour schedule.

Young, Steve   Songwriter Young is noted for his composing work with Waylon Jennings ("Lonesome, On'ry And Mean," labeled by one rock publication as one of the greatest songs to ever come out of Nashville). His own solo career died abirthing. Nevertheless, the Eagles recorded Young's "Seven Bridges Road" on their 1980 live album.

Youngbloods, The   Jesse Colin Young (vocals), Jerry Corbitt (guitar, bass), Lowell "Banana" Levinger (guitar, keyboards), Joe Bauer (drums)—Formed during the mid-1960s in Massachusetts by folkie Jesse Colin Young and Jerry Corbitt, the group wrote and recorded a song in 1967 called "Get Together," which went on to become the anthem of the waning flower power movement, one of the runaway hits at the Woodstock festival and a top 10 song in 1969. The Youngbloods' subsequent success never matched that of their one phenomenal hit, and by 1972, just before parting ways, they were reduced to cutting old Beatles songs.

1945 in Toronto, Canada, Young first gained notoriety as a member of the outstanding 1960s group the Buffalo Springfield. His songwriting— "Nowadays Clancy Can't Even Sing" (which was banned on radio stations because of the word "damn") from the 1966 *Buffalo Springfield* album and "Mr. Soul" from the 1967 *Buffalo Springfield Again* album—and his high nasal singing helped set the group apart, but his spats with Stephen Stills led to the group's breakup. Young went solo, and his second album (with the group Crazy Horse), *Everybody Knows This Is Nowhere* (1969), is justifiably considered a classic. In 1970 he linked up with one of the most commercial rock bands of all time, Crosby, Stills, Nash and Young (CSN&Y), and his work on the CSN&Y *Deja Vu* album that year (including "Helpless" and "Country Girl") established him as a major talent. However, Neil Young is nothing if not iconoclastic.

Yuro, Timi Yuro began singing in her mother's Italian restaurant in Los Angeles. She broke the charts twice, in 1961 with "Hurt" and the next year with "What's A Matter Baby." She was born on Aug. 4, 1941 in Chicago, Ill.

Zager and Evans Denny Zager and Rick Evans became overnight sensations in 1969 with their science fiction recording of "In The Year 2525," which they originally recorded and sold on their own. The song eventually became a huge hit, although the duo was never able to match it.

Zappa, Frank, and the Mothers of Invention Even now it's hard to figure Frank Zappa. His contribution to rock (if you had to close your eyes and pick one) is a healthy dose of insanity, beginning with his 1966 *Freak Out* album (featuring the original Mothers—the "of Invention" was tacked on by a nervous record company—Ray Collins, Roy Estrada, Jimmy Carl Black and Elliot Ingber. That album was a landmark in rock. For a start, it was a live double album, a first for a new group. Secondly, it's finely honed satire ("Hungry Freaks, Daddy," "Who Are The Brain Police," "Help, I'm A Rock" and "You're Probably Wondering Why I'm Here") was totally devoid of any commercial potential. And the Mothers got crazier and crazier, becoming

the premier underground group in America. Songs like "Duke Of Prunes," "America Drinks And Goes Home" and "Invocation And Ritual Of The Young Pumpkin"; the brilliant *Sergeant Pepper* parody *We're Only In It For The Money* (recorded in 1967, with the "hit" singles "Who Needs The Peace Corps," "Flower-Punk," "Take Your Clothes Off When You Dance" and the ever-popular "Hot Poop"); and

Zappa's general craziness kept the band in the public's eye, if not in their record collections. Nevertheless, Zappa (born on Dec. 21, 1940 in Baltimore, Md.) knew his music and into his manic stew he injected doses of jazz, rhythm and blues and classical strains. In 1969 the Mothers disbanded because nobody was buying Mothers' records—at least not enough people to keep what had evolved into a 12-piece

Frank Zappa

ensemble on the road—and Zappa began a series of solo projects; work with, among others, old friend Don Van Vliet, whom Zappa had originally christened Captain Beefheart; and, later, numerous resurrections of the Mothers. In 1973 he had a fluke hit with "Don't Eat The Yellow Snow," advice to a young Eskimo regarding animal hygiene, and in 1979 he scored a huge (and totally unexpected) hit with "Dancing Fool," the ultimate antidisco song. During the early years he also cut an album of 1950s music that predated the nostalgia craze (*Ruben And The Jets* in 1968) and he did a solo album of ballet music (*Lumpy Gravy* in 1968).

Zevon, Warren Originally known as a songwriter for the laid-back West Coast school (particularly Linda Ronstadt: "Hasten Down The Wind," the title track from her 1976 album, and "Poor Poor Pitiful Me," a hit for her in 1978), Zevon began cutting a string of solo albums in the late 1970s that catapulted him to stardom on his own. Central to that stardom is his songwriting talent, which is completely off the wall. His songs are little vignettes of urban violence and insanity ("Lawyers, Guns And Money," "Werewolves Of London" and "Excitable Boy" from the 1978 *Excitable Boy* album and "Jungle Work" and "Bad Luck Streak In A Dancing School" from the 1980 *Bad Luck Streak In A Dancing School* album). Not surprisingly, he has built up quite a following, and his stage shows grow progressively weirder—one tour featured a

Warren Zevon

mock firefight at the conclusion of "Jungle Work," the first rock-and-roll hymn to mercenaries. He is also probably the only rock star whose album covers have to be approved not only by record executives, but by the Bureau of Alcohol, Tobacco and Firearms as well. He also owns a .44 Magnum revolver named Willy.

Zombies, The Colin Blunstone (vocals), Ron Argent (keyboards), Paul Atkinson (guitar), Chris White (bass), Hugh Grundy (drums)— Originally launched in England in 1962, the Zombies are primarily remembered for the Ron Argent-penned "She's Not There" (1964), a rock classic. After the group's collapse in 1967, it came back with a hit, "Time Of The Season," in 1969. Argent went on to form the group Argent. Blunstone

pursued a solo career without distinction.

ZZ Top Billy Gibbons (guitar), Dusty Hill (bass), Frank Beard (drums)— Formed by Billy Gibbons in 1970, ZZ Top has become a spectacularly successful band, sticking to straight-ahead rock (sort of like Led Zeppelin gone South). The group had a hit single in 1974 with "LaGrange," a song about the whorehouse later immortalized in the Broadway production *The Best Little Whorehouse In Texas.* ZZ Top has also been responsible for the greatest single excess ever perpetrated on a rock tour when the band decided to take along a buffalo, some vultures and a few head of cattle to "bring Texas to the people." There was near panic at one concert when the vultures began cruising the audience.

INDEX

Record album titles in italic in index.

243

250

253

The author gratefully acknowledges these companies and individuals for the use of these photographs:
A & M Records, for photographs of Peter Frampton, The Police. ABC Records, Jimmy Buffett, Everly Brothers, Tompall Glaser, Tom Petty & the Heartbreakers. Arista, The Allman Brothers Band, The Grateful Dead, Kinks, Lou Reed, Patti Smith, Dionne Warwick. Asylum, J. Browne, Eagles, John Prine, Bonnie Raitt, Linda Ronstadt, John Travolta, Warren Zevon. ATCO Records, Derek and the Dominos. Atlantic, Abba, Average White Band, Crosby Stills & Nash, Keith Emerson, Lou Gramm (Foreigner), Mick Jones (Foreigner), Graham Nash, Stephen Stills. Bearsville, Todd Rundgren. Capitol Records, April Wine, Beatles, Natalie Cole, Rick Nelson. Capricorn Records, Elvin Bishop, Dobie Gray, Delbert McClinton. Casablanca Records, Kiss. CBS Records, Tina Turner with Lynn Anderson. Chrysalis, Blondie. Columbia, Johnny Cash, Elvis Costello, Bob Dylan, Billy Joel, Kris Kristofferson, Janis Ian & Kenny Loggins, Nick Lowe & Rockpile, Dave Mason, Paul McCartney, Willie Nelson, Laura Nyro, Phoebe Snow, J. D. Souther, Bruce Sprinsteen. Curb/Warner Bros., 4 Seasons & Frankie Valli. Curtom Records, Curtis Mayfield. Dark Horse Records, George Harrison. DJM Records (product of Phonogram Inc.), Papa John Creach. Elektra, Roy Acuff, The Cars, Joe Cocker, Judy Collins, Doors, Jerry Lee Lewis, Jim Morrison, Queen, Eddie Rabbitt, Neil Sedaka, Carly Simon, Television, Tom Verlaine (Talking Heads). Elektra/Asylum, Jonathan Richman. Epic Records, Jeff Beck, Boston, The Clash, The Charlie Daniels Band, The Fabulous Poodles, Dan Fogelberg, Heart, The Jacksons, Meatloaf, Ted Nugent. Fantasy, Country Joe McDonald. Fantasy/EMI, Creedence Clearwater Revival. Far Out/MCA, War. Geffen Records, Donna Summer. Grunt/RCA, Jefferson Starship. Island, Marianne Faithful, Robert Palmer, Steve Winwood & Jim Capaldi of Traffic. Kama Sutra/MGM, The Lovin' Spoonful. MCA Records, Jimmy Cliff, Elton John, Tom Jones, B.B. King, Lynyrd Skynyrd, The Oak Ridge Boys. Mercury Records (product of Phonogram), Bachman-Turner Overdrive (Randy Bachman), Bachman-Turner Overdrive (Robbie Bachman), Bachman-Turner Overdrive (Blair Thornton), Bachman-Turner Overdrive (C. F. Turner), The Dells, Peter Gabriel, Roy Orbison, Graham Parker & The Rumour, Rush, 10cc. Monco Records, Toots and the Maytals. Paradise, Leon Russell, Mary Russell. Planet/Warner Bros., Pointer Sisters. Polydor, James Brown, Ringo Starr. RCA, Paul Anka, David Bowie, John Denver, Robert Gordon, Daryl Hall and John Oates, Dolly Parton, Elvis Presley. Rocket/RCA, Cliff Richard. Rolling Stones/Atlantic, Rolling Stones. Sire, Dead Boys, Brian Eno & David Byrne of Talking Heads, Plastic Bertrand, Ramones, Talking Heads. Tamla, Smokey Robinson. United Artists, Eddie Cochran, Kenny Rogers. Warner Bros. Records, The B-52's, Fleetwood Mac, John Lennon & Yoko Ono, Peter, Paul & Mary, James Taylor, The Who. Warner/Reprise, Beach Boys, Captain Beefhart & the Magic Band, Cheech & Chong, Alice Cooper, Deep Purple, Dire Straits, The Doobie Brothers, Michael Franks, Funkadelic, Lowell George, Arlo Guthrie, Emmylou Harris, Jimi Hendrix, The Marshall Tucker Band, Van Morrison, Randy Newman, Leon Redbone, Black Sabbath, Rod Stewart, Thin Lizzy, Van Halen, Neil Young. Zappa Records (marketed by Phonogram), Frank Zappa. AIP Pictures, The Byrds, Ronettes. Columbia Pictures, Bo Diddley, Little Richard. Kenny Kertok (private collection), Chuck Berry, Bill Haley, Les Paul, John Rotten, Temptations. Phil Walden, Otis Redding.